The Literary Fantastic

The Literary Fantastic

FROM GOTHIC TO POSTMODERNISM

Neil Cornwell

Senior Lecturer in Russian Studies
University of Bristol

HARVESTER WHEATSHEAF

New York   London   Toronto   Sydney   Tokyo   Singapore

First published 1990 by
Harvester Wheatsheaf
66 Wood Lane End, Hemel Hempstead
Hertfordshire HP2 4RG
A division of
Simon & Schuster International Group

Typeset in Bembo 10½ pt
by Columns of Reading

Printed and bound in Great Britain by
BPCC Wheatons Ltd, Exeter

British Library Cataloguing in Publication Data

Cornwell, Neil
  The literary fantastic: from gothic to postmodernism
  1. Literature, Modern 19th century history and criticism
  I. Title
  809.915

  ISBN 0–7108–1376–7

---

1 2 3 4 5   94 93 92 91 90

For Katerina and Juliet

Destroy language and, with it, all things and concepts.
The rest is silence.

Meister Eckhart

All of the things we do on earth are play,
Regardless of how great and deep they seemed. . . .

Dream and waking flow into each other,
And truth and falsehood. Certainty is nowhere.

Arthur Schnitzler, *Paracelsus*

The 'creative' imagination . . . is quite incapable of *inventing*
anything; it can only combine components that are strange
to one another.

Freud

Contents

Preface   xi
Note on Transliteration and Referencing   xvii

PART ONE BACKGROUND AND THEORY   1

I   Introduction   3
II   Towards a Background   4
III   Some Definitions: Todorov *et al.*   11
IV   The Common Ground   24
V   The 'Fantastic/Fantasy' Disarray   27
VI   'Fantasy' — Basically an Impulse?   31
VII   'The Fantastic' — Basically a Genre?   34

PART TWO PRACTICE   43

1. Origins and Development   45
      Origins   45
      England   47
      America   53
      France   56
      Germany   58
      Cross-fertilisation   64

2. Tripping the Light Fantastic: from Frankenstein to
    Dracula   67
      Preamble   67
      Mary Shelley   70
      Maturin   75

Hoffmann   78
Poe   83
Le Fanu   87
Stevenson   94
Maupassant   99
Wilde   102
Stoker   106

3. Pushkin and Henry James   113
Pushkin   113
Henry James   121

4. The Twentieth Century   140
Are Genres Historically Tied?   140
Towards the Portmanteau   144
Bulgakov   159
Banville   172
Rushdie   184
Morrison   197

PART THREE   CONCLUSIONS   209

The Import of the Fantastic   211
Postscript: The Rushdie Affair   219

Notes   230
Bibliography   245
Index   260

Preface

It might well be thought that ten years of Thatcherite government in Britain would be more than enough to send anyone fleeing to the realms of escapist literature, there to seek out subversive meanings. In fact, though, the origins of this study go back much further, to undergraduate days in the late 1960s, when I read Hoffmann and Poe alongside Pushkin and Dostoevsky. My interest in the fantastic was further stimulated in the 1970s by work on Vladimir Odoevsky and discovery of Todorov's *The Fantastic* (1973), which represented, so far as I was then concerned, a new departure in criticism. I was invited to launch a seminar series in 1985 at my old college, the School of Slavonic and East European Studies of the University of London, on the fantastic in Russian literature. For this purpose I spoke on Odoevsky (chronologically first on the programme), but also began further exploration of critical approaches to the fantastic/fantasy (encountering studies by Christine Brooke-Rose, Rosemary Jackson and others, including my fellow-Russianist Edmund Little). A sabbatical year spent in Italy in 1986–87 enabled me to develop this into a forty-five page critical–theoretical survey article (published in *Essays in Poetics* in 1988). The present study represents (in Part One) a revision and development of this theoretical element, plus (in Part Two) the addition of a new dimension of textual practice.

The main purpose of Part One, having established a historical context, is to clarify the terminology used in critical discussions of the fantastic, and in particular to draw distinctions between 'the fantastic' and 'fantasy'; it is then suggested that, for pragmatic purposes directed especially at approaches to twentieth-century literature, the whole may be subsumed under the more general category of 'the literary fantastic'. 'Fantasy' may be seen as deriving predominantly from psychology, while 'the fantastic' is regarded as a basically literary construct; hence the concentration largely, in the present study, on the latter. The overall approach is far from technical and may be loosely described as at least aspiring towards a phrase, or posture, borrowed from David Bethea, that of 'structuralism with a human face' (Bethea, 1989, p. xvii). This, it is hoped, is carried on into the readings of Part Two. Readers who are impatient for textual exposition may prefer to start with Part Two. These readings, together with their introductory and linking sections, do not purport to amount to an entire history of a genre. No claims are made to comprehensiveness and lacunae certainly remain. For various reasons, the overall coverage, while remaining comparatavist, has turned out to be somewhat biased towards northern Europe (minus Scandinavia and plus America).

With regard to the nineteenth century, the writers and texts here discussed very largely choose themselves, although some eyebrows may be raised at my deliberate choice of certain works in which the use of the fantastic is merely vestigial. In the case of Henry James, there are other strong reasons for choosing *The Aspern Papers*, while, more generally, the vestigial fantastic may be seen as a useful marker for the perception of a gradual movement of the fantastic, as here argued, towards the mainstream of fiction. The axis hereby drawn between romanticism and the approach of *fin de siècle* (although the respective works by Pushkin and James were written only fifty years apart) thus takes on something of the prominence of a detailed centre-piece within the present study. This is all the more the case, I would want to argue, in that neither Pushkin nor James, central and influential figures of their respective epochs as they were, are considered to be *predominantly* writers of the fantastic. There may seem to be one cavity which might have been occupied by the Victorian (or other European) novel of sensation; this is however partially filled, I would argue, with the inclusion of Le Fanu.

When we come to the garden of forking paths which comprises the fiction of the twentieth century, my choice of Bulgakov, Banville, Rushdie and Morrison as a quartet for more detailed consideration may well be seen as highly selective, if not idiosyncratic or totally arbitrary — as, no doubt, would virtually any other choice which I might have made. I can, however, point in justification to certain threads which I see linking Bulgakov to both Banville and Rushdie, while Toni Morrison's revival of a classic fantastic approach in *Beloved* was, to me, irresistible.

Elizabeth Dipple, in her study *The Unresolvable Plot*, includes an alluring grouping of Borges, Nabokov, Calvino and Eco. As intriguing quartets, we could propose Nathanael West, Aksënov and Angela Carter, with perhaps Alasdair Gray. Or how about Bely, Grass, Tournier and Fuentes? Or Kafka, Cortázar, Kundera and Isabel Allende? A slight science-fictional bias could produce, say, Stapledon, Vonnegut, Lem and the Strugatskys. The possibilities are wide, if not limitless: we have yet to mention Zamiatin, García Márquez, Cela, Goytisolo and many others. The absence of any detailed treatment of many of these is undoubtedly a loss — none perhaps more so than Kafka and Nabokov.

The British Library Subject Index (1971–5, vol. VI, F–Ger, London, 1986) contains no entry under 'Fantastic, the', and under 'Fantasy' says merely: 'see PSYCHOLOGY, Monographs, Imagination: CHILDREN, Child Study' (p. 3196). The situation is evidently rather different in the United States, where a cult 'fantasy' industry, based by no means exclusively on 'sword and sorcery' or science fiction, has flourished for some years. The journal *Extrapolation* has now reached volume 30. There passions run high and interventions from the mainstream of literary criticism are not always warmly welcomed. For example, one fantasy adept, Roger C. Schlobin, recently displayed no qualms in denouncing what he calls 'Harold Bloom's dismally inept chapter on fantasy in *Agon*' (Schlobin, 1987, p. 8, referring to H. Bloom, 1982). Things had also reached the point at which, of a conference taking place in Florida in 1980, it could be written, in the preface to the published proceedings (Collins & Pearce, 1985A, p. xii):

> the structural analysis of Tzvetan Todorov appeared to be the most widely adopted starting point, so much so that applications of his criteria to a text soon began to draw impatient boos or groans from audiences. Thus only the most thoughtful examples of such an approach are included in this series.

Finding useful, but inadequate, for instance the claim made by Borges 'that the basic devices of all fantastic literature are only four in number: the work within the work, the contamination of reality by dream, the voyage in time and the double' (introduction to Borges, 1970, p. 18), I have found myself thrown back, thoughtfully or otherwise, and at the possible risk of boos or groans from sections of my readership, upon Todorov as a point of departure. However, I hope I have been able to take a little further the refinements and developments of Todorov's theory already begun by other commentators.

Given that this study is as concerned with critical approaches as it is with literary texts, a good deal of it is inevitably taken up with quotation, paraphrase or consideration of the words of others. This varies in degree as the work goes on: at an early stage of the theoretical Part One I use the doubtlessly pretentious phrase 'structured hetero-glossia' by way of explanation; elsewhere (for example, in discussing the work of Toni Morrison, on whom I have read no criticism) the situation is quite different. At this juncture, I would merely draw attention to the attitude of Walter Benjamin, for whom the words of the past (*others'* words, as Bakhtin would have it) were so precious that he conceived the 'ideal of producing a work consisting endlessly of quotations, one that was mounted so masterfully that it could dispense with any accompanying text' (Hannah Arendt's introduction to Benjamin, 1973, p. 47). In the absence of any such achievement, the dividing line between the astute use of multiple quotation and a merely cluttered text may well be a fine one.

Finally, by way of self-justification, I would mention that readers who, as the case may be, turn to, or persevere as far as, the Postscript on 'the Rushdie affair' will find themselves engaging with something closer in style to polemic than to scholarly discourse. The reasons for this should be fully apparent. I shall, however, add one further point here. As a Russianist by background and training, I, in common with many colleagues, have spent a good deal of my professional time defending and promoting neglected or repressed writers (in the former category, I have written on Odoevsky and Olesha; in the latter, Pasternak, Kharms and Voinovich). It is a welcome novelty for me, and no doubt for other Russianists too, to witness the switching of the epicentre of literary repression away from Moscow; but it is even more of a shock to find such an epicentre now re-formed as a fault-line stretching between Tehran and London (or a Qom–Bradford axis).

The researching of a wide-ranging topic, such as that covered in this study, throws up its share of interesting surprises. For example, who would have expected to find a striking similarity between stories written a few years apart by Vladimir Odoevsky in Russia and FitzJames O'Brien in America? The connection explored here between Pushkin and Henry James seemed briefly to be a major find; fortunately, I rediscovered in good time a slumbering awareness that my colleague A. D. P. Briggs had been there before me. A useful and frequently delightful surprise, too, was the recent plethora of essays by some of our most gifted contemporary writers, whose thoughts on literature and the novel frequently cut through what would otherwise require, and elsewhere takes, volumes of critical verbiage: I refer to the collections of essays by Carlos Fuentes, Milan Kundera, Stanislaw Lem, Italo Calvino and Umberto Eco, plus more occasional contributions by Günter Grass, Salman Rushdie, Martin Amis and others.

The debt owed to Todorov, and other theorists and critics of the fantastic, will be apparent during the course of this study. I have to thank the editors of *Essays in Poetics* for permission to incorporate material from my 1988 article into this book. On a more private level, I would like to thank the following friends and colleagues for their precise assistance, intermittent advice or relevantly fantastical conversations, as the case may be, at various stages over the last two decades or so: Andy Barratt, Mike Basker, Tony Briggs, Tim Brooke, Adrian Clarke, Julie Curtis, Carla de Petris, Julian Graffy, Martin Hall, Ron Knowles, Bill McCormack, Maggie Malone, Martyn Matthews, Chris Pike, Robert Reid and Dennis Tate, with apologies to any undeservedly omitted. I should also thank, for their support, other colleagues, particularly in the Departments of Slavonic Studies, Queen's University of Belfast, and Russian Studies, the University of Bristol, in particular Barbara Case, and the inter-library loan staff at Bristol and Boston Spa. Finally, I would like to thank Jackie Jones and others at Harvester (including readers, anonymous or otherwise) for their encouragement and constructive criticism.

This study is dedicated to two young readers who were constantly amused and intrigued by my reading of what they take to be horror literature.

Note on Transliteration and Referencing

Transliteration from the Cyrillic alphabet here follows the Library of Congress system, without diacritics (except 'ë', as in 'Solov'ëv'). The customary 'y' ending has also been retained for surname endings in the main text (as in 'Dostoevsky' and 'Tolstoy'). Occasional exceptions have also been made in order to follow conventional renditions (e.g. 'Tchaikovsky' rather than 'Chaikovsky').

Referencing in this study, in order to cut down on the number of end-notes, is included in the text and normally follows the social sciences system (e.g. 'Todorov, 1973'). All such references are listed in the Bibliography. Titles of the more commonly used sources are frequently given on first prominent occurrence within the text proper. For the sake of convenience, references to literary titles quoted in the last three sections of Chapter 4 of Part Two are given by their one-word titles or by initials (e.g. '*Beloved*' for the novel of that name, or '*MC*' for *Midnight's Children*).

Part One
BACKGROUND AND THEORY

It was agreed that my endeavours should be directed to persons and characters supernatural . . . yet so as to transfer from our inward nature a human interest and a semblance of the truth sufficient to procure for these shadows of imagination that willing suspension of disbelief for the moment, which constitutes poetic faith.

Coleridge, Biographia Literaria

I Introduction

Τὸ φαντασικόν, c'est la faculté de se créer des illusions.

P-G Castex (1951, p. 8)

Critical and theoretical interest in 'the Fantastic' (and from here on we shall generally *try* to drop the quotation marks and the capital letter) has developed considerably over recent decades. The fantastic may not as yet constitute a branch of literary theory in its own right. However, it has, at the very least, become the centre of a sizeable body of critical writing. This is particularly the case since the appearance of Tzvetan Todorov's seminal study *The Fantastic: A structural approach to a literary genre* (Todorov, 1973, first published in French in 1970). Many of the post-1970 commentators to whom reference will be made during Part One of this volume have felt a need to respond in some way to Todorov's trail-blazing book. Some have endeavoured to develop or modify his ideas on the fantastic. Others have taken issue, by polemicising with or rejecting him.

It is also clear that the notion of the fantastic cuts across many branches of literary theory. Such a notion also, indeed, cuts across traditional ideas of genre theory, although it will here be argued that it is still in relation to genre that the literary fantastic may be most profitably discussed. Nevertheless, there is no doubt that valuable insights on the fantastic are to be drawn too from narrative theory, psychoanalytical theory, theory of discourse and other branches of post-structuralism. There is also no doubt that this will continue as a developing process.

Part One of the present study will look at a number of contributions to the critical debate over the fantastic. We shall then attempt to assess the current state of the argument, hoping to provide a degree of clarification by drawing certain distinctions, or by suggesting amendments to definitions and genre categories. But first we shall take a more historical — albeit selectively so — look at the topic, by considering a number of studies, precursory and tangential to that of Todorov, in the light of their treatment (or lack of treatment) of the fantastic.[1] Much of Part One at least will comprise, to a certain extent, something of a mosaic of linked quotation, or structured heteroglossia.

First, however, a preliminary clearing of the ground is required. We are concerned here, for practical purposes, with the fantastic as it may be discerned in narrative prose fiction (in other words, the novel and the short story). The point of departure will be Todorov's notion of hesitation on the part of the reader between a natural and a supernatural (preternatural or 'marvellous') explanation of the events presented in the narrative. Poetry, in all its forms, seems to me to require, and normally to achieve, an attitude of mind and a degree of suspension of belief on the part of the reader, or listener, quite distinct from those pertaining to prose fiction.[2] Furthermore, in cases when reader hesitation of the type here envisaged might arise — perhaps in certain narrative rather than lyric poetry — the effect is likely to derive at least as much from the incantatory quality of poetic form and language as from narrative content. Similarly, drama has, of its nature, an additional in-built quality of illusion, quite apart from the problem of variations and particularities in dramatic performance and visual presentation. It seems doubtful to me that it would be worthwhile even to consider isolating the fantastic in poetry; in the case of drama, a different approach and additional considerations would be required. No less a fantasist than J. R. R. Tolkien (1964, p. 46), in his essay 'On fairy stories', actually believed that 'Drama is naturally hostile to Fantasy.'

II   Towards a Background

Just as the word 'romantic' was cast into disrepute at 'the dawn of reason in the seventeenth and eighteenth centuries' (Siebers, 1984,

p. 10), the word 'fantastic' took on a largely derogatory connotation. Indeed, the romantic and the fantastic have long been closely linked and many examples of texts identified now as belonging to the fantastic are drawn from the romantic period. The period synonyms which Siebers supplies for 'romantic' ('chimeric', 'childish', 'ridiculous', 'absurd' and 'incredible') would most of all have been applied to those romantic works containing the qualities of the fantastic and the general tendency would have been, and may still remain today, for such works, or elements, to be dismissed as far-fetched.[3]

Not surprisingly, E. T. A. Hoffmann has always been one of the most frequently cited authors in connection with the fantastic. Recent commentators apart (and, in common with a wider general interest in the fantastic, there has been something of a revival of interest in Hoffmann the writer over the past two or three decades), Hoffmann's work attracted critical articles from such exalted figures as Walter Scott and Freud (the latter's essay having become a widely discussed document).

Scott, in his essay of 1827, defended the use of the supernatural in fiction, so long as it remained 'rare, brief, indistinct' (Scott, 1968, p. 316), but he objected to what he described as 'the FANTASTIC mode of writing' or 'style of composition', p. 325), which he attributed to 'the Germans' and saw as inimical to 'our English severity of taste' (p. 326). Scott admired Hoffmann's talent as displayed in *The Entail* and accorded him the dubious honour of being 'the inventor, or at least first distinguished artist who exhibited the fantastic or supernatural grotesque in his compositions, so nearly on the verge of actual insanity, as to be afraid of the beings his own fancy created' (p. 335). 'Unfortunately', in *The Sandman*, 'his taste and temperament directed him too strongly to the grotesque and fantastic' (p. 348). Scott felt that 'it is impossible to subject tales of this nature to criticism'; their resemblance to the effects of the immoderate use of opium rendered Hoffmann's case therefore 'one requiring the assistance of medicine rather than criticism' (p. 352).[4] The influential Russian critic Belinsky is well known, at least to students of Russian literature, for his strictures on the fantastic, for example in the early work of Dostoevsky. In relation to *The Double* (1846), Dostoevsky's first really original work, he wrote, as if echoing Scott: 'In our day the fantastic can have a place only in madhouses, not in literature, and be the domain of doctors, not of poets.'[5] Dostoevsky himself was an admirer of both Hoffmann and Poe. Also in Russia, V. F. Odoevsky (himself no mean practitioner of the fantastic) bracketed Hoffmann alongside Cervantes and Sterne, and recognised a double-sidedness in Hoffmann's 'marvellous' (*chudesnoe*) —

the presence of the realistic alongside the fantastic.[6] Poe himself (admired also by Odoevsky) appeared to equate the fantastic with 'Transcendentalism' ('Eureka', in Poe, 1976, pp. 240 and 262).

In France, Victor Hugo, in his famous preface to his drama *Cromwell* (1827), was stressing the grotesque (see Kayser, pp. 56–7), while Charles Nodier, in the 1830s, described the fantastic writer as a liar, urging that: 'to make the fantastic tale interesting, it is necessary first of all to be believed, and an indispensable condition for being believed is to believe'; once this was achieved, anything was possible (Siebers, 1984, pp. 57–8). Later on, Maupassant, writing on 'Le Fantastique' in 1883, drew attention to the supernatural in terms very close to what was to be Todorov's theory:

> when men believed without hesitation, fantastic writers took no precautions in spinning their astonishing tales. . . . But, when doubt finally penetrated men's minds, the art of storytelling became more subtle. The writer looked for nuances, prowled around the boundary of the supernatural rather than crossing it. He discovered terrible effects by hovering at the limit of the possible, by throwing men into hesitation, into bewilderment. (Siebers, pp. 46–7)

'Both Maupassant and Freud', Siebers tells us (p. 47), 'psychologized the fantastic'.

Freud himself, in his 1919 essay 'The "Uncanny"' ' (*Das Unheimliche*), following his psychological ruminations on this phenomenon and his analysis of Hoffmann's *The Sandman* (to which we shall have occasion to return in more detail at a later stage) arrives, like Maupassant, at what amounts virtually to a proto-theory of the fantastic; in connection with the (frequently unsatisfactory) presentation of supernatural elements in literature:

> the writer has one more means which he can use in order to avoid our recalcitrance and at the same time to improve his chances of success. He can keep us in the dark for a long time about the precise nature of the presuppositions on which the world he writes about is based, or he can cunningly and ingeniously avoid any definite information on the point to the last. (Freud, 1955, p. 251)

The Russian psychologist Lev Vygotsky (writing in the 1920s) noted

Freud's belief that the subconscious manifestations most closely approaching art are children's games and the fantasies of day-dreaming; creativity is thus seen as the continuation of a childhood game, the basis of which is assumed to be unsatisfied desires (Vygotsky, 1971, pp. 73–5). Vygotsky cautions against excessive Freudian readings and considers that, due to the luridness of unfulfilled desires, 'Freud, when he talks about the similarities of novels and fantasies, must take trash literature as a model' (p. 79). These points, of course, arise again when psychoanalytical approaches are taken (see, for example, Burgin, 1986, p. 96 and *passim*).

Mario Praz, in his classic study *The Romantic Agony* (first published 1933) spends much time discussing literature which could be considered as belonging to, or at least bordering on, the fantastic. However, his concerns are mainly thematic. Thus he concentrates largely on plot lines, psychological penetration and erotic sensibility in a wide range of authors dealing in diabolism and sado-masochism. The nearest Praz gets to noticing the fantastic as a concept is in such comments as the following, in relation to Mary Shelley: 'All Mrs Shelley did was to provide a passive reflection of some of the wild fantasies which, as it were, hung in the air about her' (Praz, 1970, p. 116); or a reference to 'the "fantastique" (that is, *delectatio morosa* of the sadistic type)' in connection with Flaubert's *Novembre* (p. 163). We shall have occasion to refer to a much later essay by Praz in Part Two.

The grotesque, as a commonly recognised form in art and literature, has clear connections with the fantastic. Wolfgang Kayser, in his celebrated study *The Grotesque in Art and Literature* (first published in 1957) provisionally adopts the eighteenth-century view of C. M. Wieland that the basic qualities of the grotesque are the provocation of 'laughter, disgust and astonishment' (Kayser, 1981, p. 30 and *passim*), but writes also of 'the dreamlike quality of a work and the unruly fantasy which creates its own world' (p. 40). Bosch and the Bruegels (particularly 'the Hell Bruegel'), the *commedia dell'arte* and medieval traditions of annihilating humour and satanic laughter contributed to a form recognisable as 'grotesque' by the Romantic era: in the practice of Bonaventura's *Nachtwachen* and the writings of Jean Paul Richter (commonly known as Jean Paul), Hoffmann and others, and in the theory of the Schlegels and Victor Hugo (the latter's *Cromwell* preface). We may also recall Scott's tendency to regard the fantastic and the grotesque as complementary, if not synonymous (Scott, 1968, pp. 335, 348; Hayter, 1988, p. 293).

At times the 'fantastic' is here distinguished from the 'grotesque':

Kayser approves Friedrich Schlegel's 'contrasting Jean Paul's gift for the grotesque with Tieck's penchant for the fantastic' (p. 81). In other places the fantastic seems to be treated as an ingredient of the grotesque: Kayser regards Sterne as a writer of the grotesque, 'for the categories of humour, satire and irony, of fantastic wantonness or wanton phantasmagoria fail to do full justice to the form and content of *Tristram Shandy*' (p. 51). Moreover:

> The irregular progression of the narrative and the apparent arbitrariness of the narrator seem to indicate that the latter is possessed by a strange power which is secretly allied with the maliciousness of inanimate objects and man's estrangement from his fellow men. (*ibid.*)

These are qualities, one would have thought, belonging as much to the fantastic as to the grotesque. The intertwining of the two is underlined by Kayser's reference to 'that mysterious and terrifying connection between the fantastic and the real world which is so essential for the grotesque' (p. 122). Here, we might now say, the words 'fantastic' and 'grotesque' could just as easily have been reversed.

Clear distinctions between 'fantasy', 'the fantastic' and 'the grotesque' are not, therefore, drawn by Kayser. We shall come to fantasy and the fantastic later; for the moment we are concerned with fantasy/fantastic and the grotesque. E. T. A. Hoffmann is said by Kayser to be 'a master in the composition of grotesque scenes' and an exponent of 'hellish grotesque' (p. 71). Hoffmann's *The Golden Pot* is seen as a work in which, as a whole, the grotesque plays a subsidiary role; rather 'the novella turns out to be a fairy tale illuminated by allegory' (p. 72): thus, we might say, it lies well within the realm of fantasy, but somewhat less within that of the grotesque. Where what would be recognised by many more recent commentators as the genuine fantastic occurs, for example in the configuration of Coppelius, Coppola and the fairy-tale sandman in *The Sandman*, Kayser appears to see it purely in terms of artistry, in a parenthetic comment: 'It is typical of Hoffmann's art that the doubts concerning their identity are never fully resolved' (p. 73).

A number of comments made by Kayser in his concluding attempts to define the grotesque have an obvious relevance to discussions of the fantastic. 'The grotesque is the estranged world' is one concluding point (p. 184), following through earlier comments on alienation (for example, as in Bonaventura); 'the grotesque is a play with the absurd' (p. 187) and, as 'a final interpretation', 'an attempt to invoke and subdue the demonic aspects of the world' (p. 188). 'The various forms of the grotesque' are, therefore, 'the most obvious and pronounced contradictions of any kind of rationalism and any systematic use of thought' (*ibid.*). Of these 'various forms', Kayser sees two basic types: 'the "fantastic" grotesque with its oneiric worlds and the radically "satiric" grotesque with its play of masks' (p. 186).

We pass now to Mikhail Bakhtin, whose works in question were written in the 1930s, but not published until the 1960s and 70s, by which time they appear to have undergone a certain degree of revision, or updating: indeed, Bakhtin (1968, pp. 46–52) was able to incorporate into his study of *Rabelais and his World* a critique of Kayser's book, which he finds to be of considerable value, but limited by its concentration on the modern period and in particular 'the spirit of Romanticism'. Bakhtin's own attitude to the 'romantic fantastic' is ambivalent:

> In the domain of creative literature the Romanticist concept justifies deviations from all that is static and humdrum, from documentation and typification. Finally, it justifies the grotesque and grotesque fantasy as an artistic presentation of time and of things to come. These are the indubitable merits of the Romanticist appreciation. (Bakhtin, 1968, p. 125)

However:

> The negative aspect of this appreciation is its idealism, its false concept of the role and limitations of subjective consciousness. The Romanticists often added invention to reality, depicting things which never existed. Fantasy degenerated into mysticism, human freedom broke away from necessity and became a super-material force. (*ibid.*)

In his studies of the novel, such as *The Dialogic Imagination*, Bakhtin draws attention to features of the chivalric romance: hyperbolisation of time, dreams, distortions and visions, amounting to what he terms 'the unique chronotope of this type of novel — a miraculous world in adventure-time' (Bakhtin, 1981, p. 154). Certain aspects of this, Bakhtin affirms, 'in particular the subjective playing with spatial and temporal perspectives', re-emerge in the novel, among

for example 'the Romantics . . . the Symbolists, the Expressionists
. . . and occasionally among the Surrealists as well' (p. 155).
Grotesque hyperbole and other similar exaggerated effects, done to
a purpose, are the qualities gaining Bakhtin's approval among 'the
distintive features of Rabelais' artistic method, the idiosyncrasies of
his fantastic realism' (p. 169). Bakhtin's concept of the chronotope
offers obvious scope to theorists of the fantastic, while his ideas on
'authoritative discourse' have, together with the somewhat similar
discourse theory of Foucault, already made an impact.

A far more obscure Soviet theorist of the 1930s, named
I. Mirimsky, published an article in 1938 which he called 'The social
fantastic of Hoffmann'. This article, which was seized on with
delight by Mikhail Bulgakov — then hard at work on *The Master
and Margarita* (see Curtis, 1987, pp. 199–200) — as an unlikely
intervention amid the gloom of Stalinist criticism, discerns in
Hoffmann a blend of romantic poetics and social satire. The various
dualities in Hoffmann — double-levels, dualism (*dvoemirie*) and the
propensity for doubles, in a play of contrasts between the real and
the fantastic, leads to a 'chronic dualism': 'Hoffmann's style may be
defined as the realistic–fantastic' (Mirimsky, 1938, pp. 70–1,
my translation). There is then a 'rational grain in Hoffmann's
conception of the fantastic'; the phenomenon of automata (once
again the example is from *The Sandman*) serves as a metaphor of 'the
material nature of human relations in bourgeois society' (p. 81).
Hoffmann usually employs 'a whole arsenal of devices and means
with the help of which he lays bare and surmounts the mystical
enigma of his horrific scenes'; particularly important is the use of
irony, which 'destroys the seriousness of the wonders and distances
the author from his protagonists, who are subject to an unhealthy
fear and faith in everything supernatural' (p. 82).

'The power of illusion — that is the issue', writes Pierre
Macherey in the 1960s (*A Theory of Literary Production*, 1978, p. 47).
Reminding us of Platonic ideas of representation, he quotes
Nietzsche's statement that 'the artist drapes the veil of uncertainty
over things' (p. 147). Macherey approaches what might be considered the fantastic, for example in Jules Verne's *The Mysterious
Island*, by reference to 'a very specific mode of expression: the
imaginary narrative', in which 'the imaginary is the real, just as the
future is the present' (p. 171). 'The imaginary narrative' is for
Macherey 'a literary genre', and such a book belongs to 'the
literature of fantasy', involving an interaction between form and
content corresponding to 'natural theme' and 'the operations of the
"fantastic"' (pp. 172–3), in its representations of such elements as

adventure, mystery and mystification. Verne uses 'symbolisation' and allegory in the creation of his Mysterious Island (p. 215) and at one point 'nearly succumbs to the temptation of an imagery of the miraculous' (p. 219). In *Robinson Crusoe*, with which Verne's novel has a curious intertextual relationship, Macherey (p. 242) notes the early prominence of the theme of Providence, linked with 'the outline of a thematic of fantasy: vague premonitions and the devil', 'a diffuse deism', and 'a sequence of "miracles"; life on the island is a "tissue of wonders"'. However, the fantasy themes are exorcised: 'the "story" itself puts the devil to flight; it was a cannibal, an old goat . . . and Providence is quickly forgotten'; at the same time, 'behind the fantastic there also stands nature, the tricks played by nature' (p. 243).

There have in addition, of course, been broader investigations into the aesthetics of fantasy, which may include a consideration of literature. One such is Elémire Zolla's *Storia del fantasticare* (*The History of Fantasising*), a wide-ranging cultural study — literary, psychological, anthropological — of the art of fantasising.

The fantastic as such is, of course, not the main concern of critics such as Macherey or Praz — or even of Kayser and Bakhtin, whose principal preoccupations may seem closer, at least in certain of their works. Nevertheless, the kind of often imprecise skirting around, or rubbing shoulders with, the fantastic which is to be found in these and other commentators can be instructive, not least in a consideration of the borders of the fantastic, and of what the fantastic is not (or the avoidance of the fantastic), as well as of the critical history of the term itself and related notions. These issues have been concentrated on rather more systematically by Todorov and his successors, to whom we now turn our attention.

III   Some Definitions: Todorov *et al.*

One pre-Todorovian commentator, Louis Vax in 1960 (in his *L'Art et la littérature fatastiques*) forbore any formal definition of 'fantasy', confining himself instead to categories of subject matter, ranging from werewolves to personality troubles (usually extravagantly sexual) and human degeneration (see Hume, 1984, p. 13).

Todorov, however, attacked the question of the fantastic head-on in formal terms, involving an interaction between narrative (including character) and reader. His basic approach may be encapsulated as follows:

> In a world which is indeed our world . . . there occurs an event which cannot be explained by the laws of this same familiar world. The person who experiences the event must opt for one of two possible solutions. . . . The fantastic occupies the duration of this uncertainty. Once we choose one answer or the other, we leave the fantastic for a neighbouring genre, the uncanny or the marvelous. . . . The possibility of hesitation between the two creates the fantastic effect. (Todorov, 1973, p. 25–6).

The conditions required for this are elaborated further:

> The fantastic requires the fulfilment of three conditions. First, the text must oblige the reader to consider the world of the characters as a world of living persons and to hesitate between a natural and a supernatural explanation of the events described. Second, this hesitation may also be experienced by a character . . . and at the same time the hesitation is represented, it becomes one of the themes of the work. . . . Third, the reader must adopt a certain attitude with regard to the text: he will reject allegorical as well as 'poetic' interpretations. . . . The first and third actually constitute the genre; the second may not be fulfilled. (p. 33)

Todorov himself supplies remarkably few examples of works which belong, by his criteria, to what may be considered the 'pure fantastic' — in which the hesitation is sustained and remains to the end unresolved — but further examples have been found and these will be added to.[7] In any case, despite the objections of some critics, it is not clear that a paucity of perfect examples necessarily disqualifies Todorov's theoretical model and, in any case, the sub-categories which he nominates, and which have been (and will again be) further elaborated, render his system far more widely useful than some are prepared to acknowledge (such as Hume, pp. 13–20, who also quotes a number of further 'definitions', some of which amount to no more than comments). We shall return to this question.

Stanislaw Lem, in a surprisingly traditional response for so intellectually inventive a writer, sharply attacked the pretensions of structuralism (in 1973) in the form of Todorov's theory of the fantastic. Structuralism, Lem feels, is not so much 'wrong' (he agrees with Todorov, for example, that there can be no such thing as fantastic poetry) as misapplied and inadequate to the task which it takes upon itself: 'a theory of literature either embraces all works or it is no theory' (Lem, 1985, p. 232). Such a maximalist approach, of course, would leave precious little room for theoretical manoeuvre; moreover Lem himself, in his other critical writings, is rigorous enough by his own empirical lights — being fully conscious, for example, of the 'specific rules of literary games' and their relation to the 'real' world (on Lem's critique of Todorov, see also Brooke-Rose, 1983, pp. 61–2).[8]

A more coherently reasoned critique of Todorov's 'scientific' claims, his range and the 'timid approach' to borrowed (non-literary) terms in his categorisations has been made in an article by John Reichert (in Strelka, 1978), while Antonio Risco has complained of Todorov's 'excessively formalist definition' (Risco, 1982, p. 19). Harold Bloom (1982, p. 205) denies that we 'hesitate' in reading Hoffmann and others, but his Freudian–Gnostic approach confines itself to fantasy (mainly the work of David Lindsay) rather than treating what we shall understand here as 'the fantastic'.

For Eric Rabkin, in his study *The Fantastic in Literature* (Rabkin, 1976, p. 8), 'the perspectives enforced by the ground rules of the narrative world must be diametrically contradicted' in order for the fantastic to appear; he further explains: 'the truly fantastic occurs when the ground rules of a narrative are forced to make 180-degree reversal, when prevailing perspectives are directly contradicted' (p. 12). One of his main examples is Lewis Carroll's Alice books:

> The key to the fantastic . . . is not to be found in simple comparison with the real world but in examination of the reading process. We find the reader reaction that characterizes the fantastic [i.e. Alice's astonishment] when the operative ground rules are reversed. (Rabkin, 1979, pp. 20–1)

Like Todorov, Rabkin requires astonishment and recognition of this astonishment: on the part of the character in the fiction, as well as of the reader. Brooke-Rose (p. 392 n. 1) finds Rabkin's 'precise working out' of his suppositions 'theoretically unsatisfactory', being in practice too inclusive. We shall come to the question of 'inclusive' and 'exclusive' definitions shortly.

W. R. Irwin, in *The Game of the Impossible* (1976, p. 4) adopted the principle of 'overt violation of what is generally accepted as possibility', an initial rule also accepted by Brian Attebery, in his *The Fantasy Tradition in American Literature*, (1980, pp. 1–2), who attached particular importance to the presence of a vividly-realised secondary creation, and what Tolkien had called the commitment to 'secondary belief': in short, 'any narrative which includes as a significant part of its make-up some violation of what the author clearly believes to be natural law' (p. 2). Tolkien himself (1964, p. 44) had seen the fantastic as 'freedom from the domination of observed "fact" '. C. N. Manlove's *Modern Fantasy* (1975, pp. 10–11) again provided a similar definition of the somewhat broad category of fantasy literature:

> A fiction evoking wonder and containing a substantial and irreducible element of supernatural or impossible worlds, beings or objects with which the reader or the characters within the story become on at least partly familiar terms. (quoted again in Manlove, 1983, p. ix)

Two important contributions from critics who basically accept Todorov, but with some elaboration or qualification, appeared in 1981 from Christine Brooke-Rose and Rosemary Jackson.[9]

Brooke-Rose, in her book *A Rhetoric of the Unreal*, (1983) taking Todorov's principle of 'hesitation' as a point of departure, emphasises the concept of ambiguity: 'the complexity and the subtlety of the pure fantastic lies in its absolute ambiguity' (p. 229). Commenting on Todorov's distinction of 'pure fantastic' from 'uncanny' and 'marvellous', she writes:

> If the only feature that distinguishes the pure fantastic from the uncanny and the marvellous is ambiguity, which in turn is shared with some non-fantastic fiction, we must either emphasise (as Todorov does) that this ambiguity concerns only the supernatural (thus in effect falling back on the supernatural as basic element), or treat such other non-'fantastic' texts as a displaced form of the fantastic. (p. 65)

Hesitation, ambiguity and the supernatural are therefore the key elements. Brooke-Rose's main criticism of Todorov's theory is its inability to place satisfactorily, or theoretically to account for, works such as Gogol's *The Nose* and Kafka's *Metamorphosis*, where hesitation is not present in the required manner, and categories seem blurred (pp. 66–7). Furthermore, the obvious existence of ambiguity without reference to the supernatural (in various modern texts — her main example here is the work of Robbe-Grillet) prompts a need for some reconsideration of the sub-genres adjacent to the pure fantastic. Brooke-Rose's approach to this question is by way of a consideration of the categories of 'the unreal as real' (by which she means the employment of predominantly traditional 'realistic' narrative methods to treat what is in fact the marvellous, as in much of science fiction and other forms of fantasy novel); and of 'the real as unreal' (essentially an updated elaboration of the Russian Formalist term *ostranenie* — which she calls 'estrangement from the familiar', 'defamiliarisation' or 'distancing' — in what are considered to amount to baroque forms of the uncanny). Gogol and Kafka are seen as the first to employ 'the treatment of what used to be called the unreal as real' (p. 51; see also Strada, 1988, p. 133).

While also basically accepting his formula, Jackson's study, *Fantasy: The literature of subversion* (1981), wishes 'to extend Todorov's investigation from being one limited to the *poetics* of the fantastic into one aware of the *politics* of its forms' (p. 6); she also wishes to supply a corrective to Todorov in respect of a greater stress on psychoanalysis, so as 'to stretch Todorov's ideas into a more widely based cultural study of the fantastic' (p. 7). She writes of 'fantasy as a literary mode' — 'mode' in Frederic Jameson's sense, implying 'structural features underlying various works in different periods of time'; 'fantasy', she suggests, 'is a literary mode from which a number of related genres emerge': the '*langue*, from which its various forms, or *paroles*, derive' (*ibid.*). She declares: 'It is possible, then, to modify Todorov's scheme slightly and to suggest a definition of the fantastic as a *mode*, which then assumes different generic forms' (p. 35).

Jackson derives inspiration (Todorov apart) from Sartre, according to whom 'fantasy' invented supernatural regions while the religious view of the world prevailed, since when it has assumed 'its proper function': the transformation of this world (pp. 17–18). From Carroll's preface to *Sylvie and Bruno Concluded* (1893), she draws his distinction between three mental states ('ordinary', 'eerie' and 'trance-like'), which she relates to three literary modes (mimetic, fantastic and marvellous respectively);[10] thus, for her: 'the fantastic exists in the hinterland between "real" and "imaginary", shifting the relations between them through its indeterminacy' (p. 35). She also distinguishes a particular form of narrative presentation for each mode: that for the marvellous is seen as essentially authoritative narrative, that for the mimetic as 'a knowing third-person' mouthpiece, while the central narrative characteristic of the fantastic is its instability (pp. 33–4). Furthermore, from a consideration of these and other sources, Jackson concludes (p. 41): 'the fantastic, then, pushes towards an area of non-signification', while contradictions, contraventions, opposites and negations embodied in the text inspire, in reader and protagonist alike, Todorovian hesitation and 'apprehension (in the double sense of perceiving and of fearing)' (p. 49).

Without any reference to Todorov, T. E. Apter, in her *Fantasy Literature*, (1982) would seem to accept his basic argument: 'At the heart of fantasy in modern fiction is the uncertainty as to which world the tale belongs — to this one, or to a very different one?' (p. 2). But her own approach leans towards a cautious application of psychoanalysis: 'in modern fantasy at its best, the extension proceeds through psychological investigation' (p. 19). We shall return to Freudianism later.

On the subject of 'worlds', T. E. Little, in his *The Fantasts* (1984, pp. 9–10) presents an interesting formulation (developed from the approach of Tolkien, 1964). Deciding that 'a definition of Fantasy to include all the works commonly accepted as belonging to the genre would be a near impossible achievement', he goes on to essay the following, essentially generic scheme, based on the concept of worlds:

> All writers of creative fiction are subcreators of Secondary Worlds. The Secondary World of a non-fantastic writer will be as close to the Primary World as his talents and the needs of his art will allow. . . . A licence is granted to writers of 'normal' creative fiction to change the Primary World for the purpose of their art. Fantasy begins when an author's Secondary World goes beyond that licence and becomes 'other'. . . . Such a subcreation should be called a *Tertiary World*. (pp. 9–10)

This formula has a certain appeal, and no doubt a certain validity. However, the exact dividing lines between secondary and tertiary worlds, and even those between primary and secondary (see, for attempted guidelines on this, Little, 1980), do not seem sufficiently precise, and, as Little's selection of texts demonstrates, there are also gradations of tertiary world.[11] Perhaps all formulae are open to the objection that they generate either too few examples to be generally useful, or too many?

Tobin Siebers also eschews definitions as such in his study of *The Romantic Fantastic* (1984). He concentrates on what he calls the 'interference' between 'the Romantic and the fantastic', and in particular their convergence with 'those aspects of experience that venture beyond the strictly human toward a supernatural realm' and 'the superstitious nightmares of common men' (p. 9); Washington Irving's *The Spectre Bridegroom* is taken as a paradigmatic 'parable'. 'Supernaturalism', Siebers feels, is the neglected side of the fantastic: 'No critic of fantastic literature writing today', he laments, 'has developed a theory of supernaturalism'; furthermore, he declares: 'Supernaturalism is a difficult issue to discuss, however, especially today when any mention of the word risks casting one's intentions and scholarship in doubt' (p. 11).[12] According to Siebers, the natural scepticism of romantic authors towards the supernatural led to an aestheticisation of superstition, which in turn led to a transformation of its own: 'The Romantics began to lose sight of the doubt that originally permitted them to transform the supernatural into an aesthetic doctrine; and the doubters and liars often turned into true lovers of lies' (p. 57). Siebers quotes Gautier's comment on the spiritualism described in his novella *Spirite*: 'I no longer believe in it, but I did believe in it while I was writing the book' (p. 61). In keeping with Jackson's notion of 'instability' in the narrative of the fantastic, Siebers, while regarding narrative unreliability as 'a provocative notion',[13] considers that:

> the fantastic represents an exceptional case of narrative unreliability. Mérimée, Nodier, and Gautier defined the fantastic as a lie, requiring that the critical reader not only interrogate the complex relation between fantastic representation and falsehood in general, but study every lie in a fantastic story, for only then will both the aesthetic and social dimensions of the fantastic come to light. (p. 63)

The social dimension of the fantastic, for Siebers, is best revealed by an anthropological approach: 'The literary critic needs to clarify the anthropology of fantastic literature and not its metaphysics' (p. 45). A key element in this is the concept of superstition: 'Romantic and fantastic literature both thematize the relation between literature and superstition, as well as demonstrate an extraordinary awareness of social violence' (p. 13). Superstition itself (although he frequently seems to regard the word as interchangeable with 'the supernatural'), Siebers defines essentially as: 'a logic that creates representations of difference among individuals in order to facilitate social organization and stratify violent desires' (p. 45; see also p. 12: 'the logic that represents identities as differences'). The stories of Maupassant, for example, in the view of Siebers, 'like the fantastic in general, produce uncanny effects by representing the accusatory patterns of superstition' (p. 47). Siebers thus adds the dimensions of social persecution, or an awareness thereof, to the other ingredients which we have regarded as basic to the fantastic, in an interaction between what he regards as anthropology and poetics: 'Superstition in society and fantastic literature both function by turning the many against the one, and this process generates the essential feature of suspense' (p. 56). Siebers's approach, of course, while adding its social dimension, remains tied, by the very scope of his book, to the romantic period — in common with Todorov's study.

Kathryn Hume, in her book *Fantasy and Mimesis* (1984), purports to be dissatisfied with both generic definitions and Jackson's somewhat broader approach, as being 'insufficient through self-limitation' (p. 20) (although the difference between her own suggestion of 'impulse', as against Jackson's 'mode', would seem to be merely a slight one of degree):

> Whereas other critics writing on fantasy try to identify it as a genre or mode, I have tried not to isolate fantasy from the rest of literature. It is truer to literary practice to admit that fantasy is not a separate or indeed a separable strain, but rather an impulse as significant as the mimetic impulse, and to recognise that both are involved in the creation of most literature. (p. xii)

It is proposed by Hume, therefore, that 'literature is the product of two impulses': *mimesis* and *fantasy* (imitation of reality — alteration of reality), leading to 'a working definition of fantasy whose aim is to be as inclusive and as flexible as possible' (p. 20). This working definition amounts to the following: 'Fantasy is any departure from consensus reality', which can be manifested 'in innumerable variations, from monster to metaphor'. It includes (p. 21) 'transgressions of what one generally takes to be physical facts' (human immortality, travel faster than light, telekinesis, telepathy), 'technical or social innovations which have not yet taken place' (human cloning, utopian societies), 'alternate worlds and universes' and 'those stories whose marvel is considered "real"' (miracles and monsters that may once have been believed in). Hume's inclusive definition is not, however, all-inclusive: she excludes 'the realistic novel and occasional earlier picaresque and satiric tales'; 'escapist literature which is unrealistic but not a departure from what could physically happen in this world' (such as many women's magazine stories); and 'simply what we normally call fiction' — historical novels and the like, 'which use invented characters in real or imagined situations', but which 'are not trying to depart from consensus reality, for all that they describe something which did not actually happen' (p. 22). 'Raw daydream content' (*ibid.*) is therefore excluded. Despite these qualifications, Hume's definition, and indeed her book, is applicable to a pretty broad spectrum of literary texts.

Another commentator to adopt a broad, though more systematic, approach to the fantastic is the Soviet scholar, Iurii Mann. In his book *Poetika Gogolia* (*Gogol's Poetics*, 1978), Mann discusses the fantastic in Jean Paul, Hoffmann and Pushkin (*The Queen of Spades*), before passing to Gogol, in a study heavily influenced by Bakhtin's ideas of carnivalisation, but also demonstrating a considerable knowledge of western thinkers and critics — including Kayser and Auerbach, but with no apparent knowledge of Todorov. However, Mann's basic approach is close to that of Todorov; he quotes (p. 70, n. 1) Slonimsky's comment on 'the hesitations between a fantastic and a realistic–psychological motivation' in *The Queen of Spades*. His theory of the fantastic, worked out in Chapter 3 (pp. 59–132) of his study, sees the form arising as a variant of the fairy story, or the mystery story/thriller (or a combination of both, as in certain works of Hoffmann) and normally open to both a supernatural and a realistic explanation; he also mentions the categories of the 'unreal' (*irreal'noe*) and the 'strangely-unusual' (*stranno-neobychnoe*), which would correspond to Todorov's 'marvellous' and 'uncanny'. Where Mann parts company from Todorov, and indeed most others, is in his extension of his terminology from the fantastic to what would more customarily be considered structural or narrative devices and to imagery, plus various techniques of mystification and the playing down, or even the avoidance, of the fantastic. He thus employs such categories as:

1. 'The veiled (non-appearing) fantastic' (*zavualirovannaia [neiavnaia] fantastika*), which may feature as rumoured fantastic (unconfirmed by the narrator), relegation of the fantastic to the distant past or pre-history of the story, and unusual chains of cause and effect or coincidence.
2. 'The omission of the exponent of the fantastic' (*sniatiia nositelia fantastiki*), the leaving out of a character embodying

the fantastic, or even (as in *The Nose*) literal removal of the fantastic member, accompanied by a consequent parodying or reversal of the expected romantic conventions, still leaving behind a quality of 'fantasticity' (*fantastichnost'*).

3. 'The non-fantastic fantastic' (*nefantasticheskaia fantastika*), which includes (as in, for example, *Dead Souls*): 'the appearance of the uncanny in the discourse of the narrator, in the actions and thoughts of the characters, in the behaviour of things, the external appearance of objects, confusion in travel and general chaos' (p. 292) — in other words, all manner of narrational illogicalities and quirks.

These categories are seen as stages in the development of Gogol's treatment of the fantastic, leading towards a gradual retreat of the fantastic from character and plot into 'the everyday, things, people's behaviour, thought and speech' (p. 129): ultimately from content into form, or 'into style' (p. 131).

A different approach altogether to what is broadly the usual thematic material from a wide range of texts is taken by Theodore Ziolkowski in his impressive study *Disenchanted Images: A literary iconology* (1977). He is concerned with 'the cultural origins of three related magic images and with the history of their disenchantment as reflected in European literature of the past two hundred years' (p. 227). The magic images concerned are those of statues (and rings), portraits and mirrors' ('the animated statues', 'the haunted portrait' and 'the magic mirror'). The emphasis is on the process of 'disenchantment' through successive stages in the nineteenth century (from magic, to ambiguity, to psychology) and on to reanimation in the twentieth, providing a historical dimension which Todorov is said to lack (p. 230). We shall return later to some of Ziolkowski's findings.

Another interestingly variant glance at the fantastic, apparently unaffected by the Todorovian school, is to be found in a recent essay by the Italian Russianist, Vittorio Strada. Strada starts like Macherey, with a Platonic base (Plato's apparently distinct attitudes to myth, as opposed to philosophical myth such as his 'myth of the cave'), superimposing embellishments from Jean Paul and Vladimir Solov'ëv. In Strada's view, Plato's 'myth of the cave':

can point the way to a definition of the fantastic which is a form of invention on the part of a poetic reason born in the post-mythic age, an age in which the model of knowledge and of truth is constituted from an empirical and positive science, from the viewpoint of which myth, deprived of its symbolic significance, turns into pure superstition, or a primitive stage of knowledge — imperfect and superceded. (Strada, 1988, p. 130, my translation)

In intellectual myth, however, there may appear a quality of the 'modern' fantastic, as opposed to the 'supernatural' marvellous (*il prodigioso*):

as a presentiment of another reality, as an image of the invisible, as code for the unknowable. The fantastic is a form of consciousness of being in the cave, a hypothetical invention and a mental experiment in the impossible — a necessary spiritual paradox for grasping the possible. The fantastic is a poetic mythology of a disenchanted and demythologised world, the opening of an empirical reality on to a metaphysical surreality, the discovery of an enigmatic and problematic dimension of our humanity. (p. 131)

According to Jean Paul, the fantastic (or marvellous) 'must not fly like a bird of the day, nor like a bird of the night, but like a moth, the butterfly of twilight': it is in this intermediate light that the fantastic dwells. From Solov'ëv (on whom see below), Strada takes a concept of another causality: 'the fantastic, with the double causality of which Solov'ëv speaks, is the twilight butterfly of Jean Paul which flies within the penumbra, between the darkness of Plato's cave and his ideal of the sun' (p. 132).

This philosophical approach, akin in its poetic way, nevertheless, to the more mundane abstractions of genre theory, is then extended historically to encompass the rendition, in works of literature, of what are seen as myths of 'the fantastic metahistory of Russia'.[14] This stimulating approach to the fantastic lies somewhat outside the mainstream of generic debate (Strada uses both verse and prose texts without comment) but still manages to retain a certain ultimate relevance.

Among recent refinements to the Todorovian line of approach, Deborah Losse (1986) examines the distinctions and connections (in Rabelais) between concepts of the fantastic and carnival, based on Todorov and Bakhtin respectively. Margaret Carter, in her study *Specter or Delusion?* (1987), stresses the growing importance in the Gothic period attached to documents and evidence: 'The "fantastic" situation arises in a milieu where a common standard of evidence and belief is not universally accepted' (p. 9). She further emphasises the phenomenon of the 'preternatural' (such as Frankenstein's monster): 'the true explanation lies in scientific laws yet unknown to the majority of men' (p. 66). This logically extends the boundaries of discussion further towards science fiction.

Most usefully, perhaps, Amaryll Chanady makes two advances, or at least clarifications, in her *Magical Realism and The Fantastic* (1985). She strengthens, or surpasses, the concept of ambiguity in the fantastic by substituting for 'hesitation' the term 'antinomy', defined as 'the simultaneous presence of two conflicting codes in the text', standing for two different levels (such as reality and irreality, or the natural and the supernatural); since these are seen as mutually exclusive, 'the apparently supernatural phenomenon remains inexplicable' (p. 12). Rather than the reader's merely reacting to textual indications, it is, in Chanady's view, 'the antinomy of the text that produces the ambiguity of the fictional world and thus the disorientation of the reader' (p. 14).[15] The idea of contradictory codes co-existing within the text facilitates the distinction that Chanady then proceeds to make between the fantastic and magic realism: this is seen to reside mainly in 'the manner in which the irrational world view is perceived by the narrator' (p. 23). The supernatural in fantastic works is presented as a problematic or illogical intrusion in terms of the 'reality' established; in the divergent narrative tone of magic realism, however, things are rather different: 'the supernatural is not present as problematic' (*ibid.*). The main consequence of this state of affairs is that: 'Whereas there is always the suggestion of a rational explanation in the fantastic, a magico-realist text prevents the reader from even considering a rational solution' (p. 106).[16]

Before leaving the area of definitions, we might cite another definition of the supernatural (*sverkh"estestvennoe*), which may be presumed to equate closely to the fantastic, provided by the Russian semiotician, I. P. Smirnov (1985):

> The concept of the supernatural requires explanation. One of the oppositions of our cognitive practice is the distinction between what is accessible to our organs of feeling — what physically exists — and what is imagined. The supernatural arises when what is imagined is described as though it were sensibly perceived reality. (pp. 53–4, my translation)

The reality–imagination dichotomy is, of course, a recurring theme in critical approaches to the fantastic.

To conclude this section, we will make brief mention of the

approaches to the fantastic advanced by three earlier Russian writers.

Dostoevsky wrote on *The Queen of Spades* (a text which is as good a candidate as any, in most estimations, for Todorov's category of the pure fantastic):

> Pushkin who gave us almost all artistic forms, wrote *The Queen of Spades* — the epitome of the art of the fantastic. You believe that Herman really had a vision, exactly in accordance with his view of the world, and yet, at the end of the story, i.e. when you have read it through, you cannot make up your mind: did this vision come out of Herman's nature or was he really one of those who are in contact with another world. . . . That's art for you! (quoted from Mann, p. 70; see also Jackson, p. 27)

Elsewhere, Dostoevsky wrote that 'the fantastic must be so close to the real that you almost have to believe in it' (see Jackson, p. 27).[17] In his story *A Gentle Spirit*, Dostoevsky provides a curious notion of the fantastic, envisaging it in the person of a fantastic stenographer, taking down the frenzied discourse of a protagonist in extremis. Here he would seem to mean a fantastic quality inherent in the use of omniscient narration, or in the presentation of stream of consciousness. Milan Kundera, referring to Joyce's *Ulysses*, has recently alluded to 'the fantastic espionage of interior monologue' (Kundera, 1988, p. 28). In pratice, of course, Dostoevsky utilises forms of the fantastic as more usually understood — in early works such as *The Double* and *The Landlady*, and later in *Bobok* and *The Dream of a Ridiculous Man*.

Vladimir Solov'ëv, whom we have just seen (above) quoted by Strada, had also been used by Todorov (1973, pp. 25–6) in support of his theory of the fantastic. Solov'ëv, apropos of A. K. Tolstoy's prose romance *The Vampire*, commented that the interest and the significance of the fantastic

> is governed by the conviction that all that happens to the world, and particularly in human life, depends, its present and evident causes apart, also on another causality — more profound and universal, but less clear. . . . And therein lies the distinct element of what is *authentically* fantastic: this never presents itself, so to speak, in *naked* form. Its symptoms should never provoke a forced faith in the mystical sense of the events of life, but rather should give an indication, an

allusion of this sense. In that which is authentically fantastic, there remains always the formal external possibility of a simple explanation of the ordinary and common link between phenomena, but at the same time this explanation is completely stripped of internal probability. All the separate particulars must have an everyday characteristic and only the link between the whole should indicate another causality. (Solov'ëv, 1966, pp. 376, 377, my translation)

Solov'ëv was himself a mystical poet and religious philosopher; his commentary on the fantastic has usually been taken since as especially applicable to prose fiction.

Lastly, Brooke-Rose (p. 60) cites Nathalie Sarraute, 'for whom the true realists are the so-called formalists, who try hard to look at reality in a new way and to evolve new forms that will capture the new, unfamiliar reality'. Hume (p. 41) informs us that 'an electron microscope would reveal an entirely different reality from the one initially being observed'. These comments demonstrate a renewed currency for Zamiatin's notion of the fantastic (as a constituent of his concept of 'Neo-Realism') in the real in the form of reality under the microscope.[18]

IV　The Common Ground

Let us consider here the areas in which there is broad agreement, before attempting to determine where the main confusions or controversies lie. Prose fiction, in its various forms, comes down essentially to a matter of signs — or images in words — on printed paper. Linda Hutcheon's *Narcissistic Narrative* (1984) reminds us too (apropos of self-conscious [or meta-] fiction in particular) that 'a novel only becomes a living aesthetic reality when actualized by the act of being read' (p. 146). This does not seem to be disputed — nor could it reasonably be so. Furthermore, it seems to be agreed that a distinction must be made between the everyday world, or actual reality, in which author and reader both live (albeit separated — perhaps extensively — by time, distance and culture) and *any* world ever created, described or occurring in fiction.

This basic position may be demonstrated by means of a model constructed in terms of 'worlds' (as, with certain differences, by

Little and Hume). Or it may be stated in other ways, with slightly differing emphases. Brooke-Rose (p. 320) writes that:

> the very notion of mimesis is an illusion: unlike dramatic representation, narrative cannot imitate the story it is telling; it can only tell it, and give an illusion of mimesis, unless the object imitated is language (as in dialogue).

In relation to the world(s) of fiction, the fantastic/fantasy and the real/secondary world are seen to be mutually dependent. According to Jackson (p. 20):

> Fantasy re-combines and inverts the real, but it does not escape it: it exists in a parasitical or symbiotic relation to the real. The fantastic cannot exist independently of that 'real' world which it seems to find so frustratingly finite.

There is something of 'the fantastic', or an equivalent notion, in 'realism' and vice versa. Macherey's reading of Plato on resemblance in *The Cratylus* leads him to state (p. 61) that 'the idea of imitation, correctly understood, implies distortion'. Hume (p. xii) argues that 'fantasy is *an element* in nearly all kinds of literature', while Siebers maintains, in keeping with his thesis, that 'all Romantic literature inclines restlessly toward the fantastic' (Siebers, p. 13). Jackson too (1981, p. 13) stresses that, in a general sense, 'all imaginary activity is fantastic, all literary works are fantasies.'

Roger Fowler (1979) challenges any exclusion of the referential function in the novel:

> the reader has to make sense of the content by reconstructing it as a world which is plausible in terms of the world he knows. (Or, in the case of the fantastic, related to 'our' world by systematic transformations). (Fowler, p. 9; quoted from Brooke-Rose, p. 28)

Brooke-Rose goes on to state (p. 81): 'Obviously there is a realistic basis in all fantastic narrative, and even a fairy-tale will have some point of anchorage in the real, since the unreal can only seem so as against the real.' For Hutcheon (1984, p. 77), 'Fantasy is indeed the "other side of realism"; and represents historically a parallel and equally valid literary tradition'; at the same time, though, even 'the most extreme autonomous universes of fantasy are still referential; if they were not the reader could not imagine their existence'.

In relation to Balzac, Macherey (p. 268) affirms that even in the 'matter of writing a book which shall be like a world', 'the imaginary universe is not a reflection of the real universe.' A linkage similar to the foregoing is perceived by Apter; she writes:

> Fantasy in modern literature depends upon realism in literature: it depends upon the reader's ability to recognise a commonly acknowledged, or normal, world and to recognise descriptions as pertaining to, or failing to pertain to, normal conditions. The initial impact of fantasy is its deviation from the norm. (1982, p. 111)

Her loosely psychoanalytical slant provides a similar confirmation (p. 31): 'Human perception and fear create moral laws; our creations are our reality — and this recognition forms the bedrock of fantasy.'

This general area of agreement receives particular emphasis, for example, in Jackson's approach of 'mode', Hume's twin imagination/ mimetic impulses and Hutcheon's parallel literary traditions.

Hutcheon's view of fantasy/the fantastic as the obverse of realism points towards ideas, articulated particularly by Siebers and Jackson, of the fantastic as the outlet for the exclusions and taboos, the estrangements and alienation of bourgeois society. 'Fantastic literature enshrines differences', writes Siebers (p. 9); he argues that the demystification of supernatural representation, which the eighteenth-century rationalists had associated with ideological persecution, itself assumed a phase of intolerance, provoking the following reaction:

> To combat Rationalism, the Romantic assumed the voice of its victims. Suddenly, the madmen, divine idiots, and sorcerers, who had been the outcasts of the Enlightenment, became novelistic heroes, and the Romantic artist draped himself in Faustian attire. (p. 123)

However, he continues, 'the Romantic's appropriation of the victim's position did not eliminate persecution and exclusion any more than the Rationalist's recognition of the violence of religious ideology' (*ibid.*).

Fantastic literature, for Jackson (1981, pp. 3–4), can both 'tell of' and 'expel' desire; therefore:

> fantastic literature points to or suggests the basis upon which cultural order rests, for it opens up, for a brief moment, on to

disorder, on to illegality, on to that which lies outside the law, that which is outside dominant value systems.

'Literary fantasy', she claims, 'is a telling index of the limits' of 'the dominant cultural order' (p. 4). In respect of social and cultural taboos (incest, necrophilia, the un-dead), 'fantasies make up for a society's prohibitions by allowing vicarious fulfilment' (p. 70). Jackson extends her argument to viewing the fantastic as a subversive influence for social change, though fully recognising that it can, in its pure escapist form, also serve as a conservative or repressive force.

Such views of the social function and purpose of this type of literature, if not strongly argued by other recent commentators, do not seem to excite great disagreement. There would, therefore, appear to be a fairly extensive consensus for seeing a more prominent, if not autonomous, role for the fantastic element in the history of prose literature, in interlocking and mutual dependence on 'reality' within the fictionality of fictional worlds, and given to the expression of — and perhaps at times making an impression upon — particular social and psychological tendencies. To take matters any further, we have to return to the sphere of definitions and interpretations, in order to try and assess where the differences lie.

V   The 'Fantastic'/'Fantasy' Disarray

It may well be apparent by now that a certain inconsistency, not to say confusion, exists in the application of the expressions 'the fantastic', 'fantastic' (as an adjective) and 'fantasy'. This should be particularly evident from the range of quotations above, taken from a variety of critics — although there may also remain traces of it in the surrounding commentary. [Brooke-Rose shrewdly observes (in relation to criticism of *The Turn of the Screw*, her p. 132) that 'critics reproduce the very tendencies they so often notice in the governess: omission; assertion; elaboration; lying even (or, when the critics do so, let us call it error)'; while, as for theoreticians, 'It is in fact quite remarkable how often theorists abandon their own theories as soon as they analyse texts' (p. 82); furthermore, what is 'one of the plagues (or perhaps a saving grace) of literary theory' is that 'the "system" never quite gels with the practice' (p. 35).]

It may, therefore, not be excessive to suggest that much apparent disagreement and argument at cross-purposes stems from this particular lack of discrimination in terminology at the most basic level. Confusion has certainly increased since the days of the earlier studies discussed in Section III above (see for example the distinction, albeit terminologically reversed from ours, drawn between quality and genre by Rabkin, 1976, pp. 28–9). Tolkien (1964, p. 44) refers to 'the etymological and semantic connexions of *fantasy* with *fantastic*' (see also Calvino, 1987, pp. 71–3).[19] Irwin (1976) actually entitles his first chapter 'Fantasy versus the Fantastic'; however 'fantasy' is seen as 'a subgenre of prose fiction' (p. 5), while the fantastic is merely an element therein — or, indeed, with other forms of literature too (p. 8; see also Irwin on Todorov, pp. 54–5).

Even a quick glance at the titles of some of the books here discussed, from Todorov's onwards, is quite revealing. Of those who highlight 'fantasy' in their title, Apter (*Fantasy Literature*) generally uses 'fantasy' rather than 'fantastic', is clearly interested in the wider phenomenon of fantasy rather than in the fantastic, and generally sticks to her brief. Similarly, Little (*The Fantasts*), both theoretically and in his choice of texts for analysis, is concerned with fantasy worlds rather than a Todorovian genre. Jackson and Hume are more problematical and require a slightly more detailed examination.[20]

Todorov (at least in his English title, see below), Rabkin, Brooke-Rose and Siebers all highlight 'the fantastic' in their titles. Of these, Todorov and Brooke-Rose may be said to be predominantly interested in such a genre (and its sub-genres or neighbouring genres), while Rabkin and Siebers, although clearly interested in this too, are really discussing something wider.

Brooke-Rose, as might be expected, uses 'the fantastic' in its Todorovian generic sense (or 'the pure fantastic') consistently; she also uses 'fantasies' (see p. 136), as of the phenomenon — which may, in 'reality', either have 'appeared' or have been hallucinated — of the apparitions in *The Turn of the Screw*; and occasionally the word 'fantastic' as an adjective, as in the phrase 'a fantastic realism' (p. 388). She is evidently fully aware of these distinctions, but does not see any need to make an issue of spelling them out (had she been able to read Jackson (1981) and Hume, she might have felt differently). Nevertheless, she does point out some discrepancies in others. In her discussion of Lem's polemic against Todorov, she writes:

> he cites Sade, who, despite the direct expression of sexual

perversion admitted in the eighteenth century, nevertheless uses the detour of the fantastic (though not, it must be said, in the sense defined by Todorov, a fact apparently ignored by Lem). (p. 62)

It could be further emphasised that Sade is surely an author of 'fantasy', rather than of the fantastic in the sense understood by Todorov, Brooke-Rose or Chanady.

In her critique of the theorist of science fiction, Darko Suvin, Brooke-Rose observes (p. 73) that he 'dismisses what he calls the fantastic ("fantasy" in the English version), as "ghosts, horror, gothic weird"'. Suvin's *Metamorphosis of Science Fiction* is a translation (also a revised and expanded version) of his *Pour une poétique de la science fiction* published in Quebec two years earlier; perhaps his terminological exactitude had evolved in the meantime, or perhaps it varies as between French and English. Curiously, this calls to mind the fact that Todorov's original French title (1970) is *Introduction à la littérature fantastique*, with 'fantastic' as an adjective. The English title — felicitously explicit — is *The Fantastic: A structural approach to a literary genre*; perhaps Todorov has much for which to thank his translator, Richard Howard. Among French critics, Bellemin-Noël (1972) is also aware that there may be a problem. In any event, this discrepancy (noticed by Brooke-Rose, p. 67) must have been responsible for Hutcheon's being sufficiently terminologically misguided as to write, when referring to the French edition of Todorov (1984, p. 32): 'As Tzvetan Todorov has explained, *fantasy literature* [my emphasis] is a hesitation or compromise between the empirically real and the totally imaginary' (whether one here wishes to blame Hutcheon, who certainly knows as a rule what she means by 'fantasy', or Todorov's French).

More culpable perhaps in this regard is Jackson (1981). The title of her study is *Fantasy: The literature of subversion*; however, her chapter titles include 'The Fantastic as a Mode', 'Fantastic Realism' and 'Victorian Fantasies'. I am not suggesting that these titles are inaccurate in relation to the subject matter they address, or that Jackson does not understand the distinctions implied, although she is occasionally unclear (as in the quotation in Section IV above, from p. 20 of her study). Formulations such as 'the fantastic art of Sade, Goya and horror fiction' (p. 95) do not help — the adjectival use of 'fantastic' requiring special explanation, if it does not refer to the Todorovian genre of the fantastic, as here it clearly does not. Jackson is interested both in the genre of the fantastic and in the wide quality (or, in her terms, 'mode') of fantasy; it would have aided her argument had she been a little more precise in her definitions and categorisations. Petzold (1986, p. 12) notes this imprecision in Jackson (and others), but his own attempts to clarify the issue are not, to my mind, particularly helpful.

More seriously misleading — or perhaps misled — with regard to precision in this question is Hume. She addresses herself to 'fantasy', as we have seen above, in a wide sense and does not wish to subdivide it, or to treat it as genre or even 'mode'. Hume's subject is 'fantasy'; 'fantastic' she seems to regard as the adjectival form of 'fantasy' and as the opposite of 'real': for example, 'what comes into the text will seem fantastic to readers' and 'what is real and what fantastic' (p. 12). However, when she talks about 'theories of fantasy' (*ibid.* and *passim*) she includes genre-based theories, of which she proceeds to disapprove. She does, in fact, fleetingly recognise the existence of a limited sub-genre called 'the *fantastique*' (classed, along with detective stories, as 'suspense'), which itself is seen as a sub-branch of 'Literature of illusion', whose other branches are listed as pastoral, pornography, the uncanny and adventure stories (p. 55). She later elaborates a little on this, by stating that 'what Todorov calls the *fantastique*' is 'a variant form of affective literature' (p. 78). The latter term is equated with 'escapism', but refers to 'forms of escape that in one way or another raise and maintain tension' (pp. 73–4). 'The effect of fantasy in horror stories, ghost stories and the *fantastique*', we are told (p. 78), 'depends heavily on the reader's outlook.'

We are thus brought back full circle to Todorov. 'Fantasy' is here seen (by Hume) as an element which is to be found in 'the *fantastique*', as in many other literary forms. When Hume reiterates, in her concluding section (p. 195), that 'fantasy is not adequately defined as a genre', she is, of course, correct — both by her own lights and by those of most, if not all, other commentators. Where she is on dubious ground is in reading what are theories of 'the fantastic' (as a genre) as though they were in fact, or in intention, theories of the concept of fantasy (as a whole). Admittedly, she has been assisted in such a misprision (to borrow a term from Harold Bloom) by something of a history of critical imprecision. From her own brief references to 'the *fantastique*', we must suspect that Hume is herself aware of this distinction at some level. However, this awareness would seem to have been overridden by her conviction of the relative worthlessness of the genre approach, and of the relative insignificance of the genre identified by Todorov: 'One inescapable drawback of Todorov's definition is that many works conform to it up until their last pages, at which point they either explain the mystery . . . or affirm the reality of the supernatural event' (p. 14). It is not clear why this should be such an 'inescapable drawback'. Hume regards Todorov and his allies or successors as too exclusive in their definitions. Even setting aside the fact that they are not defining the same thing as she wishes to define, Todorov's model, with its adjacent categories and modifications added (by Brooke-Rose and Jackson, with further refinements remaining possible), is much less exclusive than Hume will admit.

Perhaps a consensus may now be reached that genre theory of something called the fantastic (or *fantastique*) is one thing, and that theory of a broader quality of fantasy is another. As a theorist — or perhaps rather a metacritic — of fantasy, Hume does have something to offer. It is unfortunate that the confusion outlined above has surfaced in, and thereby flawed, the early part of her book.

It may however be prudent to make one concession in the direction of Hume and others who may, to my mind, tend to confuse the terms which we have been discussing. 'The fantastic' can not sensibly be restricted absolutely to genre description; it is also used, logically enough, to refer to that quality which could, or would, put a work into the genre in question; or, in more Todorovian terms, the fantastic may be present in a work which turns out ultimately to belong (with the resolution of the fantastic issue — or the issue or quality of the fantastic) to the uncanny or the marvellous. However, this still leaves the term 'the fantastic' rather more limited currency than is commonly accorded to the word 'fantasy'.

VI   'Fantasy' — Basically an Impulse?

'Fantasy', then, denotes a wider concept — be it called a 'mode', an 'impulse' of equivalent value to mimesis, or a trans-generic literary quality ever present to some degree. Such an application of the word would seem to be more helpful, and to command wider agreement, than using it to connote, in its turn, another sub-genre (usually fiction set in a Tolkien-type other world): see for example Rabkin's comment that: 'The wide range of works which we call . . . fantastic is large, much too large to constitute a single genre. [It includes] whole conventional genres, such as fairy tales, detective story, Fantasy.' (Rabkin, 1976, p. 118). Rabkin's own approach to the fantastic, involving a 180-degree reversal to the ground rules of a narrative, is seen by Jackson (1981, p. 21) as being overrigid: 'his paradigm is *Alice Through the Looking-glass*, but more fluid fantasies do not fit his scheme.' Nevertheless, his ideas would still seem rather more applicable to the wider category of fantasy than to genre definition.[21]

As well as the wider quality of fantasy, as used by Hume and others, a narrower meaning must also be acknowledged. This is the use of the word in its oneiric sense, often in more limited sequences within works from all sorts of genres and in varying narrative forms: day-dream, pipe dreams, dreams, nightmares, reveries, hallucinations — down to wishful thinking, dreads or mere musings.[22] These may take on such a significance as to dominate a work or, in certain circumstances, push it towards the fantastic; more often, however, this is not the case and the fantasy element remains more or less incidental. This use of the word, of course, shades off into the standard psychological (non-literary) application of the term 'fantasy'.

'Fantasy' has usually been regarded as a positive quality (despite the long comparative neglect in its study and the imprecisions in the utilisation of the term). Ralph Fox, writing in the 1930s, observed that 'Sterne had all the divine gifts of the greatest novelists: he had irony, fantasy, a delight in obscenity' (Fox, 1979, p. 61); and 'It is the element of colour, fantasy and ironical vision which we have lost since the Renaissance' (p. 153). This may be contrasted with the connotation presumed in the word 'fantastic' (as already observed at the beginning of this study): 'Where Cervantes could combine imagination and poetry with humour and fantasy, we now [in the Victorian period] have the purely imaginative and poetic novel, the purely humorous and fantastic' (p. 72). Fox refers (p. 62) to 'the high fantasy of Cervantes and Rabelais'. 'High fantasy' is a term which has also been used to signify the Victorian fantasy–escapist creations of Carroll, MacDonald, Kingsley and others (see Jackson, p. 153).[23] To add yet further possible confusion, Fox (p. 72) reminds us of E. M. Forster's division (in *Aspects of the Novel*) of the novel genre into 'novels of "story", novels of "fantasy", novels of "prophecy"'.

Bakhtin (1968, pp. 344–9) writes of the origin, for Rabelais and for medieval literature, of fantasy and 'grotesquerie' in the so-called 'Indian Wonders' cycle, the Prester John legend and other exotica, the medieval mystery and 'diablerie'. Origins merge into subject matter. We have above mentioned Louis Vax in this connection. Hutcheon (1984, p. 98), with acknowledgement to Todorov, gives this a structuralist twist:

> a theory of fantasy literature must also draw upon a concept of fictive referents (at the level of both langue and parole) because surely vampires, devils, unicorns and hobbits exist only in words. Only language can allow us to conceive of the absent, the unreal, the supernatural.

The stories of Borges clearly include examples of fantasy, in the narrower and the wider sense; many of them would be acknowledged as 'fantasies', if we must allow a generic sense of the word.[24] However, 'the fantastic', even when it makes an appearance, is pushed firmly into the background, usually by the stress which the author places on problems of narrative. The work of Borges, therefore, presents an interesting case in relation to the various terms and connotations under consideration. Macherey has pointed out (p. 253) that, for instance, 'his critical essays are fictional even when they are about actual works'. Borges makes frequent, if fleeting, appearances in discussions of fantasy, metafiction and related topics. However, the phenomenon of 'magic realism' in Latin American fiction is only beginning to receive attention in works of metacriticism and theory.

In modern literature, fantasy is frequently linked to metafiction (though also, of course, to science fiction and other fictional forms); for example Hutcheon (1984, pp. 76–82) has a section treating fantasy within metafiction, to which topic we shall briefly return.

Hutcheon maintains (with acknowledgement to John Fowles) that 'All literature could be said to be "escape" literature: readers as well as authors want to create worlds as real as, but other than, the world that is'; for that matter, 'all reading (whether of novels, history or science) is a kind of "escape"' (p. 76). Hume, though (pp. 79–81), is keen to differentiate between fantasy and escapist literature: escapist, unrealistic literature is not necessarily 'fantastic' (as we have seen), while 'Fantasy is a larger and more varied realm than the literature of escape' (p. 79; escape does not constitute, obviously, one of Hume's twin basic impulses in literature). Escapist works will emphasise sensations, emotions and the revoking of responsibilities; fantasy and escape partially overlap, but escape may be subdivided into 'mimetic escape' and 'fantastic escape' (p. 80).

Other interesting theoretical points made by Hume about fantasy include its capacity for taking both 'the additive form of deliberate distortion and departure' and 'the subtractive form of omission and erasure' (p. xii). She stresses the aim of fantasy for 'richness' and 'a plethora of meanings' (p. 194) and reapplies R. S. Crane's description of plot as having three components — action, character and idea — to a conception of fantasy: 'Fantasy can likewise be seen as fantasy of action, of character, or of idea' (p. 159).

Fantasy must also be related to Todorov's category of 'the marvellous'. This relationship will be broached further in the section below. Ann Swinfen, in her *In Defence of Fantasy*, (1984, p. 5) states that 'The essential ingredient of all fantasy is "the marvellous"', regarded as 'anything outside the normal space–time continuum of the everyday world'; Manlove (in Schlobin, 1982, p. 28) considers that 'most . . . would place "fantasy" where Todorov puts his genre of "the marvellous", that is, where we are dealing with the unambiguously supernatural almost from the outset.' This may well be the case, but use of the word 'fantasy' in this particular role would tend to confirm existing confusions, rather than to remove them.

Finally, in an essay entitled 'The age of fantasy' (first published in 1982), Patrick Parrinder goes as far as to propose 'fantasy' as 'an alternative description of the characteristic style of our age' (an alternative to ' "Postmodernism", the fashionable term of the 1970s': Parrinder, 1987, p. 109). Parrinder too appears to treat 'fantasy' and 'the fantastic' as interchangeable, while displaying an awareness of what he bizarrely sees as 'a school which advocates the so-called "pure fantastic"', to wit, Todorov and Brooke-Rose (pp. 111–12). Nevertheless, with such backing from the mainstream of literary criticism, the term fantasy should have a future.

VII   'The Fantastic' — Basically a Genre?

We have been arguing that 'the fantastic' is a term whose basic use should be generic; we may also admit to the existence of a quality of the fantastic (i.e. that which puts the fantastic into 'the fantastic') and it may be all but impossible to rid ourselves of usages such as 'fantastic literature'. However, these usages should be employed with forethought. Similarly, if 'fantasy' is basically recognised to be a wide-ranging impulse or mode, then its narrower meaning must also be maintained and cautious use of fantasy as a genre can scarcely be totally excluded. However, the application of these terms needs to be more discriminatory than has usually been the case hitherto, if confusion is not to reign.

At this stage, it is time to turn our attention back to the question of genre. '*Genres*', according to Bakhtin (1981, p. 288) are 'specific organisms' which accomplish the 'stratification' of literary language and may comprise genres of 'low literature' and of 'high literature'. The novel, though, is glossed by Bakhtin's translators (p. 428) as 'defining itself precisely by the degree to which it cannot be framed by pre-existing categories'. This concept is suitably loose, particularly as we would wish to consider the short story alongside the novel (Brooke-Rose, p. 229, notes that 'pure fantastic texts are usually short, relatively: it would be impossible to keep it up over a trilogy'). Given the general aura of vagueness surrounding the word 'genre', it might be convenient to suggest that, for present purposes, the novel and the short story (and suchlike major literary entities) be regarded as 'forms'; 'genres' would encompass such categories as 'the realist novel' and, shall we say, the Gothic, the modernist, the Symbolist or the historical novel (quibbles and sub-divisions here are of course possible). If we do not wish to postulate a genre of 'the fantastic novel', we may prefer to settle for 'the fantastic' as a minor genre, or sub-genre, drawn from the novel and short-story 'forms' (Brooke-Rose, p. 64, refers to 'transitory categories, or subgenres').

Bakhtin (and Aristotle) apart, consideration of genre theory these days usually begins with the fourth essay of Northrop Frye's *Anatomy of Criticism*.[25] However, a suitable approach for present purposes is to be found in Thomas Winner's essay 'Structural and semiotic genre theory' (in Strelka, 1978), which, in structural terms, sees individual texts as performances, or the *parole*, corresponding to the *langue* of genre. More importantly, Winner's presentation of genre incorporates 'dynamically related diachronic and synchronic characteristics' (Winner, 1978, p. 264): genres are 'never static' but evolve in 'a dialectical combination of both variants and invariants' (*ibid.*), requiring, therefore, study that is both historical and comparative.

Let us now consider Todorov's schema in its diagrammatic form (having outlined it briefly above, in Section III):

Uncanny / Fantastic–Uncanny / Fantastic–Marvellous / Marvellous

The pure fantastic (PF) 'may be represented by the median line separating the fantastic–uncanny from the fantastic–marvellous. This line corresponds perfectly to the nature of the fantastic — a frontier between two adjacent realms' (Todorov, 1973, p. 44; see also Jackson, 1981, p. 32). Or, as Brooke-Rose explicates the schema with admirable clarity (pp. 64–5):

> The 'pure' fantastic is represented by the central line — a frontier between two adjacent realms. If the supernatural *eventually* receives a natural explanation, we are in the fantastic–uncanny; if the events are not supernatural but strange, horrific, incredible, we are in the uncanny (with the accent on the reader's fear, not on his hesitation). On the other side of the line, if the supernatural has to be *eventually* accepted as supernatural, we are in the fantastic–marvellous (with the accent on wonder). Presumably, then, on the left of the line, in the fantastic–uncanny, not only is the reader's hesitation resolved but his fear is purged; whereas on the right of the line, in fantastic–marvellous, this fear is turned to wonder.

That PF is represented merely by a line seems at first sight credible, particularly as Todorov suggests so few examples which actually fit such a category. However, it makes little sense to speak of PF as even a sub-genre unless we create a space in the model for it to occupy. Furthermore, the number of texts which may be, at least provisionally, assigned to it is not as small as some would have us believe (see note 7 above). The most frequently quoted candidates are James's *The Turn of the Screw*, Hoffmann's *The Sandman*, Cazotte's *Le Diable amoureux* (a short story of 1772) and Mérimée's *La Vénus d'Ille*; Brooke-Rose makes a strong case for Poe's *The Black Cat* and Jackson suggests Hogg's *Private Memoirs and Confessions of a Justified Sinner*. We have already seen it widely claimed that Pushkin's *The Queen of Spades* is a perfect example; in fact probably a plethora of Russian works could be proposed (certainly tales by Odoevsky and Gogol, Lermontov's unfinished *Shtoss* and, in more recent times, works by Bulgakov and Siniavsky would make interesting cases for consideration). Certain works normally considered to be science fiction might also qualify: Earth-based works such as the Strugatskys' *Roadside Picnic* (was the mysterious 'zone' really caused by extraterrestrial visitors, or could this belief result from a cover-up for some terrestrial disaster?) and perhaps other novels of theirs. Lem, as we have seen, one of Todorov's strongest critics, himself elsewhere suggests a suitable candidate: the short story *The Monkey's Paw*, by W. W. Jacobs. No doubt the list could be extensively added to before we ran any risk of exhausting the likely possibilities.

We may therefore propose the insertion of an actual space in the schema for PF as a first modification. Secondly, I am inclined to agree with Jackson that there is a problem over 'the uncanny'. She comments (1981, p. 32):

> [Todorov's] scheme is useful for distinguishing certain kinds of the fantastic, but its polarization of the marvellous and the uncanny leads to some confusion. For to see the fantastic as a literary form, it needs to be made distinct in literary terms, and the uncanny, or *l'étrange*, is not one of these — it is not a literary category, whereas the marvellous is.

I have difficulty in imagining what the 'pure uncanny' would be as a sub-genre, and which texts might fit it (see also Bellemin-Noël, 1971, p. 107); however, Todorov's postulation of fantastic–uncanny does make sense, as, further along the scale to the 'left', would a category of uncanny realism. The uncanny, then, would be admissible as a quality in, or as a direction for, texts which may begin in the fantastic mould, or which may be predominantly realist but contain uncanny (but not supernatural) elements (of chance, coincidence etc., but not strongly enough to provoke suspicion of a supernatural involvement). The idea of a genre of 'fear', which Brooke-Rose would appear to favour, seems to me of doubtful validity or necessity: fear is surely ultimately based either on causes which are natural and explicable (albeit horrific), or on supernatural causes; should the cause remain unresolved or undiscovered, the work may well stay within the category of PF. I would also be inclined to reject Brooke-Rose's view that Kafka's *Metamorphosis* belongs equally to the marvellous and to the uncanny (the failure of Todorov's theory to account for this work she takes to be a flaw, pp. 66–7), but we shall return to this text shortly.

It is worth noting here that even Freud's notion of the uncanny (*Das Unheimliche*) as outlined in his essay of that title is, as has been observed by Margaret Carter (p. 9), 'much closer to Todorov's fantastic than to the latter's uncanny'. Other commentators on the uncanny would appear to agree with this statement. This is the main thrust of Maria Tatar's argument: 'Uncanny events are situated at the heart of the fantastic tale. Their ambiguous character almost invariably generates the hesitation that defines the fantastic' (Tatar, 1981, p. 169). Earlier, S. S. Prawer (1965, p. 21) had referred to 'the uncanny fantasy'.

Brooke-Rose further writes (p. 310), following Todorov: 'In the "pure" uncanny there is little or no supernatural, but only the bizarre or horrific, and this opens out onto all narratives with strange or unusual events, and ultimately onto all realistic fiction.' She continues (*ibid*.): 'Between the fantastic–uncanny and the pure uncanny hovers the murder-mystery or detective-story, with its natural explanation of a perfectly natural and often chilling murder, and which does or did sometimes include strong hints of the supernatural. . .' None of this seems to me to make a persuasive case for the existence of the pure uncanny as a meaningful category; such works as may be proposed for such a category would seem to be readily ascribable to either the fantastic uncanny or to uncanny realism.[26] It is, therefore, the pure uncanny, rather than PF, which should be reduced to the status of a mere line or frontier, given that there may be a logical necessity for its at least token retention.

Brooke-Rose (p. 84) puts forward the possibility, at least, of one interesting innovation — that of joining up the ends of Todorov's linear model to form a circle. This has the virtue, for her, of

allowing the categories of realism and the marvellous to touch, and possibly thereby account for the features of realism which she discerns in science fiction: 'Could science fiction then be another, more extreme version (marvellous & realism) of a "mixed genre", in which the opposite ends of Todorov's diagram somehow join up, impossibly in his theory. . . ?'.[27] The answer to the first part of this question, at least, may be yes, but we shall return later to the question of mixed genres. Nevertheless, the possibility of positing a category of 'marvellous realism' might have certain attractions.

What I wish to propose is a return (at least for the time being) to Todorov's linear model, bearing in mind some of the comments of Jackson and Brooke-Rose, and indeed the approach of Hume, but with further extensions, a possible division and at least one sub-division. The basic division proposed is also a convenience, in that the line would otherwise be too long for most printed pages. The pure fantastic (PF) appears in both divisions: on the far right of the first set, and on the far left of the second; were the model presented as a single long line, PF would of course occupy a single central position (its double vertical lines being for emphasis). This set may

					UNCANNY	FANTASTIC–	
1.	NON-FICTION	FACTION	REALISM		REALISM	UNCANNY	PF

be said to be, in general, mimetically dominated — though it becomes less so, obviously, as we move from left to right, culminating in PF — but, following Hume's lead, we take 'fantasy' to be likely to be present, to some degree, if only in its narrower sense, almost throughout.

Realism is shown as occupying a larger space, partly because of its wide currency, but also because of the possibility of further sub-divisions (naturalism, critical realism, historical fiction etc.), but that is not the concern of this study.

Faction — fictionalised contemporary history and politics, and other forms perhaps descended from the concept of *literatura fakta* ('literature of fact', a term established by LEF [the Left Front of Art] theorists in the Soviet Union in the 1920s) — and non-fiction appear to the left. Non-fiction would embrace such forms as the 'non-fiction novel' ('the real simply reported, but more unreal than the familiar real' — Brooke-Rose, p. 102), plus memoirs and auto-biography: subjective narratives which include (consciously or otherwise) fictional and impressionistic elements. This category would shade off, to the far left, into journalism, history and, in a general sense, scientific literature. This second set may be said to be,

		FANTASTIC–			
2.	PF	MARVELLOUS		MARVELLOUS	MYTHOLOGY, etc.

in general, fantasy dominated, although some mimetic or referential elements must be present (increasingly so towards the left of the model).

Mythology, on the right, may shade off into theology and other forms of cosmogony (or the irrefutable absurd?).

Again, the category of the marvellous is shown as wider and in this case it may help to break it down into sub-divisions.

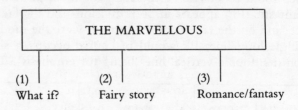

1. *What if?*[28] This would include works set in what seems to pass for 'our' world, but with a single (or at least a small number of) element(s) of the manifestly impossible. This is where Kafka's *Metamorphosis* and Gogol's *The Nose* might arguably be placed, along with other works dependent on a single major transformation. ('According to Rabkin [1976:121], there is a prescription whereby a good work of SF may make only one assumption about its narrative world which violates what is known about our world and then extrapolate the whole narrative world from that difference' — Brooke-Rose, p. 392 n. 1) Following Chanady, we may feel inclined to place magic realism here; she indeed specifically wishes to include *Metamorphosis* in the magical realist category (Chanady, pp. 48–50).[29]
2. *Fairy Story*, or similar, in which the action again takes place in what seems to be 'our' world, albeit in timeless or remote regions, but with manifold transformations (or magical elements). Animal stories might also be included under this category.
3. *Romance/Fantasy* in which the work unfolds in a world patently not 'ours': either a romance or 'faery' world, *à la* Tolkien (the word 'romance' of course presents possible difficulties, due both to its high medieval and popular modern generic connotations), or an other-planetry SF world.

Applying Little's 'worlds' schema to this sub-model, we could say that 1) *What if?* comprises 'Secondary World +'; 2) *Fairy Story* 'Secondary World ++'; and 3) *Romance/Fantasy* would be fully 'Tertiary World'.

It may also be the case (as will be suggested again later) that, by following extremes off the scheme to both left and right, we would arrive at a situation in which pseudo-scientific literature could meet the categories beyond the marvellous, thus reviving the possibility of a full (i.e. joined) circle.

There may, of course, be room for more refinements to this scheme.

Clearly, the categories represented in the diagrams above form a list apart from such purely generic terms such as 'the novel' and 'the short story'. There must, in addition, be a number of 'cross-genre' concepts: the most obvious one is 'fiction', while 'mimesis' and 'fantasy' are here also used as cross-genre concepts (whether 'modes' or 'impulses'); others may include such terms as satire, parody, the absurd, etc. Certain categories, too, may occur in more than one slot: historical fiction, for example, may be most commonly found in the areas of realism and faction, but may also crop up in other domains, such as the marvellous.

This brings us on to the question of the historical nature of genres, as well as to genre mixes, but let us now look in more detail at the nineteenth- and twentieth-century evolution of what we shall call the literary fantastic.

Part Two
PRACTICE

So, from the beginning, although it may seem that we have suddenly plunged into the realm of a rather wild mysticism, it is immediately revealed that this is a literary device.

Vladimir Solov'ëv 1966, p. 378

I hope I shall never again know a moment of terror as blank and absolute. I could not have moved or spoken to save my life. Either all the known laws of nature were nothing, or I was mad.

Edith Nesbit, 'The ebony frame', Fear, London, 1910

1   *Origins and Development*

> The human race ceased to fear God. Then came its
> punishment; it began to fear itself, began to cultivate the
> fantastic, and now it trembles before this creature of its own
> imagination.
>> Kierkegaard (quoted from Banta, 1972, p. 257, n. 2)

ORIGINS

The origins of what we have chosen to call the literary fantastic lie
in the realms of antiquity, amid a variety of mythological, folkloric
and literary traditions. Occasionally particular works of classical or
other remote literatures may beckon as formal or thematic
exemplars; *The Golden Ass* by Apuleius, dating from the second
century AD, is one such, a primitive novel written in an eccentric prose
style. Such forms of writing came and went throughout literary history
but all commentators are agreed that the second half of the eighteenth
century saw a fundamental revival and consolidation of such a style.
This coincided, in general terms, with the era of the Enlightenment,
which was followed by the French Revolution, and with the birth of
romanticism, which was accompanied by the Industrial Revolution. In
terms of prose fiction, this was the period which gave birth specifically
to the Gothic novel, or the 'tale of terror'. David Punter, concluding his
book *The Literature of Terror* (1980, p. 422), sees the 'structure' of the
Gothic tradition as follows:

> a body of material which was once the object of general belief —
> legendary, ballads, folk memories — but had begun to fall into
> disrepute due to changing habits of mind during the Renaissance,
> became during the eighteenth century a source of ambiguity and
> resonance which invited relation to contemporary anxieties.

Punter (pp. 14–15) sees the concepts of 'Gothic' and 'terror' as
intertwined in literary history. Mario Praz, in his seminal essay
introducing *Three Gothic Novels* (1968, p. 9) speaks of 'an aesthetic

45

theory of the Horrid and the Terrible' which had developed over the eighteenth centry. Devendra P. Varma, in his *The Gothic Flame* (1966, p. 103) had followed a tendency to distinguish between 'Terror' and 'Horror'. However, all these categories undoubtedly impinge upon what we here consider to be the literary fantastic.

Traditions developed, more or less simultaneously though not necessarily independently, in England, America, France and Germany and we shall attempt to see how these cross-fertilised one another and coalesced to form, by or during the second quarter of the nineteenth century, a recognisable western literary pattern of the fantastic which was to draw in other literatures and extend from the eastern seaboard of the United States in the West to St Petersburg in the East.

In addition to the inspiration of the Gothic ruin, one of the first and foremost pan-European influences was the work in engraving and sketch of Piranesi (1720–78), especially the *Carceri d'Invenzione*, a series of engravings of the most complex imaginary prisons, an endless formation of halls, vaulted spaces, staircases and balustrades, said to have been conceived under the delirium of malaria. Piranesi's visions held immense appeal for the Gothic imagination, from Walpole to Odoevsky, and not least to the opium dreamers, Coleridge and De Quincey (see Hayter, 1988, pp. 93–7). The architectural vaults complemented and represented the labyrinths of the mind in a Gothic-cum-fantastic chronotope (to use Bakhtin's term for the literary intersection of time and space) which grasped ever further towards infinity. Umberto Eco (1987, p. 237) reminds us that Panofsky 'discovered a structural homology between the plan of Gothic cathedrals and the form of medieval theological treatises'. Horace Walpole had advised English artists to study:

> the sublime dream of Piranesi, who seems to have conceived visions of Rome beyond what is boasted even in the meridian of its splendor. Savage as Salvator Rosa — fierce as Michael Angelo, and exuberant as Rubens, he has imagined scenes that would startle geometry, and exhaust the Indies to realize. He piles palaces on bridges, and temples on palaces, and scales Heaven with mountains of edifices. Yet what taste in his boldness! What labour and thought both in his rashness and details. (Walpole, *Anecdotes of Painting in England*, cited from Praz, 1968, pp. 16–17)

Sir Walter Scott, writing in 1823, commented in relation to Walpole's own *The Castle of Otranto*: 'Yet Horace Walpole has attained in composition, what, as an architect, he must have felt beyond the power of his art' (Scott, 1968, p. 88). Varma too (p. 16) finds that 'The Gothic novel is a conception as vast and complex as a Gothic cathedral. One finds in them the same sinister overtones and the same solemn grandeur.' In a similar, but more modern, vein Peter Brooks (1976, p. 19) observes:

> The Gothic castle, with its pinnacles and dungeons, crenella-
> tions, moats, drawbridges, spiraling staircases and concealed
> doors, realizes an architectural approximation of the Freudian
> model of the mind, particularly the traps laid for the
> conscious by the unconscious and the repressed. The Gothic
> novel seeks an epistemology of the depths; it is fascinated by
> what lies hidden in the dungeon and the sepulcher.

Marilyn Butler (1982, pp. 156–7), for one, has pointed up the historical context of the Gothic, seeing it as 'a product of the three decades of quickening pulse, the revolutionary era from about 1760 to about 1797, reaching a culmination in England with the mature work of Ann Radcliffe' (effectively spanning the period from *The Castle of Otranto* to *The Italian*). After 1797, she adds, all self-respecting novelists steered clear of the Gothic for about two decades. This, of course, applies mainly, if not entirely, to England. On a European scale, there is not only greater continuity and development, but the imagery and rhetoric of the Gothic spilled over into the main historical and political works of the period. Edmund Burke, in his *Reflections on the Revolution in France*, wrote of 'a vast, tremendous unformed spectre'; *The Communist Manifesto*, half a century later, has a spectre haunting Europe. This spectre, it has been pointed out (by Conor Cruise O'Brien, see Baldick, 1987, p. 19), therefore 'walks for the first time in the pages of Burke'.

ENGLAND

In England a flourishing novelistic tradition, from Defoe to Richardson, developed into sentimentalism, as well as into its contingent branch of the Gothic (see Punter, p. 28). 'Graveyard poetry' was a particularly influential sub-current in this respect, not only because of its immediate impact but also by its importance for the writers of German fiction of terror, through whom it returned as a further influence on the English Gothic (p. 33). Much of this writing is frequently subsumed too under the category of 'romance' (Ann Radcliffe's novels, for example, were subtitled 'a romance', as later was Hawthorne's *The House of the Seven Gables*, while Stevenson's *Weir of Hermiston* was styled 'an unfinished romance'). Gillian Beer sees the term as stretching from *The Faerie Queene* to *Lord Jim* (Beer, 1970, pp. 4–5) and affirms that 'the Gothic romance and the romantic movement gave new significance to the form' (p. 6); she also sees 'the criminal romance' as having represented an early reconciliation between 'novel' and 'romance', leading to the fiction of Defoe and Fielding (p. 50).

The major writers of English literature had also, as one might expect, contributed something to this development. Marilyn Butler (p. 21) draws attention to the Shakespearean features of Horace Walpole's pioneering contribution to the genre:

> *Otranto* looks uncommonly like an attempt to graft on to the novel — that modern form concerned with money, possessions, status, circumstance — the heightened passions, elemental situations, and stylized poetic techniques of the Elizabethan dramatists.

Chris Baldick, in his *In Frankenstein's Shadow* (1987, p. 40), reminds us of the importance of Milton's *Paradise Lost* as a literary source for *Frankenstein*. While, for present purposes, we do not intend to treat poetry or drama as fantastic texts, it would of course be foolish to attempt to deny the contribution of these artistic forms to the development of the tradition which we are attempting to trace (just as other cultural and art forms, both verbal and non-verbal, may also have contributed at various times). Indeed Punter (p. 130), referring to the Gothic novels of Radcliffe and Matthew Lewis, considers that 'the tradition with which they deal has less to do with the earlier development of the novel than with a longer and more diffuse poetic and dramatic tradition'; likewise there remains a strong connection between Gothic fiction and the work of many romantic poets.

In this regard we should perhaps go no further without mentioning the oft-quoted phrase of Coleridge — himself a rabid cross-fertiliser with his strong interest in German aesthetics — (from his *Biographia Literaria*, XIV), concerning the 'willing suspension of disbelief'. We should also return again to Burke, whose treatise *A Philosophical Enquiry into the Origin of our Ideas of the Sublime and*

Beautiful (1757), has been widely recognised as a central inspiration for Gothic writing (see Punter, p. 44; Praz, 1968, p. 10) for the connection it draws between 'terror' and 'the sublime', as well as for its propagation of the concept of 'astonishment'. Burke can be seen as having been answered by Piranesi (Praz, 1968, p. 16) and leads clearly enough to Sade (to whom we shall shortly return).

Walpole's *The Castle of Otranto* (1765) is universally recognised as the first Gothic novel proper.[1] From the outset, Walpole's conception of the Gothic novel was of a synthesis: 'It was an attempt to blend the two kinds of romance, the ancient and the modern', 'imagination' and 'Nature' (Walpole's 'Preface to the Second Edition' of 1798; Fairclough, 1968, p. 43). Allegedly envisaged as a combination of fantasy and realism, Walpole's novel has always been noted rather for the former quality (Punter, p. 50). *Otranto* is an aristocratic work of medieval revivalism, light in tone and tongue-in-cheek rather than seriously frightening; its introduction of the supernatural is unashamedly undiluted by doubt, let alone any element of realistic explanation. At the same time it includes many of the ingredients, in detail and in theme, of what was to follow.

The successors of *Otranto* took some years to materialise. Clara Reeve's *The Old English Baron* (1777) and Sophia Lee's *The Recess* (1783–5) were more genuinely historical and, in the latter case at least, post-medieval in setting. Both Walpole and Reeve used 'framed' narratives, in which the main text purports to be a discovered manuscript, 'edited' by the author/narrator; Lee's novel is a first-person narrative, but one which interpolates letters and manuscripts and, deriving from the epistolary novel, contrives to furnish conflicting viewpoints. These techniques, and variations thereupon, were to remain thereafter the staple fare of Gothic and fantastic fiction.

Beckford's *Vathek* (1786), which was originally written in French, is frequently considered the first important Gothic successor to Walpole's *Otranto* and indeed Beckford followed his predecessor in building his own actual Gothic castle (though in a less lasting vein, the edifice collapsed). However, *Vathek*, with its middle-eastern setting, belongs more to the literature of exotica and as such is further removed from the literary fantastic, as we understand it here, than is the general run of the Gothic tradition. As Mario Praz (1968, p. 25) has remarked, 'We are prepared to accept any improbability from *Vathek*, because it partakes of the nature of a fairy tale'. Another prominent novel by an influential figure was

William Godwin's *Caleb Williams* (1794), described as 'the first psychological pursuit story' (Aldiss, 1986, p. 32). While Godwin's theme of paranoid persecution was to be of inestimable importance to the development of the Gothic and fantastic traditions (strikingly so in the work of his daughter, Mary Shelley), his novel is in other respects remote from our concerns.

The 1790s, though, saw the heyday of the English Gothic, with the appearance of the main novels of Ann Radcliffe — *The Mysteries of Udolpho* (1794) and *The Italian* (1797) — and Matthew Lewis's *The Monk* (1796). However, even these were only stepping stones to the fantastic.

Despite its reputation, Radcliffe's *Udolpho* is by no means a pure Gothic novel. It has a historical setting, late sixteenth-century France and Italy, reminiscent to an extent of Scott and Manzoni, but with far less attention to historical events and details than was to be the case a little later with these two illustrious novelists. The emphasis at first is rather on elements of the sentimentalist novel, with more than a touch of the society novel and the quality of a proto-*Bildungsroman*: an economic base to the motivation of most of the characters is maintained throughout. Poetry is interspersed freely about the text (some of it 'original' to the heroine Emily) and much of the novel is taken up with descriptions of 'romantic' landscapes (the word 'romantic' being much used). The novel proceeds at a leisurely pace and Gothic trappings are only gradually introduced, as the love story gives way to one of suspense and the elements of terror slowly gain the upper hand. The truly Gothic belongs to the central portion, contained within volumes 2 and 3 of a four-volumed work spanning, in modern editions, some 670 pages; the quintessentially Gothic castle of Udolpho is first sighted only on page 226 (of the World's Classics text) and left for good on page 451. Not for nothing has *Udolpho* been termed 'a transitional work', 'which begins and ends as a novel of sentiment but is not quite able to account for the core of Gothic and Freudian horror in its middle sections' (Rajan, 1986, pp. 260–1).

The supernatural, which appears seriously to enter *The Mysteries of Udolpho* half way through, is neatly cleared up by the end (particularly just before the end) of this near-omniscient third-person narrative in the characteristic manner of Ann Radcliffe's brand of Gothic, the *surnaturel-expliqué*. Varma (1966, p. 33) claims that the phenomenon of the supernatural explained arose in German fiction only after 1800, whereas in England Radcliffe used it from 1789. This is certainly not the case with 'Monk' Lewis. *The Monk* achieved European notoriety for its extended use of horror, cruelty and sexuality in ways which anticipated the *école frénétique*. Furthermore, Lewis made no bones about the overt supernatural: diabolical agencies and magical devices abound in his novel. Lewis, it has been supposed, may well have known Sade's *Justine* while the 'divine Marquis' did not stint in his praise of *The Monk*, which he considered 'superior in all respects to the strange leaps of the brilliant imagination of Mrs Radcliffe' (quoted from Praz, 1968, p. 13).

Indeed, even more fascinating, perhaps, are Sade's further remarks, in his *Idées sur les romans* (1800), attempting to explain the tale of terror:

> This genre was the inevitable product of the revolutionary shocks with which the whole of Europe resounded. For those who were acquainted with all the ills that are brought upon men by the wicked, the romantic novel was becoming somewhat difficult to write, and merely monotonous to read: there was nobody left who had not experienced more misfortunes in four or five years than could be depicted in a century by literature's most famous novelists: it was necessary to call upon hell for aid in order to arouse interest, and to find in the land of fantasies what was common knowledge from historical observation of man in this iron age. But this way of writing presented so many inconveniences! The author of the *Moine* failed to avoid them no less than did Mrs Radcliffe; either of these two alternatives was unavoidable; either to explain away all the magic elements, and from then on to be interesting no longer, or never raise the curtain, and there you are in the most horrible unreality. (quoted from Praz, 1968, p. 14)

This penetrating statement, like so much of Sade, is of interest from both the historical and the psychological viewpoints. Moreover, the logic of Sade's thought here seems to lead to a demand for a synthesis of the two literary approaches which he has observed, a demand for something very like the pure fantastic.

Such a desire did not, of course, emanate from Sade alone, Coleridge seemed to approve the formula of terror-suspense-explication, but the *Quarterly Review*, for example, of May 1810 expressed dissatisfaction with contrived explanations (see Varma, p. 105), and the relatively Gothic-free twenty years following publication of Radcliffe's *The Italian* in 1797 allowed scope for synthetic development. By the 1820s, when the Gothic style was again coming to the fore, such development is generally recognised to have taken place. Karl Miller, in his book *Doubles*, (1987, p. 1) sees a combination of the romantic novel and the romantic lyric in the works of autobiography and autobiographical fiction of that decade (citing Maturin, De Quincey and James Hogg). Writing in 1824 on Ann Radcliffe, Scott displayed the following appreciation of the literary trend in question:

> There are some modern authors, indeed, who have endeavoured, ingeniously enough, to compound betwixt ancient faith and modern incredulity. They have exhibited phantoms, and narrated prophecies strangely accomplished, without giving a defined or absolute opinion, whether these are to be referred to supernatural agency, or whether these were produced (no uncommon case) by an overheated imagination, and the presages apparently verified by a causal, though singular, coincidence of circumstances. (Scott, 1968, p. 116)

Scott goes on to warn that such a method is 'an evasion of the difficulty, not a solution', but then to admit that 'perhaps, upon the whole, this is the most artful mode of terminating such a tale of wonder'.

Arguably, Mary Shelley's *Frankenstein* (1818) and Maturin's *Melmoth the Wanderer* (1820) each represent something of such a synthesis. It seems strange that so perspicacious a critic as Praz (1968, p. 25) should see Frankenstein's refusal to reveal to his narratee the manner of his animation of lifeless matter as 'a fundamental weakness which seriously hampers the suspense of disbelief'. As Scott (1968, p. 90) had pointed out, with reference to Walpole's novel, there are times when a natural explanation can be even more incredible than the supernatural (or, in the case of *Frankenstein*, rather the preternatural). Furthermore, Mary Shelley's treatment here of her 'difficulty' seems to respond to Sade's call, as highlighted in Praz's very same essay. Praz is on surer ground (p. 32; cf. Scott, 1968, p. 271, and others) in picking on 'the way in which the monster acquires a remarkable degree of education' as a 'serious obstacle to the suspension of disbelief'; these strictures notwithstanding, Praz can still conclude that 'Mrs Shelley's novel ranks as the greatest achievement of the Gothic school.' Maturin, in his *Melmoth*, is seen by Praz (1968, p. 34) as having produced 'the synthesis of all the themes of the "tales of terror" school', while Varma (p. 206) states that 'the two Gothic streams of "terror" and "horror" met in the genius of C. R. Maturin.'

We shall look a little more closely at these claims made for novels by Mary Shelley and Maturin in the next chapter. We shall also make further use of the synthetic approach to prose fiction and genre as we advance further into what Punter (in a formulation which comes close to Todorovian notions of the fantastic) calls 'paranoiac fiction':

> fiction in which the reader is placed in a situation of ambiguity with regard to fears within the text, and in which the attribution of persecution remains uncertain and the reader is invited to share in the doubts and uncertainties which pervade the apparent story. It is this element of paranoiac structure which marks the better Gothic works off from mere tame supernaturalism: they continually throw the supernatural into doubt, and in doing so they also serve the important function of removing the illusory halo of certainty from the so-called 'natural' world. (Punter, p. 404)

AMERICA

American prose before Poe has at best a patchy reputation. The Puritan and colonial traditions produced little of lasting interest or inspiration. In eighteenth-century America, in the words of the literary historian, Marcus Cunliffe:

> There were gentry and fine houses, though not many; there was litigation and slavery; there were several worthy colleges, and a quantity of schools. . . . Colonial literature might henceforth develop in modest conjunction with that of the Mother Country: for there was little to distinguish it, seemingly, from that of England. It was clumsier; it lacked the excitement of a great metropolis; a few of its words were novel; some Indian names had crept incongruously among the scriptural and classical references. But its models were English. . . . The colonial, one might say, had become provincial. (Cunliffe, 1970, pp. 37–8)

Noah Webster, the philologist, however, told his compatriots in

1789 that 'Great Britain . . . should no longer be *our* standard, for the taste of her writers is already corrupted and her language on the decline' (quoted from Cunliffe, p. 47).

English and German Gothic fiction had flooded the country by the end of the century. In the early part of the nineteenth century, Poe attended, at a tender age, school in England before imbibing European influences back on American soil. Washington Irving, another early figure of influence, travelled widely in Europe, compiling *The Sketch Book* (1819–20), *Tales of a Traveller* (1824), *The Alhambra* (1832) and others. Despite, or perhaps because of, a tendency merely to move his material from one language to another with the addition of 'some incidental ornament' (Cunliffe, p. 57), Irving achieved a considerable reputation on both sides of the Atlantic. Best remembered at home for his tale *Rip Van Winkle*, a German plot transposed to the Catskills (for a fantastic reading of which, see Brooke-Rose, pp. 106–12), Irving was also the author of such other oft-quoted stories in the fantastic vein as *The Spectre Bridegroom* and *The Adventures of the German Student*.

An earlier writer of significance, frequently dubbed the first American professional writer, was Charles Brockden Brown (1771–1810). Accorded only half a page in Cunliffe's *The Literature of the United States*, Brockden Brown's star has risen again in recent years, with the general revival of interest in Gothic fiction and with modern reprintings of his main novels. Under the influence of the social thought of William Godwin, Brockden Brown wrote Utopias before turning his attention to psychological novels with distinctly Gothic features. He referred to his novels, which he hurriedly delivered to an indifferent reading public, as 'a series of performances' (Brown, 1978, p. 3), perhaps in part because of their frantic and virtually simultaneous composition, and he dissociated himself from the traditional English and European trappings of popular terror: 'Puerile superstition and exploded manners; Gothic castles and chimeras, are the materials usually employed for this end' (Brown, 1988, p. 3). Instead, he set his works in newly independent America: the city of Philadelphia during the yellow fever epidemic of 1793 in *Arthur Mervyn* (1799–1800); *Wieland* (1798) takes place, for the most part, on the country estates of Pennsylvania; *Edgar Huntly* (1799) is essentially concerned with the settlers' lands of Delaware. Post-colonial and Indian problems figure. When further-flung sequences are required, Brockden Brown turns to Europe, and in particular to another British colony, Ireland. The origins of the Wieland family are in Saxony; the mysterious Ludloe is an Irishman with Spanish connections; Carwin is himself American, but in the unfinished sequel to *Wieland* — *Memoirs of Carwin, the Biloquist* — he sojourns in Ireland and Spain, under the strange tutelage of Ludloe; the prehistory of Clithero, the lunatic sleepwalker from *Edgar Huntly*, takes place in his native northern Ireland.

In accordance with his interests in advanced social, scientific and medical thinking of the period, Brockden Brown's works, and indeed his very characters, seem made up of delusions, manias, transformations and dreams, plus somnambulance — or, in the case of Carwin, extraordinary powers of ventriloquism. Their first-person epistolary narratives or memoirs reveal, overtly or covertly, deep psychological disturbance or ambivalence. Authentic cases of murder and insanity (such as the New York murder of 1796 which inspired the central melodrama of *Wieland*) were blended with ambiguous or perverse motivation in a manner foreshadowing Dostoevsky. Brockden Brown's characters, narrative and psychological situations may frequently be seen as metaphors for the prospects awaiting the new American Republic. The ambiguity of his approach to the Gothic is also seen as the first vital stage in the Americanisation of that tradition, in a line running from Brockden Brown through Irving, Poe, Hawthorne and Melville to Henry James (Thompson, 1973, p. 76).

In terms of his contribution to the fantastic, Brockden Brown is usually considered an exponent of the 'explained supernatural' (see, for example Punter, p. 194). The persistent question with regard to *Wieland*, as G. R. Thompson (p. 76) puts it, 'is whether the younger Wieland acts under the influence of a demonic agent when he murdered his family or whether his was merely the act of a madman influenced by environmental forces'. The supernatural disaster which befell Wieland *père* seems to have been spontaneous human combustion. However, the demonic aura surrounding the physically unprepossessing, but vocally alluring, Carwin may not be totally dispelled for many readers and in any case other possible explanations for Wieland's horrendous conduct remain: malignant intervention by a non-demonic Carwin, or relatively innocent participation by Carwin amid a series of coincidences mounted by a sinister fate. Brockden Brown's novels end somewhat hurriedly, when they are finished at all. In *Wieland*, Carwin alludes to retreating to the 'wilderness', there 'to employ myself in composing a faithful narrative of my actions' (Brown, 1978, p. 212): this companion volume (*Memoirs of Carwin*) remained incomplete, as does Carwin's motivation. One Brockden Brown specialist Norman Grabo (in his introduction to Brown, 1988, p. xi) has remarked that 'each novel is structured so as to collapse, to self-destruct somewhere along the telling — usually nearer the end than elsewhere.' Again *Wieland* (titled also 'or The Transformation') is a prime example. Clara Wieland, the first-person narrator, a young woman of advanced consciousness by most normal fictional standards of the period but apparently facing the onset of madness after her ordeal, threatens just that — personal and narrative self-destruction: 'When I lay down the pen the taper of life will expire: my existence will terminate with my tale' (Brown, 1978, p. 221); however, three years later she adds a postscript, 'saved by medicine and marriage'.

There is not only something distinctly modern about Brockden Brown's writing, but also something distinctly 'New World'; Punter (p. 197) pinpoints it as: 'his ability to explore mental worlds with precision peculiar to a situation in which those worlds were not submerged beneath the pressure of a fearsome past'. Just one of Brown's English admirers was Thomas Love Peacock, who praised *Wieland* as 'one of the few tales in which the final explanation of the apparently supernatural does not destroy or diminish the original effect' (quoted from Birkhead, 1921, p. 140). In America, his novels received a certain posthumous recognition in the 1820s, the formative years of Edgar Allan Poe. It was of course Poe who was to make the strongest American contribution to the literary fantastic, as he pursued his own synthesis of English, American and European forms.

FRANCE

It is little wonder that Todorov's study, *Introduction à la littérature fantastique* (1970) emerged from the French critical tradition. What was new about Todorov's book, which has impelled contemporary interest in the fantastic, was his attempt at a structuralist approach to genre, rather than the theme itself. The theme of the *fantastique* has long been a regular feature in French literary criticism.[2] Indeed, not only is this theme long established in critical writing in France, but in French one has to distinguish between *le fantastique* and *la fantastique*: the former refers to works of the literary fantastic, the latter to the capacity of the imagination in general (Bessière, 1974, p. 30).

The nineteenth century in France abounds with discussion of *le fantastique*, from Jean-Jacques Ampère to Maupassant. France was early in the field with an example of something at least approaching the pure fantastic, seen, of course, with hindsight (p. 95), as a synthesis of the marvellous and the everyday: Jacques Cazotte's *Le Diable amoureux* of 1772. This work was picked out by Ampère in 1828, in an article on Hoffmann, as the originator of the tradition of which Hoffmann was by then seen as the glorious culmination: '*Le Diable amoureux*, by Cazotte, a masterpiece of imagination and charm, is just about the only French work in which the supernatural is neither a ridiculous phantasmagoria nor a purely satirical frame' (quoted from Castex, 1951, p. 25, my translation).

There were works of French fiction seen as precursors to Cazotte, works featuring diabolical pacts for instance (see Bessière, pp. 70–4). At the time Cazotte was writing, a movement started in which he too became involved; this movement may be loosely termed the 'renaissance of the irrational', a reaction to the Enlightenment. The exponents of this movement, who were to have considerable influence, direct or indirect, over the development of the tradition of the literary fantastic, developed out of the serious and less serious elements of the older cabbalist, alchemical and Rosicrucian traditions (see Castex, pp. 13–24): followers of Albertus Magnus, Cornelius Agrippa and, no doubt, Paracelsus; readers of Balthazar Bekker's *Le Monde enchanté* and the Abbé de Villars's *Le Comte de Gabalis*, Castex (p. 455) divides the influential exponents of the new irrational movement into three categories. Three luminaries are considered 'apostles': Swedenborg, Martines de Pasqually and his more important protégé, Louis Claude de Saint-Martin. All three may be termed evangelical spiritualists, or theosophists; Saint-Martin was himself a follower of Swedenborg, and of Jacob Böhme. Two 'practitioners', or 'vulgarisers of illuminism' were Lavater and Mesmer, the pseudo-scientists. In the category of 'charlatans' are three notorious adventurers who dabbled in occultism as an aid to high-society chicanery: Casanova, Saint-Germain and Cagliostro. All these names recur frequently on, or behind, the pages of the literary fantastic in its nineteenth-century heyday. Illuminism, Freemasonry and preternatural science, a revival of rites and magic, had much to offer the writers of European romanticism.

Michel Foucault, in his *Madness and Civilization*, has noted a connection between the emergence of the fantastic and of a dialectical discourse of reason and unreason, the phenomenon of 'sadism', the fascination with sexual desire, death-wish and madness in the western imagination, all taking place at the end of the eighteenth century (see Bessière, pp. 62–3). We have already noted Sade's comment on the tale of terror and the revolutionary events, and his interest in the English Gothic, particularly in its most sadistic example, Lewis's *The Monk*; as observed earlier, connections can be made between the works of Sade and the fantastic.[3] Such an exploration would make an interesting separate study.

However, it was the discovery of Hoffmann in the late 1820s which led to the 'golden age' of the fantastic in France. A romantic legend of Hoffmann ('of a sick man, on the edge of madness, a prey to his hallucinations', Bessière, p. 94) was fostered in Paris, largely by one Dr David (later Johann) Ferdinand Koreff, a friend and collaborator of Hoffmann in Berlin, who had achieved literary preservation as the 'Vincent' of his friend's Serapion Brothers and who settled in France in 1822, the year of Hoffmann's death. Koreff encouraged translations of Hoffmann, by one Loève-Veimars, and thanks to these efforts, and those of the critics, Ampère (allegedly the first in France to ascribe the epithet 'fantastic' to Hoffmann) and Girardin, Hoffmann was a cult figure by 1830 (on Hoffmann's promotion in France, see Castex, pp. 42–56). Scott's generally hostile essay on Hoffmann was published in the *Revue de Paris* in 1829 and Scott was presented in literary debates as the opposing literary pole to Hoffmann, and virtually his rival. However, there was no stopping Hoffmann's reputation at this time in France, where his influence became incomparably more important than in his native Germany (Bessière, p. 94). Charles Nodier glorified Hoffmann in his essay 'Du fantastique en littérature' (1830) and he was joined by Gérard de Nerval and the young Théophile Gautier; Alexandre Dumas *père* evoked Hoffmann in his *Un bal masqué* (1833).

' "*Fantastique!*" The word was taken up everywhere like a refrain', writes Castex (p. 64) of the 1830s. The 'golden age' of the fantastic had arrived, and not only in the French prose of Nodier, Gautier and *l'école frénétique*: there was the painting of Delacroix, operas such as *Der Freischütz* and *Robert le Diable*, ballets such as *La Sylphide*, Berlioz's *La Symphonie fantastique* and a fantastic story by Jules Janin called *Hoffmann et Paganini* (1831), not to mention the real Paganini and his supposed diabolical virtuosity (Castex, pp. 58–60).

GERMANY

Eighteenth-century pre-romanticism in Germany, in the form of 'Storm and Stress' writing, grew out of a by now somewhat familiar admixture of sources. These included such varied influences as that of Rousseau and of Pietism (inspired by Jacob Böhme), Old Norse romanticism and the modern English novel, the ideas of Spinoza and Shaftesbury, and took such forms as 'the strange amalgam of liberal-minded philanthropy and mysticism in Freemasonry, or the hybridism of modern science, quackery and alchemy which the century of Enlightenment had produced' (Kohlschmidt, 1975, p. 3). As well as Old German and Old Nordic, interest returned to Neoplatonism (especially from von Baader onwards), to classical antiquity (particularly Winckelmann's study of the Greeks) and to the worlds of Ossian and Shakespeare (via Herder). The fiction of Wieland, with its motif of 'faerie', may be seen as an important stage in this development, as may the ballads of Bürger. The latter's ballad Lenore (1773) provided European and American Gothic with the archetypal figure of the revenant-bridegroom.

Such a figure makes an appearance too at the climax of Schiller's influential and popular story The Ghost-Seer (1784), itself influenced by Cazotte (Bessière, p. 93). While this story has claims to be 'the first great German fantastic work' (p. 98), strictly speaking, it supplies all the ingredients, rather than the synthesis. Its primary narrator, the Count O-, recounts a sequence of mysterious events, all of which except one (the report of a death occurring far away) are explained as the acts of a Sicilian charlatan, an imbiber of 'the infallible Count Gabolis' (Haining, 1973, p. 71). The remaining narrative, supplied by the Sicilian self-confessed impostor, re-centres attention on the story's central figure, variously posing as Armenian, Russian, officer of the Inquisition and Franciscan monk, known otherwise only 'by the name of the Incomprehensible' (p. 64). This 'Armenian', as he is most frequently styled, is presented as a demonic figure of wandering-Jewish pedigree: 'Some believe him to be the famous Apollonius of Tyana, and others the disciple of St John the Baptist, of whom it is said that he shall remain wandering on the earth until the day of judgement' (p. 66). He seems able to foretell death, detect spiritualist fraud and produce 'actual' spirits at will. The story, then, appears ultimately to remain within the realm of the supernatural; doubt, if any there be, must reside in the removes and the reliability of the narration. However, it should also be noted that the story is considered unfinished (Blackall, 1983, p. 226).

Schiller subsequently grew more suspicious of the fantastic; in the conclusion to his essay On Naive and Sentimental Poetry (1795–6), he maintains not only that 'the fantast abandons nature out of mere caprice, in order to indulge with all the less restraint the wantonness of his desires and the whims of his imagination', but that 'his phantasmagoria . . . leads likewise to an infinite fall into a bottomless abyss and can only terminate in complete destruction' (Nisbet, 1985, pp. 231–2).

There also developed in Germany a genre of popular literature known as the *Trivialromane*; it was analogous to and influential upon the English Gothic novel, as well as upon the subsequent German romantic movement. In particular there came a series of novels between 1787 and 1798, under the general title 'Days of Yore' (*Sagen der Vorzeit*), written under the pseudonym of Veit Weber (by one Leonhard Wächter). These novels were set in the Middle Ages and had occultist tendencies, secret societies which battled for causes of justice or reaction and mysteries that were usually explained at the end. They also contained contrived forms of the demonic, plus 'dark landscapes, ominous presentiments, blue flames, mysterious strangers, fateful days of the year, revenants, secret vaults, mysterious caskets, elixirs, secret writing, magic mirrors, rings and books', as well as other standard trappings of many Gothic and romantic works: 'unknown parentage, visions and dreams, warning figures, initiation rituals, journeys in the service of something, disguises for a purpose, mysterious towers, vaults, and caverns, archives, secret societies with a Superior representing their spiritual aims and an Emissary or "Genius" who is sent out to accomplish some practical aim and often guides . . . a developing hero, so that life becomes a process of education' (Blackall, p. 64).[4] Recurring character types include: 'evil monks and serene hermits, all-too-impressionable youths, androgynous females, demonic women, madmen' (ibid.). All in all, this body of 'trivial literature' seems to have furnished a roll-call of all the constituents of fantastic literature, past and future.

Other interesting transitional works of a higher literary order were supplied by Kleist and a certain mysterious 'Bonaventura'. The stories of Kleist, written in the first decade of the nineteenth century, frequently skirt the fantastic (as with *The Foundling*: what lies behind the mysterious 'doubling' of Nicolo and Colino?) or even embrace it (as with the short ghost tale *The Beggarwoman of Locarno*). Kleist's stories are frequently perceived to contain a quality of the 'uncanny' (see Cave, 1988, pp. 386–96; and Luke and Reeves's introduction to Kleist, 1978). Their prevailing ambience, in any case, seems one of constant dominion by a hostile fate, in a mysteriously malignant universe which anticipates in many ways the metaphysical absurd of Kafka or Beckett. Even more nihilistic is a strange work of 1804, entitled *The Nightwatches of Bonaventura*, which is almost as enigmatic in terms of form and genre mix as it is in terms of authorship.[5] Its structure combines confessional–chronological narration with grotesque arabesques in a 'geometrical' progression which has been seen to integrate the aesthetic precepts of Novalis with those of Friedrich Schlegel (Blackall, p. 220). Again, the overriding feeling is one of a remarkable modernity.

This brings us to a brief consideration of the impact of German romantic philosophy and aesthetics. Without getting sidetracked into the thorny question of definitions of romanticism, which would in any case lead us too far from our basic concerns, we can at least agree with Lilian Furst's statement that 'Romanticism is the culmination of that transformation of Western culture under way during the "pivotal period" of the eighteenth century' (Furst, 1984, p. 43).[6] 'The artistic revolution of the later eighteenth and early nineteenth century' (p. 36) has already been seen to be crucial to the developments which we are tracing. For example, the late eighteenth century has been identified as the period of the 'realisation of the innately fictional character of art' (p. 45) and of 'the intuition of the instability of meaning', which paved the way for 'the metamorphosis of irony' (p. 42). The romantic conception of irony, as of genre and much else, has its origins in philosophy.[7]

Paramount as literary theorists among the 'Jena Romantics' around the turn of the nineteenth century were the Schlegel brothers. Friedrich Schlegel devised an approach to irony which became known (though only from the mid nineteenth century onwards) as 'romantic irony'; it was derived from the works of such acknowledged practitioners as Socrates, Petrarch, Dante, Cervantes, Shakespeare, Sterne and Diderot (Furst, pp. 29–30). Irony thus became transformed from a rhetorical tool to a philosophical stance, having less to do with repartee or wit and rather more with a perceived universal ambivalence and paradoxicality. It was recognised by Schlegel that irony could lead to 'the necessity for the artifact not only to criticize itself, the author, or the reader, but also to "destroy" itself in a certain sense' (Wheeler, 1984, p. 20). Others saw this tendency going even further; Hegel, for one, saw the transformed phenomenon of irony in terms akin to a modern critique of deconstruction, its form 'a subjective *void*':

> The ironic . . . as an expression of the genius of individualism resides in the self-destruction of the splendid, the great, the excellent. . . . Consequently, not only is the right, the ethical and the true not to be taken seriously; furthermore, the

highest and best is reduced to nought when it contradicts and destroys itself through its appearances in certain individuals, characters and actions, and thereby becomes the ironic comment on itself. (quoted from Furst, p. 33)

Furst (p. 47) sees this transformation of irony as symptomatic of the broad political, social, philosophical and artistic change in the face of Europe of that period, summing up the process as follows:

As such it partakes of the spirit of the age; it has filiations to factors as capacious as the ascendancy of relativistic thinking in the wake of Kant's Copernican revolution and the nascent suspicion of the unsteadiness of words; the explosion of self-consciousness following from Fichte's subjectivism; the aesthetic doctrines of the Romantic movement concerning the function of poetry, the role of the artist, and the configuration of the work; the rise of the novel and the predilection for self-reflexivity; and the altered relationship between narrator and audience. In short, the metamorphosis of irony is another intimation of the avocation of that age for questioning its heritage, reassessing its values, and fashioning an ideology in keeping with its own apprehension of the universe.

These ideas can be seen reflected in (or, indeed, as a reflection of) a range of contemporary writing, including the prose of Kleist, Bonaventura, Jean Paul (Richter) and Hoffmann, as well as anticipating many of the trends which would affect literature well into the twentieth century. Referring to the fiction of Jean Paul, Furst (p. 136) states: 'The irony stems from the contradictory combination of the fiction of reality with the reality of fiction'.[8]

The novel as poetry was a fundamental romantic concept, once again worked out in detail by Friedrich Schlegel. In novels he favoured the 'arabesque' (a term derived from Goethe), the play of imagination, irony and the subjective: 'By a novel, a *Roman*, Schlegel means the "ironic, fantastic, romantic" art of Cervantes, Sterne, Diderot, Jean Paul and his own *Lucinde*' (Wellek, 1981, p. 19). In his categorisation of the novel, Schlegel distinguished four types: the 'poetic' novel, which could be either 'fantastic' or 'sentimental'; and the 'prose' novel, which in turn subdivided into the 'philosophical' or the 'psychological'; a perfect novel (such as his own *Lucinde*, 1799?) would presumably combine all four (Blackall, p. 24). By 'fantastic' Schlegel meant 'unreal material, fantasy, purely imaginative worlds' (p. 26); in his *Letter on the Novel*, he suggested the necessity of looking to Shakespeare or the 'older moderns' for 'the core of romantic fantasy' (Lacoue-Labarthe and Nancy, 1988, p. 98).

Freidrich's brother, August Wilhelm Schlegel, also saw the novel as something of an all-inclusive genre and as a romantic form, in contrast to the classical epic, a form which should be modelled on *Don Quixote. Wilhelm Meister*, and *Heinrich von Ofterdingen*' (Wellek, p. 51). René Wellek, for one, is surprised that A. W. Schlegel should have spent time in his youth translating Horace Walpole and that he should have 'seriously reviewed' such novels as Lewis's *The Monk* (p. 69). However, it may seem less than surprising to us that the kind of novelistic synthesis aimed at by the Schlegels should have left space for fantastic or Gothic forms.

Another relevant feature of romantic poetics was the cult of the fragment. This manifested itself by a propensity for unfinished works, in the device of 'manuscripts' and various other formal idiosyncrasies. Once again Friedrich Schlegel and Novalis led the way; much of the writing of these romantic theorists was itself in fragmentary form. Moreover, the concept of the fragment, the process or quest rather than completion, became in itself a part of the philosophy: '*Work in progress* henceforth becomes the infinite truth of the work' (Lacoue-Labarthe and Nancy, p. 48). Schlegel in his *Athenäum* fragments of 1798 is seen by Blackall (pp. 30–34) as 'feeling his way towards a validation' of the grotesque, the arabesque and the fantastic as a poetic form.

Some mention must also be made of the influential contribution of Schelling to romantic aesthetics. His approach is typified in the following quotation from *System of Transcendental Idealism* (1800):

What we call nature is a poem that lies hidden in a mysterious and marvellous script. Yet if the riddle could reveal itself, we would recognize in it the Odyssey of the spirit which, in a strange delusion, seeking itself, flees itself; for the land of phantasy [Phantasie] toward which we aspire gleams through the world of sense only as through a half-transparent mist, only as a meaning does through words. When a great painting comes into being it is as though the invisible curtain that separates the real from the ideal world is raised [aufgehoben]; it is merely the opening through which the characters and places of the world of fantasy, which shimmers only imperfectly through the real world, fully come upon the stage. Nature is nothing more to the artist than it is to the philosopher; it is merely the ideal world appearing under unchanging limitations, or it is merely the imperfect reflection of a world that exists not outside but within him. (quoted from Simpson, 1984, p. 129).[9]

Thus the idealist ingredient of dualism is added, or reconfirmed, within the romantic synthetic cauldron.

It was broadly speaking in these terms, though as has been pointed out 'the romantic period in general can be thought of as embracing more theoretical options than it can produce into complete coherence' (Simpson, p. 19), that romantic poetics sought a higher synthesis within art and poetry (i.e. in the novel) of a number of dualities. These included time and space, the real and the ideal, nature and spirit, the conscious and the unconscious, the finite and the infinite, unity and (or behind) plurality, complementarity and the reconciliation of opposites, fragmentariness and wholeness. As though to complicate matters further, Novalis affirmed that 'one idea can usefully have several names' (Wheeler, 1984, p. 89).

Other, less predictable, syntheses were also in the air. Friedrich Schlegel's *Athenäum* fragment 125 calls, in the name of 'wishful criticism', for a combination of Jean Paul and Peter Leberecht — that is to say of an author with a fictional character (Leberecht being one of Tieck's characters): 'The latter has precisely what the former lacks. Once united, Jean Paul's grotesque talent and the fantastic disposition of Peter Leberecht would yield an excellent romantic poet' (Lacoue-Labarthe and Nancy, p. 118). Jean Paul, it should be remembered, was also the author of an aesthetic tract (*School for Aesthetics*, 1804) and was himself concerned to distinguish 'fancy' (of a Coleridge type) from 'Phantasie' (or creative imagination, see Wheeler, p. 161). Furthermore, Schlegel, in Ideas 95, presents a fantastic image pointing out of romanticism and straight into the modernism of Borges: 'in a perfect literature all books should be only a single book, and in such an eternally developing book, the gospel of humanity and culture will be revealed' (p. 57). Novalis in his *Dialogues* too, or conversely, seems to anticipate a grotesque multiplication of books, like a proliferation of seeds (see Lacoue-Labarthe and Nancy, pp. 126–7).

CROSS-FERTILISATION

We have already seen a number of hints of cross-fertilisation at play in the literary development outlined above. These, naturally, multiply as writers of other literatures join the fray during the course of the nineteenth century. Such is the process by which literature evolves. Carlos Fuentes, writing of the literary origins of his story *Aura*, traced its basic plot to a Chinese tale, deriving in its turn from 'the traditions of the oldest Chinese literature, that tide of narrative centuries that hardly begins to murmur the vastness of its constant themes: the supernatural virgin, the fatal woman, the spectral bride, the couple reunited' (Fuentes, 1988, p. 38).

Cazotte's pioneering *Le Diable amoureux* had its influence on Schiller, Lewis and subsequently Hoffmann. The thought and fiction of Godwin was an influence on Brockden Brown. Brockden Brown and Beckford feature among the influences on Mary Shelley (Baldick, p. 36). Schiller's *The Ghost-Seer* was a favourite of Byron's; Schiller, Godwin and Brockden Brown all had an impact on Percy Shelley (Butler, p. 158). Bürger's ballad *Lenore* was translated into English by Scott; it entered Russian literature through Zhukovsky and Pushkin. Odoevsky reviewed Mary Shelley's *The Last Man*, the theme of which he later sketched in a powerful short work called 'The Last Suicide' (which formed part of *Russian Nights*, 1844). Poe's *doppelgänger* story *William Wilson* derived from a Spanish sketch by Washington Irving, in its turn based on an abandoned project of Byron's which had been drawn from Spanish literature and suggested by Percy Shelley (Miller, p. 155). We can scarcely begin to consider where the German influences on Poe led. We have already noted Hoffmann's importance in France; his influence in Russia was almost as great. Indeed, Hoffmann and Poe are already emerging as key figures on a pan-European scale.

It may no longer seem much of a surprise that among the direct influences on Odoevsky were Saint-Martin and Schelling, not to mention Hoffmann (see Cornwell, 1986). Another figure to have interested Odoevsky was Piranesi; indeed, Odoevsky wrote a fantastic story about him. As we have seen above, Schelling wrote of 'the Odyssey of the spirit'. In France, Hoffmann was called 'a new Columbus' (Castex, 1951, p. 60); in Russia, Odoevsky termed Schelling the Columbus of the soul (Cornwell, 1986, p. 91). More surprising perhaps are the similarities between Odoevsky's story *The Sylph* (1837) and *The Diamond Lens*, by the Irish–American writer Fitz-James O'Brien, written some twenty years later.[10]

If we look at the development of this tradition from another vantage point, we will see that period studies concentrating their attention on topics or approaches tangential to the fantastic tend to focus consistently on a similar range of sources, authors and texts, whether these studies are primarily concerned with Gothic or terror literature (Birkhead, 1921; Varma, 1966; Punter, 1980 and others), the romantic novel (Kiely, 1972; Blackall, 1983), Mesmerism (Tatar, 1978), melodrama (Brooks, 1976), the phenomenon of doubles (Miller, 1987) or even that of opium addiction (Hayter, 1988). By the second or third decade of the nineteenth century all the elements were assembled, with a sufficient degree of cultural cross-fertilisation under way, for the tradition of the literary fantastic to achieve full momentum.

2 Tripping the Light Fantastic: from Frankenstein to Dracula

Fantastique! Le mot est repris partout comme un refrain.

P-G Castex (1951, p. 64)

PREAMBLE

Before embarking on what will be a kind of sideways survey of the literary fantastic through the remainder of the nineteenth century — in search of unusual approaches to, brushes with, or skirtings of the fantastic, rather than straight reading of already familiar works — we should pause to emphasise a few further general points.

The tendency towards synthesis, even of elements within and close to the Gothic form, let alone those novelistic areas apart, was soon producing hybrids and parodies, as well as facilitating its own natural progression. Mention may be made of Jane Austen's posthumous *Northanger Abbey* (1818), 'which is, and is not, a Gothic novel' (Furst, 1984, p. 99) and the novels of Thomas Love Peacock. Such a clearly fantastic development as the Frankenstein myth was born from an area marked out by the 'overlapping of literary and political discourses' (Baldick, 1987, p. 17). Elements of the Gothic, and/or the fantastic, proceeded to impinge on at least certain of the works of many a prominent mainstream figure of nineteenth-century fiction: Balzac, Dickens, Melville, Galdós, Dostoevsky, Henry James and others. Even within the confines of what might be considered its own tradition, in the nineteenth century and beyond, the scope for evolution was wide enough; as Alastair Fowler (1974, p. 92), for one, has pointed out:

> The gothic novel or romance (*The Old English Baron*) yielded a gothic mode that outlasted it and was applied to forms as diverse as the maritime adventure (*The Narrative of A. Gordon Pym*), the psychological novel (*Titus Groan*), the short story

(Isak Dinesen) and the detective story, not to mention various science fiction genres (not wholly unpredictable, these last, in view of Mary Shelley's *Frankenstein*).

Although Gothic and fantastic literature had almost invariably been associated with diabolical agencies, other possibilities were now arising. Again, *Frankenstein* emerges as a key text. As Brian Aldiss, in his *Trillion Year Spree* (1986, p. 39) has noted, 'Frankenstein's is the Faustian dream of unlimited power, but Frankenstein makes no pacts with the devil'; in any case, by now ' "the devil" belongs to a relegated system of belief'. Baldick too (p. 188) recognises the 'secular logic which distinguishes Victor Frankenstein's tragedy from the spirituality of the Faust myth', a quality which serves to strengthen that novel's kinship with realism. Even by 1824, Walter Scott could write of living 'in an age of universal incredulity' (Scott, 1968, p. 116). This was apparent too, of course, in the mainstream of literature; Fredric Jameson has referred in connection with Manzoni's *The Betrothed* to: 'secularization of romance as a form, a process whereby supernatural powers are supplanted by the more psychological "miracle" of conversion' (Jameson, 1975, p. 143).

Secularity thus went hand in hand with the rise of science. Frankenstein may have educated himself on Cornelius Agrippa, Paracelsus and Albertus Magnus, but nevertheless modern-style experimentation replaces alchemy: 'The "vital spark" is imparted to the composite body. Life is created without supernatural aid. Science has taken charge. A new understanding has emerged' (Aldiss, p. 40). As well as on the pseudo-scientists mentioned in the last chapter, writers from the romantic period would draw on the 'new physics, i.e. Schelling's own speculative *Naturphilosophie*' (Wellek, 1981, p. 77), which 'provided a theoretical justification for the animation of inanimate matter' (Ziolkowski, 1977, p. 76), plus the developments in what might today be considered rather more orthodox science, such as the works of Erasmus Darwin (see Aldiss, pp. 29–32).

Karl Miller (1987, p. 49) writes that 'the story of the modern double starts with the magical science of the eighteenth century, when Mesmerists or Animal Magnetists went in for an experimental separation of the second self'. Soon the term *Doppelgänger* was coined by Jean Paul (*ibid.*; and Ziolkowski, p. 176), and 'the whole of romanticism is obsessed by this threat of an absolute loss of one's own identity' (Zolla, 1964, p. 105). Physical doubles tended to be replaced by psychic kinship as the century progressed (see

Ziolkowski, p. 182) in its performance of what Miller (p. 230) has termed 'the nineteenth century's ballet of the divided mind'. Dualism and duality, on various levels, pervade an extensive range of nineteenth-century texts and it is the duality inherent in a text which is likely to sustain the fantastic.

In addition to the psychological development which may be observed in the texts of the fantastic over this period, there is also a striking extension, to the point of elasticity, of what might be called the chronotope of the fantastic. Time and space may dissolve altogether under certain transcendental conditions (as in stories by, for instance, Hoffmann or Odoevsky). But even in terms of basic narrative spacial and temporal parameters, the traditional forms, such as the Gothic castle somewhere in Renaissance Europe, no longer satisfy. Castles occasionally survive (such as Castle Dracula) but are more commonly replaced by rambling mansions (as in Poe, or Le Fanu) or modern urban settings (Stevenson and Wilde); chronological setting is usually contemporary (nineteenth-century) or the recent past (late eighteenth-century in the case of *Frankenstein*, published in 1818). There is too a development of what Ellen Moers has pinpointed, in connection with Ann Radcliffe in particular, as the distinction between 'indoor travel' and 'outdoor travel' (Moers, 1978, p. 127).

Occasionally, however, things threaten to go, or actually do go, much further. While the chronotope of ghostly activity may remain an open question, that of the supernatural explained inevitably reverts to its natural base. The introduction of a revenant must imply a blending, or at least a bending, of chronological levels. Qualitatively different again though is the apparently, or at least relatively, immortal figure of the Wandering Jew type (presented in varying form by Schiller, Maturin, Eugène Sue), or indeed the vampire. *Frankenstein* extends spacially to the Arctic wastes; chronologically, who knows where the monster and his breed might have led? Melmoth traversed the continents and the decades at will. The chronotopical system implied in Mary Shelley's *The Last Man* introduces an even more radical departure. As we have noted above, works of this period have been recognised as the real precursors of science fiction. Scientific, or pseudo-scientific, notions replaced the supernatural or magical; at the same time, eccentricities in chronotope (taken over in part from Utopian literature) vied with what were nominally, at least, ever more realistic settings. This was to lead, over the course of the nineteenth century and on through the twentieth, to such varied forms as the urban uncanny in the

Kafka mould; the extremities of chronotope found in science fiction (from H. G. Wells to the ultimate lengths of Olaf Stapledon); and the mixed forms, with fantasy and the marvellous inserted into a closely determined reality, of the magic realists. But first the nineteenth-century developments.

MARY SHELLEY

Do not fear to think even the most not-probable.
Abraham Helsing, in Bram Stoker's *Dracula*
(Stoker, 1985, p. 129)

We have already alluded to the relative extravagance of the chronotope of *Frankenstein*, which extends spacially from Switzerland to Ireland in the West, Russia in the East and the polar regions in the North. It purports to take place in the eighteenth century but, as such, the tale contains a number of anachronisms: Walton refers to Coleridge's 'Ancient Mariner' (1798), while Frankenstein quotes Shelley's 'Mutability' (1816) and Wordsworth's 'Tintern Abbey' (1798) (*Frankenstein*, in Fairclough, 1968, pp. 276, 362 and 425). Structurally, the novel is framed by Walton's letters to his sister; within this framework comes the main narrative of Victor Frankenstein, which also includes letters and in its turn frames the monster's own narrative. Walton's final letter also includes a speech by the monster. Ultimately the novel is, as Robert Kiely (1972, p. 167) has pointed out, a triple confession 'to individuals with whom the speaker has unusually close ties'. However, it is also divisible, as Richard Freeborn (1985) has shown, into a series of journeys.

The fantastic in *Frankenstein or The Modern Prometheus* comes in the form of a single 'absurd premise', as Ziolkowski (p. 171) terms this phenomenon in the case of Erasmus Spikher's lost reflection in Hoffmann's *A New Year's Eve Adventure*, or that of the transformation of Gregor Samsa into a beetle in Kafka's *Metamorphosis*. As we have remarked in Part One, there are many fairy stories and works of science fiction in which 'only the premise is supernatural and not the story itself' (*ibid.*). Such is the case with *Frankenstein*, except that we are dealing with the preternatural, rather than the supernatural.

As a work which avoids, or departs from, the supernatural in the usual Gothic sense, *Frankenstein* retains vestiges of the supernatural in its language: the otherwise nameless monster is also termed 'daemon' and 'fiend'; an 'Angel of Destruction' is thought to assert 'omnipotent sway' over Frankenstein from the moment he leaves home (Fairclough, p. 305); he indulges in 'unhallowed arts' (p. 352), addresses the monster as 'devil' (pp. 363 and 438) and refers to 'the hellish intention of my fiendish adversary' (p. 462). Walton even finds Frankenstein 'godlike in ruin' (p. 484). This may be seen as analogous to works which deliberately depart from the fantastic, or set out to avoid it, yet retain linguistic references at least (see for example Henry James in the next chapter). In the case of *Frankenstein*, Mary Shelley's debt to Milton, highlighted by the quotation on the title page of the original 1818 edition, is also relevant.[1] There are also many other basic romantic elements to be found in *Frankenstein*: its fragmentary nature in various senses, its (Promethean) questing which ends in (disastrous) failure, the psychological 'doubling' qualities of its main characters (the monster, Victor, Walton: see Baldick, p. 44) in which the pursued equally needs the pursuer, its philosophical and scientific musings.

Particularly striking is the use of what is commonly referred to as the central image of *Frankenstein*. This is all the more so if we care to include Mary Shelley's 1831 introduction as part of the text: this detail has certainly become part of the *Frankenstein* mythology. Here we have the author's supposed dream, in which 'the pale student of unhallowed arts' is imparting the 'spark of life' into 'the hideous phantasm of a man stretched out' (Fairclough, p. 263). The realisation of this vision occurs, in Frankenstein's own narrative, in Chapter Five, beginning 'It was on a dreary night of November' (said, p. 264, to have been the first words written of the story):

> It was on a dreary night of November that I beheld the accomplishment of my toils. With an anxiety that almost amounted to agony, I collected the instruments of life around me, that I might infuse a spark of being into the lifeless thing that lay at my feet. (p. 318)

This image is reversed at the very end when Walton, hearing a hoarse voice in the cabin of the recently expired Frankenstein, enters the cabin containing the remains of his 'ill-fated and admirable friend':

Over him hung a form which I cannot find words to describe
— gigantic in stature, yet uncouth and distorted in its
proportions. As he hung over the coffin, his face was
concealed by long locks of ragged hair; but one vast hand was
extended, in colour and apparent texture like that of a
mummy. (p. 492)

It is this image, to a large extent, which has given *Frankenstein* its
lasting mythic quality. As Baldick (p. 30) eloquently puts it: 'Like
the monster it contains, the novel is assembled from dead fragments
to make a living whole; and as a published work, it escapes Mary
Shelley's textual frame and acquires its independent life outside it, as
a myth.'[2]

At the same time, Mary Shelley's 'hideous progeny' (as she
herself termed it, p. 264) is also a myth of (unnatural) birth, the
'myth of the birth of a nameless monster' (Moers, p. 96), through
an 'attempt to usurp the power of women' (Kiely, p. 164) and to
bypass the normal sexual process. The result is as grotesque as it is
calamitous. It was also to become mythic on a scale that could not
have been dreamt of in 1818.

In addition to Mary Shelley's dream, still further myth-making
circumstances attended the inception and composition of *Frankenstein*.
Ellen Moers has pointed out the undoubted connection between
Mary Shelley's literary progeny and various female circumstances in
her biography (as motherless child, precocious woman and bereaved
mother): in particular, her situation in 1816, when as Mary
Wollstonecraft Godwin she had eloped (in 1814) to become the
pregnant teenage mistress of the married Percy Bysshe Shelley. The
ghost-story competition in Switzerland in the summer of 1816,
involving Mary, Shelley, Byron and Polidori, is well known (see
the author's 1831 introduction, Fairclough, pp. 259–65). Another
member of the company that summer in Switzerland was Claire
Clairmont, Mary's half-sister who was then pregnant by Byron;
Claire was destined, as we shall see, to achieve her own fictional-
mythic afterlife as the Juliana Bordereau of Henry James's *The
Aspern Papers*.[3] However, the summer of 1816 was also the 'lost
summer' of Byron's poem 'Darkness', a prolonged wintry spell
caused by the volcanic eruptions in the southern hemisphere
(Tambora, in the East Indies) of 1815; this is thought to be the
nearest approach in historical times to the likely effects of a nuclear
winter (see Rudolf, 1984). The 1831 introduction talks of 'a wet,
ungenial summer, and incessant rain [that] often confined us for
days to the house' (p. 261). However, the 1817 preface to the novel,

generally thought to have been written by Shelley *mari*, is even more explicit:

> I passed the summer of 1816 in the environs of Geneva. The season was cold and rainy, and in the evenings we crowded around a blazing wood fire and occasionally amused ourselves with some German stories of ghosts which happened to fall into our hands. (p. 268)

It is highly likely that this unseasonable presage of disaster to come contributed to the somewhat apocalyptic mood both of *Frankenstein* and of Mary Shelley's yet gloomier *The Last Man* (1826). As Freeborn (pp. 108–9) has written: 'It matches the desolation surrounding the wanderings of Mary Shelley's monster, or a world desolated by plague such as she described in her later novel *The Last Man*'.

The Last Man is, in comparison with *Frankenstein*, a long, uneven and occasionally a rambling novel, populated by characters modelled upon Mary Shelley's entourage of the 1816 period. It depicts a semi-idealised picture of a future which proceeds to deteriorate into a situation of rapid diminution in the world's population, due to virulent plague. By the end, the first-person narrator Lionel Verney concludes himself, setting out by boat along the Tiber from the ruins of Rome, to be 'the last man' (though how he can know this is far from clear). The name Verney is thought to derive from that of Volney, author of a book known in English as *Ruins of Empire* (read also by Frankenstein's monster: Aldiss, p. 48).

Edith Birkhead (1921, p. 166) considers that *The Last Man* 'attempted a stupendous theme'; this evaluation seems all the more justified as we approach the end of the twentieth century. Brian Aldiss (introduction to Shelley, 1985, no page numbers) likens the structure of the novel to a concerto, coming in three movements:

> The first movement is of great length, almost a social novel in itself; the second movement concerns the coming of the plague and the liberation of Constantinople by Lord Raymond [Byron]; and the third is almost a travel diary coupled with the alarming mathematics of diminishing numbers.

Aldiss (p. 49) points out that here, in contrast to *Frankenstein*, 'It is the race, rather than the individual, which is now hunted down to exile and extinction'; furthermore, given the weather conditions of the summer of 1816 and the epidemics sweeping the world from 1818, much of *The Last Man* represents a symbolic transposition of reality, a 'scientific romance', rather than fantasy as such (*ibid.*). Apparently supernatural apparitions, such as the 'Black Spectre' of death, are explained away in the manner of Radcliffe.

Rosemary Jackson (1981, p. 104) points out that *The Last Man*, like *Frankenstein*, is fragmentary in narrative structure, and open ended; she further stresses the importance of distinguishing between the narrator's (male) voice and 'Mary Shelley's position, as author' (p. 103). However, these are not the only points of structural interest. The novel purports to be set well into the future, towards the end of the twenty-first century (a bold stroke in itself, it is usually thought). What seems to escape comment is the 'Author's Introduction'. This recounts how the authorial persona purports to have discovered near Naples in 1818 a quantity of manuscripts, mysteriously written in both ancient and modern languages, in the cave of the Cumaean Sibyl. The following novel is the work of the authorial persona only as translator and editor of these manuscripts, other than for a degree of transformation designed only to facilitate intelligibility: 'the main substance rests on the truths contained in these poetic rhapsodies, and the divine intuition which the Cumaean damsel obtained from heaven' (Shelley, 1985, p. 4).

Apart from being a device to distance Mary Shelley from her (Verney's) narrative, this fragmentary manuscript presentation, in itself so much in keeping with romantic and Gothic traditions but here used in a novel which is, in most senses, manifestly not Gothic, serves to raise other possibilities. The authorial persona clearly believes the manuscripts to be part of a work of prophecy dating from ancient times: 'This *is* the Sibyl's cave; these are the Sibylline leaves', she is told (p. 3). That some of the manuscripts should be written in English and Italian is therefore strange; the more so that they 'seemed to contain . . . detailed relations of events but lately passed; names, now well known, but of modern date' (*ibid.*), not to mention characters of the future seemingly modelled on idealised realisations of Shelley, Byron and others. Equally plausible, perhaps, within the logic of the fiction, is that the provenance of the manuscripts should be a pre-civilisation which had followed a similar pattern to that of our own before being destroyed by plague or, even more intriguingly, an alternative or parallel world, very like our own but not exactly it. Thus Mary Shelley seems to have introduced a further new shift into the modern novel, one which, while retaining a touch of fantastic ambiguity, puts romantic fiction firmly on the path to a particular kind of science fiction.

MATURIN

A number of fantastic texts seem to have owed their origins to their authors' dreams (as with works by Horace Walpole and Mary Shelley). Maturin's preface to his novel *Melmoth the Wanderer* (1820), however, reveals the origin of that novel to have been one of Maturin's own sermons (Maturin, 1977, p. 37). Charles Robert Maturin was a Protestant clergyman from Dublin, whose Calvinist approach to Christianity belongs to an Irish Protestant tradition as vehement and familiar today as it was to the congregations of the early nineteenth century. Indeed, the novel for which he is mainly remembered, described by Mario Praz as 'the masterpiece of the "tales of terror" school' (Praz, 1970, p. 118), can itself be considered to be a vastly extended and highly colourful sermon. It is described by Robert Kiely (p. 189) as 'a roar of outrage' against the excesses and trappings of Catholicism.[4] If *Melmoth* is essentially a sermon, its message or theme may be seen as a positive one only in part: Alethea Hayter (introduction to Maturin, 1977, p. 25) sees the ostensible theme of the whole book as 'the final inefficacy of fear to imperil the soul'. This, even in so far as it may be considered positive, seems to be outweighed by the inevitability, in a universe hostile both theologically and naturally, of an inexorable grinding down at the hands of fate, followed by death. Compensation, if anywhere, would be other worldly and seems remote.

Maturin's finest novel somehow contrives to be both derivative and original at the same time, having, as Punter (1980, p. 143) puts it 'the ability to bring ancient sources to life in a remarkable way'. The use of 'ancient sources' may even at times verge on plagiarism (see Praz, 1970, p. 177 on 'The Tale of the Spaniard' and Diderot's *La Religieuse*). The Wanderer himself seems to combine something of the Wandering Jew,[5] the Flying Dutchman, Goethe's Mephistopheles, the Byronic hero and the vampire, plus, no doubt, the odd touch from Milton's Satan, Hoffmann's Medardus (*The Devil's Elixirs*), Schiller's ghost-seer, Lewis's monk and elsewhere. The plot, which in the complexity of its presentation, its layers and its chronology would tax the powers of the most expert practitioner in the art of synopsis, basically boils down to an unspeakable satanic bargain, as a result of which Melmoth wanders the earth for 150 years. Damnation must follow unless he can persuade another representative of humanity to agree, for the purpose of extrication from some horrendous circumstance, to take his place. Despite appearing to large numbers of people under severe duress, and reducing or luring others into similar dire straits, the Wanderer is ultimately unsuccessful and hence takes his diabolical medicine.

Melmoth's activities stretch, we are led to believe, far beyond what we actually learn of them by the end of a 700-page novel. He has become a legend and a bogey within his own unnaturally extended lifetime — due not least to his preternatural abilities in travel and sudden appearance — and Monçada, one of the principal sub-narrators, is about to launch into a 'sequel' (Maturin, 1977, p. 693) when the Wanderer, mercifully, returns to his ancestral home, at the conclusion of his appointed span, to await his fate. Before this, stories within stories and manuscripts 'discoloured, obliterated and mutilated beyond any that had ever before exercised the patience of a reader' (p. 67) have accumulated from multiple sub-narrators, in a profusion amounting to what Hayter calls (p. 25) 'Chinese-box perversity'.

Apart from its qualities of synthesis, alluded to earlier and implicit from the above, wherein then lie the merits of Maturin's novel, sufficient to accord it an almost pre-eminent place, at least according to comparatively recent assessments, in the literature of terror? One factor is undoubtedly the power and psychological intensity of the changes in terror which are rung by Maturin. Just one nuance present is the disturbing feeling of guilt, which frequently draws comparison with Kafka. Another may be the appealing, if scarcely credible, even by Gothic standards, figure of Immalee (later Isidora), the child of nature seduced by Melmoth from her Indian Ocean island. Not only, with her purity and vulnerability, is she a creation a pole apart from the Wanderer himself (to whom, however, she yearns incorrigibly to be united), but she stands in the annals of terror in intriguing counterpoint, as a creature of initial innocence, to her near-contemporary, Frankenstein's monster, as well as successor to the persecuted females of Sade and Lewis. Indeed, the horrifying Gothic marriage of Melmoth and Immalee has justifiably been highlighted (Kiely, p. 202) as the novel's central image: noble savage marries demon bridegroom.

As an avowedly satanic farrago, *Melmoth*, on the face of things at least, would seem a poor candidate for the pure fantastic: as Nabokov (1964, 3, p. 353) chose to put it, 'Maturin used up all the platitudes of Satanism, while remaining on the side of the conventional angels'. What Hayter has called the 'gratuitous implausibility' of the plot (Maturin, p. 26) becomes virtually an end in itself, by its presentation through multiple viewpoint of horror upon horror, which even, or in particular, the basic protagonist young John Melmoth has difficulty in believing. The result comes over as a kaleidoscope of dreams and delirium, set largely amid monastic and inquisitorial dungeons of Piranesian proportion which seem to encompass the whole of Spain, featuring a succession of doubling subsidiaries and alter egos. In addition, Melmoth himself adopts the role of satirist of religion (Punter, p. 144) and so convincingly mouths a radicalism, allegedly diametrically opposed to the views of Maturin himself (Kiely, p. 190), that it seems no wild exaggeration to consider *Melmoth* as also something of a forerunner to Bakhtinian dialogism in the novel, normally first associated with Dostoevsky. Such doubts and the possibility of opposed or open meanings are facilitated by the very structure which is so frequently criticised: Margaret Carter (1987, p. 74) has argued that 'the fragmented, mediated narratives have the additional function of rendering problematic the omniscient narrator's straight-forward equation of Melmoth with evil', while multiple narrators in general serve to 'foreground the issue of the nature of evidence and the reliability of witnesses' (p. 81). In this novel–sermon, Maturin the artist was able to exceed the brief of Maturin the preacher by means which were to be favoured and developed by subsequent exponents of the literary fantastic.

Mention of Dostoevsky is not accidental when Maturin's influence remains an important element of his legacy. One of a number of fantastic writers to have been more influential upon foreign literatures than upon his own, Maturin provoked, as we shall see, no less a figure than Balzac to compose a sequel to his *Wanderer*. Hugo, Sue and Dumas *père* are to be counted among Maturin's other French followers. In Italy, *Melmoth* quickly had an impact upon at least one episode of Manzoni's *The Betrothed* (the theme of the unwilling novitiate) and in America found fertile ground with the young Poe. However, Maturin's most striking influence was perhaps in Russia, where he achieved some effect on the opening of, and direct allusions within, Pushkin's *Eugene Onegin* (1825–30); he made an impact too on works by Gogol and Lermontov and was even credited in the Russian edition (1834) with authorship of De Quincey's *Confessions of an English Opium Eater*.[6] Belinsky, no supporter of the fantastic in Russian literature but an occasional admirer of it in foreign writers, was impressed by the (albeit unreliable and abridged) Russian edition; Goncharov, author of the dreamily realist novel *Oblomov*, much later recalled that *Melmoth* had been all the rage in the 1830s. However, the most important impact was on Dostoevsky who, having already read Radcliffe by the age of eight[!], proceeded a decade later to read from Maturin to his fellow engineering students (Miller, 1983,

p. 104). A number of features deriving from Maturin, as from other Gothic writers, have been detected in Dostoevsky's works. Most striking are the closeness of certain passages and motifs between *Melmoth* and *The Brothers Karamazov* (Maturin's novel *Woman, or Pour et Contre* may also have been known to Dostoevsky); moreover, the plan for Dostoevsky's unfulfilled novel *The Life of a Great Sinner* bears a strong structural resemblance to *Melmoth* (p. 109). The full import of the Maturin–Dostoevsky connection has, however, yet to be thoroughly investigated.

HOFFMANN

E. T. A. Hoffmann, it will by now have been noticed, is by any standards a key figure in the development of the literary fantastic. We already have some idea of the extent of his influence in France and Russia.[7] A composer by calling, a gifted caricaturist, and a lawyer by profession, Hoffmann only took to serious writing in the last ten years or so of his life, in which time, struggling with illness and indulging in wine, he was extraordinarily productive. Many of his stories, novellas and fairy-tales (*Märchen*) form parts of greater cycle or frame-tale structures (such as *The Serapion Brothers*); his two novels apart, something of the effect of Hoffmann's work as a whole may have been therefore lost by the presentation in English of random exemplars from his stories as 'best tales'. Nevertheless, sufficient is now available to give a fair idea of the overall versatility and the dazzling power of his work.

Hoffmann developed amid the atmosphere of German romanticism and contemporaneous to, but quite apart from, the famous grouping of Jena Romantics. Later he knew, and admired the work of, Tieck, de la Motte Fouqué (with whom he collaborated on the opera *Undine*) and Chamisso. His earlier inspiration, though, seemed to come from the philosophy of Schelling, the natural science of G. H. Schubert and such foreign literary models as Cazotte and the Italian dramatist Carlo Gozzi; also important to Hoffmann were the engravings of Jacques Callot and, inevitably, the impact of Goethe (in particular that of *Faust*) and of Jean Paul. Subsequently he wrote enthusiastically of the newly translated novels of Walter Scott (in particular of *Guy Mannering*) and of Tieck's translation of *Don Quixote*. In a letter of 1814, still almost on the threshold of his literary career, he wrote to his publisher, on the completed manuscript of *The Golden Pot*:

> I am sending you without delay the enclosed, finished fairy tale with the sincere wish that it will please you with its sustained irony! To be sure, the idea of permitting the fabulous to enter boldly into ordinary life is daring and, as far as I know, has not yet been used to this extent by any German author; however, I believe a more profound interpretation lends it the needed weight. (Hoffmann, 1977, p. 221)

The entry of the fabulous (and/or the fantastic) into everyday life in narratives imbued with sustained irony was indeed Hoffmann's stock in trade.

His range extended from the near realistic to the out-and-out fairy-tale and could embrace all shades in between. He wrote musical 'ghost' tales (*Don Giovanni* and *Ritter Gluck*), a dark Gothic psychological fantasy novel (*The Devil's Elixirs*) and Gothic castle fantastic (*The Entail*), dual-level fantasies of interlocking worlds of reality and faerie or myth (*The Golden Pot* and other *Märchen*), the carnivalistic *Princess Brambilla* (designated by Baudelaire 'a catechism of high aesthetics') and the *commedia dell' arte Signor Formica*. To this may be added the extraordinary unfinished novel *Kater Murr* (combining relatively realistic memoirs of a tom-cat with fantasy adventures of the musician Kreisler) and the first modern detective story of European literature (*Mademoiselle de Scudéry*, included therefore in Cassiday, 1983) written twenty years before Poe's Auguste Dupin entered the field. Romantic irony and ambiguity in narrative form, among other devices, invariably ensure that no text by Hoffmann is ever straightforward. This propensity, together with his fantastic excesses, was long used as a stick with which to beat Hoffmann and would-be followers (from Scott in the 1820s to Zhdanov in the 1930s); however, latterly such qualities have been seen in a more favourable light.

Whole studies could be, and have been, written on Hoffmann's fantastic works and their impact upon other literatures. For present purposes, we shall confine our comments briefly to two stories, the first relatively little discussed and the second the subject of wide critical attention: *Don Giovanni* and *The Sandman*.

Don Giovanni (1812) is an early story, written at a time when Hoffmann was making the transition from musician and musical reviewer to creative writer and indeed this story is partly concerned with conveying an interpretation of Mozart's opera. As early as 1795, Hoffmann had written to his friend Hippel: 'I now own *Don Giovanni* and it provides me with many a blissful hour. I am beginning more and more to fathom Mozart's truly great genius in his compositions' (Hoffmann, 1977, p. 35). However, it has been a traditional mistake to treat the tale of 1812 as a work of opera criticism presented in a pseudo-fictional form (see Wellbery, 1980). It is rather the reverse. The interpretation is extensively romantic, in keeping with the subtitle ('A strange episode in the life of a music fanatic') and, going beyond anything warranted by opera or libretto, could not have been presented as serious musical criticism. Instead, the fourteen-page story sets up a characteristically ambivalent Hoffmannian relationship between implied author, narrator and character, not to forget reader. The 'music fanatic' [or 'enthusiast'] undergoes a kind of mystical experience in what amounts to a private viewing of an inspired performance of *Don Giovanni*. His description of the performance is strongly tinged with the opera's diabolical trappings. He appears to be visited in his box during the interval by the heroine Donna Anna. This visit transforms his appreciation of the opera into total rapture and he now sees in Donna Anna's role a religious purity which transcends her seduction by the Don, and disposes her towards love and a passion-stricken mission of intercession on her seducer's behalf. The narrator returns to his box at two in the morning for another spiritual experience involving the voice of Donna Anna wafting him (or rather herself) to, not precisely a Christian paradise, but the 'world of Atlantis' and 'the ethereal realms above' ('Don Giovanni' in Taylor, 1985, p. 116). A 'Postscript' epilogue in dialogue form informs us that 'Donna Anna' had been in a swoon during the interval, had barely kept her nerves in the second act and had then died at two o'clock in the night.

The fantastic here resides in the mystical–musical ambiance created, but more particularly in the Donna Anna visitation. Was it the Italian *prima donna* (in or out of body), or the essential Mozart–Da Ponte character (from another world of pure art), or merely an inebriated delusion (there is much talk of punch and champagne)? The narrator affirms:

> It was indeed Donna Anna. It did not occur to me to wonder how it was possible for her to be on the stage and in my box at one and the same time. As a blissful dream can bring the strangest events together, a sense of faith enabling one to grasp the meaning of supernatural phenomena and link them

naturally to the events of so-called everyday life, so the miraculous presence of this woman induced in me a dream-like state in which I could see the mysterious forces that bound her to me so tightly that even on the stage she could not have escaped from me. (p. 108)

Furthermore, the narrator addresses his narrative to 'Theodor' (pp. 108, 111, 114); Theodor is the name by which Hoffmann was known to intimates (Tatar, 1980, p. 590), rather than 'the imaginary friend to whom Hoffmann is telling his story' (translator's note, p. 108). Therefore the musical fanatic is an associate, or an alter ego, rather than 'Hoffmann' himself; 'Theodor' has apparently acted as scribe, or editor, rather than 'author', and is likely to be responsible for the epilogue. It may also be noted that there exists a camaraderie between fanatic and Theodor, whereby the former wishes to draw the latter's particular attention to 'Donna Anna's seduction' (p. 114); the narrator's interest in Donna Anna is no more purely ethereal than is his liking for wine; not for nothing does he identify with Don Giovanni as 'a *bon vivant* inordinately attracted to wine and women' (p. 112).

The Sandman (1815–16) is a more mature and psychologically complex Hoffmann story which, as we have already seen, attracted the detractions of Scott and, a century later, the deep interest of Freud in what Harold Bloom calls 'unquestionably his strongest reading of any literary text' (H. Bloom, 1982, p. 205). We refer to Freud's essay 'The "Uncanny"' at various points of this study and cannot rehearse its content again here. A recent spate of articles on *The Sandman* has demonstrated the possibility of arriving at stimulating readings both by post-Freudian means (Jones, 1986) and virtually without Freud at all (Tatar, 1980).[8]

The Sandman, as Maria Tatar points out, 'appears to be the story of a young man whose plans for marriage are thwarted by a demonic agent' (Tatar, p. 597); however, the ambiguities and contradictions are such that it is difficult to be sure of anything and the lack of critical consensus over the work in itself suggests (to Tatar, pp. 586–7) that 'the story must be located in the genre of the fantastic'. The fantastic in *The Sandman* arises in three connections: the question of whether Coppelius, Coppola and 'the sandman' are identical; that of whether Olympia is 'real', or in fact a doll; and that of whether Nathaniel is beset by mysterious powers, or is merely demented. It seems impossible to provide definitive answers to any of these points. Again, the difficulties largely stem from the narrative presentation; an epistolary beginning (between Nathaniel and his foster-sister/fiancée Clara, with the complication that Nathaniel's letter is supposedly really intended for her brother Lothario) gives way to a stylised first-person narrative from a by no means disinterested narrator, who again admits (Hoffmann, 1982, p. 100) to a certain partiality as an author (and, as in *Don Giovanni*, the narrator may have an interest too in the female character). There is a further complication if we accept Tatar's evidence (pp. 589–90) for a virtual identity here between narrator and character. Shifts in point of view and a series of repetitions, involving principally eyes and optics, looks of death, and play on the theme of dolls and automata, add to the confusion (or intrigue).

Ambivalence extends to the very texture of *The Sandman*: Malcolm Jones (1986, p. 91) has pointed out that 'the difficulty of distinguishing between "objective" narrative and free indirect speech leaves the question [arising from the struggle over Olympia] shrouded in ambiguity'. Hoffmann also introduces the device of *mise en abyme* (a fragment within the work encapsulating the action or the meaning of the whole) in the form of Nathaniel's poem (spelling out for himself delusion, deception and death through Coppelius and Clara), which occupies a central position in the story (Hoffmann, 1982, p. 105). This device is particularly common in postmodernist fiction, but is, as usual, much older than that; the term was plucked from heraldry by André Gide (McHale, 1987, p. 124). Arguably, a second such, or alternative, key statement on the work occurs in the comment, ostensibly on Olympia; made by 'the professor of poetry and rhetoric': 'The whole thing is an allegory, an extended metaphor!' (p. 121). Certainly, as Tatar affirms (1980, p. 605), Nathaniel, at least, 'insists on taking the fantastic literally'.

How Hoffmann himself takes the fantastic is less clear, except to stress its abundance in his work. He can write (in connection with *The Devil's Elixirs*, see Hoffmann, 1977, p. 225) of 'heavenly and demoniacal powers, those mysterious connections of the human spirit with all the higher principles that are hidden in nature and flash forth only now and then — which flashes we then call "coincidence"'. Hesitation on the level of plot and reader response implies the fantastic; hesitation on the level of the narrator's reflections, as Tatar points out (Tatar, 1980, p. 607) implies romantic irony. Romantic irony, while in the avant-garde of romantic poetics, has to us still a distinctly modern flavour, as does Hoffmann's emphatic play on modes of perception. Furthermore, Hoffmann is also, in *The Sandman* and elsewhere, very much a key exponent of the 'carnivalization of literature', in the Bakhtinian sense (see Jones, p. 99). Finally, it is worth noting that, wracked with his final illness, Hoffmann had to defend his position as an author of fictional fantasy, against political attack on his late story *Master Flea*, in a manner not dissimilar to well-publicised later figures:

> The humorous writer must be allowed to move freely and joyously in his world of fantasy. Should he cramp himself up in Procrustes' bed with a thousand considerations, with suspicious doubts as to how his thoughts might be misinterpreted? . . . I freely follow the flight of my fantasy as it is fired by the postulates of the tale, by the situations and the characters occurring in it, without thinking of other things that lie beyond the imaginary sphere in which the story moves. . . . It is not a matter of a satirical work dealing with world affairs and events of our time, but of the product of a humorous author's imagination which only reflects the images of real life, as if caught in a mirror, in the abstractions of humour. (Hoffmann, 1977, pp. 325, 327)

Such 'abstractions of humour' have never, of course, been universally appreciated.

POE

Hoffmann's only possible rival as the archetypal figure in the establishing of the tradition which here concerns us is Edgar Allan Poe. Poe had an immense influence on the European scene as a whole, and was particularly appreciated in France and in Russia (see Baudelaire, in Walker, 1986; and Grossman, 1973, respectively), all the more so by adherents of the Symbolist movements in those countries. Poe began to be known in both countries within his own less than extensive lifetime: from 1846 in France (Walker, p. 34), with the unattributed publication of *The Murders in the Rue Morgue*; and from 1847 in Russia, with a translation of *The Gold-Bug* (Grossman, p. 191). His impact on the horror story, the detective novel and the rise of science fiction, from the late nineteenth century into the twentieth, scarcely needs emphasis.

Poe invented the first great literary detective, Chevalier C.

Auguste Dupin. He pioneered science fiction (see Harold Beaver's selection in Poe, 1976). He developed the concept of the 'double', parallel with Dostoevsky and in anticipation of Stevenson and others, while tales such as *The Pit and the Pendulum* and *The Masque of the Red Death* are to be numbered among the best-known horror stories in world literature. Poe also excelled in the satirical absurd (as in *The Man that Was Used Up*). As we have noted earlier, *The Black Cat* has been singled out as a prime example of the pure fantastic (Brooke-Rose, 1983, pp. 117–22). There are also examples of what might be termed the 'artistic fantastic' (*The Oval Portrait*, in which the life of the artists's beautiful wife and model is apparently drained into the picture he is painting).[9] However, ambivalence on all levels is a constant feature of Poe's fiction.

Apart from one fictional work of novel length (*The Narrative of Arthur Gordon Pym of Nantucket*), the hallmark of the bulk of Poe's fiction is concision: one has only to contrast, for example, *The Fall of the House of Usher* with an Ann Radcliffe novel. David Punter has aptly characterised the structure of the Poe tale as 'a kind of story which does not move by simple narrative but by spiralling intensification' (Punter, 1980, p. 203); while, in terms of style, very often 'Poe moves directly into an incantatory mode which dissolves historical location and immediately encourages the reader to see [his tales] as parables of a continuous present rather than simply as accounts of past events' (Punter, 1988, p. 2). The language can include extravagant imagery and diverse elements of wordplay. Gothic buildings often remain, but time, and not infrequently place in its wider sense, may be indeterminate. European or further-flung settings are not unusual. All this is to be expected, given the English and Germanic influences which operated on Poe.

Once again, elements of synthesis come to the fore. G. R. Thompson, in his classic study *Poe's Fiction* (1973), comments that 'it is as if Poe sought to blend two kinds of Gothic romance: the shocking, supernatural, Teutonic tale; and the insinuated, explained, English tale' (p. 77). Crucial, in Thompson's view, was Poe's appropriation of the concept of romantic irony; his idea of the imagination derived from the Germans via Coleridge, while:

> In A. W. Schlegel's *Lectures* alone, Poe found Romantic-Ironic principles of melancholy idealism and a yearning for sublime beauty even in discord and deformity; a fascination with death as the ultimate fact of existence; a belief in the illusiveness of truth, in human alienation from actuality, and in the 'one-sidedness' of all 'serious' statements. (p. 34)

For that matter, 'the affectation of literary and philosophical learning', a supposed flaw in Poe's serious writing, is in itself seen as part of the very technique of the sensation tale (p. 47). This device is frequently presented quite self-consciously by Poe, as in *Morella*, which possesses an epigraph from Plato in the original Greek, as well as a reference to 'those mystical writings which are usually considered the mere dross of the early German literature' (Poe, 1966, p. 222). The Schlegels apart, Thompson (p. 162) pinpoints Jean Paul as an important source for Poe, with his 'annihilating' and 'satanic' humour as well as the theme of the *Doppelgänger*; in addition (pp. 110–16), he make the obvious connection between Poe and Hoffmann, stressing in particular Poe's knowledge and utilisation of Scott's essay on Hoffmann.[10]

While there are Poe tales, narrated in parable or legend form, such as *The Masque of the Red Death*, in which the supernatural strikes and remains the only convincing explanation, more typically Poe, in Thompson's words (p. 119), 'brings the reader to the edge of the supernatural, as it were, then leaves him confronting, through an "unnerved" narrator, the luminous eyes of Ligeia, or the pale figure of Madeline Usher returned from the grave'. Poe's final position, not alone among practitioners of the fantastic, seems to have been one of scepticism. In his 'prose poem' *Eureka*, dedicated to Alexander Von Humboldt, he writes:

> while all men have admitted some principle as existing behind the Law of Gravity, no attempt has been yet made to point out what this principle in particular *is*: — if we except, perhaps, occasional fantastic efforts at referring it to Magnetism, or Mesmerism, or Swedenborgianism, or Transcendentalism, or some other equally delicious *ism* of the same species, and invariably patronized by one and the same species of people. (Poe, 1976, p. 240).[11]

Poe's most problematical tales are now held to be open to multiple readings, including of course a supernatural one, and may therefore (*pace* Todorov, 1973, p. 48) be considered perfectly viable as examples of the fantastic.

Many works by Poe contain then an amalgam of the (at least potential) supernatural, the psychological and the burlesque, with satirical absurd elements of hoax or arabesque (a word which Poe also acquired from the Germans). Poe, therefore, frequently and deliberately undermines himself. In *Ligeia*, in Thompson's words, 'the clues undercutting the ostensible supernaturalism could hardly be clearer': it can be read as an occultist tale of the power of the will to effect reincarnation, or as a work concerned with the delusive power of its narrator (see Thompson, pp. 77–87). Following Hoffmann's use of *mise en abyme* in *The Sandman*, Ligeia's verses can be seen as fulfilling a similar function (Hoffmann had merely summarised Nathaniel's poem; Poe goes one better in supplying that composed by the dying Ligeia). In *The Fall of the House of Usher* we are treated to a double dose of this device: the six stanzas by the morbidly demented Roderick Usher and the reading from the 'Mad Trist'. Similarly, this story is open to supernatural (or perhaps unnatural), psychological and, no doubt, psychoanalytical interpretations (see, for example, Clayton, 1982). Once again the main uncertainty resides in the nature and the reliability of the discourse of the first person narrator.

A *Tale of the Ragged Mountains* purports to portray a case of metempsychosis, but is also apparently one of murder (of Bedloe by Templeton) and at the same time a burlesque of elements of Charles Brockden Brown's *Edgar Huntly* (see Thompson, pp. 147–52). In Poe's *Doppelgänger* tale, *William Wilson*, the existence of the physical double is put in doubt when a mirror appears to display finally the narrator's own features. Here too Ziolkowski (1977, p. 182), for one, points to three interpretations:

> The supernatural: that the double actually exists and that the murdered man is in fact physically identical with the double whom Wilson had known in his boyhood. The psychological: that the double and the murdered man are simply a figment of Wilson's deranged imagination. The equivocal: that the various doubles have a physical existence as persons, as innocent victims upon whom the crazed Wilson projects the features of his own physiognomy.

However, in the case of the mesmerist tale *The Facts in the Case of M. Valdemar*, the 'facts' are presented as 'authentic' case history. Maria Tatar (1978, p. 198) comments: 'In the final analysis, however, Poe's stories of suspended animation — more fantastic and indeed more grisly than most mesmerist tales — require from his readers a state of suspended disbelief.' Nevertheless, contrary to the view that 'the description of Mr Valdemar's body at the end [as "a nearly liquid mass of loathsome — of detestable putridity". Poe, 1976, p. 203] arouses disgust rather than speculation about the possibility of such an occurrence' (Chanady, 1985, p. 142), many contemporary readers took the story as scientific description. One reader impressed by the fantastic ambivalence (in this sense) of M. *Valdemar* was Elizabeth Barratt Browning, who, replying to the dedication accorded her in Poe's *The Raven and Other Poems* (1845), wrote:

> there is a tale of yours which I do not find in this volume, but which is going the rounds of the newspapers, about Mesmerism ('the Valdemar Case'), throwing us all into — dreadful doubts as to whether it can be true, as the children say of ghost stories. The certain thing in the tale in question is the power of the writer, and the faculty he has of making horrible probabilities seem near and familiar. (quoted from Poe, 1976, p. 394)

In *Eureka*, Poe provided his own brief critical and metaphysical formula:

> In the construction of *plot*, for example, in fictitious literature, we should aim at so arranging the incidents that we shall not be able to determine, of any one of them, whether it depends from any other or upholds it. In this sense, of course, perfection of plot is really, or practically, unattainable — but only because it is a finite intelligence that constructs. The plots of God are perfect. The Universe is a plot of God. (p. 292)

LE FANU

The reputation of Joseph Sheridan Le Fanu, while still no doubt somewhat below that of most of the other writers considered in this chapter, is once again in the ascendancy after a somewhat checkered history. Edith Birkhead (1921) gives only two passing mentions to Le Fanu; however he was taken up by M. R. James and Montague Summers between the wars and is now being accorded serious critical attention.[12] Like Maturin, Le Fanu was of Irish Huguenot stock but, unlike his predecessor in Anglo-Irish Gothicism, he did not follow his father into the Protestant ministry. Instead he studied law, but then concentrated on writing and later on his proprietorship of the *Dublin University Magazine*, an organ which did much during Le Fanu's lifetime to propagate German romanticism

(McCormack, 1980, pp. 253–4). Le Fanu became a prolific, if uneven, writer of novels and stories, both singly and in collections or cycles, and the bulk of his production falls into the English Gothic and Victorian mystery traditions. So what exactly are his credentials for consideration as a prominent contributor to the slightly more specialised tradition of the literary fantastic?

One popularly advanced claim is that Le Fanu's ghosts (or demons), in particular from the story *Green Tea* (first published 1869), seem simultaneously 'to emerge from within as well as invade from without' (see Thompson, 1982, p. 93). 'Guilt is the ghost in Le Fanu', wrote V. S. Pritchett (introduction to Le Fanu, 1947, p. 10). Also widely admired is *Carmilla*, Le Fanu's reinvigoration of the vampire story, this time with strong lesbian undertones. However, it may be possible to particularise Le Fanu's innovations a little more systematically by a brief consideration of two of his stories in isolation, then of the collection *In a Glass Darkly* (1872), followed by the most acclaimed of his novels, *Uncle Silas* (1864).

Schalken the Painter (first published 1839), although an early story, is one of the most concise and effective narratives in all Le Fanu's work. Its first-person narration, however, which purports to descend from family lore, derives, ostensibly at least, not from authorial pre-history but from an editor–narrator, ironically enough a Catholic priest (a certain Father Purcell: the story appeared in a series later collected under the title *The Purcell Papers*). *Schalken* is the first of a small cluster of Le Fanu stories with a continental setting which also share a permutation of themes (sex, the demonic, art, violence: see McCormack's introduction to Le Fanu, 1985). In this tale, Rose, ward and niece of the Flemish painter Gerard Douw and secretly loved by his pupil Godfrey Schalken, is given in marriage, for a fortune, to an apparently demonic burger of Rotterdam; following her distressed return and seemingly supernatural abduction, Schalken concentrates on his art. Years later, in the crypt of a Rotterdam church, he has a vision of Rose and her satanic bridegroom; this is strikingly recorded in one of his paintings.

Schalken the Painter is a fantastic tale in that, while the balance of the narrative would seem to tilt towards a supernatural explanation, the story does contain within it a possible rational solution: enforced marriage to a repulsive bridegroom induces distraction and flight, hysteria and suicide, the whole episode subsequently generating in Schalken guilt-induced erotic hallucination and artistic inspiration. The last words of the narrative refer to 'Rose Velderkaust, whose mysterious fate must always remain matter of speculation' (Le Fanu,

1988, p. 39). However, *Schalken* is also a notable example of what we have chosen to call the 'artistic fantastic'. It pre-dates Poe's *The Oval Portrait* (earliest version 1842) but, as W. J. McCormack has noted only briefly (Le Fanu, 1985, p. 16), it appears to have strong affinities with that most art-full of artistic stories, Balzac's *Le Chef-d'oeuvre inconnu* (1831), which in its turn owed a certain debt to Hoffmann.[13]

In fact, although the emphasis is very different (artistic theory in Balzac, demonic possession in Le Fanu), in basic construction the two stories display strong similarities. Both stories feature a pair of actual seventeenth-century painters; the young artists, Poussin and Schalken, are in both cases subservient to their established elders, Porbus and Douw. In place of Balzac's eccentric (and possibly demonic) old artist who may be a genius, Le Fanu introduces a demonic lover, who is an equal threat to the status quo, a possessor of (monetary rather than artistic) riches, but ultimately also a source for artistic inspiration. Porbus and Douw both act as middle-aged go-betweens, blurring their career and plot functions as painters and pimps. In each case the fourth character is a beautiful girl: Poussin's model and mistress, Gillette; Schalken's clandestine beloved, Rose. Schalken's picture, painted subsequent to the main action, is an artistic (and chronologically displaced) equivalent to the poetic *mise en abyme* we have noted in Hoffmann and Poe. In Balzac, a number of paintings take on varied significance (see Rudolf's essay in Balzac, 1988). Also in common between the two stories we can point to the respective successions of visitation scenes, the concentration of action in particular rooms (studios, period houses or, in Le Fanu, Gothic crypt) with verbal depictions of a strikingly pictorial quality, and the strong accent in each work on commerce. Both stories turn, their differing emphases notwithstanding (though, once again, albeit diverging forms of ambiguity are a feature of both), on a succession of tensions and choices involving such oppositions as art and love, art/love and commerce/wealth, life and death (the living and the dead in Le Fanu at least), and sexuality and death. What Le Fanu appears to have achieved in *Schalken the Painter* is a blending of the artistic *conte philosophique* with the romantic theme of the demon lover (here transposed into a particularly horrific and relatively geriatric form of revenant).

Borrhomeo the Astrologer was published anonymously in 1862, but has recently been attributed to Le Fanu (McCormack, 1980, pp. 278–9) and reprinted (Le Fanu, 1985). Subtitled, ironically or otherwise, 'A Monkish Tale', it appears to transpose, along with the spelling of his name, the positive and Christian (though, of course,

Catholic) figure of Archbishop Federico Borromeo (cousin of the saint, Carlo Borromeo), best known to us through Manzoni's *The Betrothed*, into a sacreligious natural philosopher in search of the elixir of life (and, curiously, he is shown as alchemist, rather than astrologer). 'Borrhomeo' enters into a satanic bargain to gain the secrets of alchemy's timeless quest, the price for which is to spread plague by 'anointing' the doors of the city of Milan (the setting, like that in Manzoni's novel, being the Milanese bubonic plague of 1630); he is thus relegated in Le Fanu's fiction from saintly status to the lowest of the low: one of Manzoni's mythical 'anointers' (*untori*). Held by the Inquisition, Le Fanu's protagonist fears not torture and execution, as he has imbibed the elixir; however, the rub is that his thousand years of life are to mean no more than conscious catalepsy, an immobile awareness of execution, impaling and premature burial prolonged with a vengeance. This is identical to symptoms ascribed to a drug in *The Room in the Dragon Volant* and no prizes are awarded for detecting here the hand of Poe.

This denouement has been foreshadowed, as the satanic agent emphasises at the end (Le Fanu, 1985, pp. 33–4), by the 'nightmare, as we jocularly called it' in the inn, when Borrhomeo is held rigid in a spell (another version of *mise en abyme*: satanic agents are particularly alive to 'the pleasure of the text'!). The seemingly unequivocal reliance on the supernatural in this story may, nevertheless, be seen to be tempered by two factors. The first is the use of the standard romantic device of the manuscript (in the keeping of monks: hence one meaning of the subtitle), used also, of course, in Manzoni's original. The second mitigating factor is the all too obvious, the all but self-conscious intertextual relationship in itself which seems to exist between Le Fanu's tale and the fiction (and indeed fact, or at least history, on which it was based) of Manzoni. This may be seen (as suggested by McCormack, pp. 15–16) as comparable, if in reverse (the besmirching of the sanctified, rather than the redemption of the sinner), to that existing between Maturin's *Melmoth the Wanderer* and that other of Balzac's philosophical tales, *Melmoth réconcilié*.

Le Fanu's collection *In a Glass Darkly* was published in 1872; of the five stories which comprise it, *Green Tea* had appeared in 1869, *Mr Justice Harbottle* and *The Room in the Dragon Volant* came out first in magazines in 1872, *Carmilla* was written in 1871–2, while the remaining tale, *The Familiar*, had first appeared (under the title of *The Watcher*) as early as 1851. As a collection (*In a Glass Darkly* was in fact published in three volumes: Volume I consisted of *Green Tea*, *The Familiar* and *Mr Justice Harbottle*; Volume II comprised *The*

Room at the Dragon Volant; Volume III was *Carmilla*), the series
has a certain unity. McCormack (1980, pp. 188–91) has pointed to
variations on the themes of suicide and belief. Narrative unity, of at
least a nominal sort, is another strong feature. This is established by
the prologue to *Green Tea* (Le Fanu, 1947, pp. 15–16), which may
more properly be regarded as a prologue to *In a Glass Darkly* as a
whole. Separate or disparate publication of these stories (see, for
example Le Fanu, 1970 and Le Fanu, 1988) obviously does not aid
consideration of the collection as an entity (the last integral
publication before 1990 was Le Fanu, 1947).

The principal unifying factor of *In a Glass Darkly* must lie in the
narrative presentation of the stories, in accordance with which they
derive from the papers of one Dr Martin Hesselius. There are two
points to be made in this connection: the first has to do with the
persona of Hesselius and the second with the manner in which Le
Fanu chooses to exploit this narrative ploy. Dr Hesselius, a
(German) 'medical philosopher' who pursues research into spiritualism and is the author of 'Essays on Metaphysical Medicine' (Le
Fanu, 1947, pp. 18–19), holds ideas which clearly derive from
German romantic philosophy, with an input from Swedenborg. He
may be seen, potentially at least, as something of an amalgam of the
questing Dr Frankenstein and the analytical Auguste Dupin and as
such would appear to be one of the first in a line of psychic doctors,
or occult detectives, stretching forward to embrace such luminaries
as Bram Stoker's Professor Van Helsing, William Hope Hodgson's
Carnacki ('the Ghost-Finder') and many others (on which topic, see
J. Briggs, 1977, pp. 57–64).

However, Le Fanu may not have fully realised the possibilities of
the character-type which he created. Hesselius does not dominate
the collection in the way we might expect; in fact he recedes steadily
in prominence from *Green Tea* onwards. In the first place, there is a
nameless overall narrator, Hesselius's disciple and 'medical secretary', who is engaged in editing multiple volumes of the Hesselius
papers: 'scientific' tracts plus case histories. The latter, or rather the
five main plums thereof, is what our editor in fact gives us as *In a
Glass Darkly*. These stories each contain narratives and sub-
narratives, in a manner reminiscent of Maturin.

Only *Green Tea* has its main narrative stemming from Hesselius
himself. In *The Familiar*, the story is narrated by a Dublin clergyman
and Hesselius's only role is to have scribbled a few preliminary
comments. In the case of *Mr Justice Harbottle*, Hesselius has merely
inscribed the words 'Harman's Report' and a reference to one of the
essays (Le Fanu, 1947, p. 83); the account of the story we are given,

emanating from one Anthony Harman, is even said to be inferior to another missing version. *The Room at the Dragon Volant*, presented 'simply as a story' (p. 114), is said to be cited in an essay on drugs by Hesselius, and is narrated by the protagonist, a rich young Englishman abroad named Richard Beckett. *Carmilla* is presented without the 'rather elaborate note' penned by Hesselius, except for one incomplete sentence referring to 'the profoundest arcana of our dual existence' (p. 222), along with a reference to a treatise, evidently on vampirism. The narrator is the would-be victim, a now deceased resident of Austria, though of English descent, named Laura. Even when an exorcist and vampire executioner is called for, the task is not allotted to Hesselius, but falls to one Baron Vordenburg, who is expressly brought in for the purpose.

It may be that the gradual withdrawal of Hesselius aids the process whereby Le Fanu achieves the effect which Michael Cox, who traces it back as far as *Schalken*, terms 'a synchronicity of the external themes of his fiction and personal disorientation' (introduction to Le Fanu, 1988, p. 10). Margaret Carter (1987, p. 85) draws attention to the unnamed editor's stance in awe of Hesselius, the considerable chronological and linguistic distancing, 'the nested system of narrators', and a variety of ambiguities exposed by her close reading of three of the stories; she also makes the point that there is an 'implied reader *within* the fiction, the reader in Le Fanu's secondary world who is seeking knowledge of a real-life Hesselius'. The effect of all this over the collection as a whole is to increase the doubts (or hesitations) of the real reader, as the narratives oscillate between the pure fantastic, which arguably predominates in the earlier stories, suspense and a whiff of the supernatural explained in *Dragon Volant* (a rollicking imbroglio set in immediately post-Napoleonic France), and the internally undermined supernatural *outré* which governs *Carmilla*, while ranging across what collectively amounts to a highly erratic chronotope.

It remains now to say something of *Uncle Silas*. This novel represents a large-scale expansion, and a transposition from Ireland to Derbyshire, of an early short story (first published as *Passage in the Secret History of an Irish Countess*, 1838; and secondly as *The Murdered Cousin* of 1851, reprinted in Le Fanu, 1988). Contrary to some opinions, the final work gained much from its enlargement, both in terms of the working out of the details of its surface plot and of the additional vistas upon which it now opened. Its basic story line has been bluntly simplified by Northrop Frye:

Sheridan Le Fanu's *Uncle Silas* has a heroine whose father, a somewhat dithery Swedenborgian, is obsessed by the notion that his brother Silas, who is a thoroughly bad lot, has been gravely misunderstood, and sends his daughter to Silas's house, where she very nearly gets murdered. (Frye, 1976A, p. 81)

Uncle Silas, narrated by its heroine, Maud Ruthyn, is ostensibly then a Victorian mystery novel of brooding atmosphere and protracted suspense, containing such Gothic stereotypes as the rambling mansion, the helpless maiden, a wicked uncle and a treacherous (in this case French) governess.

Maud Ruthyn, as character and narrator, has been compared to Wilkie Collins's Marian (one of the narrators of *The Woman in White*) and Henry James's governess (*The Turn of the Screw*); also, as frequently happens in first-person narratives, we are given two Mauds: 'Maud at the time of the action, and a sadder, wiser Maud, who narrates the story and who is oddly *present* throughout' (Punter, 1980, pp. 234–5). However, the textual and historical criticism of W. J. McCormack has revealed further, perhaps unexpected, horizons to Le Fanu's novel. Firstly he observes (1980, p. 150): 'In Le Fanu's fiction generally, it is possible to distinguish between the explicit treatment of the supernatural in short stories and tales, and the neglect or disguise of that dimension in the longer novels.' Moreover, and in particular, '*Uncle Silas* is best approached as a work of deception' (see Le Fanu, 1981, p. XIX).

By a careful exposition of the elaborate and often symmetrical use of landscape and journey; enclosure, windows, portraiture, portraits (and other framing devices); allusion and metaphor (in particular the deathly imagery surrounding Silas Ruthyn), McCormack arrives at a reading which requires 'abandoning belief in the separate existence of the Ruthyn brothers' (1980, p. 167). Metaphor in *Uncle Silas*, according to this view, 'tends towards symbol rather than simile' (p. 163), resulting in a symbolic pattern denoting duality both of personality (Austin and Silas Ruthyn as a 'continuum': Silas being the other-world Austin) and of setting (matter and spirit: Knowl and Bartram-Haugh being somehow simultaneous worlds). The key to this interpretation, clearly signed in the text, lies in Swedenborgian doctrine, which allows for an unknowing intermixing of the mortal and the spectral in an arena designed to manifest buried guilt and enshrouded aspirations. Of significance, in reinforcing Punter's comment above, is the develop-ment in Maud's attitude to Sweden-borgianism: doubtful and naïve at the start ('In my hazy notions of those sectaries where was mingled a suspicion of necromancy, and a

weird freemasonry, that inspired something of awe and antipathy.'
Le Fanu, 1981, p. 3), by the conclusion of the novel she has achieved
the sophistication of the assenter, if not the adept:

> This world is a parable — the habitation of symbols — the
> phantoms of spiritual things immortal shown in material
> shape. May the blessed second-sight be mine — to recognise
> under these beautiful forms of earth the ANGELS who wear
> them; for I am sure we may walk with them if we will, and hear
> them speak. (*ibid.*, p. 424)

Once again, the psyche of the narrator assumes a vital importance in
revealing, or allowing, the hidden fantastic. A romantic (or, in the case
of Swedenborg, pre-romantic) transcendental system is again utilised as
literary symbolism, rather than religious ideology. Furthermore, subsequent research by the same critic advances psychological and even
political explications of an allegorical nature.[14] The textual support
adduced, too complex and detailed to review here, already demon-strates
the presence in *Uncle Silas* of a fantastic dualism behind the surface plot of
the almost conventional mid-Victorian novel of sensation, thus prefigur-
ing the symbolist novel. If McCormack's historical evidence is also to
be credited, Le Fanu's ultimate perform-ance (to repeat Brockden
Brown's term) may now be seen as a forerunner of the twentieth-century
multi-level (or 'portmanteau') novel.

STEVENSON

Just as Le Fanu purported to be, Stevenson undoubtedly was a
defender of 'romance'. As Parrinder has pointed out (1987,
pp. 109–10), '[the] attempt to return to simple and timeless verities
of narrative involved . . . a preference for childlike over adult
reading experiences.' Much Victorian fantasy veered towards moral
and religious allegory and what has now become the 'sword and
sorcery' school; Stevenson, in *Treasure Island*, *Kidnapped* and other
famous works, turned more towards a school of 'blood and
thunder'. However, in perhaps his most striking creation, the
composite figure of Jekyll and Hyde, he achieved a mythic

formulation equalled only by Frankenstein and Dracula. Further-more, as everyone knows, 'Jekyll and Hyde' as a phrase has entered the language.

If Le Fanu's Austin and Silas Ruthyn may be construed as, in some sense at least, a double or schizoid personality, operating in dual or parallel worlds, then Jekyll and Hyde, who coexist in one world, may have descended as much from *Uncle Silas*, we may now suggest, as from the father–son paradigm of *Frankenstein* (Punter, 1980; Baldick, 1987), Poe's *William Wilson*, or the similarly drug-induced split in Hoffmann's *The Devil's Elixirs*. In addition, Le Fanu's novel *Guy Deverell* (1865) contains a protagonist named Jekyl Marlowe. This is possibly a more likely source for the name of Stevenson's hero than such contortions with *franglais* as '*Je* kill'; however, Nabokov (1980, p. 182) claims that the names of both Jekyll and Hyde are of Danish origin, meaning 'icicle' and 'haven' respectively.

Just as the shapes of fantastic prose evolve, so do those of the characters within it. Stevenson, in *The Strange Case of Dr Jekyll and Mr Hyde* (1886), reverts in narrative terms to something closer to the hoax scientific document of Poe: Oscar Wilde wrote that 'the transformation of Dr Jekyll reads dangerously like an experiment out of the *Lancet*' (Wilde, 1973, p. 61). Grafted on, as Jekyll's 'Full Statement', is an element of the confessional form, *à la* Victor Frankenstein. The narrative as a whole provides, for once, a full explanation (naturally, apart from the chemical formulae used by Jekyll). The divided self is this time explicitly derived from a single personality; rather as with *Uncle Silas* (but unlike most other *Doppelgänger* predecessors), the appearances of the component doubles are anything but identical. We therefore have the phenom-enon of the 'true' double appearing to others to be 'false'.

Once again, a key work in the fantastic tradition originated in a dream (see 'A Chapter on Dreams', appendix to Stevenson, 1987). The supernatural here has again been supplanted by the preter-natural, though vestiges of demonic vocabulary remain (Hyde is called 'Satan' by three characters, pp. 10, 19, 58, and 'that child of Hell' by Jekyll, p. 73). The setting has become the contemporary metropolis and the work has been discussed in psychological terms ranging from associations with human nature, bourgeois social repression and English imperialism. Also prominent in discussion are Darwinism, recidivism and pseudo-science: Jekyll comports himself much as a latter-day alchemist in his pursuit of 'transcend-ental medicine' (p. 58).

If the quality of the fantastic resides ultimately in the psyche of

the reader as much as within the text, then the mythic status of
Dr Jekyll and Mr Hyde has long since rendered Stevenson's novella a
victim of its own success. Not only are its plotlines too well known
to need repetition here, but few readers, one imagines, can embark
on a first reading of this text without at least some pre-knowledge
of its main events (more so even than in the case of *Frankenstein* or
Dracula). This state of affairs undermines the effects of the fantastic
to an extent, at least to the modern reader. These effects, as with
some of Poe's stories, are known to have appeared startling to
contemporaries, even though belief in the powers of 'the powders'
is likely always to have been in short supply. Nevertheless, Oscar
Wilde's dictum that 'Man can believe the impossible, but man can
never believe the improbable' (Wilde, 1973, p. 84) should not be
forgotten.

In this connection, Stevenson was a writer with his finger close to
the pulse of the realities of Victorian society, as comparisons
between *Dr Jekyll and Mr Hyde* and the Jack the Ripper phenomenon show (see C. Bloom 1988). Furthermore, through the persona
of Vivian, in his 'observation' *The Decay of Lying*, Wilde reports, or
conjects, the following:

> Shortly after Mr Stevenson published his curious psycho-
> logical story of transformation, a friend of mine, called
> Mr Hyde, was in the north of London, and being anxious to
> get to a railway station, took what he thought would be a
> short cut, lost his way, and found himself in a network of
> mean, evil-looking streets. Feeling rather nervous he began to
> walk extremely fast, when suddenly out of an archway ran a
> child right between his legs. It fell on the pavement, he
> tripped over it, and trampled upon it. Being, of course, very
> much frightened and a little hurt, it began to scream, and in a
> few seconds the whole street was full of rough people who
> came pouring out of the houses like ants. They surrounded
> him, and asked him his name. He was just about to give it
> when he suddenly remembered the opening incident in
> Mr Stevenson's story. He was so filled with horror at having
> realized in his own person that terrible and well-written
> scene, and at having done accidentally, though in fact, what
> the Mr Hyde of fiction had done with deliberate intent, that
> he ran away as hard as he could go. He was, however, very
> closely followed, and finally he took refuge in a surgery, the
> door of which happened to be open, where he explained to a
> young assistant, who happened to be there, exactly what had

occurred. The humanitarian crowd were induced to go away on his giving them a small sum of money, and as soon as the coast was clear he left. As he passed out, the name on the brass door-plate of the surgery caught his eye. It was 'Jekyll'. At least it should have been. (Wilde, 1973, p. 76)

This 'text' by Wilde provokes hesitation in the modern reader as to its veracity, just as Stevenson's story did in its own day.

'Jekyll had more than a father's interest; Hyde had more than a son's indifference' (Stevenson, 1987, p. 68) is a common quotation from *Dr Jekyll and Mr Hyde*. Stevenson's last work, *Weir of Hermiston*, subtitled 'An unfinished romance' on its posthumous publication in 1896, represents a final attempt to deal definitively with the father–son duality. It has even been said that the former work is 'a simplification or reduction' of the latter in that respect (Emma Letley's introduction to *ibid.*, p. xix). *Weir* is certainly a return by Stevenson to the romance form, with its historical and political setting of Scotland in the 1812–14 period, in the admired tradition of Scott (who is alluded to several times in the narrative). Just as Scott touched on fantastic elements in his work (as in *The Bride of Lammermoor*), so does Stevenson's *Weir* have around and within it at least a vestigial aura of the supernatural.

The predominantly omniscient third-person narration, in Stevenson's renowned style of the master story-teller, gathers pace and intensity as it approaches its break-off point and slips intermittently into the first person. The 'Introductory' page to *Weir*, presumably intended mainly as atmospheric, furnishes the novel with a mini plot summary, up to and slightly beyond its own premature ending (a veritable *mise en abyme* in prologue). The emphasis in the first paragraph is on historical and literary allusion; in the second it turns to the folkloric and the proto-fantastic:

> The Deil's Hags was the old name, but the place is now called Francie's Cairn. For a while it was told that Francie walked. Annie Hogg met him in the gloaming by the cairnside, and he spoke to her, with chattering teeth, so that his words were lost. He pursued Rob Todd (if any one could have believed Robbie) for the space of half a mile with pitiful entreaties. But the age is one of incredulity; these superstitious decorations speedily fell off; and the facts of the story itself, like the bones of a giant buried there and half dug up, survived, naked and imperfect, in the memory of the scattered neighbours. To this day, of winter nights, when the sleet is on the window and

the cattle are quiet in the byre, there will be told again, amid the silence of the young and the additions and corrections of the old, the tale of the Justice-Clerk and of his son, young Hermiston, that vanished from men's knowledge; of the two Kirsties and the Four Black Brothers of the Cauldstaneslap; and of Frank Innes, 'the young fool advocate,' that came into these moorland parts to find his destiny. (Stevenson, 1987, p. 83)

Annie Hogg and Rob Todd do not recur. However, the landmarks and the remaining characters assume central importance. 'The Deil's Hags' ('the devil's bog') already had its historical–folkloric associations; it had been the venue for the elder Kirstie's love trysts and assumes the same function in the affairs of the blighted trio of *Weir*'s main action: Aunt Kirstie herself connects events there with 'the omen, for I think there's a weird on the place' (p. 188). 'Francie's Cairn' (and therefore its putative ghost) is evidently called after the doomed Frank Innes (addressed as 'Francie' by Archie Weir, p. 177), who would apparently have been shot by Archie at that very spot. Frank Innes is himself called (in the title of Chapter VII) 'Mephistopheles'. The elder Kirstie loved to dwell on 'the supernatural or the horrific' (p. 131). Dandie Elliott's words to young Kirstie, 'You're shürely fey, lass!' (p. 155) are glossed by the narrator as 'suggested doom' (p. 156), 'ill-omened words' (p. 157) and 'ominous words' (p. 158), while the 'idea of Fate — a pagan Fate' enters (p. 158), to balance Innes's 'destiny' (from Stevenson, p. 83).

So much may reside merely in the style of narration adopted, aptly signalled by the 'Introductory' section: in other words the romance quality. It may also be argued that what is known at the time of the writer's death of 'the intended argument' (the novel breaks off mid-sentence) of its continuation (see appendix, pp. 195–7) suggests, in either of two variants, little or nothing of a fantastic nature. However, there remain, in addition to the residual atmosphere and traces of the fantastic detailed above, at least two other points of evidence. With reference to the composition of the novel, Stevenson wrote: 'The heroine is seduced by one man, and finally disappears with the other man who shot him.' In the text of *Weir* itself, to return to the 'Introductory' (p. 83), we find that 'young Hermiston' (i.e. Archie Weir) is said by the narrator to have 'vanished from men's knowledge'. We cannot now know the exact sense in which 'disappear' or 'vanish' was intended. While one would scarcely argue that this was Stevenson's intent, it cannot be denied that one way to intensify the mystification, or indeed the fantastic quality, of a work is to contrive to leave it unfinished (all the more so if it is in fragment or manuscript form). In this way, additional to its use of the vestigial fantastic, *Weir of Hermiston* takes its place, perhaps as unfinished fantastic (as well as 'unfinished romance': a subtitle which must be equally unrepresentative of Stevenson's purpose), alongside such works as Dickens's *The Mystery of Edwin Drood* and Hoffmann's *Kater Murr*.

It is for these reasons that *Weir of Hermiston* may be a more rewarding case for consideration than some of the more obvious Stevenson texts, such as *Markheim* or *Olalla*.

MAUPASSANT

We have already, in Part One, quoted Guy de Maupassant's theoretical comments, from his essay 'Le fantastique' (1883); these have been seen to approximate to the more modern approaches of H. P. Lovecraft (regarding fear) and Todorov (on hesitation). From the considerable body of novels and short stories written by Maupassant before his final insanity, a recent critic has computed a total of eighteen tales, spanning the years 1875 to 1890, as belonging to the genre of the fantastic (summarised by Rachmühl, 1983, pp. 21–9).

Le Fanu's novel *The House by the Churchyard* (1863) includes a chapter entitled 'An Authentic Narrative of the Ghost of a Hand', which contains what has been described as 'the most terrifying ghost story in the [English] language' (see introduction to Le Fanu, 1988, p. 16), a passage from which runs as follows:

He drew the curtain at the side of the bed, and saw Mrs Prosser lying, as for a few seconds he mortally feared, dead, her face being motionless, white, and covered with a cold dew; and on the pillow, close beside her head, and just within the curtains, was the same white, fattish hand, the wrist resting on the pillow, and the fingers extended towards her temple with a slow wavy motion.

Maupassant wrote two stories, with or without any knowledge of Le Fanu, on the theme of the severed hand: *La Main d'écorché* of 1875 and the better known *La Main* (1883).

In the latter work, the hand features in the framed narrative of an examining magistrate. It refers back to the fate of an Englishman living in Corsica, the land of vendetta, who keeps a dessicated hand, said to have belonged to his worst enemy, chained to the drawing-room wall. He dies of strangulation, with no sign of an assassin; the hand is broken from its chain and missing, having left, however, one of its fingers between the clenched teeth of the corpse. Investigations lead nowhere until the magistrate suffers a nightmare in which: 'I dreamed that I saw the hand, that horrible hand, running like a scorpion or a spider across my curtains and walls . . . three times I saw that hideous relic galloping round my room, using its fingers as legs' (Maupassant, 1971, p. 257). The next day it is found on the Englishman's grave, the index finger missing.

Just as the proprietor of the hand retained a cool exterior, yet kept loaded guns at the ready and periodically horse-whipped the chained hand, so does the narrating magistrate protest a cool disbelief in the supernatural, while simultaneously dwelling on details which (as pointed out by Chanady, 1985, p. 71) 'clearly belong to the code of the supernatural'. The contrasting attitude to this of the narrator and of his narratees, a group of ladies (plus the implied reader), is pointed up further by the reception given to the magistrate's rational theory ('that the rightful owner of the hand was not dead at all, and that he came looking for it with the hand he had left', Maupassant, p. 258); the ladies do not believe it and neither do most readers; and neither, one suspects, does the magistrate himself.[15]

Maupassant's best-known story in the fantastic idiom must be *Le Horla*, written in 1886, with a definitive revision following in 1887; again, this was based on an earlier story, *Lettre d'un fou*. Ziolkowski (1977, p. 190) draws a comparison here with Dostoevsky's *The Double*, with the action this time spreading over four months instead of days. However, the diary form of the second version, together with the title of the earlier story, suggest rather Gogol's *Diary* [literally 'Notes'] *of a Madman* as a point of departure, with Hoffmann, Poe and the French *fantastique* tradition as established influences. In this redaction, the diary writer feels himself gradually threatened and dominated by an invisible being which he christens 'the Horla' (French *hurler*, *hors-là*?); determining eventually to kill it, he traps it in his bedroom and burns down the house, servants and all; however, still believing it to be alive, he resolves on a final solution of suicide.

In the first version, the narration of the protagonist is framed in a case-history presentation by a learned medical expert: an authoritative authenticating figure, analogous to the magistrate of *La Main*.

The final version scraps this device and turns the confessional style narrative into a journal, thus combining immediacy with development, while sacrificing objectivity (Ziolkowski, 1977, p. 251, considers that use of the first person 'can even undermine the fantastic', while Chanady, 1985, p. 124, sees the uncertainty here as increased). As with *La Main*, there may be said to be an oscillation of rationalisations militating for and against natural and supernatural/preternatural explanations (see Neefs, 1980). What is described as 'the enigma of a writing début' (p. 236), namely the initiation of the journal (and therefore of discourse), coincides with the (subsequently supposed) arrival of the Horla, which may be from another planet (Maupassant also wrote a story called *L'Homme de Mars*), perhaps via Brazil. 'A splendid Brazilian three-master, all white and gleaming and spotlessly clean' (Maupassant, 1971, p. 314) sailed past on the opening day of the journal, saluted by its author, the narrator of *Le Horla*, who 'is and is not Maupassant' himself (Rachmühl, p. 39).

Two episodes interpolated into this second version to illustrate the apparent existence of 'outside' powers — the conversation with the monk at Mont Saint-Michel and the hypnotism scene in Paris — take on something like a *mise en abyme* significance (Rachmühl, p. 44). At the point where 'his invisible body had swallowed up my reflection' (Maupassant, 1971, p. 341) the story apes, in a new and terrifying way, the lost mirror reflection of Hoffmann's Erasmus Spikher (noted by Ziolkowski, p. 192). Interesting too is Maupassant's use of colour, rendering the whole, in Rachmühl's view (p. 53) 'a symphony in black, white and red — the colours of the fantastic'. *Le Horla* mingles Mesmerism with Darwinism (invoking a possible higher successor to man: Darwinism plus, rather than the Darwinism minus of Stevenson's recidivism). In its invading creature, which seems to come — like those of Le Fanu — simultaneously from within and without, this story furnishes something of a synthesis of most previous (and some new) models known to fantastic literature: the double, the vampire, the evil spirit (of demonic or other possession), and now the alien and the mutant. This seems to be accompanied by, or may be the product of, any of the psychological conditions hitherto known to this literary tradition: persecution mania, schizophrenia, hysteria, hypnosis, or even animal magnetism.

Maupassant's *Le Horla* thus looks both ways; its modernity has been frequently remarked upon, but at the same time it can be seen to epitomise and recapitulate many attributes of the nineteenth-century fantastic.

WILDE

Chapter XI of the 1891 version of *The Picture of Dorian Gray* has a long section, written in free indirect discourse, describing pre-dawn sensations when 'through the chambers of the brain sweep phantoms more terrible than reality itself' (Wilde, 1988, p. 101), relating the instinct perceived to lie behind 'all grotesques', Gothic art and 'the malady of reverie'.[16] It continues: 'Gradually white fingers creep through the curtains, and they appear to tremble. In black fantastic shapes, dumb shadows crawl into the corners of the room and crouch there' (p. 102). The stories of Le Fanu made a strong impression on Oscar Wilde in his Dublin youth (Philippe Jullian, in *ibid.*, p. 407); a little later (see pp. 126–7) the text alludes to a Gautier poem about the preserved hand of a murderer. We may say nothing here of Maupassant in this connection, but *Dorian Gray* too is pervaded (as *Le Horla* is said to be above) by 'the colours of the fantastic'. On the question of colour, Karl Miller (1987, p. 226) detects an irony in the colour symbolism in Wilde's protagonist and the 'dualistic name . . . for a book which belies it by being filled with colour'.

Particularly striking, though, is the use of whiteness, blackness (and grey shadow), plus variations of red, often in close proximity. Shortly after the passage featuring the white fingers (and black fantastic shapes), we find a description of the attractions held for Dorian by Roman Catholic ritual, including a priest 'with white hands moving aside the veil of the tabernacle', 'grave boys, in their lace and scarlet' and 'the black confessionals' (Wilde, 1988, p. 103). The face of the would-be avenger James Vane is seen by Dorian 'like a white handkerchief' (p. 153); the next day (but on the same page), Dorian, 'pale with terror', expects the 'shadows of his crime . . . to wake him with icy fingers', while: 'Out of the black cave of Time, terrible and swathed in scarlet, rose the image of his sin.' Such colour imagery abounds, usually related to Dorian himself (such as the red stain of blood on the portrait) or to Lord Henry (such as the crimson strawberries and white sugar, p. 160).

Allusion and suggestive imagery thus abound in *Dorian Gray* — even more so than in most works in the fantastic tradition. Although imbued with the particularly Wildean theme that 'each man kills the thing he loves', *Dorian Gray* was basically conceived, years before it was written, on 'the idea of a young man selling his soul in exchange for eternal youth — an idea that is', as Wilde said, 'old in the history of literature, but to which I have given new form'

(Ellmann, 1988, p. 293). Sources claimed or identified for Wilde's only novel are myriad: Melmoth the Wanderer (Maturin was a maternal great uncle and Wilde used the name Sebastian Melmoth in exile) has eternal youth (or, at least, eternal prime) and a portrait; Disraeli's first novel *Vivian Grey* is frequently mentioned, as is Balzac's *La Peau douce* (though Laubriet, 1971, pp. 165–8, puts in a clear plea too for *Le Chef-d'œuvre inconnu*). Gautier, Poe, Hawthorne and Stevenson obviously figure somewhere in *Dorian Gray's* lineage, as does the *Frankenstein* pattern of monster creation: Baldick (1987, p. 151) points to the frequent use in the novel of the word 'monstrous'. Literary portraits apart (haunted or otherwise), actual portraits, such as two of Baudelaire, or apocryphal ones (such as that allegedly painted of Wilde by one Basil Hall) are also brought into play. As exponents of dandyism and the epigram, Dorian and Lord Henry are distant cousins even of Pushkin's Eugene Onegin and Lermontov's Pechorin. Barbara Charlesworth (Wilde, 1988, p. 405) has written of Wilde: 'His writings, like the costume of a court jester, were a fantastic patchwork of other men's ideas in which he walked proudly as a king, thinking himself splendidly attired.' The main aesthetic ideas, which take up a sizeable portion of the text, come from Pater and Ruskin, with Huysmans's *À rebours* remaining the most probable single source for Dorian's 'golden book'.

Dorian Gray can, therefore, be readily ascribed to the growing tradition of the synthetic fantastic novel: an amalgam of Faustian bargain, *Doppelgänger* and the artistic fantastic, plus strong sub-concerns with science, Darwinism, aesthetics and psychology, a touch of mysticism (including astrology and metempsychosis), underscored by a somewhat aristocratic brand of social rebellion and a subtext of homo-eroticism. One is thus tempted to extend Baldick's observation of Dorian that 'just as his own portrait is made from himself, so he in turn appears . . . to have been assembled from parts of portraits, his life monstrously produced from multitudes of the dead' (with a Frankenstinian model implied, Baldick, p. 152) to the novel as a whole. *Dorian Gray* can itself be seen as a monstrous synthesis of foregoing works.

However, *Dorian Gray*, sometimes derided for its simplicity of plot and action as well as its derivative qualities, does bring additional subtleties to its decadent brand of Gothic revivalism. Wilde saw the three main characters of his novel as versions of himself (Ellmann, 1988, p. 301). As Charlesworth has pointed out (Wilde, 1988, p. 396), this has interesting implications for what can thereby be seen as 'internal dialogue' between the three (Lord Henry

Wotton, Basil Hallward and Dorian Gray), and all the more so for the murder of Basil. This now takes on a William Wilson-like aspect of the slaying of one's own conscience, confirmed, of course, by the final suicide by portrait-slashing: the only refraction of authorial personality to survive is, therefore, that represented by Lord Henry (standing for 'what the world thinks of me'). Given this element of self-identification, it is less surprising that (noted by Punter, 1980, p. 245; and Ziolkowski, 1977, p. 251) Wilde should utilise a narrative stance that is close to his protagonist(s). Indeed there is one occasion (only) in the book (Chapter XI, Wilde, 1988, p. 111) in which the narration slips into the first person, in a passage which is otherwise free indirect discourse: moreover the narrative 'I' there is almost equally attributable too to both Lord Henry and Dorian. As Miller has noted (1987, p. 225): 'Wilde's wit proclaimed, in equal measure, as equal partners in duality, a fiction of the second self and a theory of multiple personality.'

The surface quality of duality in *Dorian Gray*, therefore, takes on a more complex nature as Wilde plays with doubles and trebles. The three main characters stand as variant doubles one to another, as does the portrait to both Basil and Dorian (and, more obliquely, to Lord Henry as well). Dorian, Basil and the portrait stand as an interlocking trio, as do Lord Henry, Basil and Dorian. Dorian also has his opposite in Sibyl Vane, the actress who is drawn by love to prefer life to art (Ellmann, p. 298). As Miller (p. 227) has pointed out, 'art is successively said to mirror the artist, the sitter, and the spectator.' We might add that this in itself is reflected, in one of a number of *mise-en-abyme* situations occurring in this novel, in the setting of Chapter II, in which Basil, Dorian and Lord Henry are to be found respectively performing that very series of functions. This is followed by Dorian's avowed wish to exchange roles (soul and mortality) with the completed portrait: 'I would give my soul for that!' (Wilde, 1988, p. 26). Dorian thereupon suddenly and dramatically attains prophetic discourse: 'When I find that I am growing old, I shall kill myself' (*ibid.*); and, most strikingly of all, when Basil is about to take a knife to rip up the canvas, Dorian stops him with the cry: 'It would be murder!' (p. 27). This relates forward to his slaying of Basil and thence to the final scene (p. 169):

> He looked round, and saw the knife that had stabbed Basil Hallward. He had cleaned it many times, till there was no stain left upon it. It was bright, and glistened. As it had killed the painter, so it would kill the painter's work, and all that that meant. It would kill the past, and when that was dead he

would be free. It would kill this monstrous soul-life, and
without its hideous warnings, he would be at peace. He
seized the thing, and stabbed the picture with it.

Again the narrative stance is close to the hero: the 'painter's work'
becomes, or is, 'this monstrous soul-life', the knife is a mere 'thing',
the picture is 'stabbed' (a verb normally used of attacks on a
person), rather than the canvas 'ripped' (as Basil would have
performed the task, p. 27).

'Harry . . . every portrait that is painted with feeling is a portrait
of the artist, not of the sitter' (p. 10), says Basil in Chapter I, in a
sentence which prophetically links the trio of characters, but by a
false prophecy. Basil thinks the portrait reveals too much of his own
soul (i.e. of his passion for Dorian); this may be true in one sense
but, due to the fictional transformation to be brought about in the
next chapter, the portrait takes on Dorian's soul. It is a portrait of
the sitter. The sitter is able to kill the painter, but he cannot kill the
painter's work (the portrait) without killing himself. Similarly, the
spectator (Lord Henry) is also a false prophet: he underestimates his
own influence and that of his 'poisonous' book on Dorian and he
denies that Dorian could be a murderer. Who, therefore, creates the
evil Dorian? The 'good' Basil who paints him and appropriates his
soul, or the 'bad' Lord Henry, mentor of his mind (both of whom
get him 'wrong')? Or Dorian himself, the instigator of the 'devil's
bargain'?

Wilde's devil's bargain without a devil, or 'secular version of a
demonic pact' (Jackson, 1981, p. 113) brings us finally to the nature
of the fantastic in *Dorian Gray*. The text contains at least one passage
of classic (if slightly blasé) hesitation:

Besides, was it really under his control? Had it indeed been
prayer that had produced the substitution? Might there not be
some curious scientific reason for it all? If thought could
exercise its influence upon a living organism, might not
thought exercise an influence upon dead and inorganic things?
Nay, without thought or conscious desire, might not things
external to ourselves vibrate in unison with our moods and
passions, atom calling to atom in secret love or strange
affinity? But the reason was of no importance. He would
never again tempt by a prayer any terrible power. If the
picture was to alter, it was to alter. That was all. Why inquire
too closely into it? (Wilde, 1988, p. 84)

The story is ostensibly within the marvellous, but the supernatural is at best tentative. Joyce Carol Oates (Wilde, 1988, p. 427) observes that 'the *consequences* of a Faustian pact with the Devil are dramatized, but the Devil himself is absent, which suggests that the novel is an elaborate fantasy locating the Fall within the human psyche alone', and Miltonic references do support a reading of the novel as allegory of the Fall, as well as psychological allegory. Ziolkowski (p. 129) argues that it is equally possible for the reader 'to rationalize almost the entire improbable action': only Dorian and Basil see the portrait after the day of completion until its discovery, in pristine state, by the servants on Dorian's death; Dorian's sense of guilt may explain all; Basil sees the picture in poor light and speculates on impurities in the paints; Dorian may not be so utterly unchanged and even the appearance of extreme youthfulness may not be utterly unbelievable in a dandy of thirty-eight. Or does the novel belong more to the realm of fairy story (Jackson, p. 112; Baldick, p. 148), with its 'Prince Charming' motif and its single transformation of wish-fulfilment, spliced with cheap melodrama?

Wilde has intensified in *Dorian Gray* the nineteenth-century obsession with the double into ever more intricate combinations and shapes, not least the shape of the enspirited portrait. Not only do the monstrous features evolving on Dorian's portrait originate from within him in the usual sense; they also emanate jointly from within and without in another, in that blood creeps over it and even drips (Wilde, 1988, p. 168); moreover: 'It was from within [the portrait itself], apparently, that the foulness and horror had come' (p. 122). The psychological complication is merely reinforced here by the fact that this last quotation is presented from Basil's viewpoint. Wilde's portraits in *Dorian Gray*, figurative and otherwise, of his characters, of his age and (prophetically) of his own life, interrelate and interlock, it has been claimed (Ellman, p. 297; Lawler, in Wilde, 1988, p. 453), to the point of self-deconstruction. His novel carries within it also a fusion, enframed in a tight contemporary topography, of many of the devices, approaches and categorisations of the fantastic tradition.

STOKER

The final act of nineteenth-century fantastic-Gothicism brings to the stage the third great myth to have made its impact on the popular

culture of this century: after *Frankenstein* and *Dr Jekyll and Mr Hyde*
we must conclude with the imposing figure of Count Dracula. As
already remarked, just as the shapes of Gothic and post-Gothic
prose evolved over the century so did those of its protagonists —
and no one in nineteenth-century prose took on shapes more
numerous or more weird than Dracula. Furthermore, as recent
criticism has begun to reveal, *Dracula* (1897) is not such a simple
text of horror fantasy as may have once been thought.[17]

Just as we identified a central mythic image in *Frankenstein*, that of
a figure imparting the spark of life into a man stretched out, so does
Dracula have an equally memorable, and a more horrifying, central
image: that of a man (in black) bending over a woman (in white) to
suck out her life (in blood), and it should occasion no surprise to
find 'the colours of the fantastic' again to the fore. This image and
the requisite colour scheme recur prominently in the novel, but
there are two striking pictorial posings. The first is witnessed by
Mina, pursuing the supposedly somnambulent Lucy along the cliffs
of Whitby, perceiving in the distance:

> There was undoubtedly something, long and black, bending
> over the half-reclining white figure. I called in fright, 'Lucy!
> Lucy!' and something raised a head, and from where I was I
> could see a white face and red, gleaming eyes. (Stoker, 1983,
> p. 90)

Later, more in close-up, Dr Seward's diary describes the following
sexually ambivalent tableau, as he and Van Helsing burst into the
Harkers' bedroom:

> On the bed beside the window lay Jonathan Harker, his face
> flushed, and breathing heavily as though in a stupor.
> Kneeling on the near edge of the bed facing outwards was the
> white-clad figure of his wife. By her side stood a tall, thin
> man, clad in black. His face was turned from us, but the
> instant we saw it we all recognised the Count — in every
> way, even to the scar on his forehead. With his left hand he
> held both Mrs Harker's hands, keeping them away with her
> arms at full tension; his right hand gripped her by the back of
> the neck, forcing her face down on his bosom. Her white
> nightdress was smeared with blood, and a thin stream
> trickled down the man's bare breast, which was shown by his
> torn-open dress. The attitude of the two had a terrible
> resemblance to a child forcing a kitten's nose into a saucer of

milk to compel it to drink. As we burst into the room, the Count turned his face, and the hellish look that I had heard described seemed to leap into it. His eyes flamed red with devilish passion; the great nostrils of the white aquiline nose opened wide and quivered at the edges; and the white sharp teeth, behind the full lips of the blood-dripping mouth, champed together like those of a wild beast. . . . The moonlight suddenly failed, as a great black cloud sailed across the sky. (pp. 281–2)

This scene is so important that we are given a repeat summary of it by Seward (possibly with inconsistencies, at least according to Martin, 1988), as he relates the event to the revived Harker (p. 284), and a third, this time first-person, account from Mina Harker (p. 287), again highlighting black, white and red features and referring specifically back to Whitby. Again, as with *Frankenstein*, the central image undergoes a final reversal; in the culminating scene of execution, Mina sees 'the Count lying within the box upon the earth': this time it is Dracula who is in the subordinate position (in fact prone), while over him the executioners (Harker and a dying Quincey Morris) wield their deadly knives (pp. 376–7).

Just as these images of power recur analogously in key works of the last century, with or without the colours of the fantastic, so do the basic character configurations and plot functions (as we shall see again, in the case of a different pattern, in works by Pushkin and Henry James). The present pattern, and its attendant variations, we are liable to find explained in Freudian terms: the double (with its mirror and shadow connections), according to Otto Rank and Freud, was originally 'an insurance against the destruction of the ego', akin to the immortal soul, which then reversed its function to that of 'the uncanny harbinger of death', becoming finally 'a thing of terror' (Freud, 1955, pp. 235–6). On to this may be grafted the Oedipal myth with its consequent ramifications. Alternatively (or in conjunction, through a similar process of wish–fulfilment), it may be explained in terms of Jungian archetypes: this normally involves a hero and a beloved, threatened with bodily or mental enslavement by the (in some sense 'doubling') Other or Shadow, and then rescued by the intervention of a Wise Old Man. Naturally, the changes rung on these themes and the sophistications of plot-presentation invariably suggest readings which go beyond the primitive fairy-tale.

Dracula as vampire tale is commonly assumed to descend from John Polidori's *The Vampyre* (1819, to be found in Haining, 1972), via the popular *Varney the Vampire* (1847, a work of multiple authorship) and Le Fanu's *Carmilla*, with more than a touch of *Melmoth the Wanderer* (as yet another Anglo-Irish author in this field, Bram Stoker was well versed in the works of Maturin, Le Fanu and Wilde — Stoker had married Florence Balcombe, Wilde's early beloved). Vampires had, of course, occurred elsewhere in European literature, at least from Byron onwards (see Praz, 1970, pp. 78–80). A nod from Stoker to Le Fanu is to be found in *Dracula's Guest* (a discarded chapter from the novel, subsequently published as a story), in the form of a tomb inscribed to a suicide Styrian Countess (as was Carmilla), who has now become a vampiric werewolf (Stoker, 1914, p. 9). Other traditional factors to the fore include the extension of premature burial to un-dead; and details familiar from Hoffmann and Chamisso, such as reflection and shadow loss.

With regard to doubles, Jonathan Harker, figuring as the initial protagonist, is pitted against Count Dracula in what is eventually depicted as a battle for the body and soul of Mina; Harker is the one whose journey to Castle Dracula parallels that of the Count to England and whose journal provides the novel with its opening discourse. However, a closer double of Dracula ('by an unwitting irony', according to Baldick, 1987, p. 147) is the vampire hunter — 'a philosopher and a metaphysician, and one of the most advanced scientists of his day' (Stoker, 1983, p. 112) — Abraham Van Helsing, an obvious development of Le Fanu's Dr Hesselius and significantly favoured with Stoker's own Christian (*sic*) name. Baldick (p. 147) sees Van Helsing and Dracula, in their obsessive chase across Europe, as analogous to Conan Doyle's contemporaneous Holmes and Moriarty: 'They are the twin halves of a single, perversely sexualized Frankensteinian transgressor; blood brothers by proxy, the one draws blood out of women while the other pumps blood into them'. Van Helsing and Dracula also double in their delivery of broken English, although here it must be said that Dracula has the edge: not only is it impossible to agree (with Varnado, 1987, p. 109) that his accent (if accent be a quality that can be judged at all on the written page) is 'as clumsy as that of Van Helsing', but he, while sharing Van Helsing's habit of persistent reference to his English acquaintances as 'my friend. . .', is spared, as no doubt befits a villain in black, his rival's tedious repetition and garrulity.

Varnado (p. 111) writes of *Dracula*: 'Historical traditions, legends and occult lore give the book a quality that must be considered epic.' This view may have a certain validity, yet any such impression seems to be overshadowed by internal features of detail and presentation. Just as the precise contemporary setting and topography (late-Victorian London, Whitby, Exeter) contrasts strikingly with the traditional elements of Gothic castle, Transylvania and the centuries-old house of Dracula, so does the late nineteenth-century technology (phonograph, shorthand, telegram) clash with the increasingly rampant Christian religiosity. The presence in or below the text of taboo and desire, repression and status, add plausibility to a Marxist–Freudian reading, by which the privileged Victorian values of Christianity, empire and patriarchy hold sway, in a battle of penetration, over devilry, subversion and assertive female sexuality (see, for example, Cranny-Francis, 1988; Martin, 1988). Baldick (1987, p. 148) sees *Dracula* as the victory of the bourgeoisie over baronial despotism: 'Dracula is feudalism's death warmed up'. The text is peppered too with such comments as the following remark by Van Helsing to Morris:

> A brave man's blood is the best thing on this earth when a woman is in trouble. You're a man, and no mistake. Well, the devil may work against us for all he's worth, but God sends us men when we want them. (Stoker, 1983, p. 149)

It should also be noted that Dracula's status is eventually reduced from the demonic, and all that might thereby be implied, to the merely 'criminal' (p. 341); again, connections with the Ripper phenomenon come to mind. The vampire tale is also seen as a modern version of the myth of dragon-slaying, a latter-day reflection of the primordial reassertion of man-made order over the chaos of nature (see Foust, 1986).

The device of multiple narration in *Dracula* (taken from *Melmoth the Wanderer* and perhaps Wilkie Collins, but here extended to comprise a compilation of journals, letters, newspaper reports and other documents), traditionally treated as a guarantee of authenticity, can be questioned upon closer examination, as Margaret Carter has demonstrated (1987, pp. 104–5). The introductory note and epilogue which frame the narratives explicitly and self-consciously call into question the credibility of the events narrated; there is a constant questioning by the characters of their own and each other's sanity; critical events are frequently not presented directly and some documents are presented more as fiction (narrators share an ability to write in the closest proximity to spine-chilling events). This maintains, in Carter's view (p. 113), a state of the fantastic until the last four chapters and even then this is reasserted in the epilogue. The multiplicity of narrative voices which we find in *Dracula* has a disturbing propensity (noted by Baldick, p. 147), in contrast to that of *Frankenstein*, for corroboration, rather than polyphony or challenge. Could we conceivably even yet be dealing with a case of collective delusion, based on some sort of a grotesque chain of misconception?

This is only one, if the most fundamental, of a series of questions which seem to arise from a text which, taken on its own terms (whether the answers be deemed to lie within the realm of inherent ambivalence or of artistic defect), generates (as Carter points out, p. 118) a double ambiguity — for characters and for reader. Why has Dracula apparently been so unsuccessful, or so idle, for centuries (why the late nineteenth century as his point of action and England as his target)? Why are there not more vampires in the vicinity of Castle Dracula, given that Dracula and the sisters have reigned in terror there for ages? Are not the boundaries of what is possible and not possible for vampires somewhat arbitrary? What is Dracula's ultimate aim? The overall domination of vampires would scarcely appear to be a logically desirable or possible outcome if, as Van Helsing maintains (Stoker, 1983, p. 214), 'the circle goes on ever widening', as 'all that die from the preying of the Un-Dead become themselves Un-Dead, and prey on their kind.' The view, that 'his ultimate goal is to establish and maintain himself in opposition to that sacred power in which he indirectly participates' (Varnado, 1987, p. 104) hardly seems to be a sufficient answer, either to the last question or to the following one: what is the cosmographic–theurgic system implied by the existence of vampires and the nature of their relation to the God–Satan system which seems to follow from Stoker's (or Van Helsing's) use of Christian symbolism and articles of ritual? Finally, why is the execution of Dracula not carried out by the approved method (of staking and decapitation), apparently required for all other (in particular female) vampires?[18]

George Orwell cited *Dracula* in his discussion of Chesterton's category of 'good bad books'. The reader's fascination with Stoker's novel, helped along by cinema and popular mythology, has been maintained despite, or perhaps because of, the emanation of questions such as those posed above and this is likely to remain the case. It may also reside in yet another quality which *Dracula* shares with *Frankenstein*, that of 'gruesome Resurrection myth' (Aldiss, 1986, p. 145; Punter, 1980, p. 261). However, the survival of its appeal may be (perhaps alarmingly) ensured by the prominence of an unpredictable and gruesome development in the recent past of our own century. Brian Aldiss (p. 144) considers the real subject of *Dracula* to be 'that obsession of the *fin de siècle*, syphilis. *Dracula* is the great Victorian novel about VD, for which vampirism stands in as Stoker's metaphor.' Such a view can only appear even more alluring in the age of Aids, a disease with symptoms which seem to bear an uncanny resemblance to the wasting effects resulting from vampirism, at least *à la* Stoker and Le Fanu.

3   Pushkin and Henry James

The taste for the marvellous has indeed been compared to the
habit of drinking ardent liquors. But it fortunately differs in
having its limits: he upon whom one dram does not produce
the effect, can attain the desired degree of inebriation by
doubling the dose. But when we have ceased to start at
one ghost, we are callous to the exhibition of a whole
Pandemonium.

Sir Walter Scott (1968, p. 212)

PUSHKIN

As we saw in Part One, Dostoevsky hailed Pushkin's *The Queen of
Spades* as 'the epitome of the art of the fantastic'. Written in 1833,
Pushkin's story appeared at a time when Russian prose was
undergoing something of a romantic vogue; the English Gothic,
French freneticism and Hoffmann were all fashions of the day; even
Scott's articles on the supernatural in literature were being
translated.

The origins of *The Queen of Spades* have been variously traced to
Pushkin's own earlier abandoned prose fragments, to a society
anecdote involving a still living Princess Golitsyna and to an
autobiographical episode, to hidden meanings derived from Freemasonry with political overtones, to literary derivations from
French freneticism (usually Janin) and other French novels (by
Stendhal and Balzac), the Faust legend and the Hoffmann tale, as
well as the folklore–fairy-tale tradition.[1] John Bayley (1971, p. 323)
summed up some of these sources at least in the following neat
formula: 'Thus the story grew up from abandoned story-projects
and the characters in them, was grafted on to an anecdote from real
life, and given a colouring of fashionably literary *diablerie.*'

Paul Debreczeny (1983, p. 186) calls the story 'a triumph of
detached narration' and quotes the enthusiastic approval of Tolstoy
and Gide. One of the more gifted Soviet critics of the Stalin period,
A. Lezhnëv (1983, p. 126), terms it 'this most complicated of
Pushkin's stories, so difficult to understand', while Lauren Leighton
(1982, p. 15) quotes Anna Akhmatova's remark: 'How complicated

113

The Queen of Spades is! Layer upon layer', while himself designating it (p. 22) 'one of the most intriguing works in all world literature'. Strangely enough, to Lezhnëv (p. 141) the story is seen as 'avoiding contrived plot construction'; this now seems difficult to sustain in the light of detailed articles (Shukman, 1977; and Pursglove, 1985) which lay bare the actual chronology of the tale, in terms of the discrepancy between *fabula* (logical 'fable') and *siuzhet* (plot presentation within the text). Nevertheless, in a naïve sense at least, the plot appears to bear a classical simplicity. Similarly, Belinsky could regard the work as 'not a short story, but an anecdote' (see Bocharov, 1978, p. 318), while, in more recent years, A. V. Chicherin has seen concealed in it 'an extremely compressed novel' (see Debreczeny, p. 232).

Compressed *The Queen of Spades* certainly is. Some twenty-five pages in length (thirty in Rosemary Edmonds' English translation), it gives rise to a number of what are by now commonplaces in Pushkin criticism: its condensed form and precision of style are seen as almost poetic in nature; the verbal texture is seen as full of subsidiary meaning and potentially portentous connotation; scarcely a word is held to be superfluous; even some of the rhythms of poetry have been discerned in Pushkin's prose.

Such factors have led to what must rank as an astonishing body of criticism to be devoted to such a single short work of fiction. In the last twenty years or so alone, according to Debreczeny's bibliography, about thirty articles have appeared on this story; omissions and updating would put the total at more than fifty. At least half of these have been published in western countries, the product, in many cases, of Anglo-American scholarship.

Interpretations have, as may be expected in such circumstances, differed considerably. The main division has been between the purely psychologically motivated readings (sub-dividing between those which rest on a traditional basis of obsessional monetary greed leading to inevitable downfall and consequent madness, and those leaning towards a more Freudian version) and a supernatural explanation for the events which unfold. One intermediate position is to regard the work as essentially an amalgam of literary devices, a parody (of various or particular forms of the Gothic, the frenetic, Hoffmann, etc.). From this it may follow that inquiry into 'the *real* circumstances' of the events of the plot is ultimately 'irrelevant' (e.g. Debreczeny, pp. 200–01). Another intermediate position (exemplified by Rosen, 1975) is to insist on the validity of both psychological and supernatural elements within a total explanation. Leighton (1982, p. 22) stresses the 'highly complex' and 'intriguing' literary nature of the tale, which has provoked more speculation than any other Pushkin work and which is 'so deliberately ambiguous that the scholarship devoted to it is markedly ingenious' (he himself being a prime example: see Leighton, 1977a and 1977b, as well as 1982). Some scholars have gone outside the text to surmise and fill 'gaps' in the story line; others comb tirelessly, both within and without, to construct or identify systems based on numerology and/or Freemasonary.

There remains one (if not more than one) further approach: that which embraces genuine ambiguity and was pioneered by Dostoevsky. This takes on a fresh interest, and a new lease of life, given a Todorovian approach to the fantastic. It is with this approach to *The Queen of Spades* that we shall here be mainly concerned. The first task, then, is to examine the validity of such a reading of *The Queen of Spades*.

First it may be helpful to present a brief synopsis.

The tale opens in the 'present' (about 1830) during a card session in the St Petersburg rooms of a Horse Guards officer named Narumov. Among the guests is a young officer of engineers, Hermann, who is of German origin, who never gambles himself but observes the play keenly. Tomsky, another member of the company, remarks that his octogenarian grandmother, the Countess Anna Fedotovna, also does not play — despite the circumstances of an anecdote, which he then proceeds to narrate:

Sixty years before (i.e. about 1770) she was the rage of Paris, known there as *la Vénus moscovite*. Having lost a considerable sum at cards to the Duke of Orleans, which her husband refused to cover, she faced financial and social ruin. In desperation, she turned to the Count Saint-Germain, an occultist of dubious repute. Saint-Germain gave her a three-card tip, with the aid of which she retrieved her loss against the Duke. Thereafter, the Countess revealed the formula to no one, except, some years later, to a young man named Chaplitsky, who also won with it, having promised never to play again, and has since died in poverty.

In Chapter II, Tomsky discusses the possibility of introducing Narumov to his grandmother; the latter's young ward, Lizaveta Ivanovna, is disappointed that Narumov is not an engineer, as a young officer of that calling has been watching the house and attempting to pay court to her. The engineer in question is Hermann, who, having become obsessed by the secret of the three cards, finds himself drawn, as if by 'a mysterious force', to the house of the Countess; having briefly considered the feasibility of gaining the secret by becoming the lover of the eighty-seven-year-old Countess, he has spotted Lizaveta Ivanovna and decides she might be a better bet to gain access to the house. Following the receipt of a flurry of notes, Lizaveta Ivanovna (Chapter III) agrees to an assignation with Hermann, instructing him to enter the house and await her return, with the Countess, from a ball. This Hermann does, but waits in the Countess's study, rather than going up to Lizaveta's room. After the return of the ladies, Hermann emerges to confront the Countess and demand the secret. Getting no reply, other than 'It was a joke', Hermann loses control, calls the Countess an 'old witch' and threatens her with a pistol, whereupon she expires. Hermann then goes up to Lizaveta Ivanovna to confess all. Lizaveta is distraught and calls Hermann a 'monster'; nevertheless she gives him a key to enable him to leave the house unseen (Chapter IV). More from superstition than remorse, Hermann goes to the funeral service for the Countess (Chapter V). When he approaches the coffin, he thinks he sees the dead woman wink 'mockingly' at him. In his confusion, and contrary to normal habit, Hermann quaffs a quantity of wine over dinner, returns home to sleep, waking at a quarter to three in the morning, whereupon he appears to receive a visitation from an old woman, whom he recognises as the Countess. This visitor tells him that he may win by playing the three, seven and ace, in that order, at the rate of one card a day, and never again in his life; he will earn her forgiveness if he marries Lizaveta Ivanovna. The three, seven and ace, we are told in the climactic Chapter VI, become an *idée fixe* in Hermann's mind, crowding out the image of the dead Countess. He thinks of gaming in Paris, but is brought by Narumov to the gambling salon of Chekalinsky, newly arrived from Moscow. There Hermann wins on the first night with a three and on the second night with a seven, but on the third, as he thinks he holds the winning ace, his card turns out instead to be the queen of spades, whose image on the card appears to wink at him, uncannily resembling . . . — 'the old woman!'. A short 'Conclusion' reports that Hermann has gone out of his mind, Lizaveta Ivanovna has married the prosperous son of the former steward of the Countess and is bringing up a poor female relation, and Tomsky is marrying a society princess.

The question of the fantastic in *The Queen of Spades*, or rather the possibility of supernatural involvement, is generally seen as arising in connection with two things: the secret of the three cards and the ghostly visitation of the Countess to Hermann. However, as already indicated above, the concepts of ambiguity and duality are ingrained in the text at a multiplicity of levels, not least in the depiction of the main characters — and indeed of virtually all characters — in the story. There is also the question of the pervasive feeling of the presence of the 'mysterious force' and the power of a (possibly malignant) fate, which leads for instance Kodjak (1976, p. 115) to perceive in the work 'a theological vision of the world', a meaning based on evil. Kodjak, though, it should be stressed, argues for an out-and-out supernatural interpretation. For present purposes we may perhaps concentrate on the questions of the cards and the apparition.

The existence of a three-card secret is first asserted by Tomsky in an anecdote which he clearly enjoys telling and in the telling, it has been remarked (Bocharov, 1978, p. 320), he himself adopts an authorial pose. The anecdote brings not just two but three instantaneous responses: 'Chance!' said one, 'A fairy-tale!', remarks Hermann, 'perhaps the cards were marked', adds a third (Pushkin, 1948, p. 229).[2] Three lines of explanation are therefore immediately suggested, although the third is dismissed by Tomsky.[3]

The Countess was the alleged recipient of the formula — 'And indeed was any secret revealed to her?' asks Bayley (1971, p. 319). Apart from her supposed win (at Versailles), which could be fiction or rumour, it can be said that she does at least appear to know what Hermann is talking about when he demands the secret; however, her only reply, said twice, that it was a 'joke' is hardly in itself conclusive confirmation of the veracity of Tomsky's anecdote.

The secret of the three cards is directly linked with the ghostly visitation, in that this visitation provides the occasion for Hermann to acquire the arcane formula. Proponents of a realistic/psychological explanation seize upon Hermann's drunkenness on the night in question as evidence that he hallucinated the visit of the dead Countess and with it her ghostly message. John Mersereau (1983, p. 223) goes so far as to call the scene not even a hallucination but a dream (as does Briggs, 1983, p. 223). Furthermore, it has been frequently pointed out that the figures three and seven (and even the ace) seemed to be present earlier in Hermann's mind. Mersereau puts the case concisely for a psychological reading:

> The content of the dream is thoroughly motivated. The spectre begins with a preamble stating that its appearance is against its will, a fact which Hermann must realize in view of his relationship with the late Countess. The secret of the winning three cards which she reveals has already been partly established, since Hermann previously had mentioned 'calculation, restraint, and industriousness' as the three cards which would *triple* and *make sevenfold* his capital. The ace as the third card is the natural choice of a person suffering from delusions of grandeur: would the great Hermann cap his triumph with a lowly ten or knave? No, the two magical cards, three and seven, are crowned by the ace, with which Hermann identifies personally — in Russian the word ace [*tuz*] refers to a person of particular importance and prestige. Finally, forgiveness is promised if he will marry Lizaveta, a dream admonition developing from his unconscious guilt at having treated Lizaveta in a base and cruel manner. (Mesereau 1983, p. 223)

Plausible though such an explication may seem, it raises, or leaves, a number of questions which do not seem to get answered.

Even if Hermann may have subconsciously intuited, or decided upon, the values and even the sequence of the three cards, how does he know to play the cards on three separate days? There is no such procedure involved in the previous cases of the Countess and of Chaplitsky (at least, as far as we know from Tomsky's anecdote): they played their three cards one after the other. As to why the conditions should be any different for Hermann, this is another question in itself. More importantly, though, if Hermann hallucinated or otherwise imagined the formula, how is it that his cards on the first two occasions won? Indeed the formula of three-seven-ace *was* the winning one even in the final event; Chekalinsky in fact won by laying these very three cards to his left: Hermann, from whatever cause, bungled the third game by picking the queen in place of the ace.[4] Chance again, or fairy-tale? It is made clear that any idea of marked cards can be discounted as new decks are unsealed for each occasion. This is a key question for many critics; for at least one (Burgin, 1974, p. 46) reliance here on chance 'truly boggles the mind . . . and is harder to believe than the supernatural'.

Returning again to the ghostly visitation, it has been equally plausibly argued (e.g. by Kodjak, pp. 101–02) that a close reading of the text indicates that Hermann was not still drunk by a quarter to three that morning, that he was clearly awake and apparently *compos mentis*; and, furthermore, that the narrative mode employed reveals that such a visitation did in 'reality' take place.

These factors are sufficient for the tale to be placed firmly within the realm of the supernatural, at least as far as some critics are concerned (such as Kodjak or Burgin); however, having once plumped for the supernatural they then tend to proceed to develop a reading based on Faustian or other demonic systems.

However, the more closely one looks at the tersely narrated events of the ghostly visitation, the more ambiguous they become. Someone looked in at Hermann from the street, we are informed, but 'Hermann paid no attention to this' (Pushkin, 1948, p. 247). Does this imply that Hermann was unaware of someone glancing through the window, or that, deep in thought, he ignored it? Is Kodjak (p. 102) justified in stating that the narrator here assumes 'the role of eyewitness and, consequently, has become a source of objective information'? The corresponding glance through the window following the visitor's retreat *is* said to be seen by Hermann; this double perspective in perception confirms, for Kodjak at least, the objectivity, or 'reality' of the incident. As well as the glance through the window, before and after, the visit is also framed by the sound of the opening and then the banging of the outer door to the passage (which on subsequent inspection is found to be locked) and by the sound of 'shuffling slippers' (Briggs, 1983, p. 223, remarks on the symmetry of this; others, such as Pursglove, p. 18, n. 6, remark on the symmetry of the 3 a.m. death and ghostly appearance of the Countess). Additional confirmation of the actuality of this occurrence is seen by Kodjak (p. 103) in Hermann's recording of the event immediately afterwards; however, the narrator's wording of this, 'he noted down his vision' [*videnie*] would seem in fact to reopen the possibility of hallucination.

In any case, whose was the face that appeared twice at the window? According to Kodjak (p. 102) this may have been either 'the Countess' ghost itself or someone who has escorted her to Hermann's quarters'. But do ghosts require escorting? For that matter, do they need to open and close doors noisily and produce a shuffling tread?

Chance? The rational explanation here must be hallucination. Fairy-tale? The actuality of a supernatural visitation to deliver the magic information. Marked cards? In this case the suggestion would be of a hoax (Pursglove, p. 14, maintains 'there is a suggestion that the whole story of the "magic" cards was dreamed up as a cover for amorous intrigue'). Hermann does at first mistake the ghostly figure for 'his old wet-nurse', but this is the only reference to such a person in the story. A hoax theory here sounds superficially intriguing, but does not seem ever to have been put forward, no doubt for lack of supporting evidence elsewhere in the text. However, gaps and surmises from beyond the text are made to support the consequences of supernatural readings (e.g. by Burgin); a hoax theory along these lines might be no less (if no more) defensible.

It seems clear that Pushkin does not provide answers to these and many other questions. Many another minor mystery remains. We have already drawn attention to shifting authorial pose and narratorial manoevring (see Kodjak and Bocharov); this derives, according to a recent Soviet critic, from 'the accentuated indeterminacy of the authorial stance' (Murav'ëva, 1978, pp. 65–6).

Roberta Reeder (1982, p. 95) presses a parallel here with Hoffmann. As in Hoffmann's fantastic (as opposed to his 'marvellous') tales, Pushkin's narrator 'consistently provides realistic motivation for irrational events'; at the same time he uses 'such phrases as "probably" and "it seemed to him", which couch the event in either the irrational or the real.' *The Queen of Spades* operates, in a Hoffmannian manner, in three possible worlds. According to Reeder's scheme, there is the philistine world of realistic explanation (in which Tomsky and his friends live); a fantasy/make-believe world of dreams of fortunes and sentimental love (to which both Hermann and Lizaveta Ivanovna may be seen to belong); and a demonic realm of Mephistophelian dominion (in which dwell the Countess and Saint-German). Alternatively, we may prefer to return to the scheme suggested by the three lines of response to Tomsky's anecdote. This would provide a world of chance or fate, in which explanations are at least nominally rational; a world of fairy-tale, in which one may, or may not, believe; and a world of sharp practice, governed by malignant hoaxers.

Pushkin's tale, then, poses a number of questions, of which we have here discussed only the most central. Like Henry James later in the century, it would seem, he has deliberately constructed a work with such artifice as to ensure that no definitive answers may be given.

Henry James is here mentioned not by chance. If real art is essentially high drama, then it must have been the basic plot line, the configuration of central characters and, above all, the drama of confrontation present in *The Queen of Spades* which inspired one of the most artistic stories of Henry James.

Before passing to this story, however, we should first briefly consider the fantastic in relation to the work of James.

HENRY JAMES

According to Virginia Woolf, 'Henry James has only to take the smallest of steps and he is over the border. His characters with their extreme fineness of perception are already half-way out of the body'.[5] While many works by James feature characters with a high degree of psychic awareness, the use, or possible use, of the fantastic in his *œuvre* is rather more restricted. Obvious candidates for consideration are the so-called 'ghost stories'; the primary candidate has long been the celebrated *The Turn of the Screw*; mention may also be made of the unfinished novel *The Sense of the Past*.[6] James himself confessed that 'the "ghost story" . . . has ever been for me the most possible form of the fairy-tale' (James, 1984b, p. 1257).

In Volume XII of the New York edition of his works, James placed *The Aspern Papers* and followed it with *The Turn of the Screw* and then two much shorter works, *The Liar* (1888) and *The Two Faces* (1900). Given the ten-year gap between *Aspern* (1888) and *The Turn of the Screw* (1898), it is obvious that chronology played no great part in the arrangement of works. *The Novels and Tales of Henry James* (the New York edition) was planned by its author during 1906–7 and appeared from 1907 to 1909 in twenty-four volumes. This grandiose project involved rewriting, the composition of a famous series of prefaces, selection and fitting in to what was originally to have been a 'magical' number of twenty-three volumes, but eventually had to extend to a twenty-fourth (Edel, 1972, p. 329).[7] Leon Edel maintains that 'James had to juggle with stories according to their length as well as their classification by subject or theme' (p. 330). We know from letters of December 1906 that James had it in mind to put *Aspern* in the same volume as *The Spoils of Poynton* (likewise a work of considerable ambiguity, but not of the supernatural); however, his desire to include a plate of the Palazzo Capello (the house on which the setting of *Aspern* had been modelled in 1887) got the better of him and he dispatched his photographer to Venice expressly for the purpose. *The Aspern Papers* would be put instead 'with something else where its picture will still be so valuable' (James, 1984a, pp. 430–1; Edel, pp. 342–3).

Was it, therefore, totally by chance that *The Aspern Papers*, surely a psychological tale *par excellence*, ended up next to James' most overtly fantastic tale, *The Turn of the Screw*? It is intended here to show, by reading *Aspern* against Pushkin's *The Queen of Spades*, that James could have had excellent reasons, whether conscious or subconscious, for this coupling (which has indeed been felicitously continued into modern editions: see James, 1986).

James wrote a number of ghost stories: that is one way of dealing with an interest in the supernatural. Another is to write a deliberately ambiguous tale of the pure fantastic (as Pushkin, for one, had done): *The Turn of the Screw*. Yet another way of treating the fantastic is to take elements of plot, character and drama from a fantastic tale and to adapt and develop it for psychological purposes, eliminating on the way, or leaving the barest traces of, the fantastic itself. This, we suggest, is what James did, among other things, with *Aspern*.

Occasionally James would wish to 'fantasticate' an idea, as with *The Friends of the Friends* (James, 1987a, p. 190 and p. 144). In relation to *The Sense of the Past* (which he worked on in 1900 and was to return to in 1914–15) he wrote:

> The *fantasticated* is, for this job, my probable formula, and I know what I mean by it as differentiated from the type, the squeezed sponge, of *The T. of the S.* 'Terror' *peut bien en être*, and all the effective *malaise*, above all, the case demands.

The 'tone of *The Turn of the Screw* is something of which James was highly conscious and which he at times wished to recapture (e.g. for *The Sense of the Past*, see pp. 517 and 532). He also referred to 'things so fantastic as in that wanton little Tale' and the 'hideous' in 'my bogey-tale' (James, 1984a, p. 84). The deliberate manner of its construction, should this be in any doubt, is underlined by James' remark (p. 88) that 'The *T. of the S.* is a very mechanical matter'; we may now wish to disregard his verdict on it as 'inferior', though his qualifications of it as 'pictorial' and 'rather a shameless potboiler' (*ibid.*) remain of interest. In his preface to *The Altar of the Dead* (Volume XVII of the New York edition, the 'ghost volume') James wrote: 'The apparitions of Peter Quint and Miss Jessel . . . are matters as to which in themselves, really, the critical challenge (essentially nothing ever but the spirit of fine attention) may take a hundred forms — and a hundred felt or possibly proved infirmities is too great a number' (James, 1984b, p. 1260). In response to a reader's questions on *The Turn of the Screw*, James, referring to the 'questionable and ambiguous', replied 'I somehow can't pretend to

give any coherent account of my small inventions "after the fact"':
and this was in the year of publication (James, 1984a, p. 88). There
may be doubt as to whether James, like Pushkin before him, 'knew'
the answers.

The Turn of the Screw has attracted an enormous amount of critical
attention and controversy has long reigned over the perceived
alternatives of the psychological (hallucinatory) and supernatural
(ghostly apparitional) interpretations. Todorov (1973, p. 43) seizes
on this tale as an example of the fantastic. Do the ghosts really exist
or not? For Todorov, 'the answer is obvious: by maintaining the
ambiguity at the tale's heart, James has merely obeyed the rules of
the genre' (Todorov, 1977, p. 158). The case for this has been
persuasively argued in detail by Brooke-Rose (pp. 128–229) and
there is no need to rehearse the arguments again here.[8] A few brief
remarks may perhaps suffice.

Many critics of *The Turn of the Screw* have relied on 'a
paraphrased reading in which the subtle language of the original is
significantly altered to enhance the critic's case, or an appeal to
"evidence" which lies outside the text altogether' (Anthony Curtis,
Introduction to James, 1986, summarising Brooke-Rose). Many of
the imponderables of this work derive from the nature and the
content of the framing device, quite apart from the reader's response
to the tale itself — the account of the governess.

The beginning of the work now seems reminiscent of a television
series of the 1950s called 'The Tall Story Club', in which a group of
participants would gather to relate ghost, or other improbable,
stories. At the end it would be revealed which stories purported to
be true and which false: at the end of *The Turn of the Screw* there is
no such revelation. The reader is distanced from the main narrative
both in time and by a double narratorial remove. The primary
(Jamesian) narrator reproduces a manuscript which was read at a
Christmas house party by one Douglas, now deceased; the
manuscript was acquired by Douglas from a woman formerly his
sister's governess; at the time of Douglas's reading, the woman had
been dead 'these twenty years' (James, 1986, p. 146); the manuscript
purports to comprise the governess's account of events during a
previous period of employment, about ten years before. The
primary narrator has supplied the title, which he has taken from
Douglas's speech (p. 145). The 'few words of prologue' (p. 148),
putting into context the opening of the narrative of the governess,
belong to the primary narrator, supposedly reported by him from
Douglas's 'touches with which he had already worked us up'
(p. 148). The main narrative is, therefore, in a sense third-hand,

though its immediacy is supposedly guaranteed by the preservation and handing on of the manuscript; what we know of the circumstances surrounding it is second-hand. Questions, or indeed discrepancies, arise.

As a framing device it is notable — quite apart from any doubts as to reliability — for its one-endedness. There is no return to the frame at the conclusion of the governess's narrative; all we are told of subsequent events comes from the prologue and is limited to the statements that the governess never saw her employer again, and that she later gained employment with Douglas's family. The proposition that the catastrophic events concluding the account of the governess should have aroused no aftermath is utterly incredible. However, we learn nothing more of it. What can be said of the shadowy figure of the guardian (employer), or of the reliability of Mrs Grose, on which much would seem to depend? What is to be made of the re-employment of the governess? Why is the respectability of the previous governess so heavily stressed in the prologue, and the figure of Quint omitted entirely from the list of servants (p. 150)? (The names of Jessel and Quint are not in any case encountered until the tale proper.)

Much speculation has centered on the relationship between the governess and Douglas, and indeed on the 'real' identity of Douglas.[9] Any attempt at definitive answers seems inevitably to be impelled beyond the text (whether just to fill in 'gaps' or to resort to James's possible reading of Freud). Could Douglas have been the 'real' author all along? There can be no answer to that. All that can be said with any certainty is that the literary quality of the governess's account achieves a perfection in terms of the art of fiction to rival (almost to exceed!) that of The Master himself.

The Aspern Papers was written during 1887 and first published the following year. We know from the notebooks that the original inspiration was an anecdote involving the pursuit by a Shelley fanatic (one Captain Silsbee) of Shelley papers thought to be held in Florence by an aged Claire Clairmont, erstwhile mistress of Byron; the 'Shelley-worshipper' lodged with the old lady and her middle-aged niece until the elder Miss Clairmont's death, whereupon the niece offered him all the Shelley documents on one condition: marriage; 'Silsbee *court encore*' (James, 1987a, p. 33). In addition, there is brief mention of a Countess Gamba, who once burned a letter of Byron's.

The preface of 1907 (to the New York edition) reinforces the inspiration of the idea of a living throwback to the romantic period of Shelley and Byron. James's sense of the romantic and of the 'visitable past', and his feeling for Florence and Venice (see James, 1984b, pp. 1173–91; James, 1986, pp. 27–42). The change of scene from Florence to Venice apart, the main overt change made by James was the Americanisation — of both romantic poet (the invented figure of Jeffrey Aspern) and of the origins of the custodians of his prized literary remains. It is with the justification of the invention of Aspern in particular that James's remarks in his preface appear ostensibly to be concerned.

There are also included in the preface a number of remarks, consistent with the story itself (particularly in its re-written form), of interest to our own concerns in this study. In addition to allowing himself 'so much to fantasticate' (James, 1986, p. 32), James felt that his 'appropriation of the Florentine legend should purge it . . . of references too obvious' (p. 33), 'a question, in fine, of covering one's tracks' (*ibid.*). It will be suggested that Florentine tracks were not the only tracks which James covered. James also speaks (p. 35) of 'the harmless hocus-pocus' under cover of which Aspern might be supposed to have existed, as well as 'the dim and charming ghost of an adventurous lyric genius'. The preface appears, therefore, to reinforce impressions already present in the work itself of a submerged element of the supernatural, or the fantastic.

One would expect textual changes in the rewritten version of 1907 to heighten James's twin concerns — of style and drama — and this indeed turns out to be the case. Perhaps the most obviously felicitous change James made was to substitute the name of Tina for Tita, with respect to the younger Miss Bordereau; however, there were many other more minor amendments of a purely stylistic nature and the later version of the story has generally been accepted as preferable to its forerunner (see Leon Edel's view, quoted by Curtis, in James, 1986, p. 9). The sense of drama, and with it the narrator's consciousness and admission of his own dubious conduct, is heightened by a considerable number of minor changes and additions. The military imagery surrounding the narrator's quest is reinforced by the substitution of '*nom de guerre*' (James, 1986, p. 52) for the more ineffectual 'a name . . . not my own' (James, 1963, p. 283). 'Seize' (p. 291) is replaced by 'pounce' (p. 60), extending further the sense of plunder. Similarly (and at the same time continuing to enhance the already pervasive undertones of a repressed sexuality) the words 'penetration' (for 'attention', pp. 61/292; see also Preface, p. 28) and 'invasion' (three times, for more neutral words: pp. 80/313, 86/319, 130/368) are introduced. Miss Tina becomes 'my victim' (for 'Tita Bordereau', pp. 138/377) and other emotive words such as 'betray' and 'ordeal' (pp. 82/315, 81/313) are insinuated into the text.

A number of changes affect the Aspern papers themselves: 'relics and tokens' for 'documents', and 'literary remains' for 'papers' (pp. 51/281–2), 'treasure' for 'papers' twice (pp. 91/325 and 108/343; but also 'prize' for 'treasure', pp. 110/345), and 'Juliana's treasure' for 'Miss Bordereau's papers' (pp. 140/380) — the 1907 version uses the elder Miss Bordereau's first name with much greater frequency. 'The papers' also become 'my spoils' (pp. 51/282) and 'spoils' (pp. 63/294). The phrase 'my possible spoil' is added on the second page of the tale (p. 46). The introduction of this word, apparently a favourite of James — at least, after his writing of *The Spoils of Poynton* (1897) — allows him the triumph of proceeding to the Shakespearean–Venetian phrase 'strategems and spoils' (p. 141, for 'literary concupiscence'; Curtis, in James, 1986, pp. 9 and 13, notes 'spoils' as a 'crucial word' without making its complete absence from the 1888 text clear); the phrase 'battles and stratagems' had been used two pages before, in connection with the equestrian statue of the *condottiere* Bartolomeo Colleoni (pp. 139/378).

There is a further category of changes which may be seen as largely atmospheric. 'Diplomatic arts' is substituted for 'diplomatic practices' (pp. 51/282) and 'full of craft' for 'very cunning' (pp. 103/338). Such subtle enhancements of an atmosphere suggestive both of deceit ('such a treachery' is added, p. 132 — this time with the effect of ironic rebound upon the narrator himself) and at least hints of other types of mastery and allusion are augmented by various minor emendations. The tone of Miss Tina's speech resembles 'the light rustle of an old unfolded love-letter', instead of the mere 'it seemed such a direct testimony' (pp. 88/321). Referring to Juliana's strange, aged laugh (p. 92), James adds in 1907 that it was 'as if the faint "walking" ghost of her old-time tone had suddenly cut a caper'. In the case of Tina too, the 'phantasmagoric brightness' which the narrator briefly perceives in her final appearance before him is extended, here though perhaps to little advantage: 'This trick of her expression, this magic of her spirit, transfigured her' (pp. 141/381). Such textual changes can only be seen as reinforcing a network of imagery and reference already present, as we shall see, in the first edition of the work. Regardless of his real or primary intentions, James' alterations to the text of *Aspern* seem, on balance, to have strengthened the case to be presented here.

Perhaps at this stage we should present a brief synopsis of *The Aspern Papers*, which, though four times the length of *The Queen of*

Spades and, therefore, far more extensive in its atmospheric, and especially its psychological, treatment, is equally unilinear in plot and with a similarly closely restricted cast of characters.

The scene is Venice, presumably in the 1880s. The nameless narrator is an American literary scholar who is passionately involved in work on a celebrated American poet of the romantic period named Jeffrey Aspern. In the course of their researches, the narrator and his London collaborator, John Cumnor, have discovered that a mistress of Aspern's, one Juliana Bordereau, is unexpectedly still alive and living in Venice with her middle-aged niece Tina. Sensing the probable existence of unknown Aspern papers, the investigators have tried writing for information but have been unceremoniously rebuffed. The narrator arrives in Venice to try other means of access and conspires, prompted by his confidante, Mrs Prest, to pose as a lodger seeking rooms, and in particular the use of an all too rare Venetian garden, in the spacious palazzo of the now impoverished Bordereau ladies. Following a preliminary interview with Miss Tina, the narrator, using a false name but admitting to being engaged on literary work, is rented rooms by the venerable Juliana, but at an outrageous cost (about twenty times the going rate, and in gold). After six weeks devoid of contact with his landladies, the narrator chances upon Miss Tina in the garden and, making a clean breast of his true intentions if not yet of his name, endeavours to enlist her assistance (he had earlier joked with Mrs Prest of making love to the niece, p. 53). Tina confirms the existence of valuable papers and gives a cautious undertaking to help: the narrator, anticipating Juliana's death as imminent, is terrified that she might destroy the papers. From interviews with Juliana, the narrator suspects that she has guessed his secret, although Tina has not disclosed it. Sure enough, Juliana tantalises him by producing a miniature portrait of Aspern, purportedly for valuation. Following this scene, Juliana is taken ill — or so at least it would appear — and her life is despaired of. The narrator reveals his real identity to Tina and learns from her that the papers have been moved, apparently by Juliana, from their previous location. He absents himself from the house for some time, returning late at night. Finding all quiet, he cannot resist the temptation of glancing round the Bordereau quarters in the hope of locating the papers. About to rifle a wooden secretary, he is suddenly confronted by Juliana, who denounces him as a 'publishing scoundrel' (p. 125) and faints. Conscious of having lost his nerve and blown his chances, the narrator leaves Venice for a twelve-day trip. On his return he finds that Miss Juliana is dead and buried. Somewhat to his surprise, Tina receives him and makes him a gift of the Aspern portrait; still constrained by her aunt's wishes, however, she affects an unwillingness to show him the papers, unless and until he should become 'a relation' (p. 135). The narrator panics at such a suggestion and flees into the city. Returning late and sleeping on it, he seems to decide that the 'price' might be worth paying after all, but in a final interview an impressively dignified Miss Tina informs him that she has now burnt the papers. The chagrined narrator retreats from Venice — the portrait his only 'spoil'.

There is an obvious similarity between the bare plot lines of *Aspern* and those of *The Queen of Spades*: quest, plot (in the sense this time of conspiracy), double climax and failure. The two plots also share a corresponding mysterious realm of pre-history and a remarkably similar configuration of character types (with certain adjustments, developments or reversals). Particularly notable are the strikingly similar portrayals of tyrannical and shrewd females of extremely advanced (though, despite claims to the contrary — see below — of inexactly determined) age. This latter point, together with the structural similarity of the stories, has recently been noted by Carlos Fuentes, with respect to the ancestry of his own tale *Aura* (Fuentes, 1988, p. 39).[10] The similarities are even more remarkable, as we shall see below, when the two works are examined in detail.

The first and only other commentator to make this connection, and to draw attention to Henry James's apparent debt to Pushkin, to the best of our knowledge, is A. D. P. Briggs, in an article of 1972.[11] Briggs outlines the main argument as follows:

> The Pushkin and James stories share a basis which is common to an unusual degree. A very old woman (87 in Pushkin, over 90 in James) possesses something of preternatural value for a much younger man. . . . In both cases the old woman has as her companion a younger woman, about the same age as the man, timid and entirely subjugated. The man is unable to resist the temptation of completing his personal happiness by infiltrating the home of the old woman. Her apparently impregnable fortress is penetrated by his working on the

susceptibilities of the companion and hinting at honourable intentions of love or marriage. The process of infiltration leads at last to a dramatic confrontation between the bounty-seeker and the old woman, the excitement of which causes her unintended death. This climax, however, is not the end of the story; the hero's hopes may yet be realised. But no, after a second climax, he sees them dashed and is left with nothing but bitter and haunting memories. (A. Briggs, 1972, p. 54)

Seeking to identify key elements in the *Aspern* plot which do not derive from the anecdotes concerning Claire Clairmont, Silsbee and Countess Gamba, Briggs finds a common structural pattern of three stages: 'infiltration, confrontation and aftermath' (p. 57). In particular, 'melodramatic confrontation' is preferred by James to other possibilities, the pivotal point of construction being 'a meeting between the old woman and the fortune-hunter which brings about her death' (pp. 56, 57). This crucial element in plot and structure, of course (notwithstanding the difference in pace, which in the case of James allows his protagonist a number of preliminary jousts with Juliana before the fatal one), serves to bring *Aspern* particularly close to *The Queen of Spades*. Briggs further notes a number of more minor details which can only strengthen his case: the 'common fascination for eyes', especially those of the two old women, and the posthumous wink of the Countess 'which seems almost to be imitated by Aspern's portrait', and an interplay of viewing of and by the intruder between an upstairs window and the street or garden (p. 55). Plus the following further 'tangential similarities' and 'incidental affinities':

the fear, early on, that the old woman may die at any moment, the contrast between her present ugliness and her exceptional beauty of long ago, the description of her as a witch, her utter domination of her companion and yet her insistence that the bounty-hunter should do the right thing by her (neither of which formed part of the original source material), the huge palace-like house in which the old woman retains a dark impenetrable boudoir, surrounding herself with relics and mementoes, the futile gesture of a raised hand to ward off the intruder. (p. 55)

One further Pushkinian point made by Briggs (pp. 58–9) is to draw a comparison between the inclusion in *Aspern* of the 'one truly irrelevant and dispensable incident', the apparent digression describing the statue of the mounted Colleoni, and a similar passage from Pushkin — this time from the narrative poem *The Bronze Horseman* (though it may also bring to mind the Napoleon references in *The Queen of Spades*); indeed he goes as far as to suggest that the setting might have been moved from Florence (scene of the Silsbee anecdote and of the writing of *Aspern*) to Venice precisely in order to be able to include it. Covering one set of tracks, perhaps, merely exposes another.

Briggs was not, of course, concerned with tracing the fantastic in Pushkin and James. Nevertheless, it is of interest for present purposes that he should remark of *Aspern* that 'there are moments when the reader, especially one who knows *The Queen of Spades*, may doubt the possibility of an ending without a supernatural explanation' (p. 57).

We have already drawn attention above to changes made by James in the second version of the tale which seem to strengthen the presence in the text of a latent supernaturalism, including those in the preface referring to Aspern and to the 'hocus–pocus' obscuring him (James, 1986, p. 35). This can only enhance the structural parallel between Aspern and the mysteries which surround him and Saint-Germain in Pushkin's tale. This kind of imagery already encircles Aspern in the text, as the narrator remarks:

> That spirit kept me perpetual company and seemed to look out at me from the revived immortal face — in which all his genius shone — of the great poet who was my prompter. I had invoked him and he had come; he hovered before me half the time; it was as if his bright ghost had returned to earth to assure me he regarded the affair as his own no less than as mine and that we should see it fraternally and fondly to a conclusion. It was as if he had said: 'Poor dear, be easy with her; she has some natural prejudices; only give her time. Strange as it may appear to you she was very attractive in 1820. Meanwhile, aren't we in Venice together. . . ?' My eccentric private errand became a part of the general romance and the general glory — I felt even a mystic companionship, a moral fraternity with all those who in the past had been in the service of art. (p. 73).

There is surely no need now to emphasise the particular words used here any further. The epithet 'witches' in connection with the

Misses Bordereau is first attributable to Mrs Prest early on in the story ('I daresay they have the reputation of witches', p. 49); the narrator himself refers to Juliana as 'such a subtle old witch' (p. 108) and just 'the old witch' (p. 139) — thus echoing Hermann's 'You old witch!' to the Countess. Similarly, the epithet 'the divine Juliana' (pp. 60 and 92) — of 'some of Aspern's most exquisite and most renowned lyrics' (p. 59) — may be seen as parallelling Pushkin's phrase 'la Vénus moscovite'. Her 'adventurous youth' and its 'passions' (p. 93) seem to follow the example of Pushkin's Countess, while the reference to 'the queer rococo Venice of Goldoni and Casanova' (p. 85) virtually simulates Pushkin's allusions to period figures: Casanova, Montgolfier, Mesmer and others.

There is no card playing in *The Aspern Papers*, but there is a 'false card' (the narrator's visiting card with his counterfeit *nom de guerre*), which is likened to a 'magic token' (p. 54). For that matter, the alleged Mephistophelian quality of Hermann has its counterpart in James's narrator: the scholar who had had the temerity to enquire about Aspern papers had been denounced by Juliana as 'a devil' (p. 100); 'But I hope I shan't pass for a devil', the narrator remarks (p. 101); by his own admission he promptly does, however, when he confides — to Juliana herself — 'I'm a poor devil of a man of letters' (p. 105). Furthermore, he had already performed the role of tempter: 'It was I who had kindled the unholy flame; it was I who had put into her head that she had the means of making money' (p. 104); later, after Juliana's death, he tries his irony on Miss Tina: 'But don't let me stand here as if I had it in my soul to tempt you to anything base' (p. 135).

Before we go any further, what evidence is there that James is likely to have known Pushkin at all? As Briggs has pointed out, *The Aspern Papers* antedates Tchaikovsky's opera *The Queen of Spades*; we are, therefore, talking about the Pushkin story itself and there are at least two highly likely foreign sources for James: his conversations with Turgenev and his probable familiarity with Prosper Mérimée's French translation. Mérimée's *La Dame de pique* was first published in 1849, but had undergone at least five reprintings by the time James came to write *Aspern* (see Henry, 1987).[12] As with more modern editions (e.g. Mérimée, 1927), the work was presented along with its translator's original offerings, such as *Carmen*, with just a prefatory note to reveal its Russian origin. References to Pushkin in the writings of Henry James appear to be extremely rare. There is one to Pushkin as a poet, very much *en passant* in an essay on Flaubert of 1902 (James, 1984b, p. 320). There is, however, another, of much greater interest, in an 1874

review of Mérimée's *Dernières Nouvelles* (1873); this volume did not
include *La Dame de pique*, but James's review concludes with an
admiring comment on 'the extremely energetic little tale called "Le
Coup de Pistolet" [which] is a translation from Pushkin' (p. 565). It
seems highly likely (virtually certain, we might by now think from
textual evidence) that James knew other Pushkin translations by
Mérimée and that anyone who admired Pushkin's *The Shot* and
Turgenev's 'beautiful little story of "visions"' [*Prizraki*] (p. 971), as
well as Mérimée's own fantastic tale *Vénus d'Ille* (p. 564), cannot fail
to have appreciated *The Queen of Spades*.

One would scarcely expect, in all probability, to find much trace
of Mérimée's French text in a Henry James story, influential or
otherwise, and such is in fact the case. Indeed, there are even
instances in which James's text seems closer to Pushkin than to
Mérimée: James's use of the word 'witch' corresponds to that of
Pushkin, whereas Mérimée has the phrase '*maudite vieille*', which he
inappropriately uses twice (Mérimée, 1931, pp. 62, 79). However,
James does appear to display a certain proximity to Mérimée on
occasions. Pushkin's Hermann denounces the Countess, as we have
seen, as an 'old witch', only himself to be denounced by Lizaveta
Ivanovna as 'you monster!' ('*Mais vous êtes un monstre!*', Mérimée,
p. 67). James is content with the one denunciation (Juliana's
memorable 'Ah, you publishing scoundrel!', p. 125); however, in the
next chapter he refers to that whole scene as a 'midnight
monstrosity' (p. 127), which had been a mere 'nocturnal scene' in
the first version (James, 1963, p. 364). The imagining of Juliana as
'some ghastly death's head' behind her green shade (James, 1986,
p. 60) may be reminiscent of '*ce spectre cassé*' (Mérimée, p. 57),
although the angle of vision is different (Pushkin here has 'hunched
old woman'). Aspern's portrait 'seemed to smile at me with mild
mockery' (p. 134), while in Mérimée (p. 71) the dead Countess,
seemingly looking at Hermann, '*le regardait d'un œil moqueur*'. More
striking, perhaps, is James's insertion of the phrase ' "walking"
ghost' [his inverted commas] (p. 92), remarked upon already above,
into the 1907 version; Mérimée also has an ambulatory spectral
phrase applying to the Countess — '*momie ambulante*' (his rather
colourful translation of Pushkin's '*chut' zhivaia*', or 'barely alive',
p. 59). It should also be stated that at least three English translations
of Pushkin's story had been published before 1900, two of which
appeared during the 1890s.[13] James, one is tempted to surmise, may
well have glanced at an English version of *The Queen of Spades*, as
well as rereading his Mérimée, between 1887 and 1907.

Let us now, though, leave the textual detail and return to the structural comparison between the two tales which first caught our attention. There are, of course, major and obvious differences, or reversals, which scarcely need enumeration: the secret of the cards and monetary fortune are transposed, as goal of the hero's quest, into literary remains and scholarly fortune (though prosecuted with equal monomania); the hero and the younger woman in James's story are both perhaps a generation older than in Pushkin's; a St Petersburg winter setting converts to summer in Venice; a seemingly omniscient third-person narrative becomes a first-person confession. There are parallels which are only partial: Juliana, like the Countess, is miserly, but relatively impoverished, and this quality is developed into grasping calculation; unlike the Countess, though, she is a social recluse. Both younger women write letters to rebuff the would-be intruder (though at different stages of the fable) and both are ultimately unsuccessful in this regard. In Pushkin, Hermann apparently receives a ghostly visitation and feels subsequently haunted by the Countess; in James there are at least feelings of haunting: of the narrator by Aspern (noted above), and of Tina by Juliana (p. 134).

However, as mentioned already, the configuration of main characters and the basic plot functions are remarkably similar. Let us take the characters first. Hermann obviously corresponds to the narrator of *Aspern*; Saint-Germain is the counterpart of Aspern (as man of mystery from the past, and as original donor of the desired prize); the two pairs of women complement each other in all but age difference — Lizaveta Ivanovna, the Countess's 'ward', may be an impoverished relation, while Tina's relationship to Juliana (nominally that of 'niece') may be ambiguous (see Kappeler, 1980, p. 218, n. 9). So far the correspondence is extremely close. In pursuing it further, we have to think in terms of plot function rather than character matching. The function of Tomsky in *The Queen of Spades* (as the provider of information which originates the hero's quest) can be seen as shared in *Aspern* between John Cumnor and Mrs Prest. What about Chaplitsky and Chekalinsky? While there are no equivalent characters to these, their functions can be seen as being performed in each case by Tina, though this may require a word of explanation. Chaplitsky, according to one critic at least (Burgin, 1974, p. 50), may be an illegitimate son of the Countess and Saint-Germain; tenuous though this may be, he does receive the secret of the cards. Tina may be the illegitimate daughter of Juliana and Aspern (Kappeler, *loc. cit.*); this may be unprovable but (chronological difference within the fable also notwithstanding) she does see (or 'know') the papers. It could also be argued that Tina fulfils the function of Chekalinsky in the second climax, or final confrontation with the hero, proving or causing his undoing. Tina's role and importance is thus expanded somewhat beyond that of Lizaveta Ivanovna. Subsidiary characters are of minimal importance in each case.

A comparative enumeration of fifteen basic plot actions may illustrate still better the structural closeness of the two works (in order of *siuzhet* or plot presentation; 'Q' = *The Queen of Spades*, 'A' = *The Aspern Papers*):

1. Q.   Tomsky tells anecdote of grandmother's secret.
   A.   Cumnor gives narrator 'definite information as to their [the Misses Bordereau's] possession of the papers' (p. 46).
2. Q.   Countess had intrigued with Saint-Germain sixty years before and received the secret of the three cards.
   A.   Juliana had intrigued with Aspern about sixty years before and received a quantity of papers.
3. Q.   Chaplitsky, who might be the illegitimate son of the Countess and Saint-Germain, is given the secret.
   A.   Tina, who might be the illegitimate daughter of Juliana and Aspern, knows of the papers.
4. Q.   Hermann appears outside the Countess's house.
   A.   Narrator appears outside Juliana's house.
5. Q.   Lizaveta receives and eventually submits to approaches by Hermann.
   A.   Tina receives and apparently submits to approaches by the narrator.
6. Q.   Hermann clumsily tackles the Countess over her secret (his MISTAKE No. 1).
   A.   Narrator is caught by Juliana in clumsy search for papers (his MISTAKE No. 1).
7. Q.   Countess says secret was a 'joke'.
   A.   Juliana has played a protracted joke on the narrator (?).
8. Q.   Countess raises her arm and immediately dies of shock.
   A.   Juliana raises her arm, collapses and subsequently dies from the overexcitement.
9. Q.   Tomsky has told Lizaveta things about Hermann.
   A.   No equivalent (between Cumnor or Mrs Prest and Tina).
10. Q. Priest's officiation at Countess's funeral.
    A. Not a 'whisk of the curato's skirt' (p. 128) at Juliana's, but doctor's officiations.
11. Q. Dead Countess seems to wink at Hermann.

    A.   Aspern's portrait seems to smile at narrator.

12. Q. Countess's ghost appears, imparts secret and instructs Hermann to marry Lizaveta.

    A.   Juliana's will still seems to rule the Aspern papers and to hint at delivery to narrator on condition of marriage to Tina.

13. Q. Idea of winning drives guilt and marriage from Hermann's mind (his MISTAKE No. 2).

    A.   Idea of possessing papers overcomes reluctance towards marriage, but narrator's hesitation and delay are fatal (his MISTAKE No. 2).

14. Q. (Protracted) confrontation with Chekalinsky: narrator loses, turning up queen of spades (seen as Countess).

    A.   Narrator's final interview with Tina: he is too late, receives the Aspern portrait but has lost the Aspern papers.

15. Q. Epilogue: Hermann has gone mad, Lizaveta has found a husband.

    A.   Aftermath: narrator remains sad, Tina has no husband.

While by no means every action of the two stories is represented here, it could certainly not be said that the choice is insignificant or arbitrary.[14]

Discussion of plot functions invariably derives from the theory contained in Propp's *Morphology of the Folktale* (Propp, 1968) and the above attempt at actional tabulation is no exception. The proximity of the plot lines of *The Queen of Spades* to the fairy-tale has been noted by Ann Shukman who gives the following summary of the archetype:

> The classic Russian fairy tale had as its core the story of the hero who is despatched, journeys to another kingdom, acquires a magic object, overcomes the antagonist, wins the princess. . . . A standard theme of the fairytales . . . is that the hero, to achieve his aim, must receive from the donor the magic object. The donor, a distinct functionary in Propp's list, is an ambivalent figure who may assist or not, who imposes certain conditions, or tests, on the hero. (Shukman, 1977, pp. 76–7)

Hermann's overall mistake, in terms of the classic fairy-tale, is that instead of striving to win fortune and bride, he misuses the latter in his single-minded attempt to gain the former; Shukman also points out that such a reading of the story is 'to assume the actual involvement of the spirit of the dead Countess' (p. 77) — 'an unambiguous interpretation' which, strictly speaking, neither she nor we would wish to admit.

The using of 'love' to gain riches, while 'a reversal of the folktale stereotype', of course, was to become 'one of the leading subjects of nineteenth-century literature' (*ibid.*), including the work of Henry James.

The Aspern Papers has also received Proppian and other folkloric attentions in a stimulating reading by Susanne Kappeler, in the course of which she demonstrates the correspondence between *Aspern* and the structure and laws (taken from the theory of Alex Olrik) of the folktale, while holding that '*The Aspern Papers* is an exception for exhibiting them, and examples of fictions which fail to conform to them are the rule' (Kappeler, 1980, p. 13). The one major difference between the stories under consideration and the fairy-, or folk-, tale resides in the fact that the latter 'presumes a one-to-one relationship between the narrative and the fictional world it creates' (p. 7), and is, therefore, devoid of doubt and totally 'unselfconscious'.

Just as Olrik's main laws of folk literature, the 'law of three' and 'two to a scene', apply closely to *Aspern* (pp. 14–21), so they do to *The Queen of Spades*. This means that groups of three characters dominate the action at any given time. *Aspern* commences with a trio comprising the narrator, Mrs Prest and the Misses Bordereau (thus far lumped together undifferentiated), with Mrs Prest assuming the function of mediator between two opposing forces. An earlier trio chronologically would have had John Cumnor as the mediator between the same 'opponents'. This gives way later to a combination of the narrator, Miss Tina (the Misses Bordereau by now having been differentiated, with Tina becoming mediator) and Juliana. After Juliana's death, Tina, who has separated from her erstwhile 'twin' (the 'law of twins') manoeuvers into a position of antagonist, the mediating posture being adopted by the papers themselves (according to Olrik, 'magic objects' may assume the role of agents, p. 16). Behind the papers, for that matter, stand the chronological residuants of a further trio: Juliana and Aspern, Tina's function has split again, as she now stands opposed to the narrator in two capacities: that of guardian of the papers (if the narrator chooses to deal with her in that role, he will lose all), plus that of potential bride (approaching her in that function he would win all).

In *The Queen of Spades* an application of the 'law of three' yields an almost identical result. We open with three figures of significance: Hermann, Tomsky (as mediator) and the Countess. In the pre-history of the action, we could even find two additional trios: the Countess, Saint-Germain (mediator) and the Duke of Orleans; Chaplitsky, the Countess (mediator) and Zorich. We soon find ourselves with Hermann, Lizaveta Ivanovna (mediator) and the Countess. After the death of the last named, we have a rather different composition: Hermann, the card and Chekalinsky, but behind the cards stand the Countess and Saint-Germain. Once again there is a split choice offered: Hermann can concentrate solely on the three cards and fortune (and lose all), or he can take Lizaveta for bride plus the cards for fortune (and thereby win both).

The law of 'two to a scene' requires that key scenes should be between two agents only (even if a third may be insignificantly present on occasion — as when Tina's presence at interviews between the narrator and Juliana is of little apparent consequence). That the main dramatic scenes in both stories feature two key actors, or two only of consequence, needs at this stage no further illustration. The folkloric quality of the numerals two and three is, of course, particularly apt to a consideration of Pushkin's tale.

Such close resemblances do not, of course, mean that there are no structural divergences. The topographical and metaphorical device of the garden (of which Susanne Kappeler makes much) has, as far as I can see, no counterpart in Pushkin's story. The transposition of point of view has far-reaching implications (imagine *The Queen of Spades* retold by Hermann). Hermann's intentions are presented as naked self-interest from the outset; James's narrator alleges noble intentions, though these mask a similar motive of self-aggrandisement. Pushkin's impersonal [author-]narrator gives us the tale (ambiguities notwithstanding) relatively straight; James's narrator, on the other hand, 'has a vested interest [of confessional self-justification] in presenting his story in the true form of a folktale' (Kappeler, p. 22). Pushkin, as implied author, and Pushkin's narrator may be said to be at least relatively identical; James, as implied author, and his narrator are certainly not (although 'their two texts are absolutely identical', p. 24). There is, therefore, little or no 'space' between author and narrator in the case of Pushkin; in that of James, however, there is a wide 'space of irony' in view of the 'verbatim quotation of the narrator's account' (*ibid.*). In Pushkin's story, then, what is presented is 'truth', incomplete or hermeneutically contentious though it may be; in the case of James, the narrator's 'truth' is 'a mere point of view' (p. 53).

However, it is the parallels and balances between the two works which seem to be almost endless. The Countess seems to make a posthumous attempt to pass off Lizaveta Ivanovna in marriage; Juliana seems to be attempting in life (and by posthumous influence) to pass off her niece in marriage. Hermann represents Germanic values of thrift, which he proceeds to betray; James's narrator seems to stand for American chauvinism (Kappeler, p. 26), and betrays, if not that, at least the standards of his purportedly artistic and scholarly calling. Despite what we have called above the unilinear nature of the two plots, there are, in a certain sense, hidden subsidiary plots; those of the designs of other characters. There is, therefore, 'the plot of the Misses Bordereau' (p. 43) — that of an intended bargain over marriage and the papers; this is balanced by a similar plot of the dead Countess — a bargain is offered over marriage and the secret of the cards. In both cases, by the narrator (in 'reality' and in his narrative) and by Hermann, this subsidiary plot is missed or ignored — to their loss. *The Queen of Spades* also has a further subsidiary plot line: that of the aspirations of Lizaveta Ivanovna (noted by Shukman, pp. 69–70), also ignored by Hermann. The documents in *Aspern* are the folkloric equivalent of the beautiful princess (the prize, or 'spoil') and Tina is used both as the narrator's cover in his quest, and then as the means to obtain them (pp. 57–8); the secret of the cards and Lizaveta are used by Pushkin in an identical manner.

This brings us to the question of sexuality in the two works. An intensity akin to sexual desire accompanies the pursuit of both card secret and papers. In the case of James, the sexual desire seems to find a surrogate in the identification with Aspern (James, 1986, pp. 59, 73); the narrator's mimicry of Aspern has its parallel in the mimicry by Hermann of the Countess's lover of yore, as he leaves her house by the back stairway. Sexuality in *The Queen of Spades* has been noted, mainly for its voyeuristic qualities (Debreczeny, p. 233; A. Briggs, 1983, pp. 221–2) and in a sense is the more overt, due to the greater contrast between the two women in Pushkin's version. Hermann, the self-seeking parvenu ('upwardly mobile' in modern parlance); is engaged in an attempted penetration of society in all senses (though less, even abnormally so, in the obvious sexual sense): his upward infiltration from street to Countess's boudoir is a demonstration of this. We have already remarked on the repressed sexuality underlying *Aspern*, and Kappeler (p. 61) finds the narrator's 'narrative discourse adorned by metaphoric sexual language'. The pattern of infiltration, penetration into an inner sanctum and ambivalent sexuality is broadly the same in each; it only remains to point out that James ultimately emphasises this perhaps even more strongly, in that the final hiding place of the Aspern papers turns out to be within Juliana's death bed (James, 1986, p. 132).

The most striking common feature of the two works, however, centres on the use of double peripeteia. Hermann's two peripeteias, it has been noted, 'are like mirror images of each other' (Shukman, p. 70): the visit of Hermann to the Countess and the reverse posthumous visit of the Countess to Hermann. In the case of *Aspern*, the narrator's first peripeteia, his impetuous search of Juliana's apartment, is matched, less symmetrically, by his interview with the new owner of the papers, Tina (which in itself serves to surprise him: 'I was grateful to her for not treating me as if I had killed her aunt', p. 129). There is associated with all four instances an accompanying or an ensuing loss of control on the part of the hero, with catastrophic consequences. Indeed we can borrow an expression from catastrophe theory and speak here of the hero's disastrous loss of head as 'behaviour on the cusp', leading to sudden catastrophic leaps into discontinuity.[15]

In conclusion, we may note Martha Banta's statement that 'James liked to work within existing literary traditions, while expanding possibilities only hinted at by earlier writers or while discovering in them entirely new imaginative strengths' (Banta, 1972, p. 157). It was this kind of development that James brought to his 'performance' (see Kappeler, p. 4) of an essential archetypal folkloric plot: one which Pushkin had 'performed' half a century earlier. Among the tracks which James attempted to cover at various levels (see Preface, p. 33; and Kappeler, p. 57, on the narrator's attempts) were those which led back to *The Queen of Spades*. Banta writes of James (pp. 135–6): 'He carefully poured newly attained psychological insights into the receptacles of the early romancers, gothicizers, and tellers of fireside tales'. In so doing, in using *The Queen of Spades* as a highly suitable receptacle, James removed the overt elements of magic and the supernatural but permeated his resulting performance, as we have seen, with vestigial fantastic imagery, thus providing an excellent exemplar for Iurii Mann's categories of the 'veiled' and 'non-fantastic' fantastic.

Perhaps it now makes sense that James should have placed *The Aspern Papers* alongside his tale of the pure fantastic — *The Turn of the Screw* — in the New York edition. His decision to do so of itself presents us with the one track he did not cover.

4 *The Twentieth Century*

Fantastic literature deals with what can be best described as the impossible seeping into the possible, what Wallace Stevens calls 'black water breaking into reality'.

A. Manguel (1983, p. xvii)

ARE GENRES HISTORICALLY TIED?

At this point we pick up again, albeit briefly, our discussion of genre in Part One. Attitudes to genre have tended to fluctuate in recent years. Alastair Fowler (1974, p. 81) remains a staunch proponent of the concept: 'Some regard all genres as absolute. They imagine them as sets of old rules, irrelevant to Post-Romantic literature. But all literature may in fact be genre-bound, without this being consciously realized.' Paul Hernadi, in his study *Beyond Genre* (1972, p. 184), sees genre rather as a means to an end: 'the finest generic classifications of our time make us look beyond their immediate concern and focus on the *order of literature*, not on *borders between literary genres*'. Northrop Frye, in his essay 'Charms and riddles' (1976b, p. 123), hits at Hernadi's haste: 'Despite a book called *Beyond Genre*, we have not got to the subject yet, much less beyond it: we do not even know where the conception stops.'

Our own approach to genre in this study has been rather dialectical and dynamic (similar to that of Winner, 1978), which would suggest agreement with Lem's comment (1985, p. 123) that 'the evolution of literary genres is based precisely on violation of storytelling conventions which have already become static.' Our approach has also led us to seek out the procedure which Jameson terms (1975, p. 155) 'a systematic construction of that imaginary entity designated as intertextuality [which] is at work in all genre criticism'. Furthermore, it is worth noting Lem's sobering reminder (1985, p. 228) that the genre of a text depends also on the sophistication of its reader, with variations possible from 'primitive oaf' to 'experienced connoisseur'.

A frequent objection made to Todorov's model, and particularly to the category of pure fantastic (PF) itself, stems from the narrowness of the period from which examples are drawn. This has been raised by Lem and to an extent this doubt is shared by Brooke-Rose (p. 67), particularly over Todorov's treatment of Kafka, in relation to whom 'his theory no longer holds, and is bound therefore to apply only to the nineteenth-century texts examined, a particular genre with a short life (for the social and historical reasons he gives)'. The literature of the fantastic is 'nothing more than the uneasy conscience of the positivist nineteenth century' (Todorov, 1973, p. 169). Jackson (1981, pp. 25–6) considers that 'Fantastic tales proliferate during the nineteenth century as an opposite version of realistic narrative. . . . [The literature of the fantastic] is all that is not said, all that is unsayable, through realistic forms' and consequently is normally 'conceptualized only by negative terms . . . the im-possible, the un-real, the nameless', etc.

Todorov apart, obviously Siebers (1984), by the very scope and intentions of his book, and Mann (1978), of those critics here discussed, seem keen to root, or even confine, the fantastic within a limited historical (nineteenth-century) genre. Hutcheon, for one, though, seeks to warn against the consequences, for new fiction and criticism, of 'that transfer of a period description to a genre definition which threatens to distort the entire history of the novel as a mimetic form' (1984, p. 43).

Leaving aside the possibility (even the certainty) of finding twentieth-century examples to add to the list of PF works (not to mention the richer pastures of fantastic uncanny and fantastic marvellous), the 'historically limited' critique does appear to have some foundation. Examples of just about any genre, sub-genre or category can no doubt be found from within twentieth-century literature. Nevertheless, there does seem to be an increasing trend in this century, at least in 'serious' or avant-garde literature (as opposed to conventional popular counterparts), towards a break-down of genres.

Robert Scholes, in his book *Structural Fabulation* (1975, p. 1), expresses this development with panache:

Once we knew that fiction was about life and criticism was about fiction — and everything was simple. Now we know that fiction is about other fiction, is criticism in fact, or metafiction. And we know that criticism is about the impossibility of anything being about life, really, or even about fiction or, finally about anything.

In her *The Unresolved Plot*, Elizabeth Dipple (1988, p. 79) cites the case of Nabokov: 'In *Lolita*, Nabokov telescopes genres so that elements of poetic tradition coexist with the idea of the novel as romance and, even more pertinently, as detective fiction.' Hutcheon (1988, p. 9) echoes this while anticipating our own preoccupations below:

> The borders between literary genres have become fluid: who can tell anymore what the limits are between the novel and the short story collection (Alice Munro's *Lives of Girls and Women*), the novel and the long poem (Michael Ondaatje's *Coming Through Slaughter*), the novel and autobiography (Maxine Hong Kingston's *China Men*), the novel and history (Salman Rushdie's *Shame*), the novel and biography (John Banville's *Kepler*)? But in any of these examples, the conventions of the two genres are played off against each other; there is no simple, unproblematic merging.

For Dipple, indeed (p. 129), 'all sense of definition as imposed by the nineteenth century was lost long ago in the rising mists of Modernism'.

Probably any literary form has contained, and will contain, 'within itself the contesting seeds of its own transcendence' (Hutcheon, 1984, p. 38). New forms, a new synthesis, may always · be expected and this is the process which we have been endeavouring to trace throughout this study:

> Modern literature is in its way a literature of quest, a literature which first strikes the reader as being in search for its proper form rather than already possessed of that form. This quality gives it the appearance of being transitional. . .
> (Hume, p. 43)

Or, in the words of Calvino (1987, p. 61):

> Literature is a search for the book hidden in the distance that alters the value and meaning of the known books; it is the pull toward the new apocryphal text still to be rediscovered or invented.

The transition towards the present ever-transitional situation, under the influences of Symbolism and modernism, was itself marked by a mixing of the genres — as the romantic period had been very much an era of the mixing of styles. Rather than follow Todorov's explanation of the themes of the fantastic being largely taken over by psychoanalysis, it may be preferable, therefore, to see the historical prevalence of PF in particular rather as succumbing to, but at the same time having a continued existence within, the twentieth-century trend towards genre mixing and genre break-down.

It is now frequently pointed out that modern theoretical definitions of discourse developed by such as Sartre, Heidegger, de Man and Derrida were already to be found in the work of certain theorists of romanticism (e.g. by Rajan, in his *Dark Interpreter*, p. 19), operating 'in a universe already recognised as discontinuous rather than organic' (p. 15). Similarly, Eve Sedgwick (1986, p. 49) is able to write of reading De Quincey as though he were Borges.

The 'romantic fantastic', or the mainly nineteenth-century fantastic ('that of the Gothic novel and its brief aftermath' — Brooke-Rose, p. 62), though, assumes a particular importance in this process. If the roots of modernism and even post-modernism (for discussions of which, see Brooke-Rose, especially pp. 343–63; McHale, 1987; and Hutcheon, 1988) lie, as is now increasingly apparent, in romanticism, then the roots of contemporary meta-fiction and its allied forms (on which, see Brooke-Rose, pp. 364–89, Hutcheon, 1984, and Waugh, 1984) are to be found in the romantic fantastic. The fantastic and its themes seem to be clear antecedents of both metafiction, at least of certain kinds, and the trend towards literary games (see Hutcheon, 1984, pp. 82–5 and *passim.*, and Hutchinson, 1983), absurdism (Hume, pp. 91–101) and nonsense (Hutchinson, pp. 84–6). At the same time as it becomes more difficult to distinguish between fictional and nonfictional forms (the fictionality of nonfiction being increasingly recognised), so it becomes harder to distinguish between literature and other modern forms of art and popular culture. Thus from the fantastic — though also from other starting points on our linear scale of Part One — we arrive at metafiction and other contemporary trans-generic literary forms: fictional and metafictional trans-genres which dissolve, in their turn, into the multifarious realms of modern culture — from feature film, dramatised documentary, videos, advertisements and cartoons — of all recognisable genres and of none.

Nevertheless, we may return briefly to the twin basic impulses of fantasy and mimesis proposed by Hume. Regardless of, or in addition to, the posited categories of genres and sub-genres above, we may now wish to accept a basic duality, at least of stress, in prose fiction between:

Prose which primarily attempts to create, describe or operate within, a world transformed, distorted or re-created; a world which departs to a greater or lesser degree from the 'normally' perceived 'real' or historical world in which we live.

AND

Prose which primarily attempts to create, describe or to operate within, the 'real' world as 'normally' perceived (albeit usually — though not exclusively — by a narrator of above-average perception).

Such an opposition between fantasy and mimesis and between imagination and 'reality' may be set alongside, then, a series of oppositions, the relationship of which to each other, and to an interconnected cultural whole, remains to be pondered: fiction and nonfiction; the historical novel and history; memoirs/autobiography and biography; philosophy and science. Furthermore, in a final series of oppositions, there arises the relation of each and all of these latter categories to what we call reality itself. Such oppositions are of course currently being comprehensively deliberated by theorists, practitioners and critics of postmodernism (as discussed by Hutcheon, 1988).

TOWARDS THE PORTMANTEAU

In the twentieth century the literary process which gave rise to what we have called the literary fantastic may be expected to display both continuity and development. Elements of continuity may be anticipated in both genre and style, while the rise of modernism will lead to dynamic evolution turning, some would argue, in the postmodern phase at least, to breakdown and chaos, marked by extremes of minimalism on the one hand and what Henry James (1987b, p. 515) termed 'large, loose baggy monsters' on the other: Kharms, Beckett and Coover; Joyce, Pynchon and Rushdie. Form has been demonstrated to exist, however, even in *Finnegans Wake*, although wordplay and fantasy may seem to dominate.

It will be the thesis of the remainder of this study that the 'dominant', to take up a term used by Roman Jakobson in an article of 1935 (see Jakobson, 1987, pp. 41–6) and revived by Brian McHale in his study *Postmodernist Fiction* (1987, pp. 6–11), has passed steadily from the old certainties of realism to the fragmented and ambiguous challenge posed by the literary fantastic. Definable as 'the focusing point of a work of art' (Jakobson, 1987, p. 41), the term dominant was originally used by the Russian Formalists in relation to verse analysis but is acknowledged by Jakobson to have wider literary and cultural applicability. McHale sees the epistemological dominant of modernism (centered on the problem of knowledge, for example of the past) giving way to the ontological dominant of postmodernism (centered on the problem of being, the nature of our existence); this shift gives rise to the kind of 'ontological flicker' (McHale, p. 32, the hint of a meeting of two worlds) that characterises what he calls 'the postmodernist fantastic' (p. 179). We have already noted similar views of recent literary evolution, or of this shift of the dominant, in our Part One survey (e.g. Brooke-Rose, 1983; Parrinder, 1987).

As with the nineteenth century, the fantastic may be said to impinge at least upon most of the major writers of the first half of this century: Joyce, Bely, Mann, Hesse, Gide, Kafka and Musil for example. The fantastic assumed the position of dominant, as previously, only in what are generally considered to be minor works and genres: the ghost story, high fantasy, horror, science fiction. The fantastic, in one form or another, achieved, or was promoted to, dominance in just certain works of what now looks to us to be the mainstream of modernism: Kafka's *Metamorphosis*, *The Trial* and *The Castle* (by means of what Kundera, 1988, p. 113 identifies as the 'bureaucratic fantastic'), Hesse's *Steppenwolf*. As the century has progressed, it will be argued below, the fantastic has itself become the dominant in the modern novel.

This seems clearly to be the case in North America, Latin America, the British Isles, Western and Central Europe (even the German Democratic Republic can boast the more recent works of Christa Wolf). In Russia, where through historical circumstances a realist dominant continued to be artificially imposed, the tradition running from Pushkin, Gogol and Dostoevsky, through the Symbolist movement to Bely, managed to maintain itself in the work of Zamiatin and Bulgakov, to be picked up later by Siniavsky, and passed on to the Strugatsky brothers and Aksënov. However, we shall return to the contemporary scene in due course.

Returning to the beginning of the century, we find a number of areas into which strands of the literary fantastic were permeating through from the tradition traced here from the eighteenth and nineteenth centuries. By this stage, the kind of cross-fertilisation which we observed earlier had led to both synthetic and more specialised development. The synthetic effects were tending to be felt in the mainstream of prose fiction (from Henry James, and occasionally Conrad or even Hardy, on). The specialised reaction, and the real continuity, was confined still to the minor genres.

Julia Briggs, in her study *Night Visitors* (1977, p. 22) comes close to sharing the view taken by Todorov of the development of the fantastic into the twentieth century when she writes: '. . . the late nineteenth-century ghost story anticipated the advent of Freud, whose psycho-therapy aimed at reducing the night side to manageable proportions, and breaking up the potentially destructive doubleness of Victorian man.' Continuity there was, as the ghost story moved into the twentieth century: Henry James's tale *The Jolly Corner* (1908) is a complex and somewhat intense example, which even retains the motif of the mutilated hand. The ghost story, as a form in its own right, flourished in the tales of M. R. James (a great afficionado of Le Fanu) and Walter de la Mare and continued, at least on an occasional basis, thereafter.

We have alluded in Part One to the tradition of 'high fantasy'. Touching on the 'nonsense' of Edward Lear and Lewis Carroll, it matured in the allegory of Kingsley and George MacDonald (see Manlove, 1975; Prickett, 1979). In the twentieth century, this line has followed through to embrace religious allegory (C. S. Lewis), sword and sorcery (T. H. White and his modern successors), fantasy of the mind (Mervyn Peake), faery (Tolkien), animal stories (Richard Adams) and a whole spectrum of children's literature (see Manlove, 1983; Swinfen, 1984). This tradition can also extend on occasion to faery erotica: for example, Seamus Cullen's *Astra and Flondrix* (1976).

Stemming perhaps from both the high fantasy and ghost story sub-genres, but with more than a touch of Poe, is the branch of the fantastic which is usually termed 'horror'. Turn-of-the-century exemplars of this mode of fiction include Arthur Machen and William Hope Hodgson. We have already had cause to mention Hodgson as the creator of the psychic sleuth of the eponymous *Carnacki the Ghost-Finder* (1913), a kind of paranormal counterpart to Conan Doyle's Holmes. Carnacki utilises a combination of pseudo-scientific technology (his 'Electric Pentacle') and occult mumbo-jumbo (the 'Sigsand MS.' and the 'Saaamaaa ritual') to combat the 'Outer Monstrosities', which may manifest themselves as half-materialised hand or as gigantic hog. Such 'emanations' from the

'Outer Circle' purport to substantialise from gas layers left over from the formation of the earth and are somehow in psychic tune with and 'malignant towards all that we consider most desirable' (Hodgson, 1974, p. 239). This presumably tongue-in-cheek hocum (it is hard to know how serious Hodgson is; his stories seem laced with a wry humour, but he certainly has a terrified obsession with pigs!) is closely related to the undoubtedly in earnest compositions of H. P. Lovecraft and his successors in modern horror, such as Dennis Wheatley. Lovecraft penned the following recipe for the weird tale:

> A certain atmosphere of breathless and unexplainable dread of outer, unknown forces must be present; and there must be a hint, expressed with a seriousness and portentousness becoming its subject, of that most terrible conception of the human brain — a malign and particular suspension or defeat of those fixed laws of Nature which are our only safeguard against the assaults of chaos and the daemons of unplumbed space. (Lovecraft, 1973, p. 15; quoted from Chanady, 1985, p. 142)

Hodgson also occupies a surprisingly central place in a line of disembodied transcendental space flight and potted planetary history, by virtue of his novel *The House on the Borderland* (1908). This line would seem to extend from Dostoevsky's *The Dream of a Ridiculous Man* via Hodgson to Olaf Stapledon's unsurpassed and unsurpassable SF classic, *Star Maker* (1937). Stapledon, a philosophy lecturer, appears to reveal his debt to Dostoevsky (though this time to *The Notes from Underground*) by his remark that the Star Maker 'could not, for instance, make twice two equal five' (Stapledon, 1988, p. 234). It is no accident that his conception of the Star Maker marks a return to the romanticism of Schelling: 'the eternally achieved perfection of the absolute spirit' (p. 224). This creator's powers and whims seem sufficient to shape enough SF worlds to last for the rest of the century:

> In his maturity the Star Maker conceived many strange forms of time. For instance, some of the later creations were designed with two or more temporal dimensions, and the lives of the creatures were temporal sequences in one or other dimension of the temporal 'area' or 'volume'. These beings experienced their cosmos in a very odd manner. Living for a brief period along one dimension, each perceived at every

moment of its life a simultaneous vista which, though of course fragmentary and obscure, was actually a view of a whole unique 'transverse' cosmical evolution in the other dimension. In some cases a creature had an active life in every temporal dimension of the cosmos. The divine skill which arranged the whole temporal 'volume' in such a manner that all the infinite spontaneous acts of all the creatures should fit together to produce a coherent system of transverse evolutions far surpassed even the ingenuity of the earlier experiment in 'pre-established harmony'. (ibid., p. 251)

This passage and the successively sketched cosmological permutations form not only a gamut of possibilities for science fictional worlds; on a more localised earth-bound level Stapledon's texts almost read like programmatic statements for postmodernist fiction.

A more orthodox brand of SF descended, of course, by way of the novels of Jules Verne and H. G. Wells, intersecting again in Stapledon and passing down to the more serious modern practitioners: Lem, the Strugatskys, Ursula Le Guin, Ian Watson and others. While it is not part of the present book to undertake a study of SF as such, as has already been pointed out, this form of literature shares some of its origins with, and remains one of the tangential bedfellows of, what is here being treated as the fantastic. In particular, earth-based SF, set in the present or the near future, with perhaps one or two main transformations from recognisable 'reality', can provide close approaches to our tradition of the fantastic (it is not accidental that the Russian term for SF means 'scientific fantastic'). Mention must be made of the dystopian novels of Zamiatin, Huxley and Orwell. More interesting examples for us, though, are to be found among the novels of the Strugatsky brothers (we have already alluded to *Roadside Picnic; Definitely Maybe* is another);[1] the time-warped rewriting of history in Watson's *Chekhov's Journey* (1983) provides another, as does the reworking of reality by dream in Le Guin's *The Lathe of Heaven* (1971).

Le Guin's novel is set in Portland, Oregon in the fairly near future (about thirty years on from the time of writing) and is a recognisable projection of the world from a late sixties standpoint: climate has evolved through the greenhouse effect, there is a permissive drug and sex culture, the private car market has collapsed. The one major transformation from supposed reality/ normality is the capacity of the protagonist, George Orr, to dream successively into 'reality' (presumably from an infinite series of alternatives with which he is subconsciously in tune) other circumstances or world histories, which nevertheless remain basically recognisable and continuous in terms of time and place of setting, main characters and, indeed, of president of the United States: in one variant, overpopulation has gone away due to plague ten years before; there has never been a racial problem as all people are grey; George's black lawyer, Heather Lelache, is demoted to secretary and George's (grey) wife. The dreams, however, have been directed by George's increasingly megalomaniac psychiatrist, Dr Haber, who eventually takes over the dream process himself with utterly chaotic consequences. George is the only person who may be able to traverse and transcend these fragmenting and discontinuous realities to switch off Haber's elaborately programmed dream machine; he and Heather find themselves ascending an erupting Mount Hood while the buildings of Portland dissolve:

> The presentiment which had seized Heather, as she looked down from the jade sky was now a presence. It was there. It was an area, or perhaps a time-period, of a sort of emptiness. It was the presence of absence: an unquantifiable entity without qualities, into which all things fell and from which nothing came forth. It was horrible, and it was nothing. It was the wrong way.
>
> Into this, as the funicular car stopped at its terminus, George went. He looked back at her as he went, crying out, 'Wait for me, Heather! Don't follow me, don't come!'
>
> But though she tried to obey him, it came to her. It was growing out from the center rapidly. She found that all things were gone and that she was lost in the panic dark, crying out her husband's name with no voice, desolate, until she sank down in a ball curled about the center of her own being, and fell forever through the dry abyss. (Le Guin, 1974, p. 147)

We can see here an amalgam of Hodgson's pit (in *The House on the Borderland* and his Carnacki story *The Hog*) and a merging of the dimensions plotted by Stapledon, not to mention the new theory (at the time of Le Guin's writing) of black holes.

An intellectualised, metaphysical alternative world of Tlön is posited by Borges, in his celebrated story *Tlön, Uqbar, Orbis Tertius*. Hidden encyclopedias and secret books, compiled by a secret society of scholars, have amassed over centuries exhaustive expositions of this idealised realm or planet until, when the time is ripe, the ideology and thought systems of Tlön strike. The result of this total mental invasion, as Dipple (1988, p. 57) has noted, 'is put in fantastic terms in this tale of takeover':

> Almost immediately reality yielded on more than one account. The truth is that it longed to yield. Ten years ago any symmetry with a semblance of order — dialectical materialism, anti-Semitism, Nazism — was sufficient to entrance the minds of men. How could one do other than submit to Tlön, to the minute, and vast evidence of an orderly planet? . . .
> The contact and the habit of Tlön have disintegrated this world. Enchanted by its rigour, humanity forgets over and again that it is a rigour of chess masters, not of angels.
> (Borges, 1970, p. 42)

The abstract intellectual conquest plotted by Borges perhaps comes somewhere between the multi-dimensional worlds posited by SF and the more tentative worlds which attempt to protrude in works of the pure fantastic (PF). Comparison may be made too with the Terra/Anti-Terra juxtaposition in Nabokov's *Ada*.

But what has become of PF in the twentieth century? Can it still be said to survive as such? We mentioned earlier one or two minor works from the beginning of the century: certain works by W. W. Jacobs, Henry James and some further tales in the ghost story tradition are likely to qualify. We can also, however, point to more substantial examples from the recent, or contemporary, period to show that this form is alive and well and seems likely to remain so. Given the predilection for ambiguity and discontinuity, and McHale's 'ontological flicker', it should cause no great surprise that examples may be located among the works of such writers of the postmodern period as Thomas Pynchon or Doris Lessing; as we shall see later, contemporary use of the form is also made by Toni Morrison, who will no doubt soon have her own imitators.

Written in a black humorous style, full of faintly ludicrous names (such as Genghis Cohen and Mike Fallopian), Pynchon's *The Crying of Lot 49* (1966) confronts its heroine, Oedipa Maas, with increasing evidence for the existence, centuries old and still very much flourishing, of a clandestine and conspiratorial shadow (perhaps even occult) communications network ('Tristero/Trystero' and 'WASTE'). Many of the clues stem from a performance of 'The Courier's Tragedy', a supposed revenge tragedy by one Richard Wharfinger, which is outlined in great detail, so that there is considerable dependence on a spoof text which may, or may not, be a 'spoof' within the terms of the fictional world. There is a hint of 'intrusions into this world from another, a kiss of cosmic pool balls' (Pynchon, 1979, p. 86). Ultimately the possibilities appear to lie between hidden history on a wide (possibly otherworldly) scale, a gigantic hoax (perpetrated by Oedipa's benefactor, the deceased Pierce Inverarity), or a raging case of paranoia. Various interpretations have been suggested (see Tanner, 1982), but the third-person narration, largely by means of indirect free discourse, leads to no resolution, leaving the novel at the end within the realm of the pure fantastic.[2]

Brian McHale (1987, pp. 74–5), notwithstanding a propensity for absolutism in his treatment of the classification of modern/ postmodern, epistemological/ontological, justifies his claim of 'affinity between postmodernist fiction and the fantastic genre' by seeing the postmodern fantastic still as 'a zone of hesitation, a frontier — not, however, a frontier between the uncanny and the marvellous, but between this world and the world next door'. This is a particularly appropriate formulation to bring to bear on Doris Lessing's novel *The Memoirs of a Survivor*, first published 1974. This is a novel which does, within its own pages, quickly shift in the manner of McHale's pattern (though Lessing is an author not mentioned in his book), from an emphasis on time, memory and identity to a stress on interfacing worlds and the nature of being.

Lessing's narrator is a woman living in a London flat in conditions of some kind of impending or actual catastrophe: people are leaving, gangs are forming, services have broken down. She soon becomes aware of something abnormal beyond her living-room wall, where there should be just a communal corridor:

> Yet there did come that moment when I had to admit that there was a room behind that wall, perhaps more than one, even a set of rooms, occupying the same space as, or rather overlapping with, the corridor. The realization of what I was hearing, the knowledge that I had been aware of something of the kind for a long time, became strong in me, at the time that I knew I would almost certainly have to leave this city. (Lessing, 1976, p. 11)

Beyond the wall seems to lie another dimension, visions of which appear to come and go independently, as do visitations behind the wall into the other, seemingly idyllic, space–time, which may have mysterious connections with the narrator's normal reality. The narrator gathers around her what Parrinder (1987, p. 142) chooses to call a 'karass' (borrowing the term from Kurt Vonnegut's *Cat's Cradle*) of like-minded or suitable comrades (her ward, Emily; Emily's lover, Gerald; and their gang of children), with whom she is eventually led by a female from the beyond: walking 'behind that One who went ahead showing them the way out of this collapsed little world into another order of world altogether' (Lessing, p. 190).

The deliverance (if such it be) may or may not be in some sense religious (the capital 'o' of 'One' may be a positive signifier). As Parrinder comments (1987, p. 155): '*The Memoirs* is a deliberate romance, and it is essential to its quality that the questions "by whom? when? where?" are not answered. Indeed they cannot seriously be asked.' This also goes for the provenance of the narrative. The novel appears to remain within the confines of PF at least until the very end and even beyond that the basis and nature of the (first-person) narrative may be questioned: could it all be, after all, merely distraught ramblings? Taken at face value, *The Memoirs of a Survivor* provides an interesting example of the use of a series of 'worlds' in the modern novel. In terms of the fiction, world '1' would be the narrator's current restricted world (her flat); adjacent to this in time, we could posit world '1 minus 1' (the narrator's previous world, that of before the crisis, of which she retains a certain memory); adjacent in space would be 'world 1 plus 1' (the pavement and beyond, from which other characters pass to and fro, bringing her snippets of knowledge); qualitatively apart from these worlds in space–time, apparently, is 'world 2' (the world through the wall, characterised by chronological and perspectival instability).[3] The end seems to bring about a merging of these worlds, or at least a transition from one to the other, in the best spirit of the ontological dominant.

Discussion in this section has mainly taken the form of an assemblage of fictional categories or sub-genres, ingredients perhaps for the melting-pot of what is envisaged in our section title as the 'portmanteau' of the modern/postmodern and contemporary novel — or at least a certain key sector thereof. Before we go on to any further discussion or clarification of terms, there are a couple more leavening agents to be thrown in.

Some mention should now be made of the intertextual. We shall deal more fully with 'intertextuality' shortly, but for the moment let us briefly note a phenomenon which may best be termed 'intertextual [or perhaps just "textual"] dependency'. There exists a relatively small body of texts in which the intertextual quality goes beyond any normal influence, borrowing, allusion or subtext; in such texts the extent of dependency on a particular pre-text for any *raison d'être* is all but total. We have already encountered a few nineteenth-century texts of which this may be said: Verne's *The Mysterious Island* has a close relationship with Defoe's *Robinson Crusoe*; Le Fanu's *Borrhomeo the Astrologer* owes a more than considerable debt to Manzoni; even stronger is the dependency of Balzac's *Melmoth réconcilié* on Maturin's novel. This kind of 'intertextual fantastic', the dependency of one fictional world on another (created by a previous author) extends also into the twentieth century and frequently involves Gothic or near-fantastic texts. Examples include *Wide Sargasso Sea* (1966), Jean Rhys's novel of the first Mrs Rochester, the supposedly mad wife in Charlotte Brontë's *Jane Eyre*; Sue Roe's *Estella. Her Expectations* (1983), a feminist reworking based on *Great Expectations*; and *Frankenstein Unbound* (1973) by Brian Aldiss, in which an American from the year 2020, slides back by 'timeslip' to the Switzerland of 1816, where he contrives to seduce Mary Shelley, to meet her poetic–fantastic entourage at the Villa Diodati and, in an inexplicable crossing of fictional and historical worlds (and an extra couple of decades), to confront Frankenstein and his monster.

Other modes which come close to the fantastic are the absurd and surrealism. The absurd may be defined as a form in which 'an event can unexpectedly occur that contradicts the rest of the narrative' (Chanady, 1985, p. 30) — or indeed a series of such events. For Umberto Eco (1987, p. 254), it amounts to: 'literature that cheats with the given language . . . an activity that breaks down the rules and imposes others: temporary, valid in just one instance and for one current'. Kafka, once again, is frequently seen in this way; the banality, or blasé attitude, of his fantastic and/or absurd marks him out as a precursor of magical realism (McHale, 1987, pp. 76–7; Chanady, 1985, pp. 48–50). The stories of Daniil Kharms, a recently rediscovered pre-war Russian absurdist, are now belatedly entering the European canon (see Kharms, 1989; Giaquinta, forthcoming). Kharms undoubtedly had affinities with such Irish exponents of the comic–absurd–fantastic as Beckett (Jaccard, 1988) and Flann O'Brien (Maxton, 1989). Furthermore, the same might be said of Kharms as Calvino (1987, p. 48) has written of Beckett: 'a unique case, to the extent that his atrocious grimace has been suspected of containing tragic and religious elements, whether rightly or wrongly I do not know.'

Surrealism has long been associated with the fantastic (see Varma, 1966, pp. 66–7), not least by the Surrealists themselves: many surrealist images (in writing and other art forms) are thought to have literary (Gothic–fantastic) origins, while Breton, Artaud, Eluard and even Dali were all involved in reviving interest in the novels of Walpole, Lewis and Maturin (Ziolkowski, 1977, pp. 255–6). Just one experimental novel to arise out of this was André Breton's *Nadja*. Calvino (p. 47) has remarked that 'literature in the *fantastique* tradition was relaunched by the Surrealists in their struggle to destroy the barriers between the rational and the irrational in literature.' The introduction of the term 'the irrational' could, no doubt, lead to further explorations, but for present purposes we shall consider it to be encompassed by the categories just noted.

The spheres of fiction listed above, with an obvious input from the realist tradition and the historical novel, as well as from other literary and art forms — but with a fantastic mode tending to become the dominant — seem to come together, then, in what we are here calling the 'portmanteau novel'.[4] This term is intended to designate the complex, multi-levelled or multi-layered novel which has come to dominate the novel form in the second half of the twentieth century, although it also has its precursors. This may often conform to postmodernism, at least in McHale's terms of ontological preoccupation (many of these works are, or may be, multi-world, as well as multi-level), which allows for instance Bulgakov's *The Master and Margarita* (written 1929–40) to be categorised as postmodern (McHale, 1987, pp. 73–4, 174). Long novels often result (Pynchon's *Gravity's Rainbow*, Fuentes's *Terra Nostra*), but shorter examples also exist, more of novella length (*The Crying of Lot 49* by Pynchon, *Aura* by Fuentes). Short stories may be similarly considered (*John Duffy's Brother* by Flann O'Brien is an interesting case; García Márquez's *The Last Voyage of the Ghost Ship* is a more celebrated one — see Kroeber, 1988), particularly when postmodernism is defined rather as a (post-1960s) period style. However, taking the longer McHale ontological view, utterly unconscious affinities can be seen between, say, Daniil Kharms and certain American minimalist stories, such as Robert Coover's *The Marker* (1963). Just as such works vary enormously in length, they inevitably diversify and permutate the number of genre ingredients utilised.

There are naturally other terms in use to refer to what is more or less the same phenomenon as that which we are calling the portmanteau novel. McHale (1987, p. 75) arrives at what he terms 'the postmodernist fantastic'; such postmodernist fiction derives largely from SF, the historical novel, plus the fantastic (pp. 16, 79). It will on occasion contain the motif of the 'transhistorical party', involving an assembly of characters apparently from disparate historical eras or worlds (p. 17): *Terra Nostra, The Master and Margarita*. This is seen as akin to Bakhtin's ideas of carnivalisation (pp. 171–5), stretching through Menippean satire, Rabelais, Hoffmann, etc. to the modern era, to surface in various ways, we might add, in novels from *Ulysses* to *The Satanic Verses*. McHale (p. 36) also talks of the mythification or fictionalisation of sacred and profane levels, a concept of obvious relevance to the novels we shall consider by Bulgakov and Rushdie.

Linda Hutcheon, in her *A Poetics of Postmodernism*, (1988, p. ix) prefers the name 'historiographic metafiction', citing examples which include García Márquez's *One Hundred Years of Solitude*, Grass's *The Tin Drum*, Fowles's *The Maggot* and Rushdie's *Shame*. Clearly much the same kind of fiction is intended here, though perhaps with a more definite historical bias, but Hutcheon (1988, p. 50) is reluctant to be restricted by McHale's 'either/or' division: 'Historiographic metafiction asks both epistemological and onto-logical questions. How do we know the past (or present)? What is the ontological status of that past? Of its documents? Of our narratives?' Postmodernism for her is a matter of problematisation rather than synthesis (p. 221) and the questioning of historical knowledge, in particular, is seen as 'a reaction against the neoconservative appropriation of history to its own ends (a nostalgic traditionalism and need for authority)' (p. 209).

Carlos Fuentes, who writes his essays in English and his fiction in Spanish, has proposed the phrase 'potential novel', an open or 'incomplete' work (in a Bakhtinian sense): 'the post-Joycean death of the novel of realism, psychology, and linear unities in fact secretly heralded the birth of the potential novels of a Bakhtinian stripe' (Fuentes, 1988, p. 87). Examples include works by Kundera, Calvino, Grass, Goytisolo, Rushdie and Ackroyd. In his view (pp. 87–8):

These are the novels that, without thematically needing to espouse them, truly address the alterity of life in the post-industrial world, the uncertainties of life under the nuclear threat, the multiplication of communications, and the swamps of information competing for our attention today.

Such a conception of the novel has clear affinities also with Catherine Belsey's 'interrogative text', seen as illusionist, self-conscious, dialogical, open to a plurality of readings (Belsey, 1980, pp. 92, 104).

These terms all characterise very much the same trend in fiction. Of course, more limited forms or cross-currents may also be identified. In an illuminating recent study, David Bethea (1989, p. 33) seeks to establish a sub-genre of the modern Russian novel which he calls 'apocalyptic fiction', comprising Dostoevsky's *The Idiot*, Bely's *Petersburg*, Platonov's *Chevengur*, Bulgakov's *The Master and Margarita* and Pasternak's *Doctor Zhivago*. These novels, seen to share a sense of apocalypse and a subtextual dependency on the Book of Revelation, might well, in some cases at least, fit Hutcheon's category of historical metafiction; however, as a group, they may seem set apart from their western counterparts by the at least nominal Christianity of their authors, their biblical symbolism and their eschatological obsession with the destiny of Russia. Bethea also introduces (p. 34) the possible categorisation of such novels by dichotomy of critical school rather than generic or period style:

> the either/or optic of structuralism or poststructuralism — that is, they are *either* self-regulating, self-inscribing linguistic units whose 'anatomies' can be classified and dissected with the appropriate narratological *langue* (Tomashevsky, Barthes, Todorov, etc.) *or* they are generic anarchists whose chief *raison d'être* is to subvert convention and tradition and to exist in what Bakhtin would call a zone of openness with reality.

However, Bethea's treatment of them 'as verbal forms that are *simultaneously aware of their openness and closedness*, and of the boundary between *Wahrheit and Dichtung*' (*ibid.*) brings him close to other commentators whose stress is on contradiction and antinomy.

The true nineteenth-century predecessor to the portmanteau novel in many respects is what Calvino (1987, pp. 203–4) has called the 'poly-novel', such as Manzoni's *The Betrothed*, 'in which a number of novels succeed one another and cross one another's paths'. Maturin's *Melmoth the Wanderer*, with its nested narratives, and Le Fanu's *Uncle Silas*, with its duality of level, might count as other proto-examples, along with various works picked out as Menippean satire or 'anatomies' (see Frye, 1957).

There are a number of qualities likely to be found in the portmanteau novel which may need further emphasis.
1.   *Chronotope.* The tendency towards an extended or exaggerated chronotope noted in the nineteenth-century fantastic is carried further in the twentieth, reaching its ultimate in SF (Stapledon's *Star*

Maker covers the entire universe in space and time). Rather than purely the intersection of time and space in traditional setting, Bakhtin's concept of chronotope (see Bakhtin, 1981) adds an element of authorial consciousness regarding the handling of time and space and a privileging of the means or locus of transition. In the portmanteau novel, and allied fictional forms, these factors tend to be less than stable. The treatment of space and time in works by Fuentes — the novel *Terra Nostra* or the story *Aura* — would serve as a prime example.

2. *Irony.* The types of romantic irony noted earlier resurface as a prominent feature of twentieth-century fiction. Eco, who goes further than most in wishing to divorce postmodernism from any chronological period, stresses the central position of irony in a modernity which recognises the futility of iconoclasm: 'The postmodern reply to the modern consists of recognizing that the past, since it cannot really be destroyed, because its destruction leads to silence, must be revisited: but with irony. . .' (Eco, 1985, p. 67).

3. *Parody.* Far from being merely imitation by ridicule, parody tends rather to mean parallel, but with ironic departure: 'ironic playing with multiple conventions . . . extended repetition with critical difference' (Hutcheon, 1985, p. 7). The reader is likely to pick up this quality too from narratorial comment or from *mise en abyme*, a frequent feature of our older fantastic tradition, which in modern fiction 'will signal this dual ontological status' (p. 31). Forms are also parodied: the detective story, for example, in Borges, Robbe-Grillet and Nabokov; SF in Calvino and even some SF writers themselves (such as Lem, many of whose works take on wider postmodern qualities). The most celebrated case of parody in recent literature is perhaps Calvino's *If on a winter's night a traveller* (1979), which parodies many conventions of writing and reading, as well as consisting largely of a series of spoof first chapters of novelistic stereotypes. Parody is essentially seen by Hutcheon (p. 97) as a quality of double or contradictory potential, 'a way to preserve continuity in discontinuity'.

4. *Intertextuality.* We have already touched on a rather extreme category of this (the 'intertextual fantastic', above). Hutcheon (1988, pp. 124–40) provides a detailed discussion. In its wider sense, intertextuality has to do with the history of discourse (and often the discourse of history) in linguistic and philosophical terms. In its more everyday usage, it concerns the tracing of other (pre-)texts in a literary work, which may involve influence, borrowing, quotation, allusion and other familiar concepts. These things are often consciously done, all the more so in postmodern literature, but the

term can embrace the unconscious use of prior texts. Prime authors for the study of intertextuality include Nabokov (who also, in his later novels, offers the phenomenon of 'auto-intertextuality') and Borges. It is a strong feature of most portmanteau novels, none more so perhaps than Eco's *The Name of the Rose* (1980), written by a literary theorist and making particular use of Borges, Conan Doyle and a polyphony of literary and philosophical voices from various epochs. An illuminating lesson in the art of intertextuality is to be found in Fuentes's essay 'How I wrote one of my books' (Fuentes, 1988, pp. 28–45), on the composition of the problematic *Aura* (1962), just two of the sources for which, as we have already seen, were the stories by Pushkin and Henry James. Perhaps the most interesting implication of Fuentes's revelations is that his grasp of the intertextual makeup of his story (which extends forward too in *Terra Nostra*, 1975) continues to develop.

5.   *Metafiction.* A term touched on several times already, meta-fiction is primarily to be understood as self-consciousness in fictional narrative. Based on, or traced to, those original mould-breakers of post-medieval fiction — Rabelais, Cervantes, Sterne and Diderot — metafiction can provide problematic plotting and (open or even multiple) ending (John Fowles's *The French Lieutenant's Woman*) and can even confront authors with characters (Fowles's *Mantissa*). More typically it forms a part of the general uncertainty and discontinuity of much recent fiction. An early example from this century is Max Beerbohm's *Enoch Soames* (1912, included in Manguel, 1983). The metafictional quality sometimes lies in the provenance of a narrative: Stapledon's *Last and First Men* (1930) has an 'Introduction by one of the last men', the book's 'true' author who, from 2,000 million years hence, has 'seized the docile but scarcely adequate brain of your contemporary' to convey a metahistory of humankind in the solar system (from Earth to Venus, to Neptune: Stapledon, 1987, p. 15).

These qualities outlined above, it will be observed, frequently combine or overlap.

Among the upholders of the claims of Cervantes, Diderot and company to be the vital formative influences on twentieth-century fiction are not only the theorists (Bakhtin wrote a large book on Rabelais; Sterne was championed by Viktor Shklovsky), but also the novelists themselves — the very exponents of the portmanteau or postmodern novel. Bulgakov had written a dramatisation of *Don Quixote*. We have already quoted Fuentes (1988) on the 'potential novel', citing Kundera, Calvino, Grass, Rushdie and others. Fuentes's collection includes essays on Cervantes and Diderot, as well as on Borges, Garcia Márquez and Kundera. Kundera himself (1988, p. 56), as well as his beloved Central Europeans (Kafka, Broch, Musil, etc.), greatly admires Fuentes, who possesses 'a novelistic technique that makes *Terra Nostra* an immense, strange dream in which History is made and continually traversed by the same characters endlessly reincarnated'. For Kundera too, Cervantes, Sterne and Diderot (whom he has adapted: see his play *Jacques and his Master*) form the basis of modern fiction. Among the Olympians of modern literature, Lem (1985, pp. 48–9) includes Grass, Borges and Calvino; he regrets that Stapledon, as an SF writer, is automatically confined to the lower depths of trivia. Günter Grass (1988, p. 18) praises the 'two epic assaults' of Rushdie's *Midnight's Children* and *Shame*. Rushdie, for his part, has recorded his own appreciation of *The Tin Drum* (Rushdie, 1985). A line passing from Cervantes through Kafka is either claimed or implicit in all these writers. The practitioners of the portmanteau novel stem from the same origins and are kindred literary and anarchic spirits.

Portmanteaux may frequently be seen as 'baggy monsters'; they may now also frequently contain a fantastic level, or their own monster, within their baggage.

BULGAKOV

As long ago as 1968, Mario Praz referred to 'the favour recently enjoyed in some European countries (Italy for instance) by Gustav Meyrink's *The Golem* and Mikhail Bulgakov's *The Master and Margarita*' (Praz, 1968, p. 7). Praz continues (pp. 7–8):

> The terror and wonder which abound in those two novels have certainly profited also by the example of modern masters, but a reader familiar with the Gothic novels of the end of the eighteenth and the beginning of the nineteenth century will easily recognize in them themes and proceedings which were the stock-in-trade of the tales of terror. . . . And in the posthumous work of the Russian novelist there is a devilish cat who descends from Hoffmann's Kater Murr, a man who lacks a shadow like Chamisso's Peter Schlemihl, besides obvious echoes of Goethe's *Faust*, of Gogol, and the Wandering Jew.

This statement was written in the year after the main translations of Bulgakov's novel had appeared and within two years of the novel's first (truncated) appearance in print (itself over a quarter of a century after the death of its author) in Moscow in 1966–7, in the journal *Moskva*.[5] Despite the enormous attention accorded Bulgakov's novel by western Russianists (comprehensively surveyed in Barratt, 1987), it seems that discussion of it in general studies on the novel or on the fantastic has been almost non-existent. Recent, but very brief, exceptions have been Chanady (1985, p. 21), who classes *The Master and Margarita* as a work of magical realism, and McHale (1987), who, as we have noted, puts it squarely into postmodernism.

We shall here attempt to follow the lead of Praz, as well as of the two later commentators, in attempting to place *The Master and Margarita* within the progression of the literary fantastic. We shall also see subsequently that Bulgakov's novel has not itself been entirely uninfluential over the past twenty years.

Bulgakov's own life, with its dramatic turns of fortune, took on a seemingly magical quality almost on a par with that of his protagonist, the Master (see Proffer, 1984, for the fullest account). This in itself, or an early inkling thereof, may have contributed to Bulgakov's assumption of the narratorial pose of 'master story-teller', the style of narration (or *povestvovanie*) which characterises most of his prose, at least from *The White Guard* (1925). This tone, employed in various styles, dominates the narrative(s) of *The Master and Margarita* and governs the deceptive simplicity and consequent accessibility of the bulk of the text. Its readability and high entertainment quotient, based on ironic humour and sheer slapstick, a cracking episodic tempo and the allure of its fantastic–religious themes, has guaranteed *The Master and Margarita* immense popularity. This has been the case both in the Soviet Union, where even its belated publication in the 1960s seemed both amazing and daring, and abroad: even in Britain (usually not the foremost country in bestowing popularity on foreign language texts), the novel has remained continuously in print as a paperback for over twenty years (in 'Fontana', 'Flamingo' and 'Collins–Harvill' variants from the same publishing house). This is, in part, a tribute to Michael Glenny's translation which, despite certain flaws and inevitable (at the time) textual inadequacies, does successfully convey the tone and charm of the original. Bulgakov's prose, in this respect at least, is more readily translatable than the rhythmic complexities of Bely or the densely poetic texture of Pasternak (to name Bulgakov's only possible rivals in the 'greatest twentieth-century Russian novelist' stakes).

The adjective 'deceptive' is basic to any discussion of *The Master and Margarita*, more so perhaps than any word except 'mystification'. The deceptiveness behind the simplicity of Bulgakov's narrative method immediately becomes apparent upon consideration of plot summary. In Russian Formalist terms, the fable (*fabula*) is too complex to be readily communicable; it is more feasible to attempt to encapsulate the plot as presented by Bulgakov (the *siuzhet*). This can be done by outlining the opening scene and then sketching in the story-levels which all arise out of that.

The novel opens at Patriarch's Ponds in Moscow one Stalinist summer in the 1930s (or, according to some commentators, the late 1920s) with a conversation between a literary editor named Berlioz and a poet writing under the pseudonym of Ivan Bezdomny (Ivan Homeless). They are discussing the existence, or rather non-existence, of Jesus Christ apropos of an anti-religious poem of Bezdomny's which depicts Christ too realistically for Berlioz. The heat seems to have caused Berlioz to hallucinate a strange elongated figure, when they are interrupted by a mysterious foreigner who claims to have breakfasted with Kant, prophesises imminent decapitation by tram for Berlioz and mental asylum for Bezdomny, and relates a hypnotic narrative of Pontius Pilate. The foreigner, purportedly a Professor Woland, consultant in black magic, claims his version, which differs widely from gospel accounts, to be authentic on the grounds that he was there himself incognito; his other prophecies quickly come true.

This sets in motion the three basic plots of the novel, which interweave and interrelate textually and thematically until the last chapters (of thirty-two) when the plots merge and their main characters join, in an apocalyptic finale beyond time and space. A final epilogue confirms that life continues much as before in Moscow.

Plot 1 continues the opening chapter, concerning the Moscow sojourn of Woland (who appears to be a diabolical figure or agent) and his retinue, during which havoc rages in literary and theatrical (but, noticeably, not — at least overtly — political) circles. The tone is one of furious hilarity, the high point being Woland & Co's black magic show at the Variety Theatre, with merciless satire turned on to *homo sovieticus*.

Plot 2 (in the order in which they occur) is the crucifixion account, in a style of sober — almost epic historical — realism, much of it narrated in free indirect discourse via the viewpoint of Pilate. This begins in Chapter 2 and recurs in Chapters 16, 25 and 26. There are chronological and thematic parallels between the Jerusalem and

Moscow plots, as well as shared imagery, verbal echoes, down to lexical roots and sounds (see Bethea, 1989, especially p. 214ff). We shall return subsequently to the apocryphal nature and provenance of this narrative.

Plot 3 is the love and literary story of the Master (an otherwise unnamed Moscow writer) and his mistress Margarita (wife of a prominent scientist). The narrative tone here is mostly lyrical. The Master is the author of a novel on Pontius Pilate, which, having been lambasted by critical hacks, has been denied publication and burned; following a breakdown and denunciation, he takes refuge in a mental asylum.

The three plots begin to merge as follows: the Master's novel appears to correspond with Woland's narrative of Chapter 2 and its continuation; the Master happens to be in the same mental institution as Bezdomny (the clinic of Professor Stravinsky), so notes on Pontius Pilate are compared; Margarita, in order to redeem the Master and his burned manuscript, agrees to officiate at Satan's ball, a 'trans-historical party' (or apocalyptic carnival ceremony) held within a Moscow flat, but somehow in a different dimension of time and space. Following this, Margarita's wish is granted: the Master and his manuscript are restored to her.

The final merging of levels and plots takes place when the Master and Margarita transcend worlds (by means apparently of death by poisoned wine), into a further dimension (or afterlife?). This, arguably, then becomes Plot 4, in which accounts are settled; directed by Woland, but as a result of higher intercession, the Master is able to complete his novel by freeing Pilate from his double millenia of remorse; Pilate is thus enabled to re-engage in endless disputation with Ieshua (the Nazarene philosopher, whose crucifixion he had ordered through cowardice), as the pair are rewarded with 'light'; the Master and Margarita are delivered to eternal refuge, not that of 'light' but 'peace'. The epilogue returns to the more or less untouched life of Moscow, where absurd rationalities have been devised to explain certain events. The first part of it returns too to the earlier slapstick tone, thus affecting considerably the reader's final impression of the novel (noted by Barratt, 1987, p. 303). Bezdomny, now a professor of history but still the Master's 'disciple', undergoes each year his 'ontological flicker', by dreaming only on the vernal full moon (the anniversary of the events of Plots 1, 2 and 3) of Pontius Pilate and Ieshua. His first dream is a nightmare; his second a blissful one, in which the philosopher assures the Procurator that the execution never took place.

Computation of the 'plots' in Bulgakov's novel can of course vary a little, according to whether and how one counts, say, 'worlds', story-lines or narrative styles. The two plots which I have separated into Plots 1 and 3 are frequently treated as a single 'Moscow plot' (for example by Barratt, 1987, thus matching his 'Two Worlds' approach).

Alternatively, in order to clarify further the worlds and levels of *The Master and Margarita*, we could revert to the model used in our comments on Lessing's *Memoirs of a Survivor*. In terms of Bulgakov's fiction, 'World 1' would be Moscow of the 1930s, the Moscow literary and theatrical world inhabited by the Master, Margarita, Bezdomny, Berlioz and the rest. 'World 1 plus 1' would represent this world, plus the fantastic magical invasion of Woland and his retinue, whose advent brings in its wake tricks of space–time, black magic and other 'ontological flickers'. 'World 1 minus 1' is that of Jerusalem, the past, though in this case nearly two millenia previously. 'World 2' is a different dimension altogether, in which time and space are quantitatively different and into which Woland and retinue, plus the Master and Margarita, disappear to join at some level Ieshua, Pilate and Matthew the Levite (it is unclear whether, for instance, the 'light' constitutes a further dimension again). In addition to brief flickers, World 2 has a temporary incursion into 1 plus 1 for the occasion of Satan's ball. The epilogue returns to World 1, but there is still an annual 'ontological flicker' (or 'kiss of cosmic pool balls', as Pynchon would have it). Such a world scheme would amplify slightly further the 'Between Two Worlds' conception of Barratt's title.

Enough must have been said already to suggest that *The Master and Margarita* is a prime case for intertextual study. The Bible, Goethe and Dante are the first sources to strike most readers. As with Bely's *Petersburg*, there is a heavy intertextual debt in Bulgakov's writing to the fundamental stalwarts of Russian literature: Pushkin, Gogol, Tolstoy and Dostoevsky. Many less obvious Russian literary sources, parallels and prototypes have been proposed; a number have been added by Rita Giuliani (1982–4), including one old friend: A. K. Tolstoy's story *The Vampire* (the point of departure, we may recall, for Vladimir Solov'ëv's comments on the fantastic), here cited as a source for Bulgakov's vampire-witch, Hella. Much work has also been done, in western and Soviet scholarship, on Bulgakov's historical, theological and philosophical sources (see Barratt, 1987, pp. 184–97). One particularly valuable and intriguing source is Pavel Florensky's *Imaginary Quantities in Geometry*[6] in which space and time are explored by means of models which include Einstein and Dante (see Bethea, 1989, pp. 201–5).

The *Faust* connection is obvious, right from the novel's epigraph,[7] and has been thoroughly worked over (Barratt, pp. 268–302). Andrew Barratt, in the most detailed and satisfying study yet of the novel, observes that, its Soviet setting notwithstanding:

> the heart of Bulgakov's work lies elsewhere. In theme and manner, it announces its indebtedness to the art of the pre-revolutionary period, and in particular to the nineteenth-century tradition of the fantastic, as represented in the work of Gogol and Dostoyevsky. (Barratt, 1987, p. 313)

While this is undoubtedly true, as is Barratt's designation (p. 319) of the work both as 'a quintessentially "Symbolist" novel' and 'a *post*-Symbolist work' [his emphasis], other commentators are undeniably justified in laying more stress on the romantic origins and affinities of *The Master and Margarita*. Romantic in essence is Bulgakov's preoccupation with great literary personalities, their lives as well as their works; Alan Menhennet (1983, p. 5) writes:

> Indeed, Goethe belongs, with Molière, Gogol, Pushkin, Cervantes and perhaps also Hoffmann, to the pantheon of writers who form a kind of spiritual reservoir on which Bulgakov, a man aware both of the death, and of the continued life of the 'old world', seems not infrequently to have drawn in time of trouble.

We know of Bulgakov's delight with Mirimsky's article on Hoffmann's 'social fantastic', which he would read to his friends, pretending that it was a commentary on his own work (Curtis, 1987, pp. 199–200). We can, of course, discern many romantic features in Bulgakov's novel — the fantastic, the duality of worlds (*dvoemirie* in the Russian tradition), a mixture of styles, romantic irony and subjectivism, down to such details as devil's retinues and cataleptic death — and Bulgakov's 'Romantic vision' has been given due weight in the study by J. A. E. Curtis (1987, pp. 188–202).

These tendencies to romantic subjectivity gave rise to what has been termed the 'Master's theme' (Semeka–Pankratov, 1985, pp. 19–20), the timeless issue of the place of the creative artist in society, which runs through so much of Bulgakov's work. This theme, indeed, provides the main focus for Curtis's book, on

Bulgakov in the 1930s, which concentrates in particular on the treatment of the writer as fictional hero.

Influential on Bulgakov too was romantic thought. Particularly apposite here is Schelling's view that 'Every great poet is called upon to reconstruct this world . . . only a part of which his time reveals to him, into a whole, and out of this material to create his own mythology' (quoted from Semeka-Pankratov, p. 20). This statement scarcely needs further amplification in the context of *The Master and Margarita*. Mythic and dualistic though Bulgakov's fictional universe undoubtedly is, however, it would be premature and simplistic to rush to conclusions and to class Bulgakov with those proponents of 'high fantasy' or Symbolism for whom reality is (in the words of Zahorski and Boyer, 1982, p. 67) 'a mere shadowy reflection of the authentic world', holders of a world view according to which ours is seen as a Platonic shadow world, while the 'other' world is primary.

In fact caution should be the watchword in any analysis of *The Master and Margarita*. Nothing, on any level, is quite what it seems. David Bethea (1989, p. 205) qualifies his comment on the multiplicity of 'hermeneutical expectations' raised and satisfied by this text with a characteristic eloquence of his own:

> Yet its essence remains indeterminate. Reflective of both a nineteenth-century tradition of realism and fierce ethical commitment and a twentieth-century tradition of post-symbolism and destabilizing irony, the novel seems a kind of marvellous stone that with each stroke of the critic's blade reveals a new facet but that for this very reason can never be apprehended in the totality of its lapidary brilliance.

We cannot engage here in a full analysis of *The Master and Margarita*, but we can explore further, in the remaining part of this section, some aspects of this indeterminacy.

One of the prime questions to exercise the minds of commentators on *The Master and Margarita* has been that of genre. In view of the plurality of plots, we might feel inclined to consider Calvino's term, the 'poly-novel', or, following the reckoning of Barratt (p. 86), the 'double novel' (this novel containing two heroes, the Master and Pilate, 'bound together at the deepest level by a common sense of guilt over an act of "faintheartedness"'). This would, once again, be true but would not provide a very full description or characterisation of the work.

A number of other genre categories have been suggested: all, arguably, of some merit but none entirely satisfactory. Menippean satire, on the pattern of Bakhtin (1973/84), which is close to Frye's 'anatomy' (Frye, 1957) or Frye's four worlds, or levels (1976a, p. 98), was an early runner (Proffer, 1984, p. 531; previously expressed in her 1971 thesis). However, as Proffer herself acknowledges, Bulgakov's plots and episodes are far more interconnected than had been the case with these older genres. Many other attempts at generic classification, while illuminating up to a point, only fit the novel in part, as do related discussions in terms of satire, allegory or parody. Lesley Milne (1977) applies the categories of medieval mystery play and carnival, based on Bakhtin (1968 — the Rabelais book). Giuliani (1982–4) demonstrates the applicability of Proppian folk-tale functions, at least to the 'fairy-tale' story of Margarita's adventures (based on Propp, 1968); first published in 1928, Propp's study could have been known to Bulgakov. Barratt has utilised Terence Cave's concept of 'recognition plot' (later fully elaborated in Cave, 1988), with regard to the progressive unfolding of the real identity of Woland: 'the problem of identification involves a process of discovery in which we as readers — no less than Bulgakov's characters — are intimately bound up' (Barratt, 1987, p. 134). Bethea (1989, p. 223) places the novel in his category of 'apocalyptic fiction': Chapters 30–32 of *The Master and Margarita* contain 'one of the most *explicit* parodies of the Book of Revelation in Russian literature'. Persuasive and detailed though much of Bethea's argument is, and the abundance of apocalyptic imagery notwithstanding, Barratt (pp. 169–70) is surely right to point out (referring to Bethea's findings, first published in an earlier article) that the key word here is 'parody'; as Bethea himself recognises, there is no apocalypse here in the sense of the Apocalypse of John. What there does seem to be, of course, in the novel is apocalypse in the sense that Bethea (p. 181) defines it elsewhere in his study: 'a revelation from one spatio–temporality to another'.

Barratt's comments on reader–character joint participation in the search for Woland's identity are suggestive of a Todorovian type of hesitation, and constitute a level of doubt which, it might be argued, is maintained to the end. As we have seen, Chanady (1985, p. 21) admits *The Master and Margarita* to magical realism, on the grounds of narratorial belief in 'an immortal Satan and witches' sabbaths' and 'the amalgamation of a rational and an irrational world view'. Only one critic, to my knowledge, has discussed the novel expressly in terms of the Todorovian fantastic: Giuliani (1982–4, pp. 298–300), who, not surprisingly, places the novel in Todorov's category of the fantastic–marvellous, finding that reader hesitation eventually gives way to a recognition and admission of the supernatural dimension. However, given the hesitations and ambiguities which do remain at the end of the novel, we may wish to question even this seemingly incontrovertible assertion.

Much effort has been expended in attempts to pin down Woland's identity: Barratt's survey of the criticism documents this (pp. 77–101), while his own investigation comprises a solid chapter (entitled 'Who the Devil? . . .', pp. 133–72). Once again, Bethea (p. 206) has an apt comment:

> whether Woland turns out to be primarily good or evil, the Master a Christ-like figure or an ally of Satan, Margarita the Russian incarnation of Gretchen, Faust, or both are all questions which defy neat solutions and which . . . have come to be as slippery as the whereabouts of Woland and his retinue.

Bethea himself, with his apocalyptic approach, casts Woland as revelatory 'messenger from a different temporality and spatiality' (p. 41). This is not so very distant from conclusions reached in other recent studies, although the stress, or interpretation, of Woland's role or purpose, may vary. Curtis (1987, p. 173) sees Woland as 'a kind of plenipotentiary ambassador from the supernatural realm', whose task is to save the spiritual heritage of mankind. For Barratt (1987, pp. 171–2), Woland is a 'gnostic messenger', with a dual role as 'unorthodox evangelist and agent of deliverance'. Rather than Gnosticism, Gareth Williams (1990) sees the key to *The Master and Margarita* in the dualistic teachings of Manichaeism.

Just as Woland's identity, in the reader's (and characters') perception, metamorphoses in the early part of the text from foreigner, to scholar, to historian, to black magician through to supernatural agent, so have earlier critical identifications tended to metamorphose through Satan, Mephistopheles, a devil, the Devil, Platonic demiurge, or Stalin. In any case, as Barratt has pointed out (p. 171), 'we do not solve the problem of Woland's identity simply by naming him.' The epigraph, reading 'a *part* of that power which wills for ever evil, yet does forever good' (see note 7), suggests not only the ambiguity between good and evil but the response of an agent, rather than the power itself or its overlord; yet even this is not certain, as the speaker may represent a 'part' of a joint 'power' which itself represents both good and evil (either conjointly or separately). The fact that Chapter 23 of the novel is entitled 'The Great Ball at Satan's' ('Satan's Rout' in the Glenny translation) should indicate Woland's satanic identity; but this does not help very much, as little kinship with traditional devil figures, or with any known theogonic order, can be seen in Bulgakov's supernatural dimension. Similarly, Ieshua Ha-Notsri's relationship with the Jesus of Christianity is far from doctrinally faithful, while the deity is as conspicuously absent from Plot 4 (or World 2) as is Stalin from the Moscow levels and the Roman emperor from Ershalaim (as Jerusalem is named in the original).[8]

Of greater potential interest is the concept developed by Milne (1977, pp. 20–22) of Woland as satirist. Jean Paul Richter, in the heyday of German romanticism, had written: 'I can easily think of the devil, the true reversed world of the divine world, the great world-shadow which marks off the contours of the light-body, as the greatest humorist and "whimsical man"!' (Richter, 1973. p. 92; noted too by Milne). Milne continues (p. 21):

> If this interpretation of Woland's role is accepted, the novel acquires a further principle of coherence. To the configuration of 'the writer' in his various refractions we can now add the figure of the satirist Woland, as a kind of alter ego to the Master and expressing another potential in Bulgakov.

We have already seen that Woland narrates the first chapter of what subsequently seems to be the Master's novel. As well as being 'author' of the chaotic events which occur in Moscow, and of much else besides, Woland can also be taken then as co-author of the Pontius Pilate novel: there is at least a sense, as Bethea (1989, p. 192) has acknowledged, in which 'the Master's novel and Woland's are one' (see also Barratt, 1987, p. 163). We could go further. If we are looking for a hidden author or narrator, one who is present on all levels with a knowledge of all events — who has greater omniscience than Woland? Any such assertion is at best unprovable; however, it would provide a possible solution to what Barratt (p. 108) has identified as an 'epistemological paradox'.

We now seem to be entering the realms of what might be called 'the textual fantastic'. Following the 'double death'[9] of the Master and Margarita in Chapter 30, the manuscript is reconfined to the flames and they visit Bezdomny to urge him to write the continuation of the Master's novel; this is repeated in the Epilogue. However, as Barratt points out (p. 311), Bezdomny's touch of gnosis each vernal full moon is always followed by loss of memory; the novel as a whole, therefore, has a 'problem of its own provenance' and remains in a fundamental sense, in terms of its own fiction, 'unwritable'. Considering even just the Jerusalem text, we cannot but agree with Carol Avins, in her analysis of the Master and his 'readers' (or rather 'audience'):

> In Bulgakov's novel, Ivan's mind is the only earthly place where the text remains; but what remains is a fragment, and that fragment is inaccessible to awareness. The text endures neither in writing nor in conscious memory, and it will be conveyed to no one, for there is no teller. (Avins, 1986, p. 284)

But let us look again briefly at the presentation of what is generally called 'the Master's novel', the Pontius Pilate–Ieshua–Jerusalem story. The first chapter is narrated by Woland. The second is 'dreamed' by Bezdomny. The third and fourth chapters are (re)read by Margarita from the Master's resurrected manuscript ('Manuscripts don't burn.' Bulgakov, 1967, p. 326). Woland affects surprise on learning that the Master is the author of a novel about Pontius Pilate (*ibid.*). Curtis takes this surprise seriously (pp. 146, 179), but acceptance of her view here would imply serious constraints on Woland's omniscience. Barratt (p. 163) is surely on firmer ground in assuming Woland's surprise to be feigned; after all, his underling, Azazello, has already demonstrated this knowledge (Bulgakov, 1967, p. 259). Curtis (p. 179) points out the obvious, that 'nowhere in the novel does the Master himself actually narrate the story he has written' and that he seems to take remarkably little interest in it. In fact, as Avins (1986, p. 279) has noted, 'the novelist refuses to transmit the text orally' to Ivan Bezdomny. However, Woland's account and Bezdomny's dream seem to accord precisely in content, the second being a continuation of the first. A dreamer may be regarded as 'simultaneously creator and audience', although the dream here 'comes to him from an external source' (Avins, pp. 279–80). As for the chapters read by Margarita (to herself), their authenticity is presumably guaranteed by Margarita's recognition upon rereading. The Pontius Pilate novel, therefore, seems to form a single text, despite its multiple origins, though it always remains possible to question the reliability of narrators such as 'the devil' and Bezdomny (as does Williams, 1990).[10]

But is it all one novel, the Master's novel? And is that all there is of it (a total of some sixty-five pages), apart from its missing continuation which may be just a concluding passage or words? When Margarita is pulling charred remains of the manuscript from the stove, a chunk is said by the Master to be 'a chapter from somewhere in the middle of the book. I forget which' (Bulgakov, 1967, p. 170; 'kakaia-to glava iz serediny romana, ne pomniu, kakaia', Bulgakov, 1988, p. 152). On the basis of a four-chapter novel, only two chapters could be from 'the middle' and the expression kakaia-to would normally be taken as implying a total of more than two possibilities. Is it, in any case, really all the same narrative, or just near enough so in order to seem compatible to all concerned, or is this effect, as so much else, somehow illusory? In any case what is the status of this text? Is it to be taken as intuited 'truth', or is it to be viewed as 'a heretical version shared by the devil and the modern mortal' (Avins, p. 277)? These questions are ultimately unanswerable, but if the Master has somehow 'guessed' either 'the truth' or 'a truth', the implications are indeed considerable. Curtis (p. 146) quotes the leading Soviet Bulgakov scholar, Marietta Chudakova:

> The unity of the text begun by Woland and subsequently identified with the Master's manuscripts means that the Master's novel takes on the status of some sort of 'fore-text', which has existed since primordial times and has only been drawn from the darkness of oblivion into the 'bright field' of modern consciousness by the genius of the artist. 'Oh, it's just as I guessed it!' exclaims the Master as he listens to Ivanushka's [Bezdomny's] narration ['Oh, I guessed it! I guessed it all!', Bulgakov, 1967, p. 156], and behind that exclamation lies the entire aesthetic position of Bulgakov himself.

Barratt (p. 249) suggests that this may be seen as fictional expression of the Jungian 'collective unconscious'. In any event, the reader is left with what can only be an unfathomable, or an actual, 'fantastic text'.

The Master's achievement, by intuition, inspiration or guesswork, if such it be, can only be contrasted with the efforts of Matthew the Levite, the only 'disciple' of Ieshua and author of a distorted and invented version of his life, presumably intended as representative (though not in literal terms, see Curtis, pp. 147–9) of the canonical gospels. For his trouble (whether for his dedication or for his fictionalising is not clear), Matthew appears to have been accorded 'light'. Matthew's literary endeavours have frequently raised the question of literature as 'lying', inspired or otherwise (see Barratt, pp. 247–9), as opposed to the 'mysterious intuition' of true art. We have encountered the notion of literature, or fiction, as 'lying' earlier in this study: in the ideas of Nodier, the blatant hoaxing of Poe and Wilde's essay *The Decay of Lying*, while the line can be traced back at least as far as Lucian (Kern, 1982, p. 185). While 'lying' is, at various levels, a recurrent motif in the novel, a tension and an interplay between the artistic approaches of intuition, lying and mythmaking can be felt throughout *The Master and Margarita*.

There is within *The Master and Margarita* an extensive textual hierarchy of authors and characters. Bezdomny is the author of a poem on Pilate. Matthew is the author of a parchment on Ieshua. Both of these appear to be 'false'. Woland at least appears to be author/narrator of an allegedly true account of Pilate and Ieshua. Bezdomny dreams a continuation of this, but in his case this is likely to have been implanted rather than intuited. The Master is author of a novel (allegedly embodying an intuited and independent truth) involving Pilate, Ieshua and Matthew. We speculated above on the possibility of this process, or hierarchy, being taken even further by developing the notion of Woland as satirist. Bulgakov himself would be the next step, with hints beyond that of the world and history as text, author as deity and deity as author. There would, however, appear to be as many uncertainties in Bulgakov's textual hierarchy as in his cosmic hierarchy, for the penetration of which, overall, metafiction may prove to be a more incisive tool than metaphysics.

Bulgakov's treatment of the metaphysical and the supernatural remains essentially 'literary'. It stems from the romantic (and indeed pre-romantic and fantastic) literary tradition. But the seriousness of the fantastic and metaphysical levels can be questioned (as by Williams, 1990). The novel as a whole has something of a medieval (not to say biblical and timeless) air. Supernatural beings transform themselves into knights and gallop across the heavens on apocalyptic horses.[11] News is communicated by messengers, while cabalistic magic and (usually) benevolent demonry leave little room for advances in technology (an open flying limousine, chauffeured by a black crow, conveys Margarita to the infernal ball). Even telepathy is selective and localised. Woland, Ieshua (and Pilate?) have 'read' the Master's novel from their respective positions in supernatural timespace (in Russian, is one, at the risk of flippancy, to assume?). Despite what we may have said about Woland above, there does seem to be a degree of lack of omniscience about these supernaturals: they have to 'read' the novel which purportedly tells the true version of their story and their immortality.

Thus, overall, it can be argued, Bulgakov's supernatural reordering of the universe does not stand up to any real logical, or even theological, scrutiny, the seemingly harmonised nature of its otherworldly form deriving rather from a combination of literary and popular sources. Any number of indeterminacies and mystifications remain, as do the purely unanswerables: did Woland 'cause' Berlioz's death, or merely foresee it? The nature of 'peace' (earned by the Master) is spelled out: a romantic haven not unlike Dante's first circle. That of 'light' is not: we are left with just the signifier for the, presumably transcendent at yet a further remove, signified. There is a feeling of absence too in various other ways, as we have already noted: an absence of the prime figure of power at all levels (from whom or what is Woland the messenger?); and in a certain logical sense even an absence of text. The absence of ending had been the flaw in the Master's novel, while the arguments between Pilate and Ieshua are nowhere resolved within the text (unless one wishes to accept Bezdomny's Epilogue dreams as definitive ending, resolution and reconciliation, but even here there is a problem: why is it the execution of Hestas that recurs?).

That the fantastic of *The Master and Margarita* turns, in Todorovian terms, into the marvellous can scarcely be disputed. However, for such texts as Bulgakov's portmanteau novel, this classification is of course inadequate. The marvellous here is problematised (as Hutcheon, 1988, would say) to such a degree, undercut by indeterminacy, ambiguity, mystification, irony and absence, as to return the text ultimately to a higher, more complex form of the fantastic.

And yet. . . . We should, nevertheless, not forget the circumstances of the compositional and publishing history of *The Master of Margarita*. The story of Bulgakov's novel finally reaching its mass readership is almost as improbable and as close to 'faery' as is the text of the novel itself.

BANVILLE

Outside Ireland, John Banville has been mainly noted for his historical scientific trio of novels, *Doctor Copernicus*, *Kepler* and *The Newton Letter* (1976–82). Hutcheon (1988, p. 142) considers the first two of these to be examples of 'historiographic metafiction', concerned with history and discourse and the relationship between science, language and power. However, there are two other Banville novels which may in certain senses be seen as a pair, written either side of the science novels, and which are perhaps closer to our concern with the literary fantastic. These are *Birchwood* (1973) and *Mefisto* (1986). Banville's later work, shortlisted for the Booker Prize, *The Book of Evidence* (1989), shares the first-person, confessional, stream of consciousness narrative approach of the last two mentioned novels, and certain other similarities in terms of detail, psychology and fixation with memory, but in other respects, as a murderer's memoir based on an actual case and in its relative straightforwardness, is in a separate category.

Classification of Banville's works seems as yet to be a slightly uncertain exercise. *Mefisto* has frequently been considered to belong with the preceding three volumes, thus closing Banville's 'science tetralogy' (e.g. Imhof, 1989, p. 169). While the mathematical theme in *Mefisto* provides a certain logic for such a view, its youthful and fictional protagonist, as opposed to a concern with famous historical scientists, and its modern Irish setting, as well as its narrative tone, would seem to mark it off as a work apart. In fact, by the time he gets to his conclusion, Rüdiger Imhof, author of the first critical study of Banville, seems to have come round to a different view:

> There is also the remarkably rich number of correspondences and parallels between *Birchwood* and *Mefisto*. . . . These parallels in particular would suggest that Banville has not offered a tetralogy . . . but a series of five books, coerced into a harmonious whole by the first and last parts being so strikingly similar. Or it would, on the strength of the thematic correspondences between *Nightspawn*, *Birchwood* and the rest of Banville's work, be possible to maintain that the novels build up an intricately connected series of six. (Imhof, 1989, p. 173)

As suggested above, it would be possible to add *The Book of Evidence* to such a series: Freddie Montgomery is a lapsed mathematician and his narrative tone and epistemological quest bear some comparison with those of the two Gabriels, narrators *extraordinaires* of *Birchwood* and *Mefisto*, though his implied artistry may be less baroque and textually self-conscious than theirs. However, for present purposes at least, we shall disregard too the story cycle *Long Lankin* (1970) and the metafictional thriller *Nightspawn* (1971), as well as what we would suggest is a 'science trilogy', and concentrate on the chronologically dislocated pair of *Birchwood* and *Mefisto*.

Imhof (p. 72) sees these two novels as essentially Proustian and

Nabokovian respectively, with *Birchwood* as 'a book about the madeleines and madlanes of memory'.[12] Without pursuing the Proustian comparison further (Joycean 'epiphanies' might be equally close to the mark, though Proustian verbal echoes are present), it is possible to agree that *Birchwood* is not only 'an epistemological quest, but one directed at making sense of the past by remembering it and, more importantly, by writing it down in the form of a sustained narrative' (Imhof, p. 54). We can also state that these two novels could serve as a prime illustration of McHale's version of the modernist/postmodernist dichotomy in terms of epistemological and ontological dominants.

The opening and closing paragraphs (and not merely paragraphs, but pages) are often particularly significant in Banville's works, as clues to theme and structure and as a frame, and this is clearly the case in both *Birchwood* and *Mefisto*. *Birchwood* opens with musings over memories, language and the intention to write; the problem is then posed as follows: 'We imagine that we remember things as they were, while in fact all we carry into the future are fragments which reconstruct a wholly illusory past' (*Birchwood*, 1987, p. 12). By the end, even if we admit Imhof's contention (p. 57) that Gabriel Godkin 'solves all the riddles with which he so expertly has spiced his narrative', are we really much the wiser? 'So here then is an ending, of a kind, to my story. It may not have been like that, any of it. I invent, necessarily' (*Birchwood*, p. 174). And even if it was, any of it, 'like that', what meaning is to be drawn? 'There is no form, no order, only echoes and coincidences, sleight of hand, dark laughter. I accept it.' In its lack of order, the novel manages to retain to the last both its hermetic and its sealed qualities; one must make what one can of the text as it stands (which in a sense is of course true of any fiction), no more is knowable:

> I find the world always odd, but odder still, I suppose, is the fact that I find it so, for what are the eternal verities by which I measure these temporal aberrations? Intimations abound, but they are felt only, and words fail to transfix them. Anyway, some secrets are not to be disclosed under pain of who knows what retribution, and whereof I cannot speak, thereof I must be silent. (*Birchwood*, p. 175)

The reader has been all but invited to reassemble the evidence and perhaps come to different conclusions; but such an operation would be pointless. *Birchwood* somehow seems to combine an open ending with definitive closure.

Birchwood, again like other Banville novels, is constructed in distinct parts. Part I is called 'The Book of the Dead', presumably, for one reason, because most of the people in it are dead by the end of the book. Parts II and III, rather more enigmatically, are called 'Air and Angels' and 'Mercury' respectively ('Mercury' perhaps because Part III is where all the spilt parts are supposed to roll together?). Gabriel Godkin is son and heir to Birchwood, an Irish big house in headlong decline. Various circumstances persuade him that he has a missing twin sister. In Part II he runs away and joins a circus, in quest for his missing sister. Eventually, following travels and misadventures through famine and chaos he returns in Part III to Birchwood, where the remnants of his family (his father, plus usurpers from his supposed mother's side) are massacred by Molly Maguires (members of an insurgent society who disguised themselves as women), who are in their turn massacred by a tenant named Cotter. At this point Gabriel discovers (or decides) that he had no twin sister, but that his cousin Michael is his 'cold mad brother' (*Birchwood*, p. 172): 'Yes, he was my brother, my twin, I had always known it, but would not admit it. . .' (p. 168). Gabriel manages to see off his twin rival and is left alone at Birchwood to inherit and repair the house and to assemble his story.

This rather preposterous plotline, with its uncertain chronological setting (evidence within the text points to various periods from the famine of the 1840s to the Black and Tans) and its disordered presentation ('I feel I have already lived for a century and more'; 'Am I mad, starting again, and like this?', p. 11) has been recognised as a mixture (perhaps a spoof) of a number of genres: the Anglo-Irish big-house novel (which has flourished from Maria Edgeworth to Aidan Higgins) in Parts I and III; the quest romance (Part II), with a touch of the mystery story, the picaresque novel and the rationalised Gothic (Imhof, p. 59). There are a number of Gothic elements in *Birchwood*: the *Doppelgänger*-twin effect ('He had not changed. His red hair was as violent as ever, his teeth as terrible. I might have been looking at my own reflection.', *Birchwood*, pp. 168–9). Granny Godkin dies from 'spontaneous combustion' (*Birchwood*, p. 80) a Gothic motif found in *Bleak House* and Brockden Brown's *Wieland* (as noted by Imhof, p. 65), and also in Odoevsky. The circus is thought to be masterminded by Prospero, a non-existent 'withered wizard' ('so I became my own Prospero and yours', *Birchwood*, p. 172), and billed as 'Prospero's Magic Circus', a symbolic conjured up 'make-believe world' (Imhof, p. 71).[13] Imhof (pp. 64–5) suggests parallels with Le Fanu's *Uncle Silas* (the actual circus boss in *Birchwood* is an enigmatic Silas); while this may be plausible, the comparison would carry greater conviction if it were stretched to take in the more genuinely dualist *Mefisto*.

Birchwood is constructed on a pattern of circularity, in terms of plot, topography and perhaps time; in terms too of its theme of memory — and the recalling, recording and encoding thereof. It is constructed too, as Imhof (p. 62) has noted, on binary patterns; 'sets of pairs, twins, dualities and mirror symmetries'. This binary principle of composition forms just one of the links between *Birchwood* and *Mefisto*, for Gabriel Godkin too is a dab hand at algebra, as his childhood girl friend Rosie discovered:

> She stared at me with open mouth and huge eyes as I revealed to her the secrets of this amazing new world, mine, where figures, your old pals, *figgers*, yes, were put through outlandish and baffling exercises. Let x equal *whaa*. . . ? Ah yes, I won her heart with mathematics. She was still pondering those mysterious symbols, her lips moving incredulously, when I delved between her chill pale thighs and discovered there her own frail secret. She snapped her legs shut like a trap and scuttled out of my clutches, sat back on her heels and gazed at me with moony eyes, distraught, reproachful, shocked, aye, and tumescent. (*Birchwood*, p. 68)

While *Birchwood* utilises Gothic trapping and a variety of hesitations, mystifications, ambiguities and dualities, it would appear to lack any strong preternatural or supernatural element such as we have grown to expect in the fantastic. For dualism, in addition to duality, we have to turn to Banville's mature rendering of a Gabriel narrative: thirteen years on from *Birchwood* came his novel *Mefisto*.

We have already touched on a number of the similarities between *Mefisto* and *Birchwood* and these have been summarised by Imhof (pp. 167–9). *Mefisto* takes place in post-war Ireland (Gabriel Swan apparently having been born in the last year of the war, as was Banville). Part I ('Marionettes') is set in a small town, with the nearby estate and big house of Ashburn (which much resembles Birchwood). The family characters of Part I resemble to a degree those of *Birchwood*. The two Gabriels both have twin brothers (Swan's having died at birth). Part I of *Mefisto* reads in part like a grotesque big-house novel. Godkin thinks of swimming in the room on the first page of *Birchwood*; *Mefisto* opens with the chance 'swimmer', the spermatozoa that made Swan. Part II of *Mefisto* ('Angels'), like that of *Birchwood*, is described by Imhof (p. 168) as 'eerie, nightmarish, otherworldly'; it too takes place out in the world, this time 'the city' (presumably Dublin). Imhof points out (*ibid.*) the godlike qualities shared by the two Gabriels as narrators, Godkin being perhaps God's kin, while Swan, early in his narrative, lists the names of a clutch of mathematicians whose initials spell out 'Mephisto' (though we shall return to this point later).

The godlike quality of Swan, as Imhof notes, enables him to claim 'I am omniscient, sometimes' (*Mefisto*, p. 27) and the qualifying 'some-times' anticipates such disconcerting statements as 'I was standing in an overgrown orchard. No, wait, I was walking along an avenue of beeches, sycamores, something like that' (p. 34); or 'Spring came early that year — no, I'm wrong, it came late' (p. 96). 'Things are confused after that', we are told after the death of Swan's mother in a somewhat apocalyptic car crash. 'There are gaps' (p. 104); this is reinforced on the next page by 'The nun with the head-dress was gone, had winged away. . . . No, there was no nun, I invented her', while, a few lines later, the narrator can recall 'A crow flapped past low overhead, clearing its throat' (p. 105). By the end, the narrator asks himself 'Have I tied up all the ends? Even an invented world has its rules, tedious, absurd perhaps, but not to be gainsaid'; on the possibility of Felix reappearing, he muses 'Is it my imagination? Was it ever anything else?' (p. 234).

The 'formlessness' accepted at the end of *Birchwood* may or may not have evolved by the end of the later novel, through the chance, chaos and order theorising of *Mefisto*, but the metafictional uncertainties do still remain, 'invention' and 'imagination' having been conjured with to the last. Freddie Montgomery, concluding his confession which comprises *The Book of Evidence* (Banville, 1989, p. 220), insists: 'It's my story, I said, and I'm sticking to it'; quizzed on its veracity, he replies: 'True, Inspector? All of it. None of it. Only the shame.'

Imhof (pp. 154–9) discusses the mathematical symbolism in *Mefisto*, concluding that the Greek ideas of chance and Pythagorean mathematics bring Banville's investigation of science full circle and emphasising that Gabriel Swan, notwithstanding his mathematical prodigiousness, is ultimately to be viewed as 'not a mathematical wizard, but an artist figure' (Imhof, p. 159). References to chance (or 'blind chance'), chaos and order, and twinning (gemination or duality) abound in this novel, with recurrences too of what we have called the *Doppelgänger* effect. When the young Gabriel is immersed in his mathematics, we are told:

There might have been someone else inside me doing the calculating, who was surer than I, and infinitely quicker. Indeed at times this other self seemed about to crack me open and step forth, pristine and pitiless as an imago. (*Mefisto*, p. 31)[14]

This image evolves into a winged guardian angel, but one with a look that expresses 'not solicitude, but a hooded, speculative malevolence' (*ibid.*). Later, the girl Sophie 'had so throbbed in my imagination that now, when I confronted the real she, it was as if I had just parted from her more dazzling double' (p. 68). We shall come to the question of characters, or pairs of characters, as doubles shortly.

Enough has already been said for many of the resonances of the short opening paragraph of *Mefisto* (p. 3) to be recognised:

> Chance was in the beginning. I am thinking of that tiny swimmer, alone of all its kind, surging in frantic ardour towards the burning town, the white room and Castor dead. Strange, that a life so taken up with the swell and swarm of numbers should start, like a flourish between mirrors, in the banal mathematics of gemination. The end also was chance.

We have only perhaps to add that 'the burning town' must refer to the finale of Part I, that 'the white room' is the (possibly infernal) basement computer laboratory of Part II, and that the novel closes (p. 234) with the words 'In future, I will leave things, I will try to leave things, to chance', to see that we have a virtual *mise en abyme* in the very first sentences of *Mefisto*.

Another such device, at least embracing one chunk of the action of Part I, is Sophie's marionette show: 'It was my story they were telling. Everything was there, the meeting above the meadow, my first meal with them, D'Arcy's visit, Jack Kay, the kiss, everything' (p. 114). This is followed up (p. 118) with this rumination:

> I thought of the marionettes, twitching on their strings, striving to be human, their glazed grins, the way they held out their arms, stiffly, imploringly. Such eagerness, such longing. I understood them, I, poor Pinocchio, counting and capering, trying to be real.

This is one of a number of fairy-tale references (Felix applying Pinocchio allusions to Gabriel on pp. 142 and 176). Here the title of Part I ('Marionettes') is suddenly illuminated. Who, the reader wonders, is the real puppet master and in what sense? Is it Sophie, who literally pulls the strings; Mr Kasperl, who purports to rule the roost (not least over Sophie); Felix, subtle power behind the throne and clandestine master of ceremonies; or is it, all the time, our capering Pinocchio, the narrator Gabriel himself, trying to be a real boy?

Mefisto is not the most plausible of novels when it comes to plot summary. Part I is constructed from two plotlines. The first is the autobiography of Gabriel Swan; unlike his *Birchwood* namesake Godkin, he lives outside the confines of the similarly derelict big house, although his mother had formerly worked there. The second plot concerns the activities of Kasperl and retinue, ostensibly mining operations, centered on Ashburn. The two plots merge through Gabriel's involvement with Kasperl's gang (through Felix) and conclude in flames and disaster, which Gabriel somehow survives, but the others do not, except for Felix who has decamped in time. In Part II Gabriel is recovering from serious burns (the 'angels' of the title are the drugs on which he depends). Discharged from hospital, he again meets Felix, who has assembled a new gang: a Professor Kosok and a girl called Adele being its principle members. Kosok is engaged in a manic mathematical exercise in 'the white room'. As before, things end in disaster, but Gabriel extricates himself, apparently wiser: Kasperl's mathematical black book (which had survived the fire with Gabriel) has given way to 'a black book of my own' — presumably *Mefisto*.

While Part II seems to be, in a certain sense, something of a repetition of the action of Part I, there are differences and inversions, as well as many parallels. Apart from the presence of Felix and Kasperl's black notebook, there is very little continuity from, or reference back to, the world of Part I: Part II seems, as Imhof noted, 'otherworldly'. While Kasperl and Kosok both appear to be mid-European mathematical fanatics, their methods are different (Kosok's being more advanced: he regards Kasperl's black notebook as 'Antique stuff. History', p. 173). While the deaf mute Sophie is (belatedly) revealed as Kasperl's concubine, Adele (who does talk) is said (very belatedly, p. 233) to be Kosok's daughter. Felix's pimping and swindling activities of Part I appear to have been largely replaced by drug pushing in Part II. Gabriel's incipient sexual relationship with Sophie in Part I is consummated with Adele in Part II. Felix enacts a sacreligious wedding parody in Part I (p. 83); in Part II Gabriel and Adele orchestrate their own chapel altar drugs and sex act. Sophie in Part I is an innocent victim of the machinations and follies of Kasperl and Felix; Adele is at the least aided to suicide by Gabriel in Part II. Kasperl's schemes are interfered with by D'Arcy, a solicitor from the 'real' world; Kosok's work is sabotaged by a representative from the funding ministry, Miss Hackett. Gabriel's Aunt Philomena, visiting the hospital after the catastrophic car crash of Part I is asked 'Are you a relative? (p. 99); Gabriel is questioned in the same words at the same hospital (?) — no, probably another, near the city — after Adele's death (p. 231).

Part II might be seen as a reworking, a repetition, a resurrection, or some kind of alternate or variant Part I. Gabriel has gone almost literally through the fires of hell, to emerge, after 'my season in hell' (p. 123) as a rather horrific 'glazed carnival mask' (p. 132), or 'Phantom of the Opera' (p. 166). Kosok and Adele, as well perhaps as some minor figures, can be seen as approximate doubles of their Part I counterparts. Felix's gang, or something almost identical, has been somehow resurrected or reassembled: 'Here we are again!', says Felix (p. 153), having urged Gabriel before the climax of Part I to 'Cancel, cancel and begin again' (p. 117). What would in other circumstances seem just cheerful pleasantries uttered by Felix take on, in the atmosphere which is meticulously created, 'otherworldly', sinister, or just inexplicable connotations. This atmosphere needs to be examined more closely.

We have already referred to the 'guardian angel' image (p. 31), which derives from a picture on the classroom wall at the convent school (paintings frequently serve as originators of imagery in Banville). Mr Pender's 'Put-him-in-my-hands' visit to the Swan household is likened, in its effect on the family, to the appearance of a 'ghost' or 'spectre' (p. 29). There is frequently a feeling of entering new 'worlds'. 'I moved in a new medium there', says Gabriel of the Ashburn estate (p. 54); 'What a paradise it seems', says Felix of the same location, 'I sometimes wonder if we deserve this world' (p. 57). 'A new world had opened up before me', remarks Gabriel after a flirtation in Sophie's room (p. 68): at this stage, the new world could be that of sex, or that of mathematics, or indeed the 'world' of the mysterious gang of Ashburn inhabitants. Gabriel discovers too 'another world' again, more real than his own, in the old Ashburn photographs (pp. 80–81). Summer air flows in on Gabriel 'like air from another world' while he is 'lost in a dream of pure numbers' (p. 109). Mr Kasperl too is in a mathematical world of his own: 'Strange geometries amused him, their curved worlds where no parallels are possible, where there is no infinity, where all perpendiculars to a line will meet in one mad point' (p. 76).

Mini-worlds are frequently, therefore, created, or conjured up, within the text, in Part I as well as the 'otherworldly' Part II. The hospital in Part I is 'like a grand hotel in some southern clime' and, we are told, 'another species existed here' (p. 99). There is also a world beyond Gabriel in another sense, that of Kasperl and Sophie glimpsed through the crack in the door: 'a world, subtle, intricate, unsuspected, where I could never enter' (p. 117). And, as we have seen, there is also the hell into which he descends through his multiple burns: 'The being-beyond. Indescribable. Where I went, no one could follow' (p. 125). Gabriel, after his ghastly ordeal, is almost literally remade (from his own skin, rather than, Frankenstein-like, from the skin and organs of others). As recovery begins in a hospital room, 'I began to explore my little world' (p. 133).

As already noted, much of this atmospheric build-up centres on Felix. Quite often it comes from his mock-religious remarks and actions. As Kasperl appears in a doorway, 'And the dead arose and appeared to many! Felix murmured' (p. 48); a series of rhymes, one-liners and apocalyptic hints; references to hell, which take on a more serious and literal tone as Ashburn collapses into a blazing pit, caused presumably by Kasperl's maniacally irresponsible mining activities. However, Kasperl's black notebook is said to be 'thick as a wizard's codex' (p. 69) and his own room he calls 'the temple' (p. 71). An apocalyptic tension builds up as Part I draws to a close: the weather, noises at sea, and 'something was happening underground' (p. 110); there appears to be famine ('we ate the nettle soup', p. 112) and predictions of plague (p. 113). Fire soon follows.

Felix is frequently associated with wings (wing imagery abounds in *Mefisto*) and angels. He may be a guardian angel, 'malevolent' or otherwise, or a winged demon. At Jack Kay's funeral (Gabriel's grandfather declined, crushed, apparently, by Felix's flippancy), Felix appears from behind a cluster of headstones: 'He smiled at me and winked, and made a little sign, raising three fingers and sketching a sort of rapid blessing. Behind him a stained seraph towered on widespread marble wings' (p. 73). His old coat has 'wings' (p. 142); he mentions angels in Part II (pp. 162 and 227); angels in Part II also mean drugs. Of course, Gabriel, with his surname 'Swan' is also winged, as Felix frequently tells him. Crucially, just before the Part I apocalypse, Felix 'talked and talked':

— Burning away merrily down there apparently. The whole town is sitting on it. There'll be hell to pay. Oh, hell to pay! He grinned at me.
— What do you say, bird-boy? Time to fly? (*Mefisto*, p. 112)

The disaster happens on Gabriel's return to Ashburn (p. 120), after Felix himself has 'flown' by train:

Then a kind of thrumming began under my feet, faint at first, growing rapidly louder, a great drum-roll out of the earth. The floor sagged, groaning, and with a crash collapsed. The fat man and the girl sank slowly, as if into water instead of flame. His blue eye. Her smile. My hair was on fire. A red roar came up, out of the whole, and I flew on flaming wings, clutching my black book, through smoke and dust and splintering glass, into the huge cold air.

There are a number of references too, in various contexts, to secret signals, signs and significances (pp. 30, 32, 184, 202), while people at large seem to be privy to some awful secret (pp. 140, 154). Even on the most 'naïve' realist reading, devising a maximum of rational explanations, it would surely have to be admitted that there is, at the very least, a submerged fantastic level in *Mefisto*, a level of supernatural signifiers struggling to transcend mere textuality and enter the plot. In similar vein, in Part I, a rumbling inferno was gathering, as we know, in the nether regions below Ashburn; in Part II on the other hand, according to Felix, 'There is order in everything. . . . Look at this place. It seems a wilderness, but underneath it all there's a garden' (p. 161); the garden indeed comes, with spring, as the city comes alive 'with vague shrills and swoopings on all sides in the lambent, watercolour air' (pp. 185–6). An ontological order is sought, and is alleged to prevail as *Mefisto* proceeds.

If we look to a less naïve realist or even a simply metafictional reading, we inevitably turn to the strongly signalled intertextual element. 'Mefisto' is no accidental title (though its variant spelling, from the 'MEPHISTO' formed on p. 24, is to be noted), and it certainly is a work, in some sense, of Faustian striving: the *Faust* connection, in terms of character models and verbal echoes, has been documented by Imhof (pp. 160–64). Imhof (pp. 164–5) also mentions Thomas Mann, Dante, Beowulf and Shakespeare in terms of influence or allusion (plus Bram Stoker's *Dracula*, which I have failed to spot); we have already mentioned fairy-tales (Pinocchio and Cinderella are there), and could add Dickens, Maturin and Conan Doyle.

It would perhaps be more intriguing to look at *Mefisto* against another avowedly Faustian text, Bulgakov's *The Master and Margarita*. Any comparison would seem to lie in the devil's retinue complex of characters in each work: Woland, Korov'ëv, Behemoth, Azazello and Hella in Bulgakov; Felix and his two respective gangs in *Mefisto*. Felix, in appearance and dress, is not unlike a combination of Korov'ëv and Azazello, while his name at least (Felis, feline) suggests Behemoth (Bulgakov's Kater Murr). Kasperl and Kosok, being at least nominal bosses with mid-European accents and origins, suggest parodic (weaker and stouter) versions of Woland: Kasperl, with his wizard's codex, is depicted at first as a portentous figure: 'The coat, and the galoshes, incongruous on a summer day, were impressive somehow, as if they might have a secret significance, as if they might be insignia denoting some singular, clandestine authority' (*Mefisto*, p. 33). Hella, by such a scheme, would match Sophie/Adele. Banville may, of course, have drawn his demonic gangs from other sources (there is one, for instance, in Le Fanu's *Borrhomeo the Astrologer*); nevertheless it would be tempting to see the following sentence (p. 74) as a discreet nod to Bulgakov: 'Queer the landscapes that memory, that old master, chooses for its backgrounds, the twilit distances with meandering rivers and mossy brown crags, and tiny figures in costume doing something inexplicable a long way off.' What can be said with certainty is that *Mefisto* is a strangely esoteric portrait of a master as a young man.

Finally, let us return to some of the indeterminacies of *Mefisto*, which place it, I would want to argue, notwithstanding its strong metafictional and intertextual emphases, somewhere close to the pure-fantastic sector in the postmodern spectrum. The nature and tone of the narration render it difficult to claim decisively the intrusion of the marvellous (the supernatural or another dimension) into the novel at any particular point; and yet Part II, for instance, as we have noted more than once, is presented as distinctly otherworldly. Rational explanations can probably be found for almost everything. Narrative and structural quirks and signs remove all guarantees so that the novel defies definitive interpretation. Let us, in conclusion though, consider the theme of Felix the tempter.

There is little hard evidence that Felix is omnipotent or omniscient on the scale of Goethe's Mephistopheles or Bulgakov's Woland. Much of his apparent foresight may just as easily stem from native wit and cunning as from second sight. But he may clearly be seen in the role of tempter. 'You could have had her too. The hints I dropped!' he says to Gabriel of Sophie (p. 117); and 'Can't tempt you, eh?. . . . Well, there'll be another time' (p. 230), as Gabriel declines to stay with him at the end of Part II. He may, though, also be seen as guardian angel, his ambiguity extending too to the effects of his temptation and/or protection. A case could be made both ways. Felix also has, however, a curious connection, or kinship, with two apparent sub-tempters, one in each part. In Part II, Felix has apparently put the podgy computer operator Leitch up to making a homosexual pass at Gabriel (possibly as a proxy for Felix himself?). In Part I, it is the mysterious, elderly mathematics master Mr Pender, said to be 'English and a layman' (p. 23), who urges Gabriel's family to 'put him in my hands' (p. 28), possibly involving a similar approach: Mr Pender a little later is suddenly 'spirited away' (p. 30), perhaps in disgrace(?). Father Barker too, who had entertained 'high hopes' of Gabriel, 'was quietly removed' to a sanitorium (p. 30). There are, however, still further ramifications to this. It was in fact Pender from whom the 'litany of queer names' forming 'MEPHISTO' was heard; he is described as tyrannical and predatory, but with 'a liturgical aspect' (p. 24). Some, at least, of Felix's remarks sound distinctly English (rather than Irish); 'Hell down pit, lad' (p. 64). Most strikingly, though, Felix eventually says to Gabriel 'Put yourself in my hands . . . I have high hopes for you, you know' (p. 226); he calls Gabriel 'Castor' (p. 162) and refers to his burns as 'the mark of Cain' (p. 227).

So, is Felix a superhuman being possessing at least mind-reading capability with regard to Gabriel? Or is he merely a cunning and cultured rogue with a gift for the 'echoes and coincidences, sleight of hand, dark laughter' of Birchwood? Just as there is a stress on absence in Birchwood (the twin sister, Prospero) so there is in Mefisto: absence through death (p. 137); Adele is somehow absent, even when present (pp. 158, 174), yet she is somehow there in her absence after death (p. 232); the absence inherent in zero (p. 186), and in the departure of Felix (p. 230). Absent too is Gabriel's (stillborn) twin, 'my phantom brother' (p. 18). Is Felix, who knows Gabriel's mind so intimately, really tempter or guardian angel, alter ego or double? Is Gabriel Swan red haired, one wonders, like Gabriel Godkin? Would he, therefore, looking in a mirror, if he and we could see behind the 'carnival mask' of his burn-scarred skin, look like Felix, as Godkin apparently looks like Michael? Is Mefisto, then, ultimately another Birchwood after all, with Felix in some sense Gabriel's long lost un-dead twin brother?

Such questions remain unanswerable and thus Mefisto takes its place, following the nineteenth-century novels of Maturin, Le Fanu and Wilde, as a modern Irish classic of the fantastic.

RUSHDIE

In our earlier discussion of the portmanteau novel, we saw Rushdie's name mentioned alongside those of such writers as García Márquez, Fuentes, Goytisolo, Grass and Kundera; we could add the names of Pynchon and Pirsig, Cela and Tournier, Angela Carter and Alasdair Gray and others still. Such a list would be largely according to genre, at a particular stage in the development of the modern novel. There are other ways of grouping or listing writers which may serve to bring out other sides of Rushdie's literary pedigree. Timothy Brennan, in his study *Salman Rushdie and the Third World* (1989, pp. 26–7, 34), suggests two categories: firstly, Third-World authors, predominantly Latin Americans (García Márquez, Fuentes, Isabel Allende and Bharati Mukherjee); and secondly, debunkers of dubious forms of nationalism (Grass, Kundera, E. L. Doctorow and Nadine Gordimer). Another category again would be that of exiles (Kundera, Aksënov, Beckett; or earlier Conrad, Joyce, Nabokov). Rushdie himself has written on Grass as a novelist of exile (Rushdie, 1985). We shall cite further lists to which Rushdie's name has been, or should be, added at a later stage. A certain overlap in such listings is already apparent. More striking still is the quality of internationalism; Rushdie has himself said on this:

> If you are an extra-territorial writer you select a pedigree for yourself, a literary family. . . . [We] are inescapably international writers at a time when the novel has never been a more international form . . . cross-pollenation is everywhere. (quoted from Brennan, 1989, p. 60)

Midnight's Children (1981), the novel which first gained Rushdie an international reputation, is a first-person, mock-autobiographical, confessional *Bildungsroman*, metafictional in form and fantastical in content, which creates, at the same time, a mythic and parodic history of the state of India: 'India, the new myth — a collective fiction in which anything was possible, a fable rivalled only by the two other mighty fantasies: money and God' (*MC*, p. 112). *Midnight's Children* has been compared to Grass's *The Tin Drum* (in terms of physically and morally deformed heroes with magical powers), as has *Shame* (1984) to García Márquez's *One Hundred Years of Solitude* (see Brennan, p. 66). In terms of our earlier discussion of magical realism (deriving from Chanady, 1985), we can suggest that Rushdie was one of the first writers to bring that style into English writing. This is a quality, we should perhaps remind ourselves, that depends on narrative (and frequently characters' — or some of them at least) attitude to unlikely or fantastic events. Such an attitude is made plain, for example, in *Midnight's Children* (p. 200):

> No, that would be too easy. I refuse to take refuge in illness.

Don't make the mistake of dismissing what I've unveiled as mere delirium; or even as the insanely exaggerated fantasies of a lonely, ugly child. I have stated before that I am not speaking metaphorically; what I have just written (and read aloud to stunned Padma) is nothing less than the literal, by-the-hairs-of-my-mother's-head truth.

The major transformation in this novel, affirmed here as literal truth, involves the birth, at and just after midnight on 15 August 1947, simultaneous to the birth of the new state of India, of 1001 children possessed of a range of supernatural powers. 'No, I can't prove it, not any of it', we are told (*MC*, p. 440); fibbing and distortion are admitted parts of the method (pp. 443, 459), as are dreams and the traditions of eastern thought:

> 'What is truth?' I waxed rhetorical, 'What is sanity? Did Jesus rise up from the grave? Do Hindus not accept . . . that the world is a kind of dream; that Brahma dreamed, is dreaming the universe; that we only see dimly through that dream-web, which is Maya. Maya,' I adopted a haughty, lecturing tone, 'may be defined as all that is illusory; as trickery, artifice and deceit. Apparitions, phantasms, mirages, sleight-of-hand, the seeming form of things; all these are parts of Maya. If I say that certain things took place which you, lost in Brahma's dream, find hard to believe, then which of us is right?.' (*MC*, p. 211)

As well as dealing in magical powers, *Midnight's Children* is a protracted story of baby-swapping, castration, impotence and repression, of the 'disease of optimism' and the 'lie of fiction' (Brennan, p. 115), narrated, like Rushdie's other novels and in the vein of much significant postmodernist fiction, in a tone which combines the ironic, the comic, the irreverent and the horrific, often taken, some would argue, to extremes — of literariness and of taste. But such is 'the real world' (a phrase of which Rushdie, among others, has grown fond) and so it is seen by many contemporary writers. Accordingly, Rushdie would even argue that his work falls within 'realism'.[15]

A striking feature of Rushdie's style is his adoption of devices from the eastern storytelling tradition, with its interruptions, asides and anecdotes, which, used in varying ways from novel to novel, may also have been calculated to mirror the 'recital' quality of the

Koran (see Brennan, p. 125). This is combined with what is otherwise identifiable as a 'predominantly Western aesthetic' (p. 65). Rushdie's 'tripartite identity' (p. 119) has led him to centre his three major novels, *Midnight's Children, Shame* and *The Satanic Verses*, on India, Pakistan and Britain respectively, while his 'special position as an "insider/outsider"' (p. 144) has both sharpened his social and ideological insights and fuelled controversy, the latter to unprecedented extremes. Lest anyone should doubt the political import of Rushdie's novels, he makes this aspect of his fictional intent quite explicit in his journalistic writings: see particularly his essay 'Outside the Whale' (Rushdie, 1984). All these factors contribute too to Rushdie's highly inventive macaronic prose style, which has breathed new air into the tired language of the English novel.

Before going any further, it is worth quoting a couple of statements by Rushdie himself on what *The Satanic Verses* (1988) is and is not. In an open letter to Rajiv Gandhi, following the ban on the novel in his native India, Rushdie writes: 'I am accused of having "admitted" that the book is a direct attack on Islam. I have admitted no such thing, and deny it strongly.' He goes on to amplify: 'let's remember that the book isn't actually about Islam, but about migration, metamorphosis, divided selves, love, death, London and Bombay' (quoted from Appignanesi and Maitland, 1989, p. 44).

Timothy Brennan, author of the first book-length study of Rushdie's career, whose main emphasis is on Rushdie as a Third-World writer, notes the impossibility of seeing *The Satanic Verses* 'through the distorting images of the protests or what the media made of them since they overestimate the Islamic themes of a novel that is, after all, primarily about a very secular England' (Brennan, p. 147). '*The Satanic Verses* is an immigrant theodicy', says Brennan (p. 151) and, among other things, 'a grotesque imaging of racist fantasies' (p. 155), a novel which 'problematises the colonial writer's metropolitan half' (pp. 163–4). In addition to the Third-World angle, a full analysis of *The Satanic Verses* would need to take due account of Islamic history and sources. While any such complete exegesis lies beyond the scope (and competence) of the present study, it does remain possible to consider the literary devices and imagery connecting this novel — which in any event belongs to English, European and world literature — to the tradition of the literary fantastic.

Our usual approach to such obviously portmanteau novels as the patently multilayered *The Satanic Verses* has been by a consideration of levels, worlds and plots. We may begin by noting Brennan's

calculation (see pp. 152–5) of three levels of what he terms the
theodicy. The first level of this comes in, and from, the book's title:

> It alludes to an incident recorded by the ninth-century Arab
> historian Al-Tabari, in which the Prophet at first sanctioned,
> and later deemed corrupt, certain verses of the *Quran* that he
> believed had originated not from Allah but from the devil.
> (Brennan, p. 152)

This act of what amounted to (temporary) religious tolerance, to
permit the worship within the confines of Islamic doctrine of three
female deities, although apparently blasphemous in Islamic terms,
nevertheless assisted, according to this version of events, the
survival and eventual success of the new religion. At a (second)
metafictional level Rushdie, or strictly speaking his dreaming
character Gibreel (and this qualification, I would stress, could be
vital for anyone wishing to mount a defence of Rushdie from within
Islam), projects, in the novel as a whole (or, in a more concentrated
way, in the dream world of the Jahilia chapters), something like an
alternative Koran, an 'apotheosis of self-questioning', the logic of
which leads to 'the religion of doubt' (*ibid.*). This is accentuated by
the wilful distortions which the Prophet's scribe, one Salman the
Persian, introduces into the verses of the sacred Book. Thus the
'satanic verses' of tradition are renewed in a world in which 'the
supreme deity is both devil and God at once' (*ibid.*), in his capacity
as — no more and no less — the author. The third level, on this
count, is the 'twinning of opposites' (p. 153) in the persons of the
two principal characters of the main part of the book, Gibreel
Farishta and Saladin Chamcha, posing as, or enacting the roles of,
the archangel Gabriel and the fallen angel Shaitan (Satan, or Lucifer)
respectively. This, in and following the memorable opening
sequence of the novel, re-enacts Shaitan's fall in the allegorical form
of 'big-name celebrities from India being cut down to size in the
alluring and indifferent Britain' (p. 154). In tune with the theological intermingling of good and evil which the text overall
purports to propound, Gibreel and Chamcha eventually reach an
albeit somewhat unstable reconciliation.

Brennan rightly observes (p. 155) that 'the many-levelled archi-
tecture of the novel works by reflecting each level off the other
levels like the inverted images of a broken mirror': for instance,
Gibreel poses as Shaitan, as well as Gabriel. Take also the title motif
of satanic verses: in addition to being relayed (in Gibreel's dream) by
Gabriel (or was it Shaitan? or anyway, is it not all the same?) to the

Prophet (or a prophet, 'Mahound', 'an abusive name for Muhammad used by medieval European scholars who liked to portray the prophet as a crazed charlatan', Brennan, p. 155) and reinforced by Salman's tamperings, there are further refractions in store. The profane verses with which Chamcha torments Gibreel anonymously by telephone are termed satanic (*SV*, p. 445) and their diabolical effect is felt in the events of the end of the novel (p. 544). Towards the climax of the Titlipur (Arabian Sea) dream narrative, Mirza Saeed's recitation of *The Pied Piper* is denounced by Ayesha as 'Devil's verses, spoken in the Devil's tongue' (p. 484). Extensive reflections through the various levels of the novel of imagery concerned with, and references to, devils, angels, wings, flying, ghosts, imps, the parting of waters (or other elements), mountains, blasphemy and butterflies, among other things, could be detailed. Other linking devices include the use of the 'it was and it was not so' storyteller's formula, the refrain of 'to be born again, first you have to die' (and consequent play on birth, rebirth and death) and the two questions asked of a new idea (or religion, or even of something else): 'When it's weak: will it compromise?' and 'How do you behave when you win?' (see, for example, p. 369)

In terms of worlds, there is the obvious divide between the contemporary world (of the mid-1980s) and the (eighth-century?) dream world of Jahilia, presumably in Saudi-Arabia. Within the modern world are the sub-worlds, or locations of action, of London and Bombay and the lesser dream worlds of Desh and Titlipur (the former sounds like Bangladesh, but is otherwise more reminiscent of Iran; the latter is in India, 200 miles from the Arabian Sea). London is given various names, principally 'Proper London', capital of Vilayet (there is also, briefly, a model Dickensian London, constructed at Shepperton studios). There could also be said to be a number of subsidiary worlds (or 'universes') depicted in the novel, such as those of cinema (mainly Indian) and of TV advertising (mainly British) and the immigrants' world of Brickall (Brixton/ Southall); Argentina and Everest also feature in a more limited way. There are frequent references to characters facing, or seeing into, two or three worlds at a time: ontological flickers abound. However, the concept of worlds has perhaps less meaning, or is less clear cut, in *The Satanic Verses* than in many other texts, given that all levels in Rushdie are more or less equally phantasmagoric and it is difficult to determine definitively which events (if indeed any) take place in 'the real world', as even the briefest consideration of the opening section of the novel (*SV*, p. 3–10) will show.

We have already referred above to the opening as 'memorable'; it is so particularly in the sense of being startling. Angela Carter, in her review of the novel, writes:

> It kicks off *in medias res*, astonishingly: two brown men, clasped in a reluctant embrace, hurtle out of the clouds towards the English coast, singing at the tops of their voices in raucous discord. They have burst out of the exploded pod of a hijacked aircraft, to miraculously survive impact and be extraordinarily reborn. (Appignanesi and Maitland, p. 11)

It would, of course, be perfectly possible to interpret this event and its aftermath (and logically, therefore, its flashbacks too) as instant death, followed by some kind of maniacal afterlife, or protracted phantasmagoric visions at the point of death (or Rushdie's imaginative depiction thereof). Such an interpretation would solve many problems and, if sufficiently widely propagated in time, might have saved at least a modicum of trouble. Chamcha actually conjures with this idea as, transformed into a goatish demonic being, he suffers infernal torment in the back of a police van:

> What puzzled Chamcha was that a circumstance which struck him as utterly bewildering and unprecedented — that is his metamorphosis into this supernatural imp — was being treated by the others as if it were the most banal and familiar matter they could imagine. 'This isn't England,' he thought, not for the first or last time. How could it be, after all; where in all that moderate and common-sensical land was there room for such a police van in whose interior such events as these might plausibly transpire? He was being forced towards the conclusion that he had indeed died in the exploding aeroplane and that everything that followed had been some sort of after-life. If that were the case, his long-standing rejection of the Eternal was beginning to look pretty foolish. — But where, in all this, was any sign of a Supreme Being, whether benevolent or malign? Why did Purgatory, or Hell, or whatever this place might be, look so much like that Sussex of rewards and fairies which every schoolboy knew? (*SV*, p. 158)

Similar speculation, based instead on hospitalised hallucination is abandoned upon feeling a sharp kick. Detailed examination of such a passage, and in particular its last sentence, might reinforce our own doubts and questioning still further. However, the over-riding narrative tone, at least to the reader accustomed to such fiction, locates the style, or genre, not so much within the marvellous as the fantastic, at a point not far removed from magical realism: magic realism with a eastern face, one might say.

What might be more productive than a concentration on 'worlds' in the case of *The Satanic Verses* is an attempt to identify or delineate plot lines. There can be said to be three main plots in the novel. The first, and main plot, is that of Gibreel and Chamcha. This pair (of twinned opposites) fall to English soil, or rather sea initially, from a height of 29,002 feet (or the height of Everest) in hilarious black-comic manner (although the blowing up of a jumbo jet by Sikh terrorists will not be everyone's idea of a jolly chortle), as already described, at the start of the book. We are given background information on each and they soon separate in the ensuing action, to come together again subsequently at various key points of the narrative. They are each surrounded by their own subplot, involving respective families, wife and/or lovers. Gibreel is particularly associated with his mother, with the mountaineer(ess) Allie Cone, the ghost of Mrs Rekha Merchant, the Indian cinematic world of the 'theologicals' and briefly with Rosa Diamond (the near-nonagenarian former resident of Argentina).[16] Chamcha's plot is connected with his father Changez Chamchawala, his lover Zeeny in Bombay and wife Pamela in London, the television and advertising scene and, through Pamela's lover Jumpy Joshi and his own post-lapsarian English misadventures, with the immigrant milieu of the Sufyan family and the fringes of black radicalism. These twin plots intersect, mainly through Gibreel and Chamcha's meetings but also through other interrelated factors, such as Allie Cone being a member of Jumpy Joshi's martial arts class and mutual show-business acquaintances (such as the unfortunate S. S. Sisodia). When confronted with bifurcating paths, however, both Gibreel (p. 352) and Chamcha (p. 419) choose the left-hand path — the sinister or satanic road — thus becoming 'each man the other's shadow' (p. 426). This major plot line (or twinning of plots) is, apart from those features which have already been stressed (London, Bombay, love, etc.) essentially one of migration and return. Both Gibreel and Chamcha migrate to 'Ellowen Deeowen', Chamcha having done so originally long before.[17] Both eventually return to Bombay: Gibreel, beset still by demons and illusions, returns to undergo a catastrophic crack-up; Chamcha apparently overcomes his guilt and his sins to find reconciliation. The inferno of London is left behind.

The second and third (and very much the subsidiary) plot lines are both dreamed by Gibreel, to which point we shall return yet again shortly. What we shall consider to be the second plot is that of Jahilia and the birth of a religion (purveyed by the prophet Mahound and bearing at least a close resemblance to Mohammedanism), into the sacred text of which are implanted satanic verses. This takes up two of the novel's nine parts (II, 'Mahound', and VI, 'Return to Jahilia', about 75 pages in total). The first of these parts, or chapters, deals with the first of the two questions posed (as we noted earlier), that of compromise: the answer provided is that compromise would be entertained. The second one deals with the second question posed, that of behaviour in victory: here the answer falls short of magnanimity, entailing the summary execution of whores and writers ('Writers and whores, I see no difference here', *SV*, p. 392). On both counts the result would appear to be something less than the ideal.

The third plot, another set of Gibreel's dreams, also comprises two parts (IV, 'Ayesha', and VIII, 'The Parting of the Arabian Sea', again about 75 pages in total). The chapters of the main plot and the dream plots therefore alternate and the two dream plots provide a roughly symmetrical structural balance. In this dream plot, beginning in part IV, the action is split. The first narrative concerns an exiled Imam in London; his retinue includes the same names as that of Mahound in Jahilia (Salman Farsi, Khalid and Bilal). His enemy is the Empress Ayesha of Desh. The archangel Gibreel is required to fly the exiled spiritual potentate to 'the Imam's Jerusalem' (*SV*, p. 212), where the Empress, metamorphosed into the goddess Al-Lat, is overthrown and destroyed (there is repetition here and vengeance over the same goddess as in Jahilia) and the Imam returns to Desh to found a theocratic utopia beyond time. In each dream sequence Gibreel's 'own image, translated into an avatar of the archangel, re-enters the frame' (p. 216), while vengeance can itself be translated into something more loving and nostalgic, undergoing a shift into the Titlipur narrative. In this tale, Ayesha (there are four Ayeshas in total in the dream narratives, including one impostor; Ayesha, it should be noted, is the name of Mohammed's favourite wife), a saintly and simple village girl, clothed magically in butterflies, is inspired (seduced? by the archangel Gibreel, of course) to lead the community of the village of Titlipur to the Arabian Sea, which will open, enabling the pilgrims to cross the ocean floor to Mecca, where miraculous cures will be effected. The outcome of this episode can be seen either as 'drowning with a blissful smoothness in a mirage of absolute belief'

(Nisha Puri, see Appignanesi and Maitland, p. 15) or as character-istically ambiguous: 'perhaps the pilgrims drowned in the sea, perhaps the pilgrims crossed the sea' (D. J. Enright, in *ibid.*, p. 19). The waters may have parted for those who believed: it was so, it was not so.

Nisha Puri, reviewing the book for *The Indian Post*, must have provided the most eloquent appreciation yet of Rushdie's novel: 'Like an outsize Brazilian butterfly, *The Satanic Verses* soars through its many worlds on wings of pure fire as panoramic vistas stretch before and behind us linked by a series of epiphanies' (*ibid.*. p. 15).

If we care to read *The Satanic Verses* alongside the two other modern novels which have here been under detailed consideration, an astonishing degree of common ground in approach becomes apparent. Narrative tone and metafictional aspects apart, there are a number of thematic points which can be made. Rushdie shares with Banville a preoccupation with archangels and demons, angels and wings, and the tension between order and chaos. He has acknowledged the impact of Bulgakov on *The Satanic Verses*[18] and here the comparisons which can be made are quite extensive. Bulgakov and Rushdie are both fascinated by the complex dialectic of good and evil: 'Think, now: where would your good be if there were no evil and what would the world look like without shadow', says Woland to Matthew the Levite (Bulgakov, 1967, p. 405); compare Rushdie: 'This notion of separation of functions, light versus dark, evil versus good, may be straightforward enough in Islam . . . but go back a bit and you see that it's a pretty recent fabrication' (*SV*, p. 323). Both Bulgakov and Rushdie (and perhaps Banville) engage in the unleashing of diabolical figures on a modern city, with inflammatory results. Most obviously, though, Rushdie has followed Bulgakov's lead in the fictionalisation — perhaps realistic, perhaps parodic, but in both cases alternative, unorthodox, heretical — of the origins of one of the world's major religions. This involves too, in both *The Master and Margarita* and *The Satanic Verses*, an engrossment with 'messengers' of or from other worlds, changes in the 'word' (or the Word) and in the historical record, and the role of scribes and poets, both in these processes and with regard to the relationship of the writer to society or ruler, tyrant or patron.

All three writers share interests in the Satanic, the Faustian and (in some sense) the Fall, as well as in apocalypse, incarnation, reincarnation and fluidities of identity (recurring names, for example, in Banville and Rushdie). Goethe, Dante and Milton, among others, can be seen as collective common sources. If not to Banville's *Mefisto*, there is a reference in *The Satanic Verses* to the

Hungarian (Istvan Szabo) film *Mephisto*, followed by a rhymed version of the *Faust* lines which formed the epigraph to Bulgakov's novel:

> There was an art cinema next to the Friends House, and [Chamcha] was leaning against a movie poster. The film was *Mephisto*, the story of an actor seduced into a collaboration with Nazism. In the poster, the actor — played by the German star Klaus Maria Brandauer — was dressed up as Mephistophilis, face white, body cloaked in black, arms upraised. Lines from *Faust* stood above his head:
> — *Who art thou, then?*
> — *Part of that power, not understood,*
>   *Which always wills the Bad, and always works the Good.*
> (*SV*, pp. 416–17)

Finally, without at this stage going into the furore that erupted over *The Satanic Verses*, let us return to the undeniably textual point raised several times above, namely the presentation of Gibreel's dreams. Each and all of what have been identified as the subsidiary second and third plot layers, the four chapters entitled 'Mahound', 'Ayesha', 'Return to Jahilia' and 'The Parting of the Arabian Sea', are presented, as we have already stressed, as the dreams of Gibreel. Virtually all, if not all, the passages which have been singled out as offensive to Islam occur within these dream chapters. We therefore have a situation in which offence has been taken not only to what is a work of fiction, but to passages which form part of a series of fantasies, dreamed by one of the novel's characters, who has been accurately described as 'a fading and slightly demented Indian film star' (John Walsh, in Apignanesi and Maitland, p. 31). These sections, as we have indicated, form a subsidiary layer to what is in any case and by any standards an essentially phantasmagoric novel. Gibreel Farishta is neither the narrator nor the implied author of the work as a whole; neither is he in any sense to be seen as its positive hero: he is diagnosed as schizophrenic within the text and ends the novel as a murderer and suicide. As Rushdie has himself asked (in *ibid.*, p. 44). 'How much further from history could one get?'.

As a footnote to this narrative situation, let us take just one of the (probably more minor) objections voiced to the text: that 'the book calls Abraham, the revered Prophet of Jews, Christians, Muslims alike, "the bastard"' (*ibid.*, p. 79). The relevant passage reads as follows:

In ancient time the patriarch Ibrahim came into this valley with Hagar and Ismail, their son [Ismail is also Gibreel's real first name]. Here, in this waterless wilderness, he abandoned her. She asked him, can this be God's will? He replied, it is. And left, the bastard. (*SV*, p. 95)

Not only does this passage occur within the dream framework just outlined, but it is an example of free indirect discourse (or 'dual voice') in which the narrator empathises with a character, the resulting utterance being then inseparable from, and belonging equally to, both. The narrator here is the dreaming Gibreel about whom enough has been said; the character here is Hagar, who may be entitled (except perhaps in the most patriarchal of societies) to feel at least a little aggrieved in the circumstances described. The linguistic register employed, which no doubt gives principal rise to objection, stems from the unconscious of the dreamer.

Let us, however, demonstrate that the presentation of Gibreel's dreams as dreams should be crystal clear to any remotely competent reader of the novel. We could not be told more clearly that, when Gibreel is dreaming, he is dreaming (e.g. *SV*, p. 91). He is even aware himself of his own dreaming while he is doing it, and entertains quite justified doubts as to his sanity: 'O God, he cries out, O allgood allahgod, I've had my bloody chips, me. Got bugs in the brain, full mad, a looney tune and a gone baboon' (p. 92). The first dream, for example, plainly flows from the recent hijacking experience and other key elements in Gibreel's past life. 'The spring of Zamzam', revealed by Archangel Gibreel to Hagar the Egyptian (p. 91) and water source for the fantasticated city of Jahilia which is built of sand (p. 94), derives from 'the oasis of Al-Zamzam' (p. 84), where the hijacked plane containing Gibreel and Chamcha had been held for 110 days; terrorism is even represented, the enemies of the sand-built city being 'water-terrorists' (p. 118); Cone Mountain (p. 92) is associated with Gibreel's 'obsession with the mountain-climber Alleluia Cone' (p. 85).

Gibreel, who dreams of himself both as the archangel and as Shaitan, as he drifts into sleep 'passes his loving mother who has a different name for him'; this name is 'Shaitan' because the 'rascal has been putting Muslim meat compartments into Hindu non-veg tiffin-carriers' (p. 91). Gibreel's epic religious, or mock-religious, dreams are thus shown to have origins in his past, both recent and distant, to spring from his religious doubt (p. 92), and from his mother, 'who started the whole angel business' (p. 17) and from whom 'he heard a great many stories of the Prophet, and if inaccuracies had crept into her versions he wasn't interested in knowing what they were' (p. 22). One further level of motivation behind Gibreel's dream fantasies is his profession as star of the Indian 'theological' cinema (in reality 'mythologicals'), in which he has played a range of deities. The dream sequences are presented as if cinematically: 'Gibreel: the dreamer, whose point of view is sometimes that of the camera and at other moments, spectator' (p. 108). Lest anyone should be in doubt, the device could scarcely have been bared any further, while the dreaming is emphasised once more at the end of the sequence (p. 126).

Similarly, 'Ayesha' is dreamed by Gibreel following his exhausted collapse at Allie's flat feet (p. 202; made explicit p. 301). Occasionally the dreamer tries to intervene (e.g. p. 226), which serves also to remind the reader again of the device. However, the moment when 'the boundaries of the earth broke' (p. 318) and Gibreel is confronted by 'The Fellow Upstairs' (alias God, alias the author) occurs out of, rather than in, 'one of his serial dreams'. We have by then learned that Gibreel is making another 'theological', which appears to be based on 'Jahilia' (p. 272). The proposal for his comeback is a series of films ('Gibreel in Jahilia', 'Gibreel meets the Imam' and 'Gibreel with the Butterfly Girl'), incidents from 'the angel's long and illustrious career' (p. 345), purloined by Sisodia from the dream narratives heard at Gibreel's bedside (p. 347), thus encompassing all the dreams which comprise our second and third plots. At least two of these films are eventually made, with other producers, and become disastrous flops.

Thus the dream plot and 'theological' fantasies both derive from, and are reintegrated with, the main plot level of the novel. Other ways in which this is done include the satirical depiction of Mrs Torture's Proper London being taken a further parodic stage by Hind's Jahilia (p. 361):

> Who could resist her? For her eternal youth which was also theirs; for her ferocity which gave them the illusion of being invincible; and for her bulls, which were refusals of time, of history, of age, which sang the city's undimmed magnificence and defied the garbage and decrepitude of the streets, which insisted on greatness, on leadership, on immortality, on the status of Jahilians as custodians of the divine. . . . The citizens of Jahilia dragged themselves through their increasingly dangerous streets, in which murder for small change was becoming commonplace, in which old women were being raped and ritually slaughtered, in which the riots of the

starving were brutally put down by Hind's personal police force, the Manticorps; and in spite of the evidence of their eyes, stomachs and wallets, they believed what Hind whispered in their ears: Rule, Jahilia, glory of the world.

Similarly, back in 'the real world' of his demented progress through London, Gibreel 'understands now something of what omnipresence must be like, because he is moving through several stories at once. . .': Allie Cone, the Prophet, the pilgrimage to the sea, his looming confrontation with Shaitan/Chamcha, as well as 'a Gibreel who walks down the streets of London, trying to understand the will of God' (p. 457).

In what might be considered the normal way of things, the repeated emphasis placed here on dream presentation in *The Satanic Verses* might be thought a little excessive. However, what we have witnessed since the publication of this novel has been anything but normal. Without going any further at this point into the surrounding controversy, let us conclude with two quotations (out of several) from the novel which may now be seen as ironically and tragically prophetic and as *mises en abyme* for, not only the novel as text, but the whole Rushdie affair.

The first occurs in 'Return to Jahilia' (p. 374), when the captured Salman the Persian is brought before the Prophet: 'Your blasphemy, Salman, can't be forgiven', he is told. 'Did you think I wouldn't work it out? To set your words against the Words of God.' The blubbering Salman is, however, spared (unlike the poet Baal). Secondly, though, let us remember Rushdie's epigraph, taken from Defoe's *The History of the Devil*:

> Satan, being thus confined to a vagabond, wandering, unsettled condition, is without any certain abode; for though he has, in consequence of his angelic nature, a kind of empire in the liquid waste or air, yet this is certainly part of his punishment, that he is . . . without any fixed place, or space, allowed him to rest the sole of his foot upon.

MORRISON

In Rushdie's *The Satanic Verses*, two characters (first Rosa Diamond, *SV*, p. 129, and much later Chamcha, p. 540) provide identical definitions of a ghost: 'What's a ghost? Unfinished business, is what'. Such a line might have made a suitable additional epigraph for the Afro-American writer Toni Morrison's novel *Beloved* (1987).

Beloved is essentially a historical novel of slavery and its immediate aftermath. As such it belongs very much to Afro-American, or black American literature. It is also very much an example of feminist fiction, in that it exists to give voice to the voices and stories of the past, particularly (but not solely) the voices and stories of black (or 'coloured' as they are mostly termed in this text) women, which history and patriarchy have hitherto silenced. In this respect *Beloved*, together with Toni Morrison's earlier work, stands alongside the works of a number of contemporary black women writers (Alice Walker, Maya Angelou), as well as some from other backgrounds: a useful comparison could be made, for example, with the stories in Angela Carter's collection *Black Venus* (1985). However, *Beloved* is of particular interest here because it also happens to be a tale of the fantastic.

The 'present' of the novel takes place in, or just outside, Cincinatti, Ohio, in 1873–4. The main character of the novel is Sethe, an escaped slave, now aged about thirty-seven, who lives with her seemingly retarded daughter, Denver, in a house known as '124'. Her mother-in-law (Baby Suggs) died eight years earlier, her two boys have run away from home, her husband, Halle, never made his escape (from a slave farm named Sweet Home, in Kentucky) and the house is thought to be haunted by the ghost of a baby girl, Sethe's elder daughter who perished violently in infancy and was buried beneath a headstone inscribed with the single word 'Beloved' (abbreviated from 'dearly beloved'; we are never told her 'given name'). This status quo is disturbed by the arrival of Paul D, 'last of the Sweet Home men', who, after eighteen years of captivity, soldiering and wanderings, has finally found his way to Baby Suggs's house, supposed haven for the 1855 Sweet Home escapers. Paul D takes up with Sethe, having driven out the baby's ghost (or poltergeist). However, a peaceful outcome is jeopardised by the arrival of a strange young woman who soon exercises a strong hold over Sethe and Denver, and manages progressively to expel Paul D from the premises (having first contrived to become pregnant by him). She is taken by Sethe and Denver to be the revenant baby ghost, calling herself Beloved, now grown to the age she would have been. The reaction of other characters to this situation is mixed and, at the climax, a combination of internal and external circumstances is contrived which brings traumatic pressure on Sethe: Beloved vanishes (or flees), Denver has matured (or normalised) and Paul D returns to settle down to what should, at last, be a life of peace and quiet with Sethe.

However, this is only the plot line in the 'present'. Intercut with this is a past, the details of which emerge only gradually throughout the novel. This comprises in part the personal histories, narratives and misadventures of Sethe and of Paul D; these are revealed by flashbacks, reminiscences or 'rememories' in passages interspersed through the book and narratively focalised through these characters. But the past also includes, or is equally describable in terms of, the story and background of Baby Suggs and her liberation (purchased by the labour of her son Halle); life at Sweet Home and pre-Sweet Home: or the distant past; the events surrounding the 1855 escape attempt, Sethe's flight and the birth of Denver: or the past; and the intermediate events (1855–73), particularly those centering on 124: or the more recent past.

Of central importance, and first clarified at a point very slightly beyond the centre of the book (*Beloved*, pp. 148–51), is the event, stemming from what we have just termed the 'more recent past' chronological band, which in fact took place only a month after Sethe and the newly-born Denver had arrived at 124 (Baby Suggs's house). This is the horrific scene in which Schoolteacher, the new tyrannical supervisor of Sweet Home, arrives at 124 to reclaim possession, under a Fugitives' Act then in force, of the escaped Sethe and her four children. Determined to avoid this fate at any price, Sethe is prepared to kill her children and then herself and has already killed the first one — the 'crawling already? girl'. This results in the abandoning of Schoolteacher's mission and a spell in jail for Sethe (with infant Denver), commuted, in a legal *cause célèbre*, from hanging. It also causes Sethe's dual guilt and pride, the decline of Baby Suggs into a mental state in which her sole preoccupation, before death, is the protracted contemplation of colour, and the traumatisation of the remaining children (of whom the boys run away, while Denver confines herself to watching the yard) and motivates both the purported presence of the baby ghost and the subsequent appearance of the supposed revenant, Beloved, whether in search of vengeance or consolation. We shall return again to the presentation of this key scene.

So far, we have approached this novel in terms of the plot line of its 'present' and the chronological bands of its past. We have also suggested an approach through the individual plots or histories of the main characters: Sethe, Paul D, Denver and Baby Suggs. With regard to 'worlds', there is the obvious dichotomy between the world of at least relative freedom enjoyed by the black population of Cincinatti (slave-free Ohio) and the slave world, exemplified principally by Sweet Home (which, at least until the advent of Schoolteacher, had been little more than the first circle of slavery), but extending to even worse horrors. This is recorded textually in terms of 'lives': the 'better life' Sethe believed she and Denver were living, as opposed to 'that other one', from which Paul D had now emerged (*Beloved*, p. 42). Given the apparent supernatural dimension to the novel, the question of a duality of worlds in the sense traditional to the literary fantastic also must arise. Sethe thinks of an afterlife as 'on the other side' (e.g. pp. 200, 241); however, the importance to the plot of rivers does not assist the clarity of this image. There does pertain among the characters a general acceptance of a supernatural dimension. Credence, or tolerance, extended to the interplay between two worlds in this metaphysical sense is not, however, necessarily unlimited, as is shown by the reaction of Ella, a prominent Cincinatti black resident, upon hearing that '124 was occupied by something-or-other beating up on Sethe' (p. 256): 'She didn't mind a little communication between the two worlds, but this was an invasion' (p. 257).

The question of the reactions of characters, as we have seen throughout, measured too against narration or narrative tone, is important in any consideration of the fantastic. In the case of *Beloved*, the most productive approach to the text would seem to lie in an examination of narrative method. A convenient tool for this purpose is Gérard Genette's concept of 'focalization' (see Genette, 1986, pp. 189–94). Action in *Beloved* is very largely internally focalised, that is to say depicted, filtered or reflected through the consciousness of one or more characters, as opposed to external focalisation, which would be through a mode of narration which does not admit the reader to a character's thoughts, or to nonfocalised (or traditionally omniscient, or near-omniscient) narration.

There is a certain amount of narration in *Beloved* which is nonfocalised (or perhaps 'collectively' focalised): introductory sections, such as the novel's first paragraph (beginning '124 was spiteful. Full of a baby's venom. The women in the house knew it and so did the children.' *Beloved*, p. 3); link passages providing information or keeping the narrative moving; and snippets of narratorial/authorial comment within what is otherwise focalised or informational narrative (for instance, the statement 'If the white-people of Cincinati had allowed Negroes into their lunatic asylum they could have found candidates in 124', p. 250, is scarcely attributable to these candidates themselves). Much of the essential narration, however, is achieved by internal focalisation. The internal focalisation in *Beloved* can be said to be both variable, in that it switches back and forth, and multiple, in that the privilege of focalisation is bestowed on a number of characters. These include the obvious main characters, Sethe, Paul D. and Denver; Baby Suggs, introduced retrospectively, briefly on the first pages and more substantially later; Stamp Paid (the old black Pimpernel of the escapee slaves) and, much more briefly, Ella and the liberal white, Bodwin; and, most strikingly perhaps, on occasion the enigmatic Beloved (pp. 100–01, 134). We shall return shortly to some of the effects of this narrative method.

There is one short scene in which the mode of narration is markedly different. This is the vital and horrific central scene referred to above. For just four pages in the book (pp. 148–51), the focalisation is not only external to the black characters involved, but the scene is depicted from the point of view of an external white, who is tantamount to a non-existent white witness, or to a composite of some of the four white participants. We can say that this 'witness' is certainly not exclusively any one of the party, but the discourse takes on features from perhaps three of its members (Schoolteacher, one of his nephews and a slave-catcher; the fourth is the sheriff, who remains to handle things when the mission is otherwise aborted). We can say that the viewpoint is white because of the vocabulary and sentiments, which are singularly apart from the rest of the narrative discourse: 'they trotted off, leaving the sheriff behind amongst the damnedest bunch of coons they'd ever seen' (p. 151). This fiercely ironic depiction of white self-righteousness ('you just . can't mishandle creatures and expect success', p. 150) adds an impressive dramatic power to what is a crucial and indelible scene.

So central, it must again be stressed, are the events of this scene that we are given another description of it, from the point of view of Stamp Paid, who was also present and was responsible for rescuing Denver, who would have been next in line for slaughter; this time Stamp Paid is putting a stubbornly resistant Paul D in the picture (pp. 156–8). Furthermore, we get another, somewhat 'circular', account of the same event from Sethe herself, as she circles the room confronted on the matter by Paul D (pp. 162–5). Briefer references are scattered through the book.

Genette observes (1986, p. 191) that 'any single formula of focalization does not . . . always bear on an entire work' and that, for that matter, 'internal focalization is fully realized only in "interior monologue" ' (p. 193). And, sure enough, Morrison turns eventually to interior monologue in *Beloved*. Sethe is given several interior monologues: a brief one (*Beloved*, pp. 183–4), and then a more extended one addressed to Beloved (pp. 191–8). When Sethe decides she is sure who Beloved is, she locks the door on the outside world; what we are given next are 'the thoughts of the women of 124, unspeakable thoughts, unspoken' (p. 199). These follow in the form of interior monologues which emanate from Sethe (pp. 200–04), Denver (pp. 205–9) and, most interestingly and perhaps crucially, Beloved herself (pp. 210–13, 214). The novel concludes with a lyrical monologue which can only be attributed to the author/narrator.

The central question posed by the novel must inevitably be 'who is Beloved?'. Although an examination of the narrative structure may not answer this question conclusively, it is of considerable assistance in marshalling the evidence. There would appear to be three possible solutions to the riddle of Beloved's identity. First, that she is indeed the returned daughter and therefore a supernatural manifestation. Second, that she is someone else who is mistaken for the otherworldly returnee. Third, she does not exist at all but is either hallucinated into 'being' by Sethe or is collectively hallucinated by Sethe, Denver and Paul D.

The third possibility is the easiest to discuss. If Beloved were to have been hallucinated into 'reality' by Sethe, the ontological problem posed would be no less severe than were she to have been a ghost. We would seem to get nowhere with such a supposition, unless we wish to grant the possibility of severe grief and remorse being powerful enough to conjure a being back into existence. With regard to total hallucination, we might accept this as possible, given the state of mind and experiences undergone by those concerned. The only extraneous person to see Beloved before the denouement appears to have been Stamp Paid, who observes: 'from the way they describe it, don't seem like it was the girl I saw in there' (p. 265). As for the crowd of women: 'One point of agreement is: first they saw it then they didn't' (p. 267). While such possibilities of collective hallucination and mass hysteria cannot necessarily be excluded, dwelling further on them would not seem either to enhance or to explain satisfactorily the power of the book.

Acceptance of Beloved as a bona fide returnee from the dead would place the novel ultimately in the realm of the marvellous and would also have the effect of tainting the book's powerful political and social message, with a slightly sugary supernaturalism. While evidence for such a conclusion can be adduced, it does not seem to be overwhelming and is beset by contradictions. These need to be outlined in some detail. We can, however, first make the general point that, in a novel of relatively little independent (nonfocalised) narration, the supernatural feeling, the 'ghost culture' of the black characters, is mildly expressed at the outset ('baby's venom', 'spite', p. 3), but intensified as the focalisation zooms in ('Sethe and Denver decided to end the persecution by calling forth the ghost that tried them so', p. 4: dual focalisation; 'And when the baby's spirit picked up Here Boy. . .', p. 12: focalisation through Denver). A general acceptance, to one degree or another, of the supernatural throughout is, therefore, privileged by the employment of the narrative technique of internal focalisation, thus bringing *Beloved* close in this respect to magical realism. It might, however, be argued that the applicability of *Beloved* to this particular formal category is undercut by the virtual absence of any 'independent' and confirmatory narratorial voice.

Belief in the supernatural is mildly undermined too by the attitude of the male characters. Paul D, while not dismissive, does at least put the issue on a lower level: when the question of the baby ghost first arises, he remarks (p. 13): 'Reminds me of that headless bride back behind Sweet Home.' Stamp Paid is also more sceptical than most, as shown by the following exchange with Ella (p. 188):

'Your mind is loaded with spirits. Everywhere you look you see one.'
'You know as well as I do that people who die bad don't stay in the ground.'
He couldn't deny it. Jesus Christ himself didn't, so Stamp ate a piece of Ella's head cheese to show there were no bad feelings and set out to find Paul D.

However, Stamp is prepared to entertain serious thoughts of more general supernatural flickerings or murmurings: 'he believed the undecipherable language clamoring around the house [124] was the mumbling of the black and angry dead' (p. 198).

The main evidence for *Beloved*'s authenticity, in terms of a shared identity with the dead baby girl, begins with the statement, in a voice 'so low and rough' that her name is 'Beloved' (p. 52). This is followed by references to 'diamonds' ('crystal', 'earrings') of Sethe's (p. 58), her knowledge of Sethe's song (p. 176), the question of an apparent scar under her chin and, of course, her particular attachment to Sethe and the house. As the question is focalised through Denver: 'How did she know?' (p. 63). Circumstantial evidence includes her impact on Paul D (and, in extremely brief glimpses of her, on others) and the absence of the ancient dog, Here Boy, from her arrival until after her departure months later (the same animal had also suffered under the baby ghost). Some of these points at least seem hard, if not impossible, to answer by rational explanation within the limits of the text. However, does the implied author create a consistent code of the supernatural? Some of the information on Beloved is ambiguous and some might be said to be contradictory.

There are a number of statements of the order of 'Beloved came through the door and they ought to have heard her tread, but they didn't' (p. 100; see also pp. 116, 117, 123). When she visits Paul D in the shed for sexual purposes, the sequence seems to descend into dream, with Paul D waking himself by shouting 'Red heart' (p. 117), though the resultant 'pregnancy' presumably assumes some level of 'reality'. Beloved is also referred to in a more substantial manner on occasions: her breath is said to be 'exactly like new milk' (p. 98) and 'sweet air' (p. 121); a little later 'Beloved, inserting a thumb in her mouth along with the forefinger, pulled out a black tooth' (p. 133). Her 'night bucket' is carried out by Sethe (p. 242). What sort of a ghost, zombie or revenant is it, one wonders, who 'shines' for, seduces and expels the man of the house (albeit, in a sense, an interloper), gets pregnant and has other normal bodily functions including a voracious appetite? The mystery surrounding her coming and going may seem otherworldly, but some of the details are bizarre: 'the newness of her shoes' (p. 53), the freshness of her skin, her seeming emergence from the river and the incoherence of her narrative. At her departure, by which time her physical stature has, by some accounts at least, increased improbably, although she is thought by some simply to have vanished, a little boy 'put it out how he . . . saw, cutting through the woods, a naked woman with fish for hair' (p. 267).

However, let us pause to look at Beloved's narrative, such as it appears to be. By narrative we mean here not only the account which Beloved is able to give of herself, but narrative in the psychological sense, as used, for example, by Oliver Sacks (1985, p. 12):

> . . . each of us *is* a biography, a story. Each of us *is* a singular narrative, which is constructed continually and unconsciously by, through, and in us — . . . not least, through our discourse, our spoken narrations . . . historically, as narratives, we are each of us unique.

As we have seen, *Beloved* comprises, in large part, the narratives of Sethe, Paul D, Denver, Baby Suggs and, more briefly, Stamp Paid. These are delivered mainly by means of internally focalised narration and occasionally by interior monologue. As we have noted, these narrative modes are also applied through Beloved, as well as the more straightforward device, used widely throughout, of dialogue.

Beloved's narrative, then, in the sense appropriated from Sacks, can be seen to contrast strongly with those of all other characters with regard to detail and coherence. Having divulged her name as 'Beloved' and asked questions about hair and earrings, Beloved answers a number of questions about her background and her presence at 124: 'I don't have nobody', 'I was looking for this place [124] I could be in', 'She told me. When I was at the bridge she told me' [we don't know who 'she' is], 'I walked here', 'I take the shoes! I take the dress!' (all p. 65); 'dark', 'some is dead', 'the bridge', 'her face', 'the water', 'diamonds' (p. 75). The most coherent account is presented in summarised form (p. 119):

> Beloved, scratching the back of her hand, would say she remembered a woman who was hers, and she remembered being snatched away from her. Other than that, the clearest memory she had, the one she repeated, was the bridge — standing on the bridge looking down. And she knew one whiteman.

Beloved's recollections are consistent, whatever else. The fragments of narrative focalised through Beloved (pp. 100–01, 134) serve to confirm Beloved's obsession with Sethe, but not to enlighten us much further on any other score. The most extensive material for consideration here must be that contained in Beloved's two interior monologues.

The first one (pp. 210–13) contains repeated references to a female figure, flowers, a basket, crouching, 'the dead man on my face' and 'the men without skin' [presumably whites]; there is 'the little hill of dead people' and 'the woman is there with the face I want'; teeth, earrings, the sea, iron circles around necks; 'there is no one to want me   to say me my name   I wait on the bridge because she is under it   there is night and there is day' (p. 212). 'Sethe's is the face that left me', she asserts (p. 213). The second one (p. 214) is a more coherent and a punctuated repetition of the previous monologue. The conclusion (pp. 215–17) of the series of interior monologues (belonging to Sethe, Denver and Beloved) takes the form of a three-way lyrical dialogue between the women, which each appears to conclude with the statement 'You are mine'.

Beloved's narrative, in so far as it is possible now to piece it together, appears to have little if any reference to the terrible fate of the 'crawling already?' baby girl, Sethe's elder daughter. It is, however, consistent with Beloved's behaviour thereafter, when she 'gazed at her gazing face' in the creek, 'filled basket after basket' with flowers and said of Sethe that they 'had the same face' (p. 241). It may also be said to be consistent with being a representative of 'the black and angry dead', which, on a symbolic level, Beloved certainly is. Her story suggests forced transportation and drownings, which could relate to some horrific event of her early childhood (two of Baby Suggs's children perished on a slave transport boat) or could reflect a collective memory of the original slave transportations from Africa and other such horrors of murderous overcrowding. Her apparent difficulties with both memory and language accord also with these as important sub-themes of the book.

However, Beloved's narrative may also be consistent with an alternative story which has been implanted within the text. Sethe, before the 'click' (p. 175) which convinced her that Beloved was really her daughter (a conclusion which she takes some considerable time in reaching), has another theory about Beloved's past (p. 119):

> she believed Beloved had been locked up by some whiteman for his own purposes, and never let out the door. That she must have escaped to a bridge or someplace and rinsed the rest out of her mind. Something like that had happened to Ella except it was two men — a father and son — and Ella remembered every bit of it. For more than a year, they kept her locked in a room for themselves.

While the bridge remains unclarified, Stamp Paid knows of another such instance: 'Was a girl locked up in the house with a whiteman over by Deer Creek. Found him dead last summer and the girl gone. Maybe that's her. Folks say he had her in there since she was a pup' (p. 235). Such an alternative possible narrative sketched for Beloved could fit her references to crouching, the dark and a dead man lying on top of her, not to mention her flight at the sight of a white man (Bodwin). It would also provide an explanation for her acquisition of the appellation 'Beloved': 'In the dark my name is Beloved', she affirms (p. 75); 'Ghosts without skin stuck their fingers in her and said beloved in the dark and bitch in the light'

(p. 241). Such a history could therefore account too for Beloved's sexual adventures with Paul D and especially their taking the form of her all too seductive plea: 'I want you to touch me on the inside part and call me my name' (pp. 116, 263).

Such a narrative for a black girl, traumatised and terrorised to a degree beyond even Sethe, Denver and Paul D — who might be thought to be quite adequately prepared emotionally and psychologically for a reunion of hysterical misrecognition — by no means stretches credibility, either within the context of this text or, very probably, outside it. However, a rational explanation of Beloved's identity does not solve everything. Quite a bit has to depend still on coincidence (a shared obsession with earrings; a possibly maternal woman figure in her childhood who had looked like Sethe), while the question of how she could have known Sethe's song defies rationalisation (unless we grant Beloved telepathic abilities). Enough doubt would seem to pertain, therefore, for *Beloved* to remain within the category of the fantastic, even that of PF (the pure fantastic).

However, as suggested above, the figure of Beloved is intended to be a standard-bearer of symbolic significance. The book speaks of 'the black and angry dead' and carries a dedication to 'sixty million and more'. The epigraph, 'I will call them my people,/ which were not my people;/ and her beloved,/ which was not beloved' (Romans 9:25) may or may not point an answer to the riddle of Beloved's identity, but the real meaning of the book lies in its symbolic and historical promotion of a repressed people, by means of the symbolisation of mass history through fictionalised personal history. This is confirmed by the final poetic narratorial monologue and the refrain 'It was not a story to pass on' (pp. 274–5); 'Disremembered and unaccounted for, she cannot be lost because no one is looking for her, and even if they were, how can they call her if they don't know her name?' Beloved has no identity and this is the whole point. Many slaves and former slaves are labelled with the surnames of their owners. Beloved does not even have that dubious privilege. She may not have been the 'true' Beloved, and in any case was forgotten into the bargain, as 'They never knew where or why she crouched, or whose was the underwater face she needed like that' (*ibid.*). Her personal story, her narrative, in so far as it were ever known at all, was therefore forgotten and would not be passed on, like those of almost all of her class and race. How can the history of the nameless be traced?

Toni Morrison feels justified, she has let it be known at her public readings, in including ghosts as a phenomenon in her fiction, without necessarily believing or expecting anyone to believe in them *per se*, on the artistic grounds that they are no more incredible than the phenomenon of slavery now appears to be. Despite protestations that she admits no influences beyond historical and oral Afro-American sources, it is clear that Morrison, who is also a professor of English, has enlisted the tradition of the fantastic and a sophisticated narrative technique in her dealings with the unfinished business of history.

Part Three
CONCLUSIONS

. . . a book full of meaningless contradictions is as
worthless as one that holds forth about vampires and other
monstrous revenants. . .

Stanislaw Lem (1985, p. 120)

The Import of the Fantastic

The merely fantastic has only minor power.
First and Last Men (Olaf Stapledon, 1987, p. 11)

We have seen the fantastic, in the guise largely of the old-fashioned supernatural, coming through into 'modern' literature from its origins first in primitive and then in religious/theocratic societies. From a position of lurking around the Gothic and baroque margins of 'minor' works and genres in the eighteenth and nineteenth centuries, the literary fantastic in its broader sense, cross-fertilising and evolving new forms, has marched steadily towards the mainstream of literature. In the twentieth century, in the age of modernism and postmodernism and under progressive impact from the ideas generated by (or encapsulated in) psychoanalysis, existentialism and dialogism (Freud and dreams, Sartre and being, Bakhtin and carnival) the fantastic has, arguably, reached a position in which it is increasingly itself becoming 'the dominant', as it continues to develop not only its dialogical, interrogative, open and unfinished styles of discourse but also a strong social, political and ethical thrust.

These days, in the words of Antonio Risco (1982, p. 23), 'authors with great social preoccupations write in a manner which is completely fantastic for a realist reader.' Even the relatively traditionalist Northrop Frye was moved to write, in *The Secular Scripture* as early as 1976:

Fiction in the last generation or so has turned increasingly from realism to fantasy, partly because fantasy is the normal technique for fiction writers who do not believe in the permanence or continuity of the society they belong to. (Frye, 1976a, p. 138)

A number of other commentators who point towards the growing importance of fantasy, or the fantastic, in the contemporary era of fiction are cited at various stages of this study.

Our purpose at this stage is not so much the drawing together of threads from nineteenth- and twentieth-century readings — although it might be of interest to trace the development, for instance, of the treatment of shadows from Chamisso to Toni Morrison, to compare galloping statues in Pushkin, Bely and Rushdie, or to consider the re-emergence of the shadowless vampire in Bulgakov — but rather to return to the basics which arise from our historical and theoretical survey of Part One.

In any consideration of the significance of the contemporary fantastic, it would follow, the distinctions in terminology argued in Part One of this study may seem once again to blur or even dissolve. The sub-genre of PF, the fantastic *per se*, is unlikely to seem of much importance outside genre theory, although we have seen, in the case of Morrison's *Beloved*, that it can still be effectively revived. What we are left with in the wider world, however, is the quality (and the ingredients) of the fantastic and the quality of fantasy in its broader and narrower literary senses. We have conveniently subsumed all these, at the possible risk of reclouding our earlier discussion, under the term 'the literary fantastic' (rather than 'fantasy' — whether in a generic sense, the Freudian sense, or any yet more general sense still).

At this point, let us append a few concluding comments on the relation between the literary fantastic and psychoanalysis, on the uses of fantasy, language and discourse generally, and the position of fiction vis-à-vis history.

T. E. Apter (1982, p. 19) is, perhaps justifiably, cautious in her application of the psychoanalytical approach, stressing rather 'psychological fact' as the basis for 'the fantasist's reality'. While it may not be unusual for literary works which approach or enter the realm of the fantastic to contain within themselves features conducive to a psychoanalytical reading, it is unfortunate if such a reading is applied, or imposed, in an exclusively 'vulgar Freudian' manner, as though the tenets of psychoanalysis were an authority beyond dispute. In any case, Apter (p. 6) comments: 'Psychoanalytic interpretation tends to constrict language within the sphere of unconscious personal or human history, forcing its references back to repressed desires and discarded beliefs despite its desperate attempts to delineate human reality'. Gilles Deleuze (1980, pp. 293–4) has written:

Bad psychoanalysis has two ways of deceiving itself: it can believe that it has discovered identical subject matters, which necessarily can be found everywhere, or it can believe that it has found analogous forms which create false differences. In doing either, psychoanalysis fails on both grounds: those of clinical psychiatry and literary criticism.

We may remind ourselves again that Todorov had placed the fantastic in a limited period, its themes having subsequently become the privileged domain of psychoanalysis; however, we may also note Julia Kristeva's view of modern literature as having, in a sense conversely, taken over from psychoanalysis and become 'its strangest rival' in a potentially dangerous 'exploration of the limits of meaning' (see Brooke-Rose, 1983, p. 341–2).

Turning to Freud himself, it may be worth recalling Italo Svevo's comment that 'Freud is of more value to writers than to sick patients' (Hutcheon, 1984, p. 51), while Apter (p. 142) considers that 'Freud, the greatest representative of psychoanalysis, is also among the greatest fantasists'. Of latterday Freudians too, Lacan, we are told, treats Poe's story *The Purloined Letter* as 'an allegory of psychoanalysis, but also considers psychoanalysis as a model of fiction' (Selden, 1985, pp. 83–4).

An object lesson in the advisability of caution with regard to dogmatic psychoanalytic readings of literature is contained in no less an example than Freud's essay 'The "Uncanny"' of 1919, which Harold Bloom (1982, p. 205), as we have already seen, had called 'unquestionably his strongest reading of any literary text'.[1] Another such text to be treated with similar caution is Freud's essay on Dostoevsky. Freud's own 'certainty' in his interpretation of Hoffmann's *The Sandman* derives, Hertz (1980, p. 304) observes, from a dubious reading practice which totally ignores Hoffmann's 'vivid, shifty and extravagant' narration:

> Freud retells the story, occasionally quoting from the text, but what is remarkable is that everything he includes within quotation marks has already appeared within quotation marks in *The Sandman*: that is, he quotes nothing but dialogue, things said by Nathanael or by some other character; the words of the narrator have completely disappeared, replaced by Freud's own, and we have the illusion of watching Nathanael's actions through a medium considerably more transparent than Hoffmann's text.

What is lost from Freud's reading is 'the story's power — what makes it an instance of Romantic irony at its most unsettling or, if you like, of the uncanny — . . . its shifting between the registers of the psychological/daemonic and the literary' (Hertz, p. 313), or, quite simply, an appreciation of 'point of view'.

The notion of Freud as fantasist suggests other possibilities of tracing fantasy, or the literary fantastic in yet another form, within the spheres of science and scholarship (or pseudo-scholarship). Bakhtin, discussing elemental force and cosmic terror (in relation to Rabelais) writes:

> We must take into consideration the importance of cosmic terror, the fear of the immeasurable, the infinitely powerful, the starry sky, the gigantic material masses of the mountains, the sea, the cosmic upheavals, elemental catastrophies — these constitute the terror that pervades ancient mythologies, philosophies, the systems of images, and language itself with its semantics. An obscure memory of cosmic perturbations in the distant past and the dim terror of future catastrophies form the very basis of human thought, speech and images. (Bakhtin, 1968, p. 335)

This passage reads like a virtual summary of the studies of Immanuel Velikovsky, which purport to chart the effects and remembrance of a series of cosmic cataclysms in our own solar system in a not so very remote era of antiquity and caused (in the 1940s and 50s in particular) a considerable scientific and scholarly furore.[2] This is a case in which, to return momentarily to the revised generic model presented here in section VII of Part One (p. 39), the far left of nonfiction (scientific literature) and the far right of mythology (cosmogony) would appear to bend to meet each other, thus again forming the generic circle hinted at in the same section. Furthermore, it might be observed, had Velikovsky worked his complex researches (which, embracing so many disciplines, became thereby the harder either to affirm or refute) into any kind of fictional form, they would have remained uncontroversial. Fantasy has equally, of course, been recognised as a tool of science.

Brooke-Rose (p. 61), in tune with Frye and others quoted earlier, claims that 'we are witnessing a return of serious attention to romance: science fiction . . . Tolkien, Lovecraft, and others, as well as comic strips, a return to the Gothic in the mass media etc.'.

Jackson (1981, p. 155) is concerned that much 'high fantasy' and romance (Tolkien, MacDonald and Kingsley, C. S. Lewis and Ursula Le Guin for instance) function 'as conservative vehicles for social and instinctual repression' (although it is not clear why Le Guin should be included in this company; in the view of Moylan, 1986, p. 91, 'anarcho-communism informs her narrative').[3] According to Jackson (1981, p. 173), 'fantasies moving towards the realm of the "marvellous" are the ones which have been tolerated historically and widely disseminated socially.' Fantasy, when thus purveyed, she believes (p. 175), has been allowed to surface 'in a manner close to Freud's notion of art as compensation, as an activity which *sustains* cultural order by making up for society's lacks': Gothic fiction, in its day, and pornography are seen as analogous. Jackson herself seeks to discover more subversive effects within the literary fantastic, while Siebers (1984, p. 45) finds that 'as a literature that represents the logic of superstition and descends into every conceivable kind of violence, the Romantic fantastic seems a poor form of escapism' but that, on the contrary, 'it may be a means of examining and reinterpreting social formations'.

In her treatment of the fiction of Paolo Volponi, for example, Hutcheon (1984, p. 111) notes that in this novelist's work ' "culture" both contains and is constituted by language' and the reform of society would require the reform of the language it uses, while 'the language of a society reflects, or rather is, its limitation.' This is a theme which has engaged many feminist theorists and writers, while, at the literary critical level, Jackson (1981, p. 175) stresses that 'an understanding of the subversive function of fantastic literature emerges from *structuralist* rather than merely *thematic* readings of texts.'

Discourse in general in the modern world, we may now agree, has expanded to a vast industry of unprecedented and incredible proportions, a point made equally by critics such as Brooke-Rose and by writers such as Fuentes and Lem. Kundera and Eco, in their different ways, draw attention to the abundance of kitsch which can be seen as definitively undermining 'the logical distinction between Real World and Possible Worlds' (Eco, 1987, p. 14). Popular literary forms of culture are one thing (on which see, for example, Pawling, 1984, and Radford, 1986); quite another is the generation of the fantastic by technological and visual means, including the simulation of extra 'worlds' or dimensions by computer graphics. All these factors seemingly combine to devalue the fantastic in everything but popularity, yet (or perhaps consequently?) the literary fantastic as here discussed is in anything but decline.

At the same time, Brooke-Rose maintains (p. 389): 'everyone knows that real power, whether political, economic, social, psychological or even mystical, functions silently and has no need of the semblance of speech, even though it never ceases to use that semblance to persuade that we participate'. The power of the word in modern fiction can be seen with great effect, from Morrison to Rushdie, and in the case of the latter, at least, we can now say that it has not provoked silence. Such a view of the paradox of discourse, in any case, presumably owes much to Foucault, but is also close to Bakhtin's conception of an 'authoritarian discourse' which is at the same time an 'internally persuasive discourse' (Bakhtin, 1981, p. 342). It is, in particular, the literary and cinematic fantastic which, in Jackson's view (1981, p. 176), has consistently 'tried to erode the pillars of society by un-doing categorical structures'. Karl Kroeber (1988, p. 139) is similarly hopeful of the modern application of fantasy:

> Today, even more than during the Napoleonic era, it is fantasy that most rapidly allows us to recover the power of thus using language creatively, to reassert our human power to overcome the strength of human creations which function to dehumanize us by confining us within reified structures of our own making.

On another literary and political time and plane, perhaps, this strikes a chord with the intentions of Joyce — a writer who increasingly privileged language in utilising various forms of the literary fantastic — in order, in the words of Seamus Deane (1984, p. 138), 'to break the back of bourgeois syntax and create a new kind of fiction' in the perpetration of 'the act of writing as an act of rebellion, and rebellion as the act of writing' (p. 141). In an earlier age, according to Bakhtin (1968, p. 439), 'Rabelais's basic goal was to destroy the official picture of events.'

This official picture, or history, is, in any case, untrustworthy (ask Morrison, or Rushdie!). According to Foucalt (1986, p. 89), following Nietzsche, 'the true historical sense confirms our existence among countless lost events, without a landmark or a point of reference', while even truth is doubtful: 'truth is undoubtedly the sort of error that cannot be refuted because it was hardened into an unalterable form in the long baking process of history' (ibid., p. 79). On the plane of fiction too, for Borges's Pierre Menard, 'Historical truth . . . is not what happened; it is what we judge to have happened' (Borges, 1970, p. 69); or, to put it in the words of Fuentes (1988, p. 62) 'Art gives life to what history killed. Art gives voice to what history denied, silenced, or persecuted. Art brings truth to the lies of history.' Meanwhile, as the old certainties continue to slip in many parts of the world, those 'reified structures of our own making' are breaking down.

Given 'the fantastic metahistory of Russia', for example, in a situation in which the fantastic is as real as reality is fantastic, Strada (1988, p. 140) re-reads Russian literature 'in a fantastic key'. Similarly, Siebers (1984, p. 125) notes, in relation to Hawthorne, that 'the historical events connected with religious persecution in New England and the witchcraft delusion of Salem composed in his estimation a Gothic more horrifying than the story-teller could ever imagine.' This attitude scarcely needs extension to more recent events and has been reiterated by — once again — Rushdie and Morrison. Events in Eastern Europe, in the light of the fiction of Kafka and Kundera, or the theatre of the absurd of Havel, are a prime example. Balzac's observation that 'reality has taken great pains to imitate fiction' is re-phrased by Fuentes (p. 94) to read 'reality constantly surpasses the imagination of its inventors.' Elsewhere he goes on to say: 'By proposing the possibility of the verbal imagination as no less a reality than historical narrative, the novel becomes perpetually new, announcing an imminent world' (Fuentes, 1989b, p. xli).[4]

If the fantastic in history can be taken as read — from relativist and absolute positions alike — then what of current reality? Jackson (1981, p. 180) sees what she terms 'the modern fantastic' as representing 'dissatisfaction and frustration with a cultural order which deflects or defeats desire'. Hutcheon (1984, p. 77) views the literary fantastic as providing 'the freedom — or the "escape" — of an ordered vision, perhaps a kind of "vital" consolation for living in a world one usually perceives and experiences only as chaos'. In a similar vein, Apter (p. 111) has the following to say on the relation of 'fantasy' to 'normal conditions':

The initial impact of fantasy is its deviation from the norm. The further and more fascinating impact of fantasy arises from its connections to the norm, from the way in which it highlights the instability, inconsistency or underlying pre-posterousness of the normal.

This relation between fantasy and 'normality' can be linked with the idea of social reality as a fictional construct, an approach which is seen as going back at least as far as Kurt Vaihinger's 1911 'fictionalist' philosophy of the 'as if' (noted by McHale, 1987, p. 37).

It has, therefore, become almost a commonplace to have noted that, in modern literature, the turning away from realistic representation has taken the path of the fantastic, the absurd and the carnivalesque: to arrive at new forms 'merely showing the real, in its unique "idiocy", as the fantastic which it is', or as 'a fantastic realism' (Brooke-Rose, p. 388). At perhaps a lower general level, Burgin (1986, p. 105) stresses that 'common fantasy structures contribute to the construction of "reality" in the realm of representations' in what he calls 'the total environment of the "society of the spectacle"' (p. 106). This returns us once again to the kitsch and the popular culture which worry or intrigue Eco and Kundera.

With regard to political history, recent and ongoing, Seamus Deane (1984, p. 138) is close to Fuentes and others cited above in suggesting that 'fiction realizes the potential history fails to achieve.' As is often the case, however, such a formulation could just as easily be reversed: history may involve the fulfilling of fantasy. One ambitious attempt to investigate and substantiate such a hypothesis is Klaus Theweleit's two-volume study *Male Fantasies* (*Männer-phantasien*, 1977–8), dealing with the mentality and writings of the pre-Nazi *Freikorps* (see Carter and Turner's article in Burgin, 1986).

As for the ongoing, Martin Amis (1987, p. 26) has reminded us of a theme long established in science fiction, but remarkably little treated, he estimates, in the mainstream of fiction, in his assertion that 'nuclear weapons could bring about the Book of Revelation in a matter of hours'. This sentence by Amis compellingly entwines historical absurd with literary fantastic, in both cases *par excellence*. Here we go then, 'from monster to metaphor' again, by way of phallic symbol. However, as he chillingly adds: 'Of course, no dead will rise; nothing will be revealed'.

At what Foucault (1986, p. 265) terms society's present 'threshold of modernity', when 'the life of the species is wagered on its own political strategies', in the age of Aids and at a moment when the planet appears poised for ecological disaster — for as long, indeed, as the 'Frankenstein syndrome' of man-induced doomsday remains high on the agenda of probability — the continued need for monstrous revelations from the literary fantastic is disturbingly guaranteed.

Postscript

THE RUSHDIE AFFAIR

Any denunciation of acts of the imagination by secular or religious authorities strikes at the very heart of freedom — the freedom to imagine
Article 19 (Appignanesi and Maitland, 1989, p. 110)

In asking for the withdrawal of this sacrilege, Muslims are neither showing intolerance, imposing censorship, nor infringing anyone's freedom of expression.
Sultan Shahin (Appignanesi and Maitland, 1989, p. 113)

To burn a book is not to destroy it. One minute of darkness will not make us blind.
Salman Rushdie (*TLS*, October 6–12, 1989, p. 1089)

It was not originally envisaged that the work of Rushdie would figure to any great degree in this book. However, the situation was soon altered, at a relatively late stage in planning and preparation, by publication of *The Satanic Verses* in September 1988 and by the furore which developed a few months later. Rushdie forced his way into this study by the brilliance of his writing and he has been forced into it by the unprecedented nature and development of the 'Rushdie affair'. The life of a writer of the fantastic has been under severe threat — ultimately because of the fantastic form and content of his prose fiction.

At a reading at The Watershed in Bristol, on 30 September 1988 (a few days after publication of *The Satanic Verses* and as the first reviews began to appear), said by Rushdie to be the first public reading from the novel (I do not know how many more followed, if any), a large and appreciative audience was left in little doubt over

219

the content and the tenor of *The Satanic Verses*. That the audience included many Afro-Caribbeans and Asians is certain. How many of these were Muslims (and their distribution as to Shiite, Sunni, Sufi or other allegiance) I have no way of knowing. What I do know is that not a whimper of protest at what Rushdie appeared to be doing in his fiction was heard. What happened thereafter — at first in India, Pakistan and elsewhere, and subsequently in Bradford, Tehran and elsewhere — is now already history.[5]

Near the end of *The Satanic Verses*, a minor character warns that 'all metaphors are capable of misinterpretation' (*SV*, p. 537). This prescient statement is in tune with Tom Moylan's paraphrase of Michael Ryan: 'Metaphor holds open our perception of reality to otherness, to historical change. . . . Thus Ryan links metaphor and sedition as linguistic and political activities that share the challenge to the forces of containment, authority, totality.' (Moylan, 1986, p. 213) Thus, it follows, the forces of containment, authority ad totality not infrequently react to metaphor in maximalist and hysterical terms. Ironically or otherwise, Rushdie's character had India in mind when expounding her follow-up theory (*SV*, *ibid.*):

> Society was orchestrated by what she called *grand narratives*: history, economics, ethics. In India, the development of a corrupt and closed state apparatus had 'excluded the masses of the people from the ethical project'. As a result, they sought ethical satisfactions in the oldest of the grand narratives, that is, religious faith. 'But these narratives are being manipulated by the theocracy and various political elements in an entirely retrogressive way. . .' . 'Battle lines are being drawn up in India today,' she cried. 'Secular versus religious, the light versus the dark. Better you choose which side you are on.'

India apart, this statement has obvious relevance to a number of other states and societies. The grand narrative of Islamic faith, or at least certain of its influential representatives, has declared war on the person and text of Salman Rushdie.

'Burn the books and trust the Book', cries a henchman of the Khomeini-like Imam in one of the dreams of which *The Satanic Verses* is made up (*SV*, p. 211). The novel includes many prophetic statements of this order. Elizabeth Dipple (1988, p. 137) is writing of Eco's *The Name of the Rose* when she observes:

> Books and their denotation in the life of the mind, of the spirit, of society, and of the individual can actively lead to

death which, in this novel, easily comes from ideological controversies and from pursuing the wrong text of forbidden knowledge.

Death from books! But not in the modern age, surely? Linda Hutcheon (1988, p. 70) has the position of women and black writers in mind when she notes: 'The right of expression (however unavoidably implicated in liberal humanist assumptions) is not something that can be taken for granted by the ex-centric'. Such statements, drawn from outside Rushdie and Rushdie-criticism, take on a startling new dimension in the light of the Rushdie affair.

Brian McHale (1987, p. 36), characterising postmodernist writing, points out that 'Entities [or personalities] can change their ontological status in the course of history, in effect migrating from one ontological realm or level to another':

> For instance, real world entities and happenings can undergo 'mythification', moving from the profane realm to the realm of the sacred. Or mythological entities can, with the erosion of the belief-system that sustains them, lose their status of *superior* reality, 'realer' than the real world, and deteriorate to the status of 'mere' fictions.

Such a process of mythification and fictionalisation effectively describes what is perceived to occur in such texts as *The Satanic Verses*, Bulgakov's *The Master and Margarita* and D. H. Lawrence's *The Man Who Died*. Rushdie has subsequently spoken of 'a conflict between the sacred text and the profane text, between revealed literature and imagined literature' (Appignanesi and Maitland, 1989, p. 29). Islam (or fundamentalist Islam, at least), being 'the religion of the book *par excellence*' (Amir Taheri, *ibid.*, p. 94) and, like the Inquisition (in the view of Marina Warner, *ibid.* p. 208), engaged primarily in 'a struggle for control of the word', obviously does not take this sort of thing lightly.

The literary case for *The Satanic Verses* (or, at least, a literary case) has, it is hoped, been made in our Part Two section on Rushdie. There is no need to go over those arguments again here. Neither can one realistically expect, say, the finer points of poststructuralist mumbo-jumbo to cut much ice with the mullahs of Qom (although a short course in the basics of literary criticism would do most British politicians no harm, for a start). The problems, though, which Islam can have with literature (and, indeed therefore, literature with Islam) would appear to be immense. The status of

Rushdie's novel as a work of fiction and the devices employed of distancing, by means of dream and symbolic representation, are regarded, as John Walsh has pointed out (Appignanesi and Maitland, pp. 31–3), as no excuse for anything, and especially for 'filthy language'. Indeed, according to Malise Ruthven (in *ibid.*, p. 205), the concept of the novel is a recent and troublesome implant in the Muslim world: 'The form itself comes close to blasphemy in the sense that it creates an alternative reality to that established by the Creator.' There is no answer that a western literary critic can make to that one! However, such an attitude may go some way towards explaining why *The Satanic Verses* has caused more offence while, as a work of fiction, being 'a good deal less subversive of Islamic orthodoxy than other more scholarly works published in Britain' (Ruthven, *ibid.*, p. 204). This is not to say, however, that Islam has not had recent difficulties with *The Oxford English Dictionary*, or age-long and explosive objections, ever vibrant today, to Dante.

Without wishing to hold up institutionalised Christianity as one of the all-time beacons of tolerance, one can at least agree with John Calder (*Guardian*, letters, 11 March 1989) that 'Anything can happen in dreams and in Christian terms only a 13th-century Inquisitor would hold a person responsible for their dreams' (well, all right, perhaps three or four centuries later would be nearer the mark; Giordano Bruno certainly did not come off too well in 1600). However, Rushdie's Muslim critics (or such of his adversaries as may be sufficiently dissociated from the advocacy of murder to be dignifiable with this calling) persist in the use of such phrases as 'a thin veil of fiction' (Syed Ali Ashraf, in Appignanesi and Maitland, p. 25) and 'thinly disguised as a piece of literature' (Mughram Al-Ghamdi, *ibid.*, p. 58).

Enough alternative Muslim voices have been raised, deploring out-and-out dogmatism and threats of violence, for us to agree with Arnold Wesker (*Independent*, 25 July 1989, p. 19) that 'We are here dealing with a special mentality which cannot bear deviation from its own perceptions and beliefs.' Elsewhere (*Independent*, letters, 29 May 1989), Wesker had pointed out that 'the view that violence is a way of asserting your belief is an infantile view', while, in any case, 'to murder the thinker does not murder the thought.' One is reminded too of Robert M. Pirsig's comment on fanaticism:

> You are never dedicated to something you have complete confidence in. No one is fanatically shouting that the sun is going to rise tomorrow. They *know* it's going to rise

tomorrow. When people are fanatically dedicated to political or religious faiths or any other kinds of dogmas or goals, it's always because these dogmas or goals are in doubt. (Pirsig, 1976, p. 146)

Tariq Ali has rightly stressed (Ali and Brenton, 1989, p. 22) that, for those who may feel the need so to do, 'the only way to combat Rushdie is through a battle of ideas'.

As Dipple (1988, p. 66) has written, 'One of Borges's favorite terms or ideas is that of the heresiarch — the arch heretic who questions all before him, and particularly all forms of established dogma.' The pedigree of the heretic in European literature goes back through Zamiatin (see note 18 to Part One) and Bruno to the poets that Plato would have excluded from his Republic. The twentieth century, particularly when under the sway of Hitler and Stalin, has instructed us afresh in the repression of writers. It has also, though, demonstrated the power of texts to survive: Tariq Ali aptly quotes in comment on the Rushdie affair the famous dictum from Bulgakov's *The Master and Margarita* that 'manuscripts don't burn' (Ali and Brenton, p. 21).

Here the battle lines certainly are drawn, sides must be chosen and one thing is for sure: it can be no part of a modern, secular democratic society to act as the thought police for absolute interpretations of any religious dogma, or to countenance the witch-hunting of scapegoats or heretics.

One absolutely essential issue to be laid to rest in connection with this affair, and with any critique of its fundamentalist Muslim protagonists, is the spectre of racism. Firstly, it is hard to see how support for Rushdie — an Indian by birth — by, for example, white literati can be construed as 'racism' in any normal definition of the word. Secondly, it must be emphasised, as by Michael Foot (*Independent*, letters, 24 July 1989), that all this 'has nothing whatever to do with racism but everything to do with the bigotry inherent in all religions which must be constantly curbed in the name of our common humanity'. In other words, fundamentalist religion, from whatever quarter, is bad news, as any survey of the world's trouble spots will soon show. The Muslim community in Britain, as elsewhere, has a right to demand tolerance; it does not, however, have a right to expect that tolerance to be extended to toleration of its own complete intolerance and of the ugly consequences which may flow therefrom.

The furore over *The Satanic Verses*, it might be argued, has anyway little enough to do with religion in any meaningful (even

Islamic) sense, but plenty to do with political, patriarchal and theocratic authoritarianism: in Iran, in Pakistan and in Bradford. It has to do not with the reading of books (and certainly not with the reading of a book which is generally agreed to be long and difficult by almost any standards), but with the instilling of hatred into children, of the creation thereby of fall guys and targets — the figure of the heretic and the scapegoat, used for social, racial and often financial disadvantage. The desired effect, for the perpetrators of such campaigns, is that of substitution: a surrogate for the real and legitimate politics which would threaten their own power structure.

Two further questions immediately arise at this point: can the writer of imaginative fiction be guilty of blasphemy and should there be any law of blasphemy? The answer to these two questions, for a multitude of possible reasons, must in each case be a resounding no. The privately brought prosecution, by Mary Whitehouse, and conviction of the editor of *Gay News* for the 1977 printing of James Kirkup's poem, 'The love that dares to speak its name', has already brought the law, and the country's cultural name, into sufficient disrepute. Ironically, Kirkup has himself now come out against publication of a paperback edition of *The Satanic Verses* (*Independent on Sunday*, 4 February 1990, p. 21), on the grounds that he finds the novel 'tedious'.

Timothy Brennan (1989, p. 144) mentions 'the way *The Satanic Verses* would be manipulated by the British press', as 'a fable of Western freedom vs. Oriental fanaticism'; in so far as this is true, it is surely only the case (a factor he omits from his argument) *after* the Bradford book burning. Before that, outside its literary reviews in the quality press and gossip over the size of Rushdie's advance, the novel has attracted little publicity. Furthermore, the campaign was anything but spontaneous, as a study of documents and correspondence in *The Rushdie File* (Appignanesi and Maitland, 1989; see also Hitchens, 1989) reveals. A cogent and plausible explanation for much of this is provided by Aziz Al-Azmeh (see Appignanesi and Maitland, pp. 69–74): this commentator draws attention to the classic method adopted by the book's inquisitors — that of citing statements torn out of context — and their totalitarian, and spurious, aspirations to represent all Muslims. He continues:

> Few Muslims — even practising ones — are Islamists in cultural and political terms, although in Britain, as elsewhere, few are willing to contest the issue with cantankerous activists backed by deep (well-endowed) coffers. In fact this

kind of political and cultural zealotry is very new in Muslim
history, which only emerged from an insignificant subculture
when its patrons, from some of the most archaic groups in
the Muslim world, became spectacularly rich after the oil
boom. (*ibid.*, p. 71)

Amir Taheri informs us (writing on 13 February 1989):

A demand for Rushdie to be judged by Khomeini is believed
to have been made by a number of British Muslims in a
petition sent via the Islamic embassy in London several weeks
ago. Once he received the demand, Khomeini could not
remain silent. (*ibid.*, p. 92; see also p. 56)

Furthermore:

Khomeini's motives for giving his order are not entirely
religious. In the last few months he has suffered a number of
humiliating setbacks: the ceasefire with Iraq, the election of a
woman prime minister in Pakistan and, with the Soviet
withdrawal from Afghanistan, the failure of his protégés to
secure a prominent role in the assembly organized by the
Mujahidin in Rawalpindi. He also wants to point a finger at
Pakistan and Saudi Arabia as half-hearted defenders of the
faith. (*ibid.*, pp. 94–5)

The same situations pertain for Khomeini's successors.

Arguments over the relative morality in international relations of
Iran and other states (as put by Ali A. Muzrui, in *ibid.*, pp. 220–8)
do nothing to mitigate Iranian actions. Nor, for that matter, should
perceptions be altered by arguments as to the inconsistencies, or lack
of moral fibre, of the British literary or media establishment with
regard to any other matters of cultural or journalistic freedom
(justified or otherwise as such criticisms may be in their own terms).
Any attention paid to such equivocations can serve only the aims of
Shabbir Akhtar, who wishes to bolster 'the temper of militant
wrathfulness which is essential to the preservation of religious
traditions in secular society' (*ibid.*, p. 229; and p. 240).

As Christopher Hitchens has emphatically stated, 'the Salman
Rushdie case *has* no analogue and no precedent'; 'when last did a
head of government *claim* to be soliciting the murder of a citizen of
another country, for pay, for the offence of literary production?'
(Hitchens, 1989, p. 11).

The Rushdie affair has brought civil commotion to the streets and incitement to murder to the television screens of many a country, complete with undertones of international terrorism. People have been killed in demonstrations and by assassination. Media policy, particularly that of television in this country, appears to be one of giving prominence to the protestors on the one hand, and of ignoring the grotesque realities of the situation on the other. The famous BBC quality of 'balance' is being employed, or so it would appear, to see 'fair play' between Rushdie's supporters and his detractors, as though the matter concerned a perfectly normal and legal disagreement, or a minor dispute within, say, the SDP. One phone call or remonstration from the present writer brought forth the comment from a 'World This Weekend' producer: 'Didn't you think there was a touch of Devil's advocate there?'. The ironies of this remark require no elaboration. Incitement to murder is not infrequently reported in such terms as 'calls for the implementation of the death penalty'. No charges of incitement have yet been brought. In some ways such supine official and semi-official posturing, extending from politicians and interviewers even at times to hitherto respected writers, is even more disturbing than the events which lie behind it.

Rushdie writes exclusively in English and his works belong to English literature; they also belong to world literature. Earlier, in Part Two, it was said that further lists of writers would be proposed to which Rushdie's name should be added. One such list, provided within the text of the play *Iranian Nights* (Ali and Brenton, 1989, p. 20), consists of: 'Dante, Christopher Marlowe, Oscar Wilde, Omar Khayyam, James Joyce, Al Ma'avi, D. H. Lawrence, Naguib Mahfouz, Sean O'Casey, Faiz, Bertolt Brecht, Vasili Grossman, Gabriel García Márquez' — all persecuted or censored authors. A shorter one is contained in Tony Harrison's BBC television film *The Blasphemers' Banquet* (1989); this comprises the 'blasphemers' Omar Khayyám, Molière, Voltaire and Byron.

My own list would be of writers of the fantastic, attacked or repressed specifically for their imaginative works. These include Hoffmann who, as we have seen in Part Two, had to defend himself from his deathbed; and Zamiatin, who was driven out of Soviet literature following the publication abroad of a pirated edition of his pre-Orwellian novel *We* (banned in the Soviet Union from 1920 until 1988). Another writer, of the absurd and the fantastic, who could be included is Daniil Kharms, arrested for being an eccentric, and dying of starvation in a prison hospital during the siege of Leningrad. More recently comes the name of Andrei Siniavsky who, as author, under the pseudonym of Abram Terts, of a collection of novellas known subsequently as *The Fantastic World of Abram Terts*, remains perhaps the only author (along with his co-defendant in the infamous Daniel and Siniavsky case of 1966) to have been tried and convicted in court (of subversion against the state) purely on the basis of his literary texts. Like Rushdie (and like Kharms), Siniavsky predicted his own fate in his fiction and the 'World Statement', published by The International Committee for the Defence of Salman Rushdie and his Publishers (in a number of newspapers on 2 March 1989) includes among the many signatories the name of Andrei Siniavsky (USSR/France). We may care to note that John Banville and Toni Morrison also signed this document.

Mention, once again, of the imagination and of Siniavsky and Zamiatin brings us back full circle to *The Satanic Verses* itself. Nisha Puri's review called the novel 'a work of truly daring creativity which recognises few frontiers beyond which the imagination must not float' (Appignanesi and Maitland, p. 13), while Carlos Fuentes, as to be expected, one of Rushdie's most effectively trenchant supporters, writes of 'the Ayatollah's crusade against the freedom of the imagination' (*ibid.*, p. 247). At one stage Rushdie's Gibreel, exasperated at his own dreaming, exclaims: 'if I was God I'd cut the imagination right out of people and then maybe poor bastards like me could get a good night's rest' (*SV*, p. 122). This may be an intentional echo of Zamiatin's *We*, which culminates in the nightmare of 'fantasiectomy', an enforced operation to remove the faculty of imagination. In any case, Rushdie has once again second-guessed what would be the logical end of fundamentalist aspirations.

We have already drawn attention to many of the disturbing factors surrounding the Rushdie affair. The effects on literature include the bombing of bookshops and the intimidation of publishers. Beyond this, the short-term and long-term effects on society and race relations are as yet incalculable, and the dénoue-ment of the affair unforseeable, while the ironies are many. The novel has received unheard-of publicity, instead of remaining a relatively obscure text for the literary élite. World sales are high and the translations are flowing. How many people actually read it is another matter: George Steiner (on BBC's 'Newsnight' in February 1989) claimed not to be able to get beyond page 5, while at an Albert Hall protest meeting attended by more than 5,000 people, a show of hands revealed that only one person in the hall had read the offending book (*Guardian*, 2 October 1989, p. 3). Many English literary figures affect a posture of boredom (see Hitchens, 1989;

compare the response in Britain to the award of the 1989 Nobel Prize to Cela). The apparent necessity for a large price to be put on Rushdie's head is perhaps the most grotesque irony, for religious and other reasons: 'Why was the money necessary in the first place? Khomeini had offered any Muslim assassin a one-way ticket to Heaven' (Ali and Brenton, p. 21).

So much for the many minusses. Can there be said to be any plusses? Fuentes thinks so (Appignanesi and Maitland, p. 246):

> An author who is looking for the truth has been condemned to death by a priestly hierarchy, whose deep insecurity is disguised by their pretension to holding the truth. The Ayatollahs, nevertheless, have done a great service to literature, if not to Islam. They have debased and caricatured their own faith. But they have shifted the wandering attention of the world to the power of words, literature and the imagination, in ways totally unforeseen in their philosophy.

Elizabeth Dipple (1988, p. 120) speculates that '*The Name of the Rose* is the most unread bestseller in history.' Linda Hutcheon (1988, p. 20) also perceives a tendency in the modern novel to bridge the gap between élite and popular art and remarks on 'the paradox of novels like *The French Lieutenant's Woman* or *The Name of the Rose* themselves being at once popular best-sellers and objects of intense academic study'; this is achieved, she argues, by the 'use and abuse [of] the conventions of both popular and élite literature', in such a way as to '*use* the invasive culture industry to challenge its own commodification processes from within'. García Márquez is reported to be currently writing soap opera. Hence too the phenomenon of Rushdie's huge advance for *The Satanic Verses* (now hideously balanced by the price on his head), which stems from bizarre developments in the economics and hype of publishing and not, as some Islamic commentators purport to think, from a combination of pan-western conspiracy and will of God (see, for example, the extract from Khomeini's message published in the *Guardian*, 6 March 1989, p. 21).

'All this fuss over a book?' is a comment still heard. According to Hutcheon (1988, p. 71), postmodern literature has managed 'to break down the barrier between academic discourse and contemporary art (which is often marginalized, not to say ignored, in the academy)'. Rushdie has contributed notably to this process over the past decade. With *The Satanic Verses*, at a single stroke and at a terrifying price, his unique and fantastic 'performance' (to revive and broaden the term used by Charles Brockden Brown) has contrived to demarginalise the position of modern literature, not just in the academy but in society at large. Even literary criticism is no longer the frivolous fringe activity it was once thought to be.

AFTERWORD

At the present time of writing, after the recent first anniversary and renewal of Khomeini's *fatwa*, the situation shows little sign of advancing further and no sign of resolution. Rushdie's 7,000-word essay 'In Good Faith' (*Independent on Sunday*, 4 February 1990, pp. 18–20) stresses the fictionality of *The Satanic Verses*, while outlining, in far greater detail than writers are usually willing to supply, the compositional principles behind the novel. Works by William Blake and Mikhail Bulgakov are confirmed as 'the two books that were most influential on the shape of this novel'. Unusual insights are vouchsafed through unprecedented circumstances. Rushdie's Herbert Read Memorial Lecture (6 February 1990) had to be delivered by Harold Pinter. In this piece, Rushdie argues that literature should not be given the status of the sacred, but, at least, 'the privilege of being the arena of discourse, the place where the struggle of languages can be acted out' (Salman Rushdie, *Is Nothing Sacred?*, p. 15, published as a pamphlet by Granta, Cambridge). The particular struggle of languages which has engaged us here has now been chronicled by Malise Ruthven, in his book *A Satanic Affair: Salman Rushdie and the rage of Islam* (London: Chatto & Windus, 1990).

June 1990

Notes

NOTES TO PART ONE

1. Fuller and varying accounts of precursors in critical approaches to the fantastic may be found in the introductory chapters to the studies by, for example, Brooke-Rose, Jackson, Little and Hume: see bibliography. Petzold (1986, p. 12) points out that Todorov's use of 'the fantastic' (*le fantastique*) follows 'common usage exemplified by Roger Caillois, among others' (i.e. Roger Caillois, *Au coeur du fantastique*, Paris, 1965). See also (below) the examples from Praz, Vax etc., demonstrating twentieth-century currency for the term, as well as the earlier French tradition of its usage.

2. That all poetry is 'fantasy' would seem to be an even greater truism than the frequently made similar statements regarding prose (e.g. Little, 1980, p. 67: 'In a sense, all creative fiction is Fantasy'). Treatments of fantasy in poetry are, therefore, likely to concern themselves with psychoanalytical concepts such as 'unconscious fantasy' (e.g. John Fletcher's essay, in Burgin, 1986). A sufficient degree of verisimilitude is unlikely to be achieved in the forms normally thought of as poetry for the Todorovian notion of the fantastic, based on hesitation, to come into play. In this policy, as in a number of others, we follow Todorov's lead (see Todorov, 1973, pp. 58–60), a point with which even Lem — one of Todorov's sharpest critics — agrees (Lem, 1985, p. 241 n.). Freud (1955, p. 250) also appears to agree with this approach to the supernatural remaining within a 'poetic reality', as in Dante or Shakespeare. Cf. Irwin (Schlobin, 1982, pp. 52–3) quoting Herbert Read's view that only narrative fiction illustrates 'fantasy'; and Tolkien (1964, pp. 46–7) on *Macbeth*. See also on this Ziolkowski (1977) pp. 249–50.

3. During the eighteenth century, the word 'Gothic' also was 'a synonym for the barbarous' until Horace Walpole transformed its fortunes (see Varma, 1966, pp. 10–13).

4. Scott had personal experience of opium, in common with other writers of the period: on this and its effects upon *The Bride of Lammermoor* (1819), see Hayter, 1988, pp. 292–4. Scott could subsequently recollect writing nothing of the incident contained in this novel, which was later much admired by Wilkie Collins (himself a laudanum addict). In addition to his article on Hoffmann, Scott made interesting comments on the supernatural in pieces on Walpole, Ann Radcliffe, Maturin and Mary Shelley (see Scott, 1968), to which later reference will be made.

230

5.   V. G. Belinskii, *Polnoe sobranie sochinenii*, 13 volumes, Moscow, 1956, vol. X, p. 41; see also Introduction to Fyodor Dostoevsky, *The Double: Two Versions*, translated by Evelyn Harden, Ann Arbor (Ardis), 1985, p. xiv.

6.   V. F. Odoevskii, *Russkie nochi*, Leningrad (Literaturnye pamiatniki: Nauka), 1975, p. 189; English translation by Olga Koshansky-Olienikov and Ralph E. Matlaw: V. F. Odoevskii, *Russian Nights*, New York (Dutton), 1965, p. 27.

7.   Todorov's examples are not however quite as few as is sometimes claimed. He provides no specific listing, but seems to claim firmly the following works for the 'genre': James, *The Turn of the Screw*; Mérimée, *La Vénus d'Ille*; Cazotte, *Le Diable amoureux*; John Dickson Carr, *The Burning Court*. In addition, he frequently refers to tales by Maupassant and Nerval's *Aurélia* as likely genuine examples, plus works by Hoffmann and Poe. There is no suggestion that he considers such a roll-call to be exhaustive. He further expends considerable discussion on works which ultimately resolve themselves into either the fantastic–uncanny (such as Potocki, *The Saragossa Manuscript* and Nodier, *Inès de las Sierras*) the fantastic–marvellous (Gautier, *La Morte amoureuse* and Villiers de l'Isle-Adam, *Véra*). Todorov's imprecision in his categorisations derives partly from the abstract nature of his interest in genre and partly, despite his avowed excursions into genre theory, from an overriding emphasis rather on the qualities inherent in the fantastic (and near fantastic), as revealed perhaps (see below) in the original French title of his book.

8.   In another essay, Lem indicates that he equates the fantastic with the impossible, which can, by means of convention ('a tacit agreement between writer and reader') occur even within realism: 'For example, the thoughts of a dying man are often detailed in quite realistic fiction even though it is impossible, therefore fantastic, to read the thoughts of a dying man out of his head and reproduce them in language' (Lem, 1985, p. 32). He further proceeds to a generic classification of his own (p. 35): 'If the depicted world is oriented positively towards man, it is the world of the classical fairy tale, in which physics is controlled by morality, for in a fairy tale there can be no accidents that result in anyone's death, no irreparable damage to the positive hero. If it is oriented negatively, it is the world of myth ("Do what you will, you'll still become guilty of killing your father and committing incest"). If it is neutral, it is the real world — the world that realism describes in its contemporary shape and that science fiction tries to describe at other points on the space–time continuum.'

9.   With the exception of Todorov, most, if not all, of the recent commentators on the fantastic are to be considered critics (or perhaps 'metacritics') rather than genuine theorists; even Brooke–Rose, who has a particularly rigorous critical mind, puts herself in the former category.

10.   See the Preface to *Sylvie and Bruno Concluded*, in Carroll, 1939, p. 464.

11.   On the creation of other worlds see, for example, Hutcheon, 1984,

pp. 87–103; Aldiss, 1986; Wendland, 1985; and McHale, 1987. Aldiss (p. 98) sees Hardy's Wessex as a dreamworld. A distinction should also be made between 'other worlds' and 'possible worlds': cf. Brooke-Rose, p. 393 n. 2: 'The term "possible worlds", like "alternative world" has now become accepted for a certain type of SF which postulates a different version of history (if Napoleon had won Waterloo etc.)'. The question might also be raised as to whether the latter class of world belongs more properly to science fiction, or to some branch of the historical novel (see Little, 1980, p. 71 for distinctions between science fiction and 'Fantasy' — treated in detail by Wendland, and Kroeber, 1988). Such considerations only serve to complicate further Little's model. For a somewhat different approach again to 'worlds', see Hume (pp. 9–13), while Petzold (p. 14), again following Tolkien, appears to see no need to go beyond a 'secondary world'.

12. This state of affairs, if it be true, does certainly not inhibit some scholars: see, for example, Varnado, 1987.

13. Siebers (p. 62) warns strongly — vituperatively even — against overdoing the search for the untrustworthy narrator: 'Narrative unreliability is a provocative notion, but its usefulness may be deceiving, especially in the case of fantastic representation. The idea of narrative unreliability has become the brightest gemstone in the showcase of modern textual theory, and literary critics do not tire of polishing it to a high gloss for special exhibition. Whether a narrator's unreliability derives from jealousy, greed, insanity, or the author's irony, it is held forth and extolled as precious, avant-garde, and quintessentially modern. Traps of narration are often hailed as the only objects worthy of study, and students of narrative theory strive to uncover lies everywhere, until they identify the ultimate lie as language itself. In *The Rhetoric of Fiction*, Wayne C. Booth warns of the dangers of such 'deep reading', attributing it to the practice of viewing older works of fiction from the perspective of modernist literature, and yet the quest for unreliabilty continues' (see Booth, 1961, pp. 364–74, on Henry James).

14. Strada's concept of 'metahistory' is not to be confused with that of, say, Hayden White (in his *Metahistory: The historical imagination in nineteenth-century Europe*, Baltimore, 1973). For Strada (1988, pp. 133–4): 'Meta-history is an illumination which, across the images of poetic reason, reveals in an "alienated" [*straniata*] perspective the community [that exists between] the already dead, the not yet born and the still living — that is to say that entirety of individual and general destinies past, present and future which is called "history". This fantastic–poetic metahistory recreates a mythology of its own, bound up with the poetic myth of tradition.'

15. Chanady refers mainly to French and Spanish theoretical sources. Todorov apart, she draws most inspiration perhaps from Bessière (e.g. Bessière, 1976, p. 31, quoted by Chanady, p. 12).

16. We may well, therefore, wish to locate magic realism within the

Todorovian 'marvellous'. On the history of the term magic (or 'magical') realism and the varying interpretations of the origin and nature of the concept, see Chanady, pp. 17–21 and 26–7: for example, some commentators see magic realism as a purely Latin-American phenomenon, while others trace it to Kafka or (even) Proust (p. 20). See also Risco, 1982, for a classification of Spanish works along Todorovian (and wider) lines.

17. This quotation from Dostoevsky is invoked by the Soviet writer Aitmatov in the Foreword to his novel *The Day Lasts More Than A Hundred Years* (1980), in which the author confesses to the use 'for the first time in my writing career' of 'science-fictional plot elements'. It is unfortunate that the English translator here employs the word 'fantasy' for the original *'fantasticheskii siuzhet'* giving a different (and inaccurate) impression: see Chingiz Aitmatov, *The Day Lasts More Than A Hundred Years*, translated by John French, London (Futura), 1984, p. 7.

18. *A Soviet Heretic: Essays by Yevgeny Zamyatin*, edited and translated by Mirra Ginsburg, Chicago, 1970, pp. 41–2. Zamiatin's critical essays are all too often neglected.

19. There is also the connection with the word 'fancy'; on this see Irwin's essay (in Schlobin, 1982), 'From fancy to fantasy: Coleridge and beyond'.

20. Burgin, 1986 (*Forms of Fantasy*) deals with 'fantasy' as a general phenomenon, heavily influenced by Freudian and post-Freudian psychoanalysis; the contributors seem obsessed by primal scenes and castration complexes; literature is of rather secondary importance in this collection and questions of genre (or 'the fantastic') do not arise. Attention is drawn to the variant spellings of 'fantasy'/'phantasy' (as translations of *Phantasie*) — see, e.g., p. 32 n. 40; 'fantastic' occurs here only as the adjective of 'fantasy' (cf., in a literary context, Little, 1980, and others). On 'phantasy', in the Jungian sense, see Irwin, 1976, pp. 6–7.

21. Attebery (p. 2), as we have seen already, seems even wider: '*Any narrative which includes as a significant part of its make-up some violation of what the author clearly believes to be natural law — that is fantasy*' [my emphasis].

22. Cf. Gillian Beer's claim in connection with 'romance', seeming to include both sequences within works and whole genres: 'daydream, allegory, history, fairy-tale, horror-tale, psychological fantasy. All could be claimed as romances' (Beer, 1970, p. 66).

23. Sub-divisions of (non-science-fiction) fantasy have of course been supposed: Zahorski and Boyer (in Schlobin, 1982) discuss 'high fantasy' and 'low fantasy'; Parrinder (1980, p. 22) identifies what he terms 'anti-science science fiction'; cf. what Punter (1980, p. 421) calls 'shadows' of the Gothic. Wolfe (in Schlobin, 1982, p. 13) posits an eight-point plan of the structure of fantasy.

24. Obviously it is impossible to legislate particular terms, or usages, out of existence in critical terminology. We can only attempt to clarify and to urge greater precision.

25. Frye, 1957: 'Rhetorical criticism: theory of genres' (see especially 'Prose fiction', pp. 303–14). See also Frye (1976a), as well as Dubrow (1982), Hernadi (1972), Jameson (1975) and various essays in Strelka (1978).
26. Cf. Tatar (1981, p. 182): 'With knowledge, the intellectual uncertainty created by an uncanny event yields to conviction, and the fantastic gives way either to the marvelous or to the strange.'
27. As we have seen (note 8 above). Lem also wishes to equate science fiction with realism.
28. 'What if?' is also the question posed in Robert Scholes's formulation of 'structural fabulation', though in his case it is angled more firmly in the direction of science fiction (see Scholes, 1975, pp. 102–4).
29. For such a work to be in this category of the marvellous, as opposed to 'fantastic uncanny' or 'uncanny realism', the crucial test would be the impossibility (as opposed to the merely weird or uncanny nature) of the transformation. To take the works cited, the transformation in *Metamorphosis*, or the independence of the nose in Gogol's story, would surely not be 'believable' to any reader, other than on a fairly-tale or marvellous level. Stories featuring doubles, by contrast (taking works by Dostoevsky, Hoffmann, Poe as examples), seem to be in a different category: given the existence, or possible existence, of 'doubles', *alter egos*, look-alikes and impostors, plus 'divided-self'-type psychology, paranoia and possibilities of conspiracy, as well as the supernatural last resort, the chance of committed reader participation (or genuine doubt — on the part of protagonist, narrator and reader) seems much greater. Consideration must also be given (as Chanady would stress) to the tone of narration.

NOTES TO PART TWO

1. ORIGINS AND DEVELOPMENT

1. For a more detailed account of precusors to the Gothic novel, or tale of terror, see Punter, 1980, Ch. 2 'The origins of Gothic fiction' (especially pp. 22–49). I am indebted to Punter for a good deal of the discussion which follows.
2. Before Todorov, see (cited here) Castex (1951) and Vax (1960). Other such studies include: Marcel Schneider, *La Littérature fantastique en France* (Paris, 1964); and Roger Caillois, *Au coeur du fantastique* (Paris, 1965). Much earlier came Joseph H. Retinger, *Le Conte fantastique dans le romantisme français* (Paris, 1908). After Todorov, and not without her own critique of Todorov (see pp. 54–9), the line is continued by Irène Bessière (1974).
3. On this see comments made in Part One; for further observations, see Bessière, pp. 38–41 and 217–18.

4. The quality of 'genius' was frequently held in special awe during the romantic period; for example Fichte saw it as 'a supernatural inclination in man' (see Simpson, 1984, p. 98).

5. Among the suspected authors of this work, consideration has been given to Schelling, Hoffmann and Jean Paul Richter, as well as various minor figures: on this work see Gerald Gillespie's introduction to 'Bonaventura' (1972) and Blackall (1983, pp. 209–20).

6. For a recent survey of the varied definitions of European (as well as Russian) romanticism, see the introduction and various contributions to Reid (1986).

7. For details of this process, and an anthology of key texts and extracts, see Simpson (1984), Wheeler (1984) and Nisbet (1985). The bulk of these three volumes has now been conflated into a single volume: *The Origins of Modern Critical Thought: German aesthetic and literary criticism from Lessing to Hegel*, edited by David Simpson, Cambridge (Cambridge University Press), 1989. See also Lacoue-Labarthe and Nancy, 1988.

8. Furst (pp. 236–7) discusses 'romantic irony' and modern fiction under the term 'Romantic Modernism'. She summarises the differences between traditional and romantic irony on pp. 225–9. The 'shift in narrative', seen by Furst to arise from this development, in the relation of reader, narrative and text (p. 234) may be seen as qualitatively analogous to that discussed in Part One perceived in the differentiation drawn between the pure fantastic and magic realism.

9. Simpson has pointed out (1984, p. 269, n. 25) the similarity in argument and imagery with Shelley's *A Defence of Poetry*.

10. *The Sylph* may be found in English translation in Proffer (1979) and in Korovin (1984); it will also be included in a collection of Odoevsky stories, translated by the present author, which is due to be published by Bristol Classical Press in 1991. *The Diamond Lens* may be found in volume XV of Hammerton (no date). O'Brien (1828–62) could conceivably have known of Odoevsky's story, if not in Russian then in German translation (of 1839 or 1844). However, a more likely explanation lies in the common source of *Le Comte de Gabalis*.

2. TRIPPING THE LIGHT FANTASTIC

1. See the facsimile reproduced in *Frankenstein* (Fairclough, 1968, p. 257):

> Did I request thee, Maker, from my clay
> To mould me man? Did I solicit thee
> From darkness to promote me? —
>
> *Paradise Lost* (X, 743–5)

2. There is, of course, an abundance of literature on *Frankenstein*, but see in particular Baldick (1987) and Hammond (1986) on the myth and its follow-through (plus Forry, 1987). See also Aldiss (1986), pp. 25–52,

Moers (1978), Kiely (1972), Punter (1980), Suvin (1979), Kroeber (1988) etc.; for a contemporary (1818) review, see Scott (1968).

3. This is pointed out by Freeborn, 1985, p. 108. Particularly interesting, in view of the Henry James–Pushkin connection which we shall be stressing (involving *The Aspern Papers* specifically) are Claire Clairmont's own Russian connections (see Freeborn, p. 107).

4. Most books on the Gothic or 'terror' deal with *Melmoth the Wanderer*: the best account is possibly that by Kiely (1972, pp. 189–207), but see also Punter (1980, pp. 141–9), Sedgwick (1986, pp. 15–35), Carter (1987) and Alethea Hayter's introduction to Maturin (1977).

5. For a characteristically idiosyncratic note on the literary history of the Wandering Jew, see Nabokov (1964, 3, pp. 354–7).

6. On Maturin's Russian impact see Miller (1983); those with a knowledge of Russian, however, are referred to the far more substantial account by Alekseev (1978). Dubious attributions at this period were not unusual; Lewis's *The Monk* had earlier been attributed in Russian translation, also for blatant economic reasons, to the more famous Ann Radcliffe. It is interesting, for that matter, that Poe at one stage thought *Confessions of an English Opium-Eater* to be a brilliant hoax by Coleridge (Thompson, 1973, p. 83).

7. On Hoffmann in France, see Castex (1951) and Bessière (1974). On his impact in Russia, see Passage (1963), Ingham (1974), plus the following Soviet studies: A. B. Botnikova, *E.T.A. Gofman i russkaia literatura* (Voronezh, 1977); *Khudozhestvennii mir E.T.A. Gofmana*, ed. I. F. Belza and others (Moscow, 'Nauka', 1982). See also the present author's contribution to Reid (1986), on Hoffmann and Odoevsky, and, on the latter's interest in Hoffmann's *Don Giovanni*, Cornwell (1986, p. 147).

8. From the plethora of literature on *The Sandman*, much of it engaging also with Freud, see: Scott (1968), Freud (1955), Mirimsky (1938), Prawer (1965), Hertz (1980), Tatar (1980), Jackson (1981, pp. 64–72), Culler (1983, pp. 261–8), Wright (1984, pp. 142–50), Frisch (1985), Jones (1986).

9. Connections may be drawn between *The Oval Portrait*, *The Portrait* by Gogol, Hawthorne's *The Prophetic Pictures* and later works by such authors as Wilde, Zola and James (see Ziolkowski, 1977, Chapter 3 'The Haunted Portrait').

10. See Scott, 1968. For a list of sources connecting Poe and Hoffmann, see Thompson, 1973, pp. 219–20, n. 28.

11. Note Poe's traditional use of the word 'fantastic' (cf. also *Eureka*, Poe 1976, p. 262). On Poe's scepticism, see Thompson, 1973, pp. 146–7, 157, 160.

12. The standard work on Le Fanu is now McCormack (1980); there are also useful sections on particular Le Fanu works in general studies, such as J. Briggs (1977, pp. 44–51), Punter (1980;, pp. 230–7) and M. Carter (1987, pp. 84–93).

13. The first (1831) version of *Le Chef-d'œuvre inconnu* was subtitled '*Conte*

fantastique' (Laubriet, 1971, p. 203). Balzac knew Hoffmann's friend Dr Koreff in Paris in the 1820s and was an avid reader of Hoffmann; among the Hoffmann stories cited as possible sources for *Le Chef-d'œuvre* are *Baron Von B's Bow*, *Signor Formica*, *The Choosing of the Bride* and *The Jesuit Chapel in G* (see *ibid.*, pp. 31–40). Another beneficiary of Balzac's tale was Henry James (see *ibid.*, pp. 153–64); see also note 9 above. It may also be worth noting that Balzac, like Le Fanu, took a considerable interest in Swedenborg (see Laubriet, 1980, pp. 288–301). Incidentally, Swedenborgianism is seen by Solmi, 1978, p. 63, as a plausible derivation for science fiction.

The original version of 'Strange event in the life of Schalken the painter' (1839), with some annotations, is reprinted in *Field Day: Anthology of Irish Literature*, vol. I, London (Faber), 1990, pp. 1231–42.

14. The main textual evidence for the Swedenborgian reading is presented in McCormack, 1980, pp. 148–94. Hints of psychological and political readings are given in McCormack's introduction to Le Fanu, 1981. Fuller historical and political arguments are advanced in McCormack, 1985, pp. 182–98. The Irish background to *Uncle Silas*, transposition of setting to England notwithstanding, generates a plot which, among other things, is 'allegoric of the Big House philosophy' (*ibid.*, p. 187). In his own 'A preliminary word' to the novel, Le Fanu is at pains to distance himself from the 'sensation novel', preferring instead an association with 'the legitimate school of tragic English romance', inspired by Scott (Le Fanu, 1981, pp. xxvii–xxviii).

15. Any third explanation would appear to have insurmountable flaws. There could not have been any normal intruder: 'No door or window had been forced, no piece of furniture broken into. The two watchdogs had slept through the night undisturbed.' (Maupassant, 1971, p. 256); the victim 'carefully locked himself in his room' (p. 257). Could the victim, in a maniacal seizure, not have broken the chain and attacked himself with the dreaded hand? Perhaps, but it would be hard to believe that he could, while biting off one finger, have inflicted on his neck 'five holes which looked as if they had been made with iron spikes' (p. 256).

16. *The Picture of Dorian Gray* was first published in *Lippincott's Monthly Magazine* in July 1890; an enlarged version, now considered standard (five extra chapters were included, as well as certain revisions and expurgations made) appeared in book form in 1891. Both texts, with annotations, and valuable background and criticism, are included in the Norton edition (Wilde, 1988). On the origins of *Dorian Gray* see also Praz, 1970, pp. 354–60 and, in general, J. Briggs, 1977, pp. 83–93.

17. On *Dracula* see the following selection of material: Punter, 1980, pp. 256–63; Jackson, 1981, pp. 118–22; Foust, 1986; M. Carter, 1987, pp. 101–18; Varnado, 1987, pp. 95–114; Cranny-Francis, 1988; Martin, 1988. Most of these sources contain further references to *Dracula* criticism, which has grown in recent years.

18.   One assumes that Punter (1980, p. 258) was aware of the pun when he wrote: 'It is impossible to tell whether what is at stake is Dracula's personal longevity or his total identification with his line.'

3.   PUSHKIN AND HENRY JAMES

1.   The fullest account of *The Queen of Spades*, its origins and background, in English is to be found in Debreczeny, 1983, pp. 186–238 (plus bibliography, pp. 260–4). The most accessible general introduction to Pushkin is A. Briggs (1983); see also Bayley (1971). Other specific articles or essays will be quoted in the text.

2.   Quotations in the text refer to Aleksandr Pushkin, *Polnoe sobranie sochinenii*, vol. 8, Academy of Sciences edition, Moscow, 1948, pp. 227–52. The most obtainable English translation is that by Rosemary Edmonds (in Pushkin, 1962 and its reprints), pp. 153–83; this is also included in Manguel, 1983. Other translations are included in *The Complete Prose Tales of Alexandr Sergeyevitch Pushkin*, translated by Gillon R. Aitken, 1966 and 1978; and Alexander Pushkin, *Complete Prose Fiction*, translated by Paul Debreczeny, 1983. As Edmonds's translation does not always suit my reading (e.g. for 'staraia ved'ma' she has 'old hag', rather than 'old witch'), I have preferred to make my own.

3.   The first two ideas contain, it does not seem to have been remarked, possible ambiguities in themselves. 'Chance' (*Sluchai!*) may connote either sheer coincidence or perhaps a more guided stroke of fate, in any event a supposedly 'rational' explanation; 'Fairy-tale' (*Skazka!*) may indicate dismissal as nonsense, or, on the other hand, a magic charm or presence. See also, however, Williams (1989), which appeared after this chapter had been written.

4.   See the diagrammatic representation of the three games in J. Forsyth's notes to A. S. Pushkin, *Pikovaia dama*, Blackwell's Russian Texts (formerly Bradda Books, Letchworth, 1963, p. 86), Oxford, 1985, p. 62. On the rules of the game ('Faro'), see Debreczeny, pp. 196–9; and Nabokov, 1964, vol. 2, pp. 258–61.

5.   Virginia Woolf, 'The ghost stories', in *Henry James: A Collection of Critical Essays*, edited by Leon Edel, Englewood Cliffs, N.J. (Prentice-Hall), 1963, p. 50.

6.   The 'ghost volume' of the New York edition (Volume XVII, 1909) of James' works contains 'The altar of the dead', 'The beast in the jungle', 'The private life', 'Owen Wingate', 'The friends of the friends', 'Sir Edmund Orme', 'The real right thing', 'The jolly corner' and 'Julia Bride'; the last named story was inserted for non-thematic reasons (Edel, 1972, p. 346). For a slightly different listing, in ghostly and occult terms, see Banta, 1972, pp. 51–2. On *The Sense of the Past* in this respect see Banta, pp. 136–53; also Ziolkowski, pp. 134–40.

7.   James's fixation on the number 23 derives probably from Balzac's works

(complete in '23 huge octavo volumes') but Leon Edel speculates also on the significance to James of the combination of 2 and 3 and remarks that 'triangular relations are at the heart of his novels' (Edel, 1972, pp. 329–30).

8. Brooke-Rose, limits her study of previous criticism of *The Turn of the Screw* to two collections of essays: Gerald Willen (ed.), *A Casebook on Henry James's 'The Turn of the Screw'*, New York, 1971; and the essays accompanying Henry James, *The Turn of the Screw*, edited by Robert Kimbrough, Norton Critical Editions, New York, 1966. See also E. A. Sheppard, *Henry James and 'The Turn of the Screw'*, Auckland University Press, 1974; Banta 1972; Eli Siegel, *James and the Children*, New York (Definition Press), 1968. Many general books use *The Turn of the Screw* as a example: e.g. Bayley, 1988; Booth, 1961; J. Briggs, 1977; Punter, 1980; Varnado, 1987, etc.

9. Was Douglas 'really' a revived Miles (see Curtis, in James, 1986, p. 18)? Certainly not, unless we are to suppose that he was also a total liar (when asked 'if the experience in question had been his own . . . his answer was prompt. "Oh thank God, no!" ', p. 146).

10. Fuentes (p. 39) also includes in his comparison 'the cruelly mad Miss Havisham of Charles Dickens's *Great Expectations*, who is herself the English daughter of the ancient countess of Pushkin's *Queen of Spades*'. While there are certain atmospheric similarities and a broadly similar trio of characters in Miss Havisham, Estella and Pip, it is doubtful whether Pip can be said to stand in the same relationship as his alleged counterparts to either of the women characters and the pattern of denouement is certainly different. However, it should be said that Fuentes is principally concerned in his comments with the old women — 'the witches who consciously mothered Aura' (p. 38, referring to his own eponymous tale).

11. In addition to A. Briggs, 1972, the same author published another article in the same year on a similar theme: 'Someone else's sledge: Further notes on Turgenev's *Virgin Soil* and Henry James's *The Princess Casamassima'*, *Oxford Slavonic Papers*, New Series, vol. V, 1972, pp. 52–60. This particular unacknowledged use by James of themes from a Russian author does seem now to have been absorbed into the mainstream of James criticism: Roger Gard, in James 1987b, p. 495, comments that 'it is strange that James [in his preface to *Casamassima*] does not mention Turgenev's *Virgin Soil* as a possible inspiration for this novel. He reviewed it in 1877 [see James, 1984b, pp. 1000–06] . . . and there are many striking similarities of subject.'

12. It has traditionally been considered that Pushkin's 'eighteenth-century style', 'French in essence', enabled Mérimée to translate *The Queen of Spades* 'virtually word for word', or so Mérimée himself thought (see Mersereau, 1983, p. 225). Even in this century Mérimée's translation has frequently been reprinted as 'perfect'; however, for more considered comment see Henry, 1987, pp. 278–81: while Mérimée remains syntactically close to Pushkin, he makes errors, adds words or phrases, and tends to subjectivise the text. There are also omissions — usually minor, but these do include all the epigraphs. Interestingly, he also weakens the signs

of the fantastic (references to 'cabalistics' and 'galvanism' go out, but there is at least an isolated instance of the opposite effect). The preferred, perhaps, of other French versions on offer, is the revision of Mérimée made by André Meynieux, in A. Pouchkine, Œuvres complètes, 2e éd., Tome 1, Lausanne (l'Age d'Homme), 1973, first published 1958 (see Henry, p. 281; see also the annotations to Mérimée, 1931).

13. An anonymous translation of The Queen of Spades appeared in Blackwood's London Library in 1858; a translation by Mrs Sutherland Edwards was published in 1892 and a third by T. Keane in 1894: see Maurice B. Line, A Bibliography of Russian Literature in English Translation to 1900 (Excluding Periodicals), London (The Library Association), 1963, pp. 27–8.

14. The plot actions, or functions, for The Queen of Spades used here are adapted from those used by Roberta Reeder for the purpose of comparison with Hoffmann's tales (Reeder, 1982, pp. 92–4). See also for this approach Shukman, 1977 and Petrunina, 1980.

15. On the 'cusp catastrophe' see Alexander Woodcock and Monte Davis, Catastrophe Theory, Harmondsworth (Penguin), 1978, pp. 55–61.

4.   THE TWENTIETH CENTURY

1. Roadside Picnic is the accurately translated title of 'Piknik na obochine', while Definitely Maybe is an unrecognisable rendering of 'Za milliard let do kontsa sveta'.

2. McHale (1987, pp. 24–5, 74) also finds this novel to be within the fantastic; for him, the failure of Oedipa to 'break through the closed circle of her solipsism' and its epistemological premises keeps The Crying of Lot 49 within modernism, unlike Gravity's Rainbow, which transcends solipsism by means of its 'postmodernist poetics of ontology'.

3. In terms of our discussion of Part One, based on Little, Tolkien, etc., what we have just called 'World 2' would of course be a 'tertiary world' and 'Worlds 1' would be variations on a normal fictional 'secondary world'; this allows for the prior existence of a 'primary world', i.e. the actual world of author and reader.

4. 'Portmaneau novel' is a term which has been used by Patrick Parrinder, and which I exploit here with his permission. This term is not, of course, to be confused with 'portmanteau word', which was coined by Lewis Carroll and has since been applied to the punning and multilingual wordplay of Finnegans Wake (see Attridge, 1988: 'Unpacking the portmanteau'). These usages are, though, analogous with regard to levels and openness of meaning. Attridge also writes (pp. 152–3) of 'the multilingual portmanteau', 'the portmanteau style' and 'the portmanteau method'. On the micro-level, he remarks (p. 154): 'Every word in every text is a portmanteau, a combination of sounds that echo through the entire language and through every other language, and back through the history of speech.' On the macro-level, however, he also refers to 'the portmanteau text' (p. 152).

5. *The Master and Margarita* is a novel with a complicated compositional, textual and publishing history (for a detailed account see Barratt, 1987, pp. 39–76); this extends also to the available translations (*ibid.*, pp. 74–6). Bulgakov (1973) is the definitive Russian text; all earlier editions are defective to one degree or another. Bulgakov (1988) is the nearest thing yet to an academic edition, in that it includes an introduction, an afterword and several variant passages; its main text appears to be that of 1973. Of the two existing English translations, both first published in 1967, that by Michael Glenny is based on a more complete text. Ardis (publishers of a Bulgakov 'Complete Works' in Russian, of which Bulgakov, 1988, is volume 8) have announced the preparation of a new and complete English translation.

6. Pavel Florensky, *Mnimosti v geometrii. Rasshirenie oblasti dvukhmernykh obrazov geometrii (Opyt novogo istolkovaniia mnimostei)*, Moscow, 1922. This work is not only known to have been in Bulgakov's possession, but was assiduously annotated by him (Barratt, 1987, p. 300).

7. Unfortunately, Glenny's translation of the epigraph is a trifle inaccurate: in answer to the question 'Say at last, who art thou?', Glenny has the rejoinder: 'The power I serve / Which wills forever evil / Yet does forever good'. A more correct translation would begin 'I — am a part of the power. . .'. This slip could tend to mislead readers concerned with the question of Woland's identity.

8. The Roman emperor does seem to make one phantasmal appearance, in Ch. 2 (the first chapter of the Jerusalem text). When Pilate has read the further evidence against Ieshua, his mood changes: 'Probably caused by the increased blood-pressure to his temples, something happened to the Procurator's sight. He seemed to see the prisoner's head vanish and another appear in its place, bald and crowned with a spiked golden diadem . . . there was a sound as of distant trumpets, muted and threatening, and a nasal voice could be heard arrogantly intoning the words: "The law pertaining to high treason. . ." ' (Bulgakov, 1967, p. 38).

9. The 'death' of the Master and Margarita has been highlighted by a number of critics (Bethea, 1989, for one, mentions it on pp. 39, 150 and 224–5). Given its double nature (ostensibly by poison in one location, and simultaneously apparently by heart attack in another), in itself fitting the novel's 'two worlds' schema, it is surely to be considered merely the means of breaking through space–time, rather than physical death in the usual sense, let alone an act of crime. Glenny's translation does not help the reader's impression here by rendering the word *poverzhennykh* ('subdued' or 'defeated'), in the narrator's discourse, as 'murdered' (Bulgakov, 1967, p. 417). Curtis (1987, p. 180) however points out that it is in fact 'Iyeshua's intervention through his surly ambassador Matvey which brings about the lovers' premature deaths, opening the way for the fulfilment of the Master's destiny and the redemption of his art' and quotes Florensky's views on transition through death, concluding (p. 181)

that it is in 'a non-religious sense that we should understand the Master and Margarita's elevation to an Empyrean realm, where they retain a notional physical reality even though they have left their bodies behind'. The conducting by the demon Azazello of the Master and Margarita to another dimension could equally be seen as a parodic reversal of the Angel leading Adam and Eve out of paradise at the end of Milton's *Paradise Lost*.

10. Is Bezdomny's second Epilogue dream, in which Ieshua swears to Pilate that the crucifixion did not take place, to be seen as 'reliable'? And, if so, then in what sense? Bethea (1989, p. 205) links the unwriting of history with the reversal of time at the speed of light[!], based on Florensky. If this dream is not perceived as 'reliable', what of his earlier dreaming of the second chapter of the Master's novel?

11. A number of commentators have noted the absence of Hella from Woland's retinue at the point of transfiguration and flight to the beyond. Most assume this to be an oversight on Bulgakov's part (his final revisions being incomplete at the time of his death). For Bethea, however (1989, p. 226 and n. 90) her absence is 'logical', as Woland, Behemoth, Koroviëv and Azazello 'are transformed into Bulgakov's version of the Four Horsemen of the Apocalypse'. Incidentally, an attempt to continue the conversation between Pilate and Ieshua outside the text is made by Chingiz Aitmatov, in his novel *Plakha* (1986): English translation as *The Place of the Skull*, trans. Natasha Ward (Faber, London), 1989.

12. Imhof (1989, p. 52) may or may not have exaggerated slightly in claiming that 'the godfather of *Birchwood* is Marcel Proust'; if not, it is odd that he does not appear to see any Proustian connection in the choice of the name Swan (albeit with one 'n') for the protagonist of *Mefisto*: all the more so, as he refers (p. 166) to Gabriel's use of form in his narration as 'simply Swan's way of establishing sense'.

13. What McHale (1987, p. 251, n. 31) calls 'the postmodernist travelling circus motif' turns up again briefly in *Mefisto* (p. 10). It has clear affinities with carnivalisation, magic etc. (McHale, p. 174: cf. *The Master and Margarita*) and is no doubt extendable to devil's retinues elsewhere. Apart from instances noted here (and by McHale), a prime example is Angela Carter's novel *Nights at the Circus* (1984).

14. *Mefisto* (p. 141) contains this comment on city life: 'What is it, this sense of something impending, as if a crime is biding its time here, waiting to be committed?' *The Book of Evidence*, conversely, includes the following reaction by Freddie to his crime: 'Now I had struck a blow for the inner man, that guffawing, fat foulmouth who had been telling me all along I was living a lie. And he had burst out at last, it was he, the ogre, who was pounding along in this lemon-coloured light, with blood on his pelt, and me slung helpless over his back' (Banville, 1989, p. 124). A little later (p. 151) this inner phenomenon is referred to as 'that fat monster inside me' and 'Bunter' (see also p. 95). Dostoevskian echoes are patently present in *The Book of Evidence*; Banville had earlier named one of the *Long Lankin* stories 'The Possessed' and had opened *Nightspawn* with a paraphrase of

the beginning of *The Notes from Underground* (noted by Imhof, pp. 35, 41, 48).

15. Rushdie (e.g. at The Watershed, Bristol, on 30 September, 1988) has spoken of realism as an attempt to respond seriously to the world around us, even when using phantasmagorical means. The world is not what it seems and reality is not 'realistic' any more: therefore monsters may be required in books, to reflect our monstrous age.

16. 'Although he never mentions it, Rushdie obviously chooses Argentina as Rosa's mental refuge because of the dissonance the idea of "Argentina" is bound to have in a country still high from its imperial adventures in the Falklands', writes Brennan (1989, p. 162). While this may be true, in literary terms Rushdie acknowledges W. H. Hudson as a source for material on Argentina (*SV*, p. 549), while the 'Argentinian plot' would appear to owe something to both the gaucho stories of (the Argentinian) Borges and *Aura* by (the Mexican) Fuentes.

17. The theme of the *chamcha* is a constant one in Rushdie's main novels: the word means (literally 'spoon', hence Gibreel's nickname for Chamcha of 'Spoono') collaborator or toady, the type of citizen of the Indian subcontinent who strives to be more British (or perhaps English) than his imperial masters (see Brennan, 1989, pp. 85–9, 120). *The Satanic Verses* can ultimately be seen as a story of the 'de-chamcha-isation' of Chamcha (who had, ironically, simplified/anglicised his name from Salahuddin Chamchawala to Saladin Chamcha), the modern post-colonial chamcha figure.

18. Bristol, 30 September, 1988: brief conversation following reading. In his 'Acknowledgements' (*SV*, p. 549), Rushdie concludes, after naming a few specific quotations or borrowings: 'The identities of many of the authors from whom I've learned will, I hope, be clear from the text.'

NOTES TO PART THREE

1. On Freud's essay 'The "Uncanny"', see our section on Hoffmann in Part Two above, and related references, Jackson (1981), pp. 64–72, Kroeber (1988), pp. 88–94, and especially Hertz (1980).

2. Immanuel Velikovsky finally published the first volume in his documentation of cosmic and global catastrophies, *Worlds in Collision*, after considerable difficulty, in 1950; a number of further volumes followed. They became large-selling paperbacks to a cult readership in the 1970s. On the Velikovsky controversy, see *Velikovsky Remembered* by the editors of *Pensée*, London (Abacus), 1978; and, for example, Carl Sagan, 'Venus and Dr Velikosky' in his *Broca's Brain: Reflections on the Romance of Science*, New York (Random House), 1979. A lesser example, imbued with a good deal of fantasy in the opinion of many, is the thesis of extraterrestrial visitations proposed in the books of Erich von Däniken.

3. Manlove (1983) also devotes a chapter on Ursula Le Guin to what he

terms 'Conservatism in Fantasy'; he draws a distinction in this respect between Le Guin's fantasy, such as the 'Earthsea' trilogy, and her science fiction (see pp. 36–7).

4. A similar view is advanced by Hans Robert Jauss: 'The horizon of expectations of literature is differentiated from the horizon of expectations of historical life by the fact that it not only preserves real experiences but also anticipates unrealized possibilities, widens the limited range of social behaviour by new wishes, demands, and goods, and thereby opens avenues for future experience' (Jauss, 1974, p. 37).

5. For background to the Rushdie affair, see Brennan (1989). On the Rushdie affair, original press coverage apart, Appignanesi and Maitland (1989) is an essential dossier of reviews, correspondence and statements in the progress of the 'affair' up to April 1989 (the book was originally commissioned by Collins, 'with some enthusiasm', but then rejected by 'senior management'; it was published by Fourth Estate, following some difficulties in finding a printer). See also the following: Tariq Ali and Howard Brenton, *Iranian Nights*, London (Nick Hern Books), 1989 (this play ran briefly at The Royal Court Theatre in April 1989 and was televised on Channel Four; the title as originally proposed, 'A Mullah's Night Out', was dropped under pressure for the less contentious 'Iranian Nights'); Fay Weldon's 'Chatto Counter Blast' *Sacred Cows*; and the pamphlets *The Crime of Blasphemy — Why It Should be Abolished* and *World Statement: Writers and readers in support of Salman Rushdie*, both London (The International Committee for the Defence of Salman Rushdie and his Publishers), 1989. One particularly effective intervention is Christopher Hitchens's article in *London Review of Books* (26 October 1989). Rushdie has himself in this period published a poem, under the title '6 March 1989' (*Granta* 28, 1989, p. 29), and a number of book reviews.

Bibliography

1. SOME USEFUL ANTHOLOGIES

Almansi, Guido and Béguin, Claude (eds) 1987. *Theatre of Sleep: an Anthology of Literary Dreams*, (Picador, London). First published Pan 1986.

Bishop, Morris (ed.) 1971. *A Romantic Storybook*, (Cornell University Press, Ithaca and London).

Cassiday, Bruce (ed.) 1983. *Roots of Detection: The art of deduction before Sherlock Holmes*, (Ungar, New York).

Castex, Pierre-Georges (ed.) 1963. *Anthologie du conte fantastique français*, (Librarie José Corti, Paris).

Fairclough, Peter (ed.), intro. Mario Praz, 1968. *Three Gothic Novels, The Castle of Otranto*, Horace Walpole; *Vathek*, William Beckford; *Frankenstein*, Mary Shelley (Penguin, Harmondsworth).

Haining, Peter (ed.) 1972. *Great British Tales of Terror: Gothic stories of horror & romance 1765–1840* Volume I, (Gollancz, London).

Haining, Peter (ed.) 1973. *Great Tales of Terror from Europe and America: Gothic stories of horror and romance 1765–1840*, (Penguin, Harmondsworth). First published 1972.

Hammerton, Sir J. A. (ed.) no date. *The Masterpiece Library of Short Stories: The thousand best complete tales of all times and all countries*, 10 double-volumes (Educational Book Co., London).

Korovin, Valentin (comp.) 1984. *Russian 19th-Century Gothic Tales*, (Raduga, Moscow).

Manguel, Alberto (ed.) 1983. *Black Water: The anthology of fantastic literature*, (Picador, London).

Proffer, Carl R. (ed.) 1979. *Russian Romantic Prose: An anthology*, (Translation Press, Ann Arbor).

Rabkin, Eric S. (ed.) 1979. *Fantastic Worlds: Myths, tales and stories*, (Oxford University Press, New York and Oxford).

Silverberg, Robert and Greenberg, Martin H. (eds) 1988. *The Mammoth Book of Fantasy All-Time Greats*, (Robinson, London). First published as *The Fantasy Hall of Fame*, 1983.

Stratting, J. J. (ed.) 1968. *European Tales of Terror*, (Fontana, London).

Taylor, Ronald (trans.) 1985. *Six German Romantic Tales: Heinrich von Kleist, Ludwig Tieck, E. T. A. Hoffmann*, (Angel, London).

245

2. MAIN PRIMARY SOURCES, USED OR QUOTED

(non-fictional works by primary-source authors are listed under Secondary sources).

Balzac, Honoré de 1988. *Gillette or The Unknown Masterpiece*, trans. with essay by Anthony Rudolf (Menard Press, London).

Banville, John 1987a. *Birchwood*, (Paladin, London). First published 1973.

Banville, John 1987b. *Mefisto*, (Paladin, London). First published 1986.

Banville, John 1989. *The Book of Evidence*, (Secker & Warburg, London).

'Bonaventura', 1972. *The Night Watches of Bonaventura/Die Nachtwachen des Bonaventura*, ed. and trans. Gerald Gillespie, Edinburgh Bilingual Library (6) (Edinburgh University Press, Edinburgh).

Borges, Jorge Luis 1970. *Labyrinths: Selected stories and other writings*, ed. Donald A. Yates and James E. Irby (Penguin, Harmondsworth). First published 1964.

Brown, Charles Brockden 1978. *Wieland or The Transformation: An American tale. Memoirs of Carwin the Biloquist*, ed. Sydney J. Krause and S. W. Reid (Kent State University Press, Kent, Ohio).

Brown, Charles Brockden 1988. *Edgar Huntly: Or, memoirs of a sleep-walker*, ed. Norman S. Grabo (Penguin, Harmondsworth).

Bulgakov, Mikhail 1967. *The Master and Margarita*, trans. Michael Glenny (Collins & Harvill, London).

Bulgakov, Mikhail 1973. *Romany: Belaia gvardiia. Teatral'nyi roman. Master i Margarita* (Khudozhestevennaia literatura, Moscow).

Bulgakov, Mikhail 1988. *Sobranie sochinenii*, vol. 8, ed. Ellendea Proffer (Ardis, Ann Arbor).

Fuentes, Carlos 1975. *Aura* [bilingual edition], trans. Lysander Kemp (Farrar, Strauss & Giroux, New York).

Hodgson, William Hope 1974. *Carnacki the Ghost-Finder*, intro. Gerald Suster (Sphere, London).

Hodgson, William Hope 1988. *The House on the Borderland* (Robinson, London).

Hoffmann, E. T. A. 1963. *The Devil's Elixirs*, trans. Ronald Taylor (John Calder, London).

Hoffmann, E. T. A. 1967. *The Best Tales of Hoffmann*, ed. with intro. E. F. Bleiler (Dover, New York).

Hoffmann, E. T. A. 1969. *Selected Writings of E. T. A. Hoffmann*, ed. and trans. Leonard J. Kent and Elizabeth C. Knight, 2 volumes (University of Chicago, Chicago & London).

Hoffmann, E. T. A. 1971. *Three Märchen of E. T. A. Hoffmann*, trans. with intro. Charles E. Passage (University of South Carolina, Columbia, SC).

Hoffmann, E. T. A. 1982. *Tales of Hoffmann*, trans. R. J. Hollingdale (Penguin, Harmondsworth).

Irving, Washington 1985. *Washington Irving's Sketch Book: The classic artist's edition of 1863* (Avenel Books, New York).

James, Henry 1963. *The Complete Tales of Henry James*, ed. Leon Edel, vol. 6, 1884–88 (Hart-Davis, London).

James, Henry 1986. *The Aspern Papers and The Turn of the Screw*, ed. Anthony Curtis (Penguin, Harmondsworth).

Kharms, Daniil 1989. *The Plummeting Old Women*, trans. and intro. Neil Cornwell, 'Afterword' Hugh Maxton (Lilliput, Dublin).

Kleist, Heinrich von 1978. *The Marquise of O- and Other Stories*, trans. David Luke and Nigel Reeves (Penguin, Harmondsworth).

Le Fanu, J. Sheridan 1947. *In a Glass Darkly*, intro. V. S. Pritchett (John Lehmann, Paulton and London).

Le Fanu, J. Sheridan 1970. *The Best Horror Stories* (Sphere, London).

Le Fanu, J. Sheridan 1981. *Uncle Silas*, ed. W. J. McCormack (The World's Classics, Oxford University Press, Oxford).

Le Fanu, J. Sheridan 1985. *Borrhomeo the Astrologer: A monkish tale*, intro. W. J. McCormack (Tragara Press, Edinburgh).

Le Fanu, J. Sheridan 1988. *The Illustrated J. S. Le Fanu: Ghost stories and mysteries by a master Victorian storyteller*, ed. and intro. Michael Cox (Equation, Wellingborough).

Le Guin, Ursula K. 1974. *The Lathe of Heaven* (Panther, London, 1974). First published 1971; in UK Gollancz 1972.

Lessing, Doris 1976. *The Memoirs of a Survivor* (Picador, London). First published 1974.

Maturin, Charles Robert 1977. *Melmoth The Wanderer: A tale*, ed. with intro. Alethea Hayter (Penguin, Harmondsworth).

Maupassant, Guy de 1971. *Selected Short Stories*, trans. with intro. Roger Colet (Penguin, Harmondsworth).

Mérimée, Prosper 1931. *Œuvres complètes de Prosper Mérimée: Etudes de littérature russe*, tome premier Pouchkine–Lermontof, ed. Henri Mongault (Champion, Paris).

Morrison, Toni 1988. *Beloved*, (Picador, London). First published 1987.

Poe, Edgar Allan 1966. *Complete Stories and Poems of Edgar Allan Poe*, (Doubleday, Garden City, NY).

Poe, Edgar Allan 1976. *The Science Fiction of Edgar Allan Poe*, ed. Harold Beaver (Penguin, Harmondsworth).

Pushkin, Aleksandr 1948. *Polnoe sobranie sochinenii*, vol. 8 (Academy of Sciences, Moscow–Leningrad, 1937–59).

Pushkin, Alexander 1962. *The Queen of Spades and Other Stories*, trans. Rosemary Edmonds (Penguin, Harmondsworth).

Pynchon, Thomas 1979. *The Crying of Lot 49*, (Picador, London).

Radcliffe, Ann 1980. *The Mysteries of Udolpho*, ed. Bonamy Dobrée (The World's Classics, Oxford University Press, Oxford).

Rushdie, Salman 1982. *Midnight's Children*, (Picador, London).

Rushdie, Salman 1988. *The Satanic Verses*, (Viking, London).

Shelley, Mary *Frankenstein: or the modern Prometheus*, see Fairclough, 1968 (above).

Shelley, Mary 1985. *The Last Man*, intro. Brian Aldiss (London, Hogarth).
Stapledon, Olaf 1987. *Last and First Men: A story of the near and far future*, (Penguin, Harmondsworth).
Stapledon, Olaf 1988. *Star Maker* (Penguin, Harmondsworth).
Stevenson, Robert Louis 1987. *The Strange Case of Dr Jekyll and Mr Hyde and Weir of Hermiston*, ed. with intro. Emma Letley (The World's Classics, Oxford University Press, Oxford).
Stoker, Bram 1914. *Dracula's Guest and Other Weird Stories* (Routledge, London).
Stoker, Bram 1983. *Dracula*, intro. A. N. Wilson (The World's Classics, Oxford University Press, Oxford).
Wilde, Oscar 1988. *The Picture of Dorian Gray: Authoritative texts, backgrounds, reviews, criticism*, ed. Donald L. Lawler (A Norton Critical Edition, Norton, New York and London).
Zamyatin, Yevgeny 1972. *We*, trans Bernard Guilbert Guerney (Penguin, Harmondsworth).

3. SECONDARY SOURCES CITED OR CONSULTED

Aldiss, Brian, with David Wingrove, 1986. *Trillion Year Spree: The history of science fiction*, (Gollancz, London).
Alekseev, M. P. 1978. 'Charlz Robert Met'iurin i russkaia literatura', in *Ot romantizma k realizmu: iz istorii mezhdunarodnoi sviazei russkoi literatury*, ed. M. P. Alekseev (Nauka, Leningrad, pp. 3–55).
Ali, Tariq and Brenton, Howard 1989. *Iranian Nights* (Nick Hern, London).
Amis, Martin 1987. 'Introduction: Thinkability', in his *Einstein's Monsters* (Cape, London, pp. 7–28).
Appignanesi, Lisa and Maitland, Sara (eds) 1989. *The Rushdie File*, (Fourth Estate, London).
Apter, T. E. 1982. *Fantasy Literature: An approach to reality* (Macmillan, London).
Attebery, Brian 1980. *The Fantasy Tradition in American Literature: from Irving to Le Guin* (Indiana University Press, Bloomington).
Attridge, Derek 1988. 'Unpacking the portmanteau, or Who's afraid of *Finnegans Wake?*', in *On Puns: The foundation of letters*, ed. Jonathon Culler (Blackwell, Oxford, pp. 140–55).
Avins, Carol 1986. 'Reaching a reader: The Master's audience in *The Master and Margarita*', *Slavic Review*, pp. 272–85.
Bakhtin, Mikhail 1968. *Rabelais and His World*, trans. Helene Iswolsky (MIT Press, Cambridge, Mass. and London). Original first published 1965.
Bakhtin, Mikhail 1973/1984. *Problems of Dostoevsky's Poetics* (1) trans. R. W. Rotsel (Ardis, Ann Arbor, 1973); (2) ed. and trans. Caryl Emerson, intro. Wayne C. Booth (Manchester University Press, Manchester, 1984). Original first published 1929, enlarged 1963.
Bakhtin, Mikhail 1981. *The Dialogic Imagination: Four essays by M. M. Bakhtin*, ed. Michael Holquist, trans. Caryl Emerson and Michael Holquist (University of Texas, Austin, Texas). Original first published 1975.

Baldick, Chris 1987. *In Frankenstein's Shadow: Myth, monstrosity and nineteenth-century writing*, (Clarendon Press, Oxford).

Banta, Martha 1972. *Henry James and the Occult: The great extension* (Indiana University Press, Bloomington).

Barratt, Andrew 1987. *Between Two Worlds: A critical introduction to 'The Master and Margarita'*, (Clarendon Press, Oxford).

Bayley, John 1971. *Pushkin: A comparative commentary*, (Cambridge University Press, Cambridge).

Bayley, John 1988. *The Short Story: Henry James to Elizabeth Bowen*, (Harvester Wheatsheaf, Hemel Hempstead).

Beer, Gillian 1970. *The Romance*, (Methuen, London).

Bellemin-Noël, Jean 1971. 'Des formes fantastiques aux thèmes fantasmatiques', *Littérature*, no. 2, pp. 103–18.

Bellemin-Noël, Jean 1972. 'Notes sur le fantastique (textes de Théophile Gautier)', *Littérature*, no. 8, pp. 3–23.

Belsey, Catherine 1980. *Critical Practice*, (Methuen, London).

Benjamin, Walter 1973. *Illuminations*, ed. Hannah Arendt, trans. Harry Zohn (Fontana, London). First published Cape 1970. Original published as *Schriften* 1955.

Bessière, Irène 1974. *Le Récit fantastique: la poétique de l'incertain*, (Larousse, Paris).

Bethea, David M. 1989. *The Shape of Apocalypse in Modern Russian Fiction*, (Princeton University Press, Princeton).

Birkhead, Edith 1921. *The Tale of Terror: A study of the Gothic romance*, (Constable, London).

Blackall, Eric A. 1983. *The Novels of the German Romantics* (Cornell University Press, Ithaca and London).

Bloom, Clive *et al.*, 1988. *Nineteenth-Century Suspense: From Poe to Conan Doyle*, ed. Clive Bloom, Brian Docherty, Jane Gibb and Keith Shand (Macmillan, London).

Bloom, Clive 1988. 'The House that Jack Built: Jack the Ripper, legend and the power of the unknown', in C. Bloom *et al.*, 1988 (above), pp. 120–37.

Bloom, Harold 1982. *AGON: Towards a theory of revisionism*, (Oxford University Press, New York and Oxford).

Bocharov, S. G. 1978. 'The Queen of Spades', *New Literary History*, vol. 9, 1978, pp. 315–32, trans. Ann Feltham (from Bocharov's *Poetika Pushkina*, Moscow, 1974).

Booth, Wayne C. 1961. *The Rhetoric of Fiction*, (University of Chicago, Chicago).

Brennan, Timothy 1989. *Salman Rushdie and The Third World: Myths of the nation*, (Macmillan, London).

Briggs, A. D. P. 1972. 'Alexander Pushkin: a possible influence on Henry James', *Forum for Modern Language Studies*, vol. VIII, no. 1, pp. 52–61.

Briggs, A. D. P. 1983. *Alexander Pushkin: A critical study*, (Croom Helm, London).

Briggs, Julia 1977. *Night Visitors: The rise and fall of the English ghost story*, (Faber, London).

Brooke-Rose, Christine 1983. *A Rhetoric of the Unreal: Studies in narrative and structure, especially of the fantastic*, (Cambridge University Press, Cambridge). First published 1981.

Brooks, Peter 1976. *The Melodramatic Imagination: Balzac, Henry James, melodrama and the mode of excess* (Yale University Press, New Haven and London).

Burgin, Diana Lewis 1974. 'The mystery of "Pikovaja Dama"': A new interpretation', in *Mnemozina: Studia litteraria russica in honorem Vsevolod Setchkarev*, ed. Joachim T. Baer and Norman W. Ingham (Fink, Munich, pp. 46–56).

Burgin, Victor *et al.*, 1986. *Formations of Fantasy*, ed. Victor Burgin, James Donald and Cora Kaplan (Methuen, London and New York).

Burgin, Victor 1986. 'Diderot, Barthes, Vertigo', in Burgin *et al.*, 1986 (above), pp. 85–108.

Butler, Marilyn 1982. *Romantics, Rebels and Reactionaries: English literature and its background 1760–1830*, (Oxford University Press, New York and Oxford).

Calvino, Italo 1987. *The Literature Machine: Essays*, trans. Patrick Creagh (Secker & Warburg, London). Original first published 1982.

Campra, Rosalba 1981. 'Il fantastico: una isotopia della trasgressione', *Strumenti critici: Rivista quadrimestale di cultura e critica letteraria*, XV, 2, June 1981, pp. 199–231.

Carroll, Lewis 1939. 'Preface to *Sylvie and Bruno Concluded*', in *The Complete Works of Lewis Carroll*, (Nonesuch, London).

Carter, Albert Howard, III 1987. *Italo Calvino: Metamorphosis of fantasy*, (UMI Research Press, Ann Arbor).

Carter, Erica and Turner, Chris 1986. 'Political somatics: notes on Klaus Theweleit's *Male Fantasies*', in Burgin *et al.*, 1986 (above), pp. 200–13.

Carter, Margaret L. 1987. *Specter or Delusion? The supernatural in Gothic fiction*, (UMI Research Press, Ann Arbor and London).

Castex, Pierre-Georges 1951. *Le Conte fantastique en France de Nodier à Maupassant* (Librairie José Corti, Paris).

Cave, Terence 1988. *Recognitions: A study in poetics* (Clarendon Press, Oxford).

Chanady, Amaryll Beatrice 1985. *Magical Realism and the Fantastic: Resolved versus unresolved antinomy*, (Garland, New York and London).

Clayton, David 1982. 'On realistic and fantastic discourse', in Slusser *et al.* (below), pp. 59–77.

Collins, Robert A. and Pearce, Howard D. (eds) 1985a. *The Scope of the Fantastic — Theory, Technique, Major Authors. Selected essays from the first international conference on the fantastic in literature and film*, (Greenwood, Westport, Conn. and London).

Collins, Robert A. and Pearce, Howard D. (eds) 1985b. *The Scope of the Fantastic — Culture, Biography, Themes, Children's Literature. Selected essays from the first international conference on the fantastic in literature and film*, (Greenwood, Westport, Conn. and London).

Cornwell, Neil 1986. *V. F. Odoyevsky: His life, times and milieu* (Athlone, London; Ohio University Press, Athens, Ohio).

Cornwell, Neil 1988. 'Critical approaches to the literary fantastic: Definitions, genre, import', *Essays in Poetics*, vol. 13, no. 1, pp. 1–45.

Coyle, William (ed.) 1986. *Aspects of Fantasy: Selected essays from the second international conference on the fantastic in literature and film*, (Greenwood, Westport, Conn. and London).

Cranny-Francis, Anne 1988. 'Sexual politics and political repression in Bram Stoker's *Dracula*', in C. Bloom *et al.* (above), pp. 64–79.

Culler, Jonathan 1983. *On Deconstruction: Theory and criticism after structuralism*, (Routledge, London).

Cunliffe, Marcus 1970. *The Literature of the United States*, third edition, revised (Penguin, Harmondsworth). First published 1954.

Curtis, J. A. E. 1987. *Bulgakov's Last Decade: The writer as hero*, (Cambridge University Press, Cambridge).

Day, Gary 1988. 'Figuring out the Signalman: Dickens and the ghost story', in C. Bloom *et al.* (above), pp. 26–45.

Deane, Seamus 1984. 'Fiction as history — history as fiction', in *Joyce in Rome: the genesis of Ulysses*, ed. Giorgio Melchiori (Bulzoni, Rome).

Debreczeny, Paul 1983. *The Other Pushkin: A study of Alexander Pushkin's prose fiction*, (Stanford University Press, Stanford).

Deleuze, Gilles 1980. 'The schizophrenic and language: Surface and depth in Lewis Carroll and Antonin Artaud', in Harari, 1980 (below), pp. 277–95.

Dipple, Elizabeth 1988. *The Unresolvable Plot: Reading contemporary fiction*, (Routledge, New York and London).

Dubrow, Heather 1982. *Genre*, (Methuen, London and New York).

Eco, Umberto 1985. *Reflections on 'The Name of the Rose'*, trans. William Weaver (Secker & Warburg, London). Original first published 1983.

Eco, Umberto 1987. *Travels in Hyperreality: Essays*, trans. William Weaver (Picador, London). Published as *Faith in Fakes* (Secker & Warburg, London, 1986).

Edel, Leon 1972. *Henry James: The master 1901–1916*, (Hart-Davis, London; Lippincott, Philadelphia).

Ellmann, Richard 1988. *Oscar Wilde*, (Penguin, Harmondsworth). First published Hamish Hamilton 1987.

Fletcher, John 1986. 'Poetry, gender and primal fantasy', in Burgin *et al.*, 1986 (above), pp. 109–41.

Forry, Steven Earl 1987. ' "The foulest toadstool": Reviving Frankenstein in the twentieth century', in Morse, 1987 (below), pp. 183–209.

Foucault, Michel 1986. *The Foucault Reader*, ed. Paul Rabinow (Penguin, Harmondsworth). First published Pantheon 1984.

Foust, Ronald 1986. 'Rite of passage: The vampire tale as cosmogonic myth', in Coyle, 1986 (above), pp. 73–84.

Fowler, Alastair 1974. 'The life and death of literary forms', in *New Directions in Literary History*, ed. Ralph Cohen (Routledge, London, 1974, pp. 77–94).

Fowler, Roger 1979. 'Linguistics and, and versus, poetics', *Journal of Literary Semantics*, 8, 1979, pp. 3–21.

Fox, Ralph 1979. *The Novel and the People*, preface Jeremy Hawthorn (Lawrence & Wishart, London). First published 1937.

Freeborn, Richard 1985. 'Frankenstein's Last Journey', *Oxford Slavonic Papers*, New Series, vol. XVIII, pp. 102–19.

Freud, Sigmund 1955. 'The "Uncanny"', *The Standard Edition of the Complete Psychological Works of Sigmund Freud*, vol. XVII (Hogarth Press, London, pp. 217–56). Also in Sigmund Freud, *Collected Papers*, vol. IV (Hogarth Press, London, 1925, pp. 368–407). Original first published 1919.

Frisch, Shelley L. 1985. 'Poetics of the uncanny: E. T. A. Hoffmann's "Sandman"', in Collins & Pearce, 1985a (above), pp. 49–55.

Frye, Northrop 1957. *Anatomy of Criticism: Four essays*, (Princeton University Press, Princeton, NJ).

Frye, Northrop 1976a. *The Secular Scripture: A study of the structure of romance*, (Harvard University Press, Cambridge, Mass.).

Frye, Northrop 1976b. *Spiritus Mundi: Essays on literature, myth and society*, (Indiana University Press, Bloomington and London).

Fuentes, Carlos 1988. *Myself with Others: Selected essays*, (Deutsch, London).

Fuentes, Carlos 1989a. 'Words Apart', in Appignanesi and Maitland, 1989 (above), pp. 245–9. First published in the *Guardian*, 24 February 1989.

Fuentes, Carlos 1989b. 'New novel, new world', *The Modern Language Review*, vol. 84, part 4, pp. XXXI–XLII.

Furst, Lilian R. 1984. *Fictions of Romantic Irony in European Narrative, 1760–1857*, (Macmillan, London).

Genette, Gérard 1986. *Narrative Discourse*, trans. Jane E. Lewin (Blackwell, Oxford). First published 1980. Original published 1972.

Giaquinta, Rosanna, forthcoming. 'Elements of the fantastic in Daniil Kharms's "Starukha"', in *Essays and Materials on Daniil Kharms*, (Macmillan, London).

Giuliani, Rita 1982–4. 'Demonologia e magica nel *Maestro e Margherita* di M. A. Bulgakov', *Ricerche Slavistiche*, vol. XXIX–XXXI, 1982–4, pp. 269–304.

Grass, Gunter 1988. 'The writer, always a man of his time', in *In the Prison of his Days: A miscellany for Nelson Mandela on his 70th birthday*, ed. W. J. McCormack (Lilliput, Mullingar, Co. Westmeath), pp. 12–22.

Grossman, Joan Delaney 1973. *Edgar Allan Poe in Russia: A study in legend and literary influence*, (jal-verlag, Würzburg).

Gutsche, George J. and Leighton, Lauren G. (eds) 1982. *New Perspectives on Nineteenth-Century Russian Prose*, (Slavica, Columbus, Ohio).

Hammond, Ray 1986. *The Modern Frankenstein: Fiction becomes fact*, (Blandford, Poole).

Harari, Josué V. (ed.) 1980. *Textual Strategies: Perspectives in post-structuralist criticism*, (Methuen, London). First published Cornell University Press, 1979.

Hayter, Alethea 1988. *Opium and the Romantic Imagination: Addiction and creativity in De Quincey, Coleridge, Baudelaire and others* (Crucible, Wellingborough). First published Faber 1968.

Henry, Hélène 1987. 'Note sur les traductions en français de *La Dame de pique*', *Revue des études slaves*, vol. 59, nos. 1–2, pp. 277–84.

Hernadi, Paul 1972. *Beyond Genre: New directions in literary classification*, (Cornell University Press, Ithaca and London).

Hertz, Neil 1980. 'Freud and the Sandman', in Harari, 1980 (above), pp. 296–321.

Hitchens, Christopher 1989. 'Siding with Rushdie', *London Review of Books*, 26 October 1989, pp. 11–15.

Hoffmann, E. T. A. 1977. *Selected Letters of E. T. A. Hoffmann*, ed. and trans. Johanna C. Sahlin (University of Chicago, Chicago and London).

Hokenson, Jan 1985. 'Todorov and the Existentialists', in Collins and Pearce, 1985a (above), pp. 33–9.

Hokenson, Jan and Pearce, Howard (eds) 1986. *Forms of the Fantastic: Selected essays from the third international conference on the fantastic in literature and film*, (Greenwood, New York).

Hughes, Glyn Tegai 1979. *Romantic German Literature*, (Edward Arnold, London).

Hume, Kathryn 1984. *Fantasy and Mimesis: Responses to reality in Western literature*, (Methuen, New York and London).

Hutcheon, Linda 1984. *Narcissistic Narrative: The metafictional paradox*, (Methuen, New York and London). First published Wilfred Laurier University Press 1980.

Hutcheon, Linda 1985. *A Theory of Parody: The teachings of twentieth-century art forms*, (Methuen, New York and London).

Hutcheon, Linda 1988. *A Poetics of Postmodernism: History, theory, fiction* (Routledge, New York and London).

Hutchings, Stephen 1988. 'Discourse, story and the fantastic in the short stories of Leonid Andreyev', *Essays in Poetics*, vol. 13, no. 2, pp. 1–25.

Hutchinson, Peter 1983. *Games Authors Play*, (Methuen, London and New York).

Imhof, Rüdiger, 1989. *John Banville: A critical introduction*, (Wolfhound, Dublin).

Ingham, Norman W. 1974. *E. T. A. Hoffmann's Reception in Russia*, (jal-verlag, Würzburg).

Irwin, W. R. 1976. *The Game of the Impossible: A rhetoric of fantasy*, (University of Illinois, Urbana).

Irwin, W. R. 1982. 'From fancy to fantasy: Coleridge and beyond', in Schlobin, 1982 (below), pp. 36–55.

Jaccard, Jean-Philippe 1988. 'Daniil Harms dans le contexte de la littérature de l'absurd russe et européene', in *Schweizerische Beiträge zum X. Internationalen Slavistenkongress in Sofia, September 1988*, ed. Peter Brang (Peter Lang, Bern, pp. 145–69). English translation in *Essays and Materials on Daniil Kharms*, ed. Neil Cornwell (Macmillan, London, forthcoming).

Jackson, Rosemary 1981. *Fantasy: The literature of subversion* (Methuen, London and New York).

Jackson, Rosemary 1986. 'Narcissism and beyond: A psychoanalytic reading of Frankenstein and fantasies of the double', in Coyle, 1986 (above), pp. 43–53.

Jakobson, Roman 1987. *Language in Literature*, ed. Krystyna Pomorska and Stephen Rudy (Belknap, Cambridge, Mass.).

James, Henry 1984a. *Henry James Letters*, ed. Leon Edel, vol. IV, 1895–1916 (Belknap, Cambridge, Mass.).

James, Henry 1984b. *Literary Criticism: French writers, other writers. The Prefaces to the New York Edition*, (Library of America, New York).

James, Henry 1987a. *The Complete Notebooks of Henry James*, ed. Leon Edel and Lyall H. Powers (Oxford University Press, New York and Oxford).

James, Henry 1987b. *The Critical Muse: Selected literary criticism*, ed. Roger Gard (Penguin, Harmondsworth).

Jameson, Fredric 1975. 'Magical Narratives: Romance as genre', *New Literary History*, vol. 7, pp. 135–63. Revised in Jameson 1981.

Jameson, Frederic 1981. *The Political Unconscious: Narrative as a socially symbolic act*, (Methuen, London; Cornell University Press, Ithaca).

Jauss, Hans Robert 1974. 'Literary history as a challenge to literary theory', in *New Directions in Literary History*, ed. Ralph Cohen (Routledge, London, pp. 11–41).

Jones, Malcolm V. 1986. ' "Der Sandmann" and "the uncanny": a sketch for an alternative approach', *Paragraph*, 7, pp. 77–101.

Kappeler, Susanne 1980. *Writing and Reading in Henry James*, (Macmillan, London).

Kayser, Wolfgang 1981. *The Grotesque in Art and Literature*, trans. Ulrich Weisstein (Columbia University Press, New York). First published Indiana University Press, 1963. Original published 1957.

Kern, Gary 1982. 'The search for fantasy: From primitive man to pornography', in Slusser *et al.* (below), pp. 175–94.

Kiely, Robert 1972. *The Romantic Novel in England*, (Harvard University Press, Cambridge, Mass.).

Kodjak, Andrej 1976. ' "The Queen of Spades" in the context of the Faust legend', in *Alexander Puškin: A symposium on the 175th anniversary of his birth*, ed. Andrej Kodjak and Kiril Taranovsky (New York University Press, New York, pp. 87–118).

Kodjak, Andrej *et al.* 1985. *Myth in Literature*, ed. Andrej Kodjak, Krystyna Pomorska and Stephen Rudy (Slavica, Columbus, Ohio).

Kohlschmidt, Werner 1975. *A History of German Literature 1760–1805*, trans. Ian Hilton (Macmillan, London). Original published 1965.

Kroeber, Karl 1988. *Romantic Fantasy and Science Fiction*, (Yale University Press, New Haven and London).

Kundera, Milan 1988. *The Art of the Novel*, trans. Linda Asher (Faber, London; Grove Press, New York). First published as *L'Art du roman*, 1986.

Lacoue-Labarthe, Philippe and Nancy, Jean-Luc 1988. *The Literary Absolute: The theory of literature in German romanticism*, trans. Philip Barnard and Cheryl Lester (State University of New York Press, Albany). Original published 1978.

Laubriet, Pierre 1961. *Un Catéchisme esthétique: 'La Chef-d'œuvre inconnu' de Balzac*, (Didier, Paris).

Laubriet, Pierre 1980. *L'Intelligence de l'art chez Balzac*, (Slatkine, Geneva). First published 1961.

Le Guin, Ursula K. 1989. *The Language of the Night: Essays on fantasy and science fiction*, ed. Susan Wood, revised edition ed. Ursula K. Le Guin (Women's Press, London; Putnam's, New York). First published 1979.

Leighton, Lauren G. 1977a. 'Numbers and numerology in "The Queen of Spades"', *Canadian Slavonic Papers*, vol. 19, p. 417–43.

Leighton, Lauren G. 1977b. 'Gematria in "The Queen of Spades": A Decembrist puzzle', *Slavic and East European Journal*, vol. 21, no. 4, pp. 455–69.

Leighton, Lauren G. 1982. 'Puškin and Freemasonry: "The Queen of Spades"', in Gutsche and Leighton, 1982 (above), pp. 15–25.

Lem, Stanislaw, 1985. *Microworlds: Writings on science fiction and fantasy*, ed. Franz Rottensteiner (Secker & Warburg, London). First published Harcourt Brace Jovanovich 1984. Essay 'Todorov's fantastic theory of literature', first published 1973.

Lezhnёv, A. 1983. *Pushkin's Prose*, trans. Roberta Reeder (Ardis, Ann Arbor). Original published 1937.

Little, T. E. 1980. 'Towards a definition of fantasy', *Essays in Poetics*, vol. 5, no. 2, pp. 66–83.

Little, T. E. 1984. *The Fantasts*, (Avebury, Amersham).

Losse, Deborah N. 1986. 'Rabelaisian paradox: Where the fantastic and the carnivalesque intersect', *The Romantic Review*, vol. 77, pp. 322–9.

Lovecraft, Howard, P. 1973. *Supernatural Horror in Literature*, (Dover, New York). First published in *The Recluse*, 1927; revised form New York 1945.

McCaffery, Larry 1982. 'Form, formula and fantasy: Generative structures in contemporary fiction', in Slusser *et al.* 1982 (below), p. 21–37.

McCormack, W. J. 1980. *Sheridan Le Fanu and Victorian Ireland*, (Clarendon Press, Oxford).

McCormack, W. J. 1985. *Ascendancy and Tradition in Anglo-Irish Literature from 1789 to 1939*, (Clarendon Press, Oxford).

McHale, Brian, 1987. *Postmodernist Fiction*, (Methuen, New York and London).

Macherey, Pierre 1978. *A Theory of Literary Production*, trans. Geoffrey Wall (Routledge, London). Original published 1966.

Mandelker, Amy and Reeder, Roberta (eds) 1988. *The Supernatural in Slavic and Baltic Literature: Essays in honor of Victor Terras*, (Slavica, Colmbus, Ohio).

Manlove, C. N. 1975. *Modern Fantasy: Five studies*, (Cambridge University Press, Cambridge).

Manlove, C. N. 1982. 'On the nature of fantasy', in Schlobin, 1982 (below), pp. 16–35.

Manlove, C. N. 1983. *The Impulse of Fantasy Literature*, (Macmillan, London).

Mann, Iurii 1978. *Poetika Gogolia*, (Khudozhestvennaia literatura, Moscow).

Martin, Philip 1988. 'The vampire in the looking-glass: Reflection and projection in Bram Stoker's *Dracula*', in C. Bloom, 1988 (above), pp. 80–92.

Maxton, Hugh 1989. 'Kharms and Myles: An afterword', in Kharms, 1989 (above), pp. 93–100.

Menhennet, Alan 1983. 'Hoffmann, Bulgakov and the "Fantastic Tradition"', *Strathclyde Modern Language Studies*, vol. III, pp. 3–20.

Mersereau, John, jun. 1983. *Russian Romantic Fiction*, (Ardis, Ann Arbor).

Miller, Karl 1987. *Doubles: Studies in literary history* (Oxford University Press, Oxford). First published 1985.

Miller, Robin Feuer 1983. 'Dostoevsky and the tale of terror', in *The Russian Novel from Pushkin to Pasternak*, ed. John Garrard (Yale University Press, New Haven, pp. 103–21).

Milne, Lesley 1977. *The Master and Margarita — A Comedy of Victory*, (Birmingham Slavonic Monographs, no. 3, Birmingham).

Mirimsky, I. 1938. 'Sotsial'naia fantastika Gofmana', *Literaturnaia uchëba*, no. 5, pp. 63–87.

Moers, Ellen 1978. *Literary Women*, (Women's Press, London).

Morse, Donald E. (ed.) 1987. *The Fantastic in World Literature and the Arts: Selected essays from the fifth international conference on the fantastic in the arts*, (Greenwood, New York and Westport).

Moylan, Tom 1986. *Demand the Impossible: Science fiction and the utopian imagination*, (Methuen, New York and London).

Murav'ëva, O. S. 1978. 'Fantastika v povesti Pushkina "Pikovaia dama"', in *Pushkin: issledovaniia i materialy*, vol. 8, pp. 62–9.

Nabokov, Vladimir 1964. Commentary to Aleksandr Pushkin, *Eugene Onegin: A novel in verse*, trans. Vladimir Nabokov, 4 vols. (Routledge, London; Princeton University Press, Princeton, 1964).

Nabokov, Vladimir 1980. *Lectures on Literature*, ed. Fredson Bowers (Weidenfeld & Nicolson, London).

Neefs, Jacques 1980. 'La représentation fantastique dans "Le Horla" de Maupassant', *Cahiers de l'Association internationale des Etudes françaises*, no. 32, pp. 231–45.

Nepomnyashchy, Catharine Theimer 1982. 'Andrei Sinyavsky's "You and I": A modern day fantastic tale', *Ulbandus Review*, vol. 2, no. 2, pp. 209–30.

Nisbet, H. B. (ed.) 1985. *German Aesthetic and Literary Criticism: Winckelman, Lessing, Hamann, Herder, Schiller, Goethe*, (Cambridge University Press, Cambridge).

Palumbo, Donald (ed.) 1988. *Spectrum of the Fantastic: Selected essays from the sixth international conference on the fantastic in the arts*, (Greenwood, New York).

Parrinder, Patrick 1980. *Science Fiction: Its criticism and teaching*, (Methuen, London).

Parrinder, Patrick 1987. *The Failure of Theory: Essays on criticism and contemporary fiction*, (Harvester Wheatsheaf, Hemel Hempstead).

Passage, Charles E. 1963. *The Russian Hoffmannists*, (Mouton, The Hague).

Pawling, Christopher (ed.) 1984. *Popular Fiction and Social Change*, (Macmillan, London).

Petrunina, N. N. 1980. 'Pushkin i traditsiia volshebnoskazachnogo povestvovaniia (k poetike "Pikovoi damy")', *Russkaia literatura*, no. 3, pp. 30–51.

Petzold, Dieter 1986. 'Fantasy fiction and related genres', *Modern Fiction Studies*, vol. 32, no. 1, p. 11–20.

Pirsig, Robert M. 1976. *Zen and the Art of Motorcycle Maintenance: An inquiry into values*, (Corgi, London). First published Bodley Head 1974.

Porter, Laurence M. (guest ed.) 1988. *L'esprit créateur*, vol. XXVIII, no. 3.

Prawer, Siegbert S. 1965. *The 'Uncanny' in Literature*, (Westfield College, London).

Praz, Mario 1968. 'Introductory Essay' to *Three Gothic Novels* (Penguin, Harmondsworth, pp. 7–34). See Fairclough, 1968 ('Anthologies' above).

Praz, Mario 1970. *The Romantic Agony*, trans. Angus Davidson, 2nd edition, foreword Frank Kermode (Oxford University Press, Oxford). First published in English 1933.

Prickett, Stephen 1979. *Victorian Fantasy*, (Harvester Press, Brighton).

Proffer, Ellendea 1984. *Bulgakov: Life and work*, (Ardis, Ann Arbor).

Propp, V. 1968. *Morphology of the Folktale*, trans. Laurence Scott, 2nd edition revised and ed. Louis A. Wagner (University of Texas, Austin and London). First published 1958. Original published 1928.

Punter, David 1980. *The Literature of Terror: A history of Gothic fictions from 1765 to the present day*, (Longman, London and New York).

Punter, David 1988. 'Edgar Allan Poe: Tales of dark heat', in C. Bloom, 1988 (above), pp. 1–13.

Pursglove, Michael 1985. 'Chronology in Pushkin's *Pikovaya dama*', *Irish Slavonic Studies*, no. 6, pp. 11–18.

Rabkin, Eric S. 1976. *The Fantastic in Literature*, (Princeton University Press, Princeton).

Rachmühl, Françoise 1983. *Le Horla et autres contes fantastiques: Guy de Maupassant*, 'Profile d'une oeuvre' (Hatier, Paris).

Radford, Jean (ed.) 1986. *The Progress of Romance: The poetics of popular fiction*, (Routledge, London).

Rajan, Tilottama 1980. *Dark Interpreter: The discourse of romanticism*, (Cornell University Press, Ithaca and London). Paperback 1986.

Reeder, Roberta 1982. 'The Queen of Spades: A parody of the Hoffmannian tale', in Gutsche and Leighton, 1982 (above), pp. 73–98.

Reichert, John 1978. 'More than kin and less than kind: the limits of genre theory', in Strelka, 1978 (below), pp. 57–79.

Reid, Robert (ed.) 1986. *Problems of Russian Romanticism*, (Gower, Aldershot).

Richter, Jean Paul [Johann Paul Friedrich] 1973. *Horn of Oberon: Jean Paul Richter's 'School for Aesthetics'*, intro. and trans. Margaret R. Hale (Wayne State University Press, Detroit).

Risco, Antonio 1982. *Literatura y Fantasía*, (Taurus, Madrid).

Rosen, Nathan 1975. 'The Magic Cards in *The Queen of Spades*', *Slavic and East European Journal*, vol. 19, no. 3, pp. 255–75.

Rudolf, Anthony 1984. *Byron's Darkness: Lost summer and nuclear winter*, (Menard Press, London).

Rushdie, Salman 1984. 'Outside the Whale', *Granta* 11, pp. 125–38.

Rushdie, Salman 1985. 'On Günther Grass', *Granta* 15, pp. 179–85.

Sacks, Oliver 1985. 'Excesses', *Granta* 16, pp. 7–22.

Schlobin, Roger C. (ed.) 1982. *The Aesthetics of Fantasy Literature and Art*,

(University of Notre Dame, Notre Dame, Ind.; Harvester Wheatsheaf, Hemel Hempstead).

Schlobin, Roger C. 1987. 'From the old on to the new: New directions in fantasy criticism and theory', *Extrapolation*, vol. 28, no. 1, 1987, pp. 3–9.

Scholes, Robert 1975. *Structural Fabulation: An essay on the fiction of the future*, (University of Notre Dame, Notre Dame, Ind.).

Scholes, Robert, 1985. *Textual Power: Literary theory and the teaching of English*, (Yale University Press, New Haven and London).

Schwartz, Murray M. and Schwartz, Albert 1975. ' "The Queen of Spades": A psychoanalytic interpretation', *Texas Studies in Literature and Language*, XVII, pp. 275–88.

Scott, Sir Walter 1968. *On Novelists and Fiction*, ed. Ioan Williams (Routledge, London).

Sedgwick, Eve Kosofsky 1986. *The Coherence of Gothic Conventions*, (Methuen, New York and London). First published Arno Press 1980.

Selden, Raman 1985. *A Reader's Guide to Contemporary Literary Theory*, (Harvester Wheatsheaf, Hemel Hempstead).

Semeka-Pankratov, Elena 1985. 'Bulgakov's diabolic myth: Symbolism of *A Theatrical Novel*', in Kodjak *et al.*, 1985 (above), pp. 19–48.

Shukman, Ann 1977. 'The short story: Theory, analysis, interpretation', *Essays in Poetics*, vol. 2, no. 2, pp. 27–95.

Siebers, Tobin 1984. *The Romantic Fantastic*, (Cornell University Press, Ithaca and London).

Simpson, David (ed.) 1984. *German Aesthetic and Literary Criticism: Kant, Fichte, Schelling, Schopenhauer, Hegel*, ed. David Simpson (Cambridge University Press, Cambridge).

Skarda, Patricia J. 1989. 'Vampirism and plagiarism: Byron's influence and Polidori's practice', *Studies in Romanticism*, vol. 28, pp. 249–69.

Slusser, George E. *et al.* 1982. *Bridges to Fantasy*, ed. George E. Slusser, Eric S. Rabkin and Robert Scholes (Southern Illinois University Press, Carbondale).

Smirnov, I. P. 1985. *Porozhdenie interteksta (elementy intertekstual'nogo analiza s primerami iz tvorchestva B. L. Pasternaka* (Wiener Slawistischer Almanach, Vienna).

Solmi, Sergio 1978. *Saggi sul fantastico: dall'antichità alle prospettive del futuro*, (Einaudi, Turin).

Solov'ëv, Vladimir Sergeevich 1966. *Sobranie sochinenii V. S. Solov'ëva*, 2nd edition, vol. IX (Prosveshchenie, St Petersburg, no date). Reprinted Brussels, 1966.

Strada, Vittorio 1988. 'Il fantastico e la storia', in his *Simbolo e storia: aspetti e problemi del Novecento russo*, (Marsilio, Venice, pp. 129–40). First published *Prometeo*, vol. 5, no. 17, March 1987.

Strelka, Joseph P. (ed.) 1978. *Theories of Literary Genre*, (Pennsylvania State University Press, University Park and London).

Suvin, Darko 1979. *Metamorphosis of Science Fiction*, (Yale University Press, New Haven and London). Revised English edition of his *Pour une poétique de la science fiction*, 1977.

Swinfen, Ann 1984. *In Defence of Fantasy: A study of the genre in English and American literature since 1945*, (Routledge, London).

Tanner, Tony 1982. *Thomas Pynchon*, (Methuen, London and New York).

Tatar, Maria M. 1978. *Spellbound: Studies on mesmerism and literature*, (Princeton University Press, Princeton).

Tatar, Maria M. 1980. 'E. T. A. Hoffmann's "Der Sandmann": Reflection and romantic irony', *MLN*, vol. 95, pp. 585–608.

Tatar, Maria M. 1981. 'The houses of fiction: Toward a definition of the uncanny', *Comparative Literature*, vol. 33, p. 167–82.

Thompson, G. R. 1973. *Poe's Fiction: Romantic Irony in the Gothic Tales*, (University of Wisconsin, Madison).

Thompson, G. R. 1982. 'The apparition of this world: Transcendentalism and the American "ghost" story', in Slusser *et al.*, 1982 (above), pp. 90–107.

Todorov, Tzvetan 1973. *The Fantastic: A structural approach to a literary genre*, trans. Richard Howards (Case Western Reserve, Cleveland and London). Original published as *Introduction à la littérature fantastique*, Paris 1970.

Todorov, Tzvetan 1977. *The poetics of Prose*, trans. Richard Howard (Blackwell, Oxford). Original published as *La Poétique de la prose*, Paris 1971.

Tolkien, J. R. R. 1964. 'On fairy stories', in his *Tree and Leaf*, (Allen & Unwin, London). First published 1947 (based on a lecture of 1938).

Varma, Devendra P. 1966. *The Gothic Flame*, (Russell & Russell, New York). First published 1957.

Varnado, S. L. 1987. *Haunted Presence: The numinous in Gothic fiction*, (University of Alabama, Tuscaloosa and London).

Vax, Louis 1960. *L'Art et la littérature fantastiques*, (Presses Universitaires de France, Paris).

Vygotsky, Lev Semenovich 1971. *The Psychology of Art*, (Massachusetts Institute of Technology Press, Cambridge, Mass.). Original published as *Psikhologiia iskusstva*.

Walker, I. M. (ed.) 1986. *Edgar Allan Poe: The critical heritage*, (Routledge, London and New York).

Waugh, Patricia 1984. *Metafiction: The theory and practice of self-conscious fiction*, (Methuen, London).

Weldon, Fay 1989. *Sacred Cows*, Chatto Counter Blasts no. 4 (Chatto & Windus, London).

Wellbery, David 1980. 'E. T. A. Hoffmann and romantic hermeneutics: An interpretation of Hoffmann's "Don Juan"', *Studies in Romanticism*, vol. 19, pp. 455–73.

Wellek, René, 1981. *A History of Modern Criticism 1750–1950. 2. The Romantic Age*, (Cambridge University Press, Cambridge). First published 1955.

Wendland, Albert 1985. *Science, Myth and the Fictional Creation of Alien Worlds*, (UMI Research Press, Ann Arbor).

Wheeler, Kathleen M. (ed.) 1984. *German Aesthetic and Literary Criticism: The romantic ironists and Goethe*, (Cambridge University Press, Cambridge).

Wilde, Oscar 1973. *De Profundis and Other Writings*, intro. Hesketh Pearson (Penguin, Harmondsworth).

Williams, Gareth 1989. 'Convention and Play in *Pikovaja Dama*', *Russian Literature*, vol. XXVI, pp. 523–38.

Williams, Gareth (1990). 'Some difficulties in the interpretation of Bulgakov's *The Master. and Margarita* and the advantages of a Manichaean approach. With some notes on Tolstoi's influence on *The Master and Margarita*', *Slavonic and East European Review*, vol. 68, no. 2, pp. 234–56 .

Winner, Thomas G. 1978. 'Structural and semiotic genre theory', in Strelka, 1978 (above), pp. 254–68.

Wolfe, Gary K. 1982. 'The encounter with fantasy', in Schlobin, 1982 (above), pp. 1–15.

Wright, Elizabeth 1984. *Psychoanalytical Criticism: Theory and practice*, (Methuen, London).

Zahorski, Kenneth J. and Boyer, Robert H. 1982. 'The secondary worlds of high fantasy', in Schlobin, 1982 (above), pp. 56–81.

Zamiatin, Evgenii 1970. *A Soviet Heretic: Essays by Yevgeny Zamyatin*, ed. and trans. Mirra Ginsburg (University of Chicago, Chicago).

Zanger, Jules 1982. 'Heroic fantasy and social reality: *ex nihilo nihil fit*', in Schlobin, 1982 (above), pp. 226–36.

Ziolkowski, Theodore 1977. *Disenchanted Images: A literary iconology*, (Princeton University Press, Princeton).

Zolla, Elémire 1964. *Storia del fantasticare*, (Bompiani, Milan).

Index

absurd, the, 5, 9, 41, 70, 84–5, 143, 153,
    162, 217–18
Ackroyd, Peter, 155
Adams, Richard, 146
Agrippa, Cornelius, 57, 68
Aitmatov, Chingiz, 233, 242
    Day Lasts more than a Hundred Years,
    The, 233
    Place of the Skull, The (Plakha), 242
Akhmatova, Anna, 113–14
Akhtar, Shabbir, 225
Aksënov, Vasilii, xiii, 145, 185
Al-Azmeh, Aziz, 224–5
Al-Ghamdi, Mughram Ali, 222
Albertus Magnus, 57, 68
Aldiss, Brian, 50, 68, 73–4, 111–12, 153,
    232, 235
    Frankenstein Unbound 153
Ali, Tariq, 223, 226, 228, 244
Ali Ashraf, Syed, 222
Allende, Isabel, xiii, 185
Amis, Martin, xiv, 218
Ampère, Jean-Jacques, 56, 57, 58
Angelou, Maya, 198
Appignanesi, Lisa, 187, 190, 193, 194,
    219–22, 224, 227–8, 244
Apter, T. E., 16, 26, 28, 212–13, 217
Apuleius, 45
    Golden Ass, The, 45
Arendt, Hannah, xiv
Aristotle, 35
Artaud, Antonin, 154
Attebery, Brian, 14, 233
Attridge, Derek, 240
Auerbach, Erich, 19
Austen, Jane, 67
    Northanger Abbey, 67
Avins, Carol, 169–70

Bader, Franz Xavier von, 59
Bakhtin, Mikhail, 9–11, 19, 21, 32, 35, 46,
    77, 82–3, 155–8, 166, 211, 214, 216
    see also carnivalisation; chronotope
Baldick, Chris, 47, 65, 67–8, 71–2, 95,
    103, 106, 109–11, 235
Balzac, Honoré de, 26, 67, 77, 89–90, 103,
    113, 153, 217, 237–8
    Chef-d'oeuvre inconnu, Le, 89, 103, 236–7
    Melmoth reconcilié, 90, 153
    Peau douce, La, 103

Banta, Martha, 45, 139, 238
Banville, John, xii, 142, 172–84, 193, 227,
    242
    Birchwood, 173–7, 179, 184, 242
    Book of Evidence, The, 173, 177, 242
    Doctor Copernicus, 172
    Kepler, 142, 172
    Long Lankin, 173, 242
    Mefisto, 173–4, 176–84, 193, 242
    Newton Letter, The, 172
    Nightspawn, 173, 242
Barratt, Andrew, 160, 162–70, 241
Barthes, Roland, 156
Baudelaire, Charles-Pierre, 79, 83, 103
Bayley, John, 113, 117, 238, 239
Beaver, Harold, 84
Beckett, Samuel, 60, 144, 153, 185
Beckford, William, 49, 65
    Vathek, 49
Beer, Gillian, 48, 233
Beerbohm, Max, 158
    Enoch Soames, 158
Bekker, Balthazar, 57
Belinsky, Vissarion, 5, 77, 114, 231
Bellemin-Noël, Jean, 29, 37
Belsey, Catherine, 155
Bely, Andrei, xiii, 145, 156, 160, 163, 212
    Petersburg, 156, 163
Benjamin, Walter, xiv
Berlioz, Hector, 58
Bessière, Irène, 56–9, 232, 234, 236
Bethea, David, xii, 156, 162, 164–8, 241–2
Birkhead, Edith, 56, 66, 73, 87
Blackall, Eric A., 59–63, 66, 235
Blake, William, 229
Bloom, Clive, 96
Bloom, Harold, xiii, 13, 30, 81, 213
Bocharov, S. G., 114, 117, 120
Böhme, Jacob, 57, 59
'Bonaventura', 7–8, 60, 62, 235
    Nachtwachen (The Nightwatches of
    Bonaventura), 7, 61
Booth, Wayne C., 232, 239
Borges, Jorge Luis, 33, 64, 143, 149–50,
    157–9, 216, 223, 243
    Tlön, Uqbar, Orbis Tertius, 149–50
Bosch, Hieronymus, 7
Boyer, Robert H., 165, 233
Brecht, Berthold, 226
Brennan, Timothy, 185–9, 224, 243–4

261

Brenton, Howard, 223, 226, 228, 244
Breton, André, 154
  Nadja, 154
Briggs, A. D. P., xiv, 117, 119, 128–31, 138, 238–9
Briggs, Julia, 91, 146, 236–7, 239
Broch, Hermann, 159
Brontë, Charlotte, 153
  Jane Eyre, 153
Brooke-Rose, Christine, xi, 13–15, 24–5, 27–9, 31, 34–40, 54, 84, 123, 141, 143, 145, 213–16, 218, 230–2, 239
Brooks, Peter, 47, 66
Brown, Charles Brockden, 54–6, 65, 86, 94, 175, 228
  Arthur Mervyn, 54
  Edgar Huntly, 54–5, 86
  Memoirs of Carwin the Biloquist, 55
  Wieland or The Transformation, 54–6, 175
Browning, Elizabeth Barratt, 87
Bruegel, Peter II ('Hell'), 7
Bruno, Giordano, 222–3
Bulgakov, Mikhail A., 10, 36, 145, 154–6, 158, 159–72, 182–3, 193, 212, 221, 223, 229, 241–2
  Master and Margarita, The, 10, 154–6, 159–72, 182, 193, 221, 223, 241–2
  White Guard, The, 160
Büger, Gottfried August, 59, 65
  Lenore, 59, 65
Burgin, Diana Lewis, 118–20
Burgin, Victor, 7, 218, 230, 233
Burke, Edmund, 47–9
Butler, Marilyn, 47–8, 65
Byron, Lord George Gordon, 65, 72, 74–5, 109, 124, 226
  Darkness, 72

Cagliostro, Giuseppe Balsamo, 57
Caillois, Roger, 230, 234
Calder, John, 222
Callot, Jacques, 78
Calvino, Italo, xiii, xiv, 28, 142, 153–9, 165
  If on a winter's night a traveller, 157
carnivalisation, 19, 21, 79, 82–3, 155, 162, 166, 180, 211, 218, 242
Carr, John Dickson, 231
  Burning Court, The, 231
Carroll, Lewis, 13, 15, 32, 146, 231, 240
  Sylvie and Bruno Concluded, 15, 231
  Through the Looking Glass, 32
Carter, Angela, xiii, 184, 190, 198, 242
  Black Venus, 198
  Nights at the Circus, 242
Carter, Erica, 218
Carter, Margaret, 21–2, 37, 77, 92, 110–11, 236–7
Casanova di Seingalt, Giacomo Girolamo, 57, 131

Cassiday, Bruce, 79
Castex, Pierre-Georges, 3, 57–8, 65, 67, 234, 236
catastrophe theory, 139, 240
Cave, Terence, 60, 166
Cazotte, Jacques, 36, 57, 59, 65, 78, 231
  Diable amoureux, Le, 36, 57, 65, 231
Cela, Camilo José, xiii, 184, 227
Cervantes, Miguel de, 5, 32, 61–2, 158–9, 164
  Don Quixote, 63, 78, 158
Chamisso, Adalbert von, 78, 109, 159, 212
Chanady, Amaryll, 22, 29, 40, 86, 100–1, 147, 153, 160, 166, 185, 232–4
Charlesworth, Barbara, 103
Chesterton, G. K., 111
Chicherin, A. V., 114
chronotope, 9–10, 46, 69–70, 92, 156–7
  see also Bakhtin
Chudakova, Marietta, 170
Clairmont, Claire, 72, 124, 129, 236
Clayton, David, 86
Coleridge, Samuel Taylor, 1, 46, 48, 51, 64, 70, 84, 233, 236
  Biographia Literaria, 1, 48
  Rime of the Ancient Mariner, The, 70
Collins, Robert A., xiii
Collins, Wilkie, 93, 110, 230
  Woman in White, The, 93
Conrad, Joseph, 146, 185
  Lord Jim, 48
Coover, Robert, 144, 154
  Marker, The, 154
Cortázar, Julio, xiii
Cox, Michael, 92
Crane, R. S., 34
Cranny-Francis, Anne, 110, 237
Cullen, Seamus, 146
  Astra and Flondrix, 146
Cunliffe, Marcus, 53–4
Curtis, Anthony, 123, 125–6, 239
Curtis, J. A. E., 10, 164–5, 167, 169–70, 241

Da Ponte, Lorenzo, 80
Dali, Salvador, 154
Daniel, Iulii, 227
Däniken, Erich von, 243
Dante Alighieri, 61, 163–4, 172, 182, 193, 222, 226, 230
Darwin, Erasmus, 68
Darwinism, 95, 101, 103
de la Mare, Walter, 146
de Man, Paul, 143
De Quincey, Thomas, 46, 52, 77, 143, 236
  Confessions of an English Opium Eater, 77
Deane, Seamus, 216, 218
Debreczeny, Paul, 113–14, 138, 238
Defoe, Daniel, 47–8, 153, 197

History of the Devil, The 197
Robinson Crusoe, 11, 153
Delacroix, Eugène, 58
Deleuze, Gilles, 212
Derrida, Jacques, 143
Dickens, Charles, 67, 99, 182, 189, 239
  Bleak House, 175
  Great Expectations, 153, 239
  Mystery of Edwin Drood, The, 99
Diderot, Denis, 61–2, 75, 158–9
  Religieuse, La, 75
Dinesen, Isak (Karen Blixen), 68
Dipple, Elizabeth, xii, 142, 150, 220–1,
  223, 228
Disraeli, Benjamin, 103
  Vivien Grey, 103
Doctorow, E. L., 185
Doppelgänger see doubles
Dostoevsky, Fëdor M., 5, 23, 55, 67,
  77–8, 84, 100, 113, 115, 145, 147,
  156, 163–4, 213, 231, 233–4, 242–3
  Bobok, 23
  Brothers Karamazov, The, 78
  Double, The, 5, 23, 100, 231
  Dream of a Ridiculous Man, The, 23, 147
  Gentle Spirit, A, 23
  Idiot, The, 156
  Landlady, The, 23
  'Life of a Great Sinner, The', 78
  Notes from Underground, The, 242–3
doubles, 10, 52, 65–6, 68–9, 71, 84–6, 95,
  101, 103–4, 106, 108–9, 175, 177–8,
  184, 234
Doyle, Sir Arthur Conan, 109, 146, 158,
  182
Dubrow, Heather, 234
Dumas, Alexandre, *père*, 58, 77
  Bal masqué, Un, 58

Eco, Umberto, xiii, xiv, 46, 153, 157–8,
  215, 218, 220
  Name of the Rose, The, 158, 220, 228
Edel, Leon, 121, 125, 238–9
Edgeworth, Maria, 175
Edmonds, Rosemary, 114, 238
Einstein, Albert, 164
Ellmann, Richard, 102, 104, 106
Eluard, Paul, 154
Enright, D. J., 193

Fairclough, Peter, 49, 70–1, 235
fairy story, 4, 8, 19, 25, 32, 40, 70, 78–9,
  106, 108, 113, 120, 135–7, 166,
  178–9, 182, 233–4, 238
Faiz, 226
fantastic, pure (PF), 12, 14, 28, 34–41, 51,
  76, 84, 92, 122, 141, 143, 150–2,
  183, 207, 212, 235

fantastique, le, 6–7, 30–1, 56, 58, 67, 100,
  154, 230
fantasy, xi, 8–11, 14–16, 18–19, 25–7,
  27–34, 62–3, 70, 79, 83, 106–7, 144,
  146, 211–12, 214–18, 230, 232–3
  high fantasy, 32, 145–6, 165, 215, 233
  Victorian fantasy, 29, 32, 94
Faustian qualities *see* Goethe
Fichte, Johann Gottlieb, 62, 235
Fielding, Henry, 48
Flaubert, Gustave, 7, 131
  Novembre, 7
Fletcher, John, 230
Florensky, Pavel, 163, 241–2
Foot, Michael, 223
Formalism, Russian, 15, 24, 145, 161
Forster, E. M., 32
Forsyth, James, 238
Foucault, Michel, 10, 57, 216, 218
Fouqué, Friedrich Freiherr de la Motte, 78
  Undine, 78
Foust, Ronald, 110, 237
Fowler, Alastair, 67, 140
Fowler, Roger, 25
Fowles, John, 33, 155, 158
  French Lieutenant's Woman, The, 158, 228
  Maggot, The, 155
  Mantissa, 158
Fox, Ralph, 32
Freeborn, Richard, 70, 73, 236
Freud, Sigmund, 5–7, 13, 16, 37, 47, 50,
  81, 108, 110, 114, 124, 146, 211–15,
  230, 233, 236, 243
  'The "Uncanny"', 6, 37, 81, 213–14, 243
  see also psychoanalysis
Frye, Northrop, 35, 92–3, 140, 156, 166,
  211, 214, 234
Fuentes, Carlos, xiii, xiv, 65, 128, 154–5,
  157–9, 184–5, 215, 217–18, 227–8,
  239, 243
  Aura, 65, 128, 154, 157–8, 239, 243
  'How I wrote one of my books', 158
  Terra Nostra, 154–5, 157–9
Furst, Lilian, 61–2, 67, 235

Galdós, Pérez Benito, 67
Gandhi, Rajiv, 187
García Márquez. Gabriel, xiii, 154–5, 159,
  184–5, 226, 228
  Last Voyage of the Ghost Ship, The, 154
  One Hundred Years of Solitude, 155, 185
Gard, Roger, 239
Gautier, Théophile, 17, 58, 102–3, 231
  Morte amoureuse, La, 231
  Spirite, 17
Genette, Gérard, 200–2
genre, 3–4, 10, 15, 18, 21, 28, 30–1, 31–4,
  34–41, 51, 60–3, 81, 140–4, 156,

165–6, 185, 212, 214, 231, 233–4
ghost story, 30, 69, 72–3, 79, 87–8, 119,
    121, 145–6, 198–208
Giaquinta, Rosanna, 153
Gide, André, 82, 113, 145
Gillespie, Gerald, 235
Giuliani, Rita, 163, 166
Glenny, Michael, 160, 167, 241
Godwin, William, 50, 54, 65
    Caleb Williams, 50
Goethe, Johann Wolfgang von, 62, 75, 78,
    159, 163–4, 183, 193
    Faust, Faustian/Mephistophelian
        qualities, 26, 68, 75, 78, 98, 103,
        106, 113, 119–20, 131, 159, 164,
        167, 182–3, 193, 194
    Wilhelm Meister, 63
Gogol, Nikolai V., 14–15, 19–20, 36, 40,
    77, 100, 145, 159, 163–4, 234, 236
    Dead Souls, 20
    Diary of a Madman, 100
    Nose, The, 14, 20, 40, 234
    Portrait, The, 236
Goldoni, Carlo, 131
Goncharov, Ivan, 77
    Oblomov, 77
Gordimer, Nadine, 185
Gothic, the, 21, 35, 45–53, 54–6, 58–60,
    63, 66, 67–9, 71, 74, 76–9, 84, 88,
    102–3, 106–7, 113–14, 143, 153–4,
    159, 175–6, 211, 214–15, 217, 230,
    233–4, 236
Goya, Francisco de, 29
Goytisolo, Juan, xiii, 155, 184
Gozzi, Carlo, 78
Grabo, Norman S., 55
Grass, Günter, xiii, xiv, 155, 158–9, 184–5
    Tin Drum, The, 155, 159, 185
Gray, Alasdair, xiii, 184
Grossman, Joan Delaney, 83
Grossman, Vasilii, 226
grotesque, the, 5–10, 32, 63, 72

Haining, Peter, 59, 108
Hardy, Thomas, 146, 232
Harrison, Tony, 226
Havel, Vaclav, 217
Hawthorne, Nathaniel, 48, 55, 103, 217,
    236
    House of the Seven Gables, The, 48
    Prophetic Pictures, The, 236
Hayter, Alethea, 7, 46, 66, 75–6, 230, 236
Hegel, Georg Wilhelm Friedrich, 61
Heidegger, Martin, 143
Herder, Johann Gottfried, 59
Hernadi, Paul, 140, 234
Hertz, Neil, 213–14, 236, 243
Hesse, Hermann, 145
    Steppenwolf, 145
Higgins, Aiden, 175

Hitchens, Christopher, 224–5, 227, 244
Hitler, Adolf, 223
Hodgson, William Hope, 91, 146–7, 149
    Carnacki the Ghost-Finder, 91, 146, 149
    House on the Borderland, The, 147, 149
Hoffmann, E. T. A., xi, 5–8, 10, 13, 19,
    36, 57–8, 62, 65, 69–70, 75, 78–83,
    85–6, 89, 95, 99–101, 109, 113–14,
    120, 155, 159, 164, 213, 226, 230–1,
    234–7, 240
    Devil's Elixirs, The, 75, 79, 82, 95
    Don Giovanni, 79–81, 82, 236
    Entail, The, 5, 79
    Golden Pot, The, 8, 79
    Kater Murr, 79, 99, 159, 182
    Mademoiselle de Scudéry, 79
    Master Flea, 83
    New Year's Eve Adventure, A, 70, 101
    Princess Brambilla, 79
    Ritter Gluck, 79
    Sandman, The, 5–6, 8, 10, 36, 79, 81–2,
        86, 213, 236
    Signor Formica, 79, 237
    Undine, 78
Hogg, James, 36, 52
    *Private Memoirs and Confessions of a
        Justified Sinner, The*, 36
horror, 29–30, 46, 52, 84, 107, 145–6, 233
Howard, Richard, 29
Hugo, Victor, 6–7, 77
    Cromwell, 6–7
Humboldt, Alexander von, 85
Hume, Kathryn, 11–12, 18–19, 24–6, 28,
    30–4, 38, 142–3, 230, 232
Hutcheon, Linda, 24–6, 29, 33, 141–4,
    155–7, 172, 213, 215, 217, 221, 228,
    231
Huchinson, Peter, 143
Huxley, Aldous, 148
Huysmans, Georges Charles (Joris-Karl),
    103
    A rebours, 103

Imhof, Rüdiger, 173–7, 182, 242–3
intertextuality, 140, 152–3, 157–8, 163,
    182–3
irony, 8, 32, 61–2, 79, 82, 84, 102, 157,
    160, 164–5, 172, 214, 235
Irving, Washington, 17, 54–5, 65
    Adventures of the German Student, The, 54
    Alhambra, The, 54
    Rip Van Winkle, 54
    Sketch Book, The, 54
    Spectre Bridegroom, The, 17, 54
    Tales of a Traveller, 54
Irwin, W. R., 13, 28, 230, 233

Jaccard, Jean-Philippe, 153
Jack the Ripper, 96, 110
Jackson, Rosemary, xi, 14–18, 23, 25–32,

36–8, 74, 105–6, 141, 215–17, 230, 236–7, 243
Jacobs, W. W., 36, 150
  Monkey's Paw, The, 36
Jakobson, Roman, 145
James, Henry, xii, xiv, 36, 55, 67, 71–2, 93, 108, 113–39, 144, 146, 150, 158, 231–2, 236–8
  Altar of the Dead, The, 122, 238
  Aspern Papers, The, xii, 72, 121–2, 124–39, 236
  Friends of the Friends, The, 122, 238
  Jolly Corner, The, 146, 238
  Liar, The, 121
  Novels and Tales of Henry James, The (New York edition), 121–2, 124–6, 139, 238
  Sense of the Past, The, 121–2, 238
  Spoils of Poynton, The, 121, 126
  Two Faces, The, 121
  Turn of the Screw, The, 27–8, 36, 93, 121–4, 139, 231, 239
James, M. R., 87, 146
Jameson, Frederic, 68, 140, 234
Janin, Jules, 58
  Hoffmann et Paganini, 58
Jauss, Hans Robert, 244
Jean Paul, 7–8, 19–21, 62, 64, 68, 78, 85, 168, 235
  School for Aesthetics, 64
Jones, Malcolm V., 81–3, 236
Joyce, James, 23, 144–5, 155, 185, 216, 226
  Finnegans Wake, 144, 240
  Ulysses, 23, 155
Jullian, Philippe, 102
Jung, Carl Gustav, 108, 170, 233

Kafka, Franz, xiii, 14–15, 37, 40, 60, 70, 76, 141, 145, 153, 159, 217, 233
  Castle, The, 145
  Metamorphosis, 14, 37, 40, 70, 145, 234
  Trial, The, 145
Kant, Immanuel, 62, 161
Kappeler, Susanne, 133, 136–9
Kayser, Wolfgang, 6–9, 11, 19
Kern, Gary, 171
Kharms, Daniil, xiv, 144, 153–4, 226–7
Khomeini, Ayatollah, 220, 225, 227–9
Kiely, Robert, 66, 70, 72, 75–7, 236
Kierkegaard, Søren, 45
Kingsley, Charles, 32, 146, 215
Kingston, Maxine Hong, 142
  China Men, 142
Kirkup, James, 224
Kleist, Heinrich von, 60, 62
  Beggarwoman of Locarno, The, 60
  Foundling, The, 60
Kodjak, Andrej, 117–20
Kohlschmidt, Werner, 59
Koreff, David (Johann) Ferdinand, 58, 237

Kristeva, Julia, 213
Kroeber, Karl, 154, 216, 232, 236, 243
Kundera, Milan, xiii, xiv, 23, 145, 155, 158–9, 184–5, 215, 217–18
  Jacques and his Master, 159

Lacan, Jacques, 213
Lacoue-Labarthe, Philippe, 63–4, 235
Laubriet, Pierre, 103, 237
Lavater, Johann Kaspar, 57
Lawler, Donald L., 106
Lawrence, D. H., 221, 226
  Man Who Died, The, 221
Le Fanu, Joseph Sheridan, xii, 69, 87–94, 95, 99, 102, 109, 112, 146, 153, 156, 175, 183–4, 236–7
  Borrhomeo the Astrologer, 89–90, 153, 183
  Carmilla, 88, 90–2, 109
  Familiar, The (The Watcher), 90–1
  Green Tea, 88, 90–1
  Guy Deverell, 95
  House by the Churchyard, The, 99
  In a Glass Darkly, 88, 90–2
  Mr Justice Harbottle, 90–2
  Room in the Dragon Volant, The, 90–2
  Schalken the Painter, 88–9, 92
  Uncle Silas, 88, 92–4, 156, 175, 237
Le Guin, Ursula K., 148–9, 215, 243–4
  Earthsea Trilogy, The, 244
  Lathe of Heaven, The, 148–9
Lear, Edward, 146
Lee, Sophia, 49
  Recess, The, 49
Leighton, Lauren, 113–15
Lem, Stanislaw, xiii, xiv, 12–13, 28–9, 36, 140–1, 148, 157, 159, 209, 215, 230–1, 234
Lermontov, Mikhail, 36, 77, 103
  Hero of our Time, A, 103
  Shtoss, 36
Lessing, Doris, 150–2, 163
  Memoirs of a Survivor, The, 151–2, 163
Letley, Emma, 97
Lewis, C. S., 146, 215
Lewis, Matthew Gregory 'Monk', 48, 50–1, 58, 63, 65, 75–6, 154, 236
  Monk, The, 50–1, 58, 63, 236
Lezhnëv, A., 113–14
Lindsay, David, 13
Little, T. E. (Edmund), xi, 16, 25, 28, 40, 230, 232–3, 240
Losse, Deborah, 21
Lovecraft, H. P., 99, 147, 214
Luke, David, 60

Ma'avi, Al, 226
McCormack, W. J., 88–91, 93–4, 236–7
MacDonald, George, 32, 146, 215
McHale, Brian, 82, 145, 150–1, 153–5, 160, 174, 218, 221, 232, 240, 242

Machen, Arthur, 146
Macherey, Pierre, 10–11, 20, 25–6, 33
magic(al) realism, 22, 33, 40, 70, 153, 160,
    166, 185, 191, 232–3, 235
Mahfouz, Naguib, 226
Maitland, Sara, 187, 190, 193–4, 219,
    221–2, 224, 227–8, 244
Manguel, Alberto, 140, 238
Manlove, C. N., 14, 34, 146, 243–4
Mann, Iurii, 19–20, 23, 139, 141
Mann, Thomas, 145, 182
Manzoni, Alessandro, 50, 68, 77, 90, 153,
    156
    Betrothed, The, 68, 77, 90, 156
Marlowe, Christopher, 226
Martin, Philip, 108, 110, 237
marvellous, the, 4–5, 12, 14–15, 19, 21, 31,
    34, 35–41, 70, 120, 141, 166, 172,
    183, 202, 215, 231, 233–4
Maturin, Robert Charles, 52–3, 69, 75–8,
    87, 90–1, 103, 109, 153–4, 156, 182,
    184, 230, 236
    Melmoth the Wanderer, 52, 75–8, 90, 103,
    109, 110, 156, 236
    Woman, or Pour et Contre, 78
Maupassant, Guy de, 6, 18, 56, 99–101,
    102, 231, 237
    Horla, Le, 100–1, 102
    'Le Fantastique', 6, 99
    Lettre d'un fou, 100
    Main, La, 99–101
    Main d'écorché, La, 99
Maxton, Hugh, 153
Melville, Herman, 55, 67
Menhennet, Alan, 164
Mephistophelian qualities see Goethe
Mérimée, Prosper, 17, 36, 131–2, 231,
    239–40
    Carmen, 131
    Dame de pique, La, 131–2
    Dernières Nouvelles, 132
    Vénus d'Ille, La, 36, 132, 231
Mersereau, John, 117–18, 239
Mesmer, Franz Anton, 57, 66, 68, 85–7,
    101, 131
Mesmerism see Mesmer
metafiction, 24, 33, 143, 155, 158, 171,
    182–3, 185
Meyrink, Gustav, 159
    Golem, The, 159
Miller, Karl, 52, 65, 68–9, 102, 104
Miller, Robin Feuer, 78, 236
Milne, Lesley, 166, 168
Milton, John, 48, 71, 75, 106, 193, 242
    Paradise Lost, 48, 235, 242
Mirimsky, I., 10, 164, 236
mise en abyme, 82, 86, 89–90, 97, 101, 104,
    157, 178, 197
modernism, 35, 64, 142–3, 145, 174, 211,
    235

Moers, Ellen, 69, 72, 236
Molière, Jean-Baptiste, 164, 226
Montgolfier, J. M., 131
Morrison, Toni, xii, xiv, 150, 197–208,
    212, 216–17, 227
    Beloved, xii, 198–208, 212
Moylan, Tom, 215, 220
Mozart, Wolfgang Amadeus, 80
    Don Giovanni, 80
Mukherjee, Bharati, 185
Munro, Alice, 142
    Lives of Girls and Women, 142
Murav'ëva, O. S., 120
Musil, Robert, 145, 159
Muzruf, Ali A., 225

Nabokov, Vladimir, xiii, 76, 95, 142, 150,
    157–8, 174, 185, 236, 238
    Ada, 150
    Lolita, 142
Nancy, Jean-Luc, 63–4, 235
Neefs, Jacques, 101
neo-realism, 24
Nerval, Gérard de, 58, 231
    Aurélia, 231
Nesbit, Edith, 43
    Ebony Frame, The, 43
Nietzsche, Friedrich, 10, 216
Nisbet, H. B., 60, 235
Nodier, Charles, 6, 17, 58, 170, 231
    Inès de las Sierras, 231
Novalis, 61, 63–4
    Dialogues, 64
    Heinrich von Ofterdingen, 63

Oates, Joyce Carol, 106
O'Brien, Conor Cruise, 47
O'Brien, Fitz-James, xiv, 65, 235
    Diamond Lens, The, 65, 235
O'Brien, Flann, 153–4
    John Duffy's Brother, 154
O'Casey, Sean, 226
Odoevsky, Vladimir F., xi, xiv, 5, 6, 36,
    46, 65, 69, 175, 231, 235–6
    Last Suicide, The, 65
    Russian Nights, 65, 231
    Sylph, The, 65, 235
Olesha, Iurii, xiv
Olrik, Alex, 136
Ondaatje, Michael, 142
    Coming Through Slaughter, 142
Orwell, George, 111, 148, 226
Ossian, 59

Paganini, Niccolò, 58
Panofsky, Erwin, 46
Paracelsus, 57, 68
parody, 41, 114, 157, 166, 185, 193
Parrinder, Patrick, 34, 94, 145, 151–2, 233,
    240

Pasqually, Martines de, 57
Pasternak, Boris, xiv, 156, 160
  Doctor Zhivago, 156
Pater, Walter, 103
Pawling, Christopher, 215
Peacock, Thomas Love, 56, 67
Peake, Mervyn, 146
  Titus Groan, 68
Pearce, Howard D., xiii
Petrarch, Francesco, 61
Petzold, Dieter, 30, 230, 232
Pinter, Harold, 229
Piranesi, Giovanni Battista, 46, 49, 65, 77
Pirsig, Robert M., 184, 222–3
Plato, 20–1, 25, 223
  Cratylus, The, 25
Platonic ideas, 10, 20, 165, 167
Platonov, Andrei, 156
  Chevengur, 156
Poe, Edgar Allan, xi, 5–6, 36, 54–6, 65,
    69, 77, 79, 83–7, 89–90, 95–6, 103,
    146, 171, 213, 231, 234, 236
  Black Cat, The, 36, 84
  'Eureka', 6, 85, 87, 236
  Facts in the Case of M. Valdemar, The,
    86–7
  Fall of the House of Usher, The, 84–6
  Gold Bug, The, 83
  Ligeia, 85–6
  Man that Was Used Up, The, 84
  Masque of the Red Death, The, 84–5
  Morella, 85
  Murders in the Rue Morgue, The, 83
  Narrative of Arthur Gordon Pym of
    Nantucket, The, 68, 84
  Oval Portrait, The, 84, 89, 236
  Pit and the Pendulum, The, 84
  Purloined Letter, The, 213
  Tale of the Ragged Mountains, A, 86
  William Wilson, 65, 86, 95, 104
Polidori, John, 72, 108
  Vampyre, The, 108
postmodernism, 34, 82, 143–5, 150–2,
    154–5, 157, 160, 174, 183, 211, 240
Potocki, Jan, 231
  Saragossa Manuscript, The, 231
Prawer, S. S., 37, 236
Praz, Mario, 7, 11, 46, 49, 51–2, 75, 109,
    159–60, 230, 237
Prickett, Stephen, 146
Pritchett, V. S., 88
Proffer, Ellendea, 160, 166
Propp, Vladimir, 135, 166
Proust, Marcel, 173, 233, 242
Punter, David, 45–6, 48–9, 53, 55–6, 66,
    75, 77, 84, 93, 95, 104, 111, 233,
    234, 236–9
Puri, Nisha, 193, 227
Pursglove, Michael, 114, 119–20
Pushkin, Aleksandr S., xi, xii, xiv, 19, 23,
    36, 65, 77, 103, 108, 113–39, 145,
    158, 163–4, 212, 236, 238–40
  Bronze Horseman, The, 130
  Eugene Onegin, 77, 103
  Shot, The, 132
  Queen of Spades, The, 19, 23, 36, 113–39,
    238–40
psychoanalysis, 3, 7, 16, 26, 86, 143, 146,
    211–13
  see also Freud
Pynchon, Thomas, 144, 150–1, 154, 184
  Crying of Lot 49, The, 150–1, 154, 240
  Gravity's Rainbow, 154, 240

Rabelais, François, 9–10, 21, 32, 155, 158,
    166, 214, 216
Rabkin, Eric S., 13, 28, 31–2, 40
Rachmühl, Françoise, 99, 101
Radcliffe, Ann, 47–8, 50–2, 69, 74, 77, 84,
    230, 236
  Italian, The, 47, 50–1
  Mysteries of Udolpho, The, 50
Radford, Jean, 215
Rajan, Tilottama, 50, 143
Rank, Otto, 108
Read, Herbert, 229, 230
Reeder, Roberta, 120, 240
Reeve, Clara, 49
  Old English Baron, The, 49
Reeves, Nigel, 60
Reichert, John, 13
Reid, Robert, 235, 236
Retinger, Joseph H., 234
Rhys, Jean, 153
  Wide Sargasso Sea, 153
Richardson, Samuel, 47
Richter, Johann Paul Friedrich see Jean Paul
Risco, Antonio, 13, 211, 233
Robbe-Grillet, Alain, 15, 157
Roe, Sue, 153
  Estella, Her Expectations, 153
romance, 9, 40, 48–9, 68, 84, 94, 97–9,
    152, 214–15, 233
Rosen, Nathan, 114
Rousseau, Jean-Jacques, 59
Rudolf, Anthony, 72, 89
Rushdie, Salman, xii, xiv, 142, 144, 155,
    158–9, 184–97, 212, 216–17,
    219–29, 243–4
  'In Good Faith', 229
  'Is Nothing Sacred?', 229
  Midnight's Children, 159, 185–7
  'Outside the Whale', 187
  Satanic Verses, The, 155, 187–97, 219–29,
    243–4
  Shame, 142, 155, 159, 185, 187
Ruskin, John, 103
Ruthven, Malise, 222, 229
Ryan, Michael, 220

Sacks, Oliver, 204
Sade, Marquis de, 28–9, 49, 51–2, 57–8, 76
    Idées sur les romans, 51
    Justine, 51
Saint-Germain, 'Count', 57, 115, 130,
    133–4, 136–7
Saint-Martin, Louis-Claude de, 57, 65
Sarraute, Nathalie, 24
Sartre, Jean-Paul, 15, 143, 211
Schelling, Friedrich Wilhelm Joseph von,
    63–4, 65, 68, 78, 147, 165, 235
    Naturphilosophie, 68
    System of Transcendental Idealism, 63–4
Schiller, Friedrich, 59, 65, 69, 75
    Ghost-Seer, The, 59, 65
    'Naive and Sentimental Poetry, On',
    59–60
Schlegel, August Wilhelm von, 7, 61, 63,
    84
    Lectures, 84
Schlegel, Karl Wilhelm Friedrich von, 7–8,
    61–4
    Athenäum, 63–4
    'Letter on the Novel', 62
    Lucinde, 62
Schlobin, Roger C. xiii, 34, 230, 233
Schneider, Marcel, 234
Scholes, Robert, 141–2, 234
Schubert, G. H., 78
science fiction (SF), 15, 22, 29, 33, 38, 40,
    68–70, 74, 83, 145, 147–50, 154,
    156–7, 159, 214, 218, 232–4, 237,
    244
Scott, Sir Walter, 5, 7, 46–7, 50, 52, 58,
    65, 68, 78–9, 81, 85, 97, 113, 230,
    236–7
    Bride of Lammermoor, The, 97, 230
    Guy Mannering, 78
    'On the Supernatural in Fictitious
    Composition', 5, 58
Sedgwick, Eve Kosofsky, 143, 236
Selden, Raman, 213
Semeka-Pankratov, Elena, 164–5
Shaftesbury, 3rd Earl of, 59
Shahin, Sultan, 219
Shakespeare, William, 48, 59, 61–2, 182,
    230
    Macbeth, 230
Shelley, Mary, 7, 50, 52–3, 65, 68, 70–4,
    75, 153, 230
    Frankenstein, 22, 48, 52, 67–9, 70–4, 76,
    91, 95–6, 103, 107–8, 109, 111, 153,
    181, 218, 235
    Last Man, The, 65, 69, 73–4
Shelley, Percy Bysshe, 65, 70, 72–4, 124,
    235
    'Defence of Poetry, A', 235
    Mutuality, 70
Shklovsky, Viktor, 158
Shukman, Ann, 114, 135, 138, 240

Siebers, Tobin, 6, 17–18, 25–6, 28, 141,
    215, 217, 232
Silsbee, Captain, 124, 129–30
Simpson, David, 64, 235
Siniavsky, Andrei, 36, 145, 226–7
    Fantastic World of Abram Terts, The,
    226–7
Slonimsky, Mikhail, 19
Smirnov, I. P., 22
Socrates, 61
Solov'ëv, Vladimir, 20–1, 23–4, 43, 163
Spenser, Edmund, 48
    Faerie Queene, The, 48
Spinoza, Baruch, 59
Stalin, Joseph, 10, 113, 167–8, 223
Stapledon, Olaf, xiii, 70, 147–8, 149,
    156–9, 211
    First and Last Men, 158, 211
    Star Maker, 147–8
Steiner, George, 227
Stendhal, 113
Sterne, Laurence, 5, 8, 32, 61–2, 158–9
    Tristram Shandy, 8
Stevens, Wallace, 140
Stevenson, Robert Louis, 48, 69, 84, 94–9,
    101, 103
    Kidnapped, 94
    Markheim, 99
    Olalla, 99
    *Strange Case of Dr Jekyll and Mr Hyde,
    The*, 94–7, 107
    Treasure Island, 94
    Weir of Hermiston, 48, 97–9
Stoker, Bram, 70, 91, 106–12, 182
    Dracula, 67, 70, 95–6, 107–12, 182,
    237–8
    Dracula's Guest, 109
Strada, Vittorio, 15, 20–1, 217, 232
Strelka, Joseph P., 35, 234
Strugatsky, Arkadii and Boris, xiii, 36,
    145, 148
    Definitely Maybe, 148, 240
    Roadside Picnic, 36, 148, 240
Sue, Eugène, 69, 77
Summers, Montague, 87
Surrealism, 10, 153–4
Suvin, Darko, 29, 236
Svevo, Italo, 213
Swedenborg, Emanuel, 57, 85, 91, 93–4,
    237
Swinfen, Ann, 34, 146
Symbolism, 10, 35, 83, 94, 143, 145, 164,
    165

Taheri, Amir, 221, 225
Tall Story Club, The, 123
Tanner, Tony, 151
Tatar, Maria, 37, 66, 81–2, 86, 234, 236
Taylor, Ronald, 80
terror, literature of, 45–6, 48–9, 51–2, 57,

66, 75–6, 108, 159, 236
Terts, Abram *see* Siniavsky
Tiedk, Ludwig, 8, 64, 78
Theweleit, Klaus, 218
Thompson, G. R., 55, 84, 85–6, 88, 236
Todorov, Tzvetan, xi, xiii, xv, 3, 6,
    11–16, 18–21, 23, 28–31, 33, 34–41,
    53, 56, 85, 99, 115, 123, 141, 143,
    146, 156, 166, 172, 213, 230–4
Tolkien, J. R. R., 4, 14, 16, 28, 31, 40,
    146, 214–15, 230, 232, 240
Tolstoy, A. K., 23, 163
    Vampire, The, 23, 163
Tolstoy, Lev N., 113, 163
Tomashevsky, Boris, 156
Tournier, Michel, xiii, 184
Turgenev, Ivan S., 131–2, 239
    'Visions' (*Prizraki*), 132
Turner, Chris, 218

uncanny, the, 12, 14–15, 19–20, 30–1,
    35–40, 60, 70, 108, 141, 214, 231,
    234
    see also Freud

Vaihinger, Kurt, 217
vampires/vampirism, 33, 69, 75, 92, 101,
    108–12, 163, 209, 212
Varma, Devendra P., 46–7, 50–2, 66, 153,
    230
Varnado, S. L., 109–11, 232, 237, 239
Vax, Louis, 11, 33, 230, 234
Velikovsky, Immanuel, 214, 243
Verne, Jules, 10–11, 148, 153
    Mysterious Island, The, 10–11, 153
Villars, Abbé de, 57
    Comte de Gabalis, Le, 57, 59, 235
Villiers de l'Isle-Adam, P. H., 231
    Véra, 231
Voinovich, Vladimir, xiv
Volponi, Paolo, 215
Voltaire, 226
Vonnegut, Kurt, xiii, 152
    Cat's Cradle, 152
Vygotsky, Lev, 6–7

Walker, Alice, 198
Walker, I. M., 83

Walpole, Horace, 46–9, 52, 63, 75, 154,
    230
    Castle of Otranto, The, 47–9
Walsh, John, 194, 222
Warner, Marina, 221
Watson, Ian, 148
    Chekhov's Journey, 148
Waugh, Patricia, 143
Weber, Veit, 60
    Sagen der Vorzeit ('Days of Yore'), 60
Webster, Noah, 53
Weldon, Fay, 244
Wellbery, David, 80
Wellek, René, 62–3, 68
Wells, H. G., 70, 148
Wendland, Albert, 232
Wesker, Arnold, 222
West, Nathanael, xiii
Wheatley, Dennis, 147
Wheeler, Kathleen, 61, 64, 235
White, Hayden, 232
White, T. H., 146
Whitehouse, Mary, 224
Wieland, Christoph Martin, 7, 59
Wilde, Oscar, 69, 95–7, 102–6, 109, 171,
    184, 226, 236, 237
    'Decay of Lying, The', 96–7, 171
    Picture of Dorian Gray, The, 102–6, 237
Williams, Gareth, 167, 169, 171, 238
Winckelmann, Johann Joachim, 59
Winner, Thomas, 35, 140
Wolf, Christa, 145
Wolfe, Gary K., 233
Woolf, Virginia, 121, 238
Wordsworth, William, 70
    Tintern Abbey, 70

Zahorski, Kenneth J., 165, 233
Zamiatin, Evgenii, xiii, 24, 145, 148, 223,
    226–7, 233
    Soviet Heretic, A, 233
    We, 226–7
Zhdanov, Andrei, 79
Zhukovsky, Vasilii A., 65
Ziolkowski, Theodore, 20, 68–70, 86, 101,
    104, 106, 154, 230, 236, 238
Zola, Emile, 236
Zolla, Elémire, 11, 69